Recent Developments in the South China Sea Dispute

The South China Sea region contains potentially huge deposits of petroleum and natural gas, important shipping lanes and fishing areas, and is subject to a number of maritime territorial disputes. This edited volume analyses the most recent developments in the South China Sea dispute, looking at the positions taken by China, the ASEAN countries and the United States. In recent years maritime joint development zones have emerged as an important means to overcome deadlock in relation to maritime jurisdictional claims. This book tests the applicability of joint development regimes in this region and explores the prospect of joint development of resources as a way to successfully manage the conflict in the South China Sea. Eminent scholars in the field of South China Sea studies have contributed original chapters to the volume, covering such issues as the legal framework for joint development, the challenges faced by joint development and the way forward for the region.

The book will be of interest to researchers and students of International Law, Maritime Law, Political Science and Asian Studies.

Wu Shicun is President of the China National Institute for South China Sea Studies, a sole national-level think-tank in China specializing in South China Sea studies. His research focuses on the history and geography of the South China Sea, ocean boundary delimitation, international relations and regional security issues.

Nong Hong is Director of the Research Center for Oceans Law and Policy at the National Institute for South China Sea Studies. Her research takes an interdisciplinary approach to examining international relations and international law, with a focus on ocean governance in East Asia, the law of the sea, international security, international dispute settlement and conflict resolution.

Recent Developments in the South China Sea Dispute

The Prospect of a Joint Development Regime

Edited by Wu Shicun and Nong Hong

Routledge
Taylor & Francis Group
LONDON AND NEW YORK

First published 2014
by Routledge
2 Park Square, Milton Park, Abingdon, Oxfordshire OX14 4RN

and by Routledge
711 Third Avenue, New York, NY 10017

First issued in paperback 2016

Routledge is an imprint of the Taylor & Francis Group, an informa business

British Library Cataloguing in Publication Data
A catalogue record for this book is available from the British Library

Library of Congress Cataloging-in-Publication Data

Recent developments in the South China Sea dispute : the prospect of a joint development regime / Shicun Wu, Nong Hong.

pages cm

Includes bibliographical references and index.

ISBN 978-0-415-73505-6 (hardback) -- ISBN 978-1-315-81869-6 (ebk) 1. South China Sea--International status. 2. Marine resources development--Law and legislation--South China Sea Region. 3. South China Sea Region--Economic conditions. 4. Marine resources development--South China Sea Region--International cooperation. I. Wu, Shicun, editor of compilation. II. Hong, Nong, editor of compilation.

KZA1692.R43 2014

341.4'480916472--dc23

2013046254

ISBN 13: 978-1-138-68512-3 (pbk)
ISBN 13: 978-0-415-73505-6 (hbk)

Typeset in 10/12 Baskerville MT by
Servis Filmsetting Ltd, Stockport, Cheshire

Contents

Notes on contributors

Ramses Amer is associated fellow, Institute for Security & Development Policy, Sweden. His major areas of research include security issues and conflict resolution in Southeast Asia and the wider Asia-Pacific, and the role of the United Nations in the international system. He is the author of *The Sino-Vietnamese Approach to Managing Boundary Disputes* (Maritime Briefing, vol. 3, no. 5, International Boundaries Research Unit, University of Durham, 2002). He is co-editor, with Carlyle A. Thayer, of *Vietnamese Foreign Policy in Transition* (Institute for Southeast Asian Studies and St. Martin's Press, 1999); with Keyuan Zou, of *Conflict Management and Dispute Settlement in East Asia* (Ashgate, 2011); with N. Ganesan, of *International Relations in Southeast Asia: Between Bilateralism and Multilateralism* (Institute of Southeast Asian Studies, 2010); with Ashok Swain and Joakim Öjendal, of *Globalization and Challenges to Building Peace* (Anthem Press, 2007); of *The Democratization Project: Opportunities and Challenges* (Anthem Press, 2009); and of *The Security-Development Nexus: Peace, Conflict and Development* (Anthem Press, 2012).

Rommel C. Banlaoi is manager of the South China Sea Program at the Center for Intelligence and National Security Studies of the Philippine Institute for Peace, Violence and Terrorism Research. He was a recipient of the Albani Philippine Peace Prize Award in 2011 for peace and national security education. He currently serves as vice president of the Philippine Association of Chinese Studies and is a senior fellow of the Yuchengco Center at De La Salle University in Manila, the Philippines. He currently teaches at the Department of International Studies at Miriam College, the Philippines, where he specializes in political analysis, Philippine government and constitution, global issues and international peace and security.

Robert Beckman is the director of the Centre for International Law (CIL), a university-wide research centre at the National University of Singapore (NUS) which was established in 2009. In addition to serving as director of the Centre, he also heads its Ocean Law and Policy programme and its research projects on the South China Sea and international maritime crimes. Professor Beckman received his JD from the University of Wisconsin and his LLM from Harvard Law School. He is an Associate Professor at the NUS Faculty of Law, where he has taught for more than thirty years. He currently teaches Ocean Law & Policy in Asia and Public International Law at the NUS Faculty of Law. Professor Beckman is an expert on the issues of law of the sea in Southeast Asia, including piracy and maritime security. He served for several years as a regional resource person in the workshops on Managing Potential Conflicts in the South China Sea. He has represented Singapore at various meetings on maritime security at the Council for Security Cooperation in the Asia-Pacific and has worked for many years on legal and policy issues relating to the Straits of Malacca and Singapore. He lectures in the summer diploma programme at the Rhodes Academy of Oceans Law & Policy in Rhodes, Greece. He is also an Adjunct Senior Fellow in the Maritime Security Programme at the S. Rajaratnam School of International Studies, Nanyang Technological University.

Irene Chan is a senior research analyst with the China Programme at the S. Rajaratnam Institute of International Studies, Nanyang Technological University. Her research interests are South China Sea issues, regional security, Sino-US relations and China's ethnic minority politics.

Vannarith Chheang is currently serving as an Executive Director of the Cambodian Institute for Cooperation and Peace and is a member of the ASEAN Institute of International Studies, the Council for Security Cooperation in the Asia-Pacific, the Network of ASEAN Defence Institutions and the Economic Research Institute for ASEAN and East Asia. He earned a BA in International Relations from the Diplomatic Academy of Vietnam (2002), an MA in International Relations from the International University of Japan (2006), a Graduate Certificate in Leadership from the East West Center in Hawaii (2008) and a PhD in Asia Pacific Studies from the Ritsumeikan Asia Pacific University in Japan (2010). His research interests include the political economy of regional integration in Southeast Asia, regional security issues, security sector governance and reform, and development cooperation.

Hasjim Djalal was born in West Sumatra, obtained a BA from the Indonesian Academy for Foreign Service in Jakarta (1956), and an MA (1959) and PhD (1961), both from the University of Virginia. He graduated from the Indonesian National Defense Institute in 1971. He was Director of Treaty and Legal Affairs of the Indonesian Department of Foreign Affairs (1976–1979) and Director General for Policy Planning (1985–1990). He has served at the Indonesian embassies in Belgrade, Guinea (Africa), Singapore, Washington DC and as ambassador/deputy permanent representative of Indonesia to the UN in New York (1981–1983) and ambassador to Canada (1983–1985), Germany (1990–1993) and ambassador-at-large for the Law of the Sea and Maritime Affairs (1994–2000).

Ralf Emmers is Associate Professor and Coordinator of the Multilateralism and Regionalism Programme at the S. Rajaratnam School of International Studies, Nanyang Technological University, Singapore. He completed his

MSc and PhD in the International Relations Department of the London School of Economics. His research interests cover security studies and international relations theory, maritime security, international institutions in the Asia-Pacific, and the security and international politics of Southeast Asia. Dr Emmers is the co-Series Editor of the Warwick Studies in Globalisation (Routledge) and an Editorial Board member of *Pacific Review*. Dr Emmers is the author or editor of eleven books and monographs and has contributed numerous journal articles and book chapters in edited volumes. His recent books include *Resource Management and Contested Territories in East Asia* (Palgrave Macmillan, 2013) and *Geopolitics and Maritime Territorial Disputes in East Asia* (Routledge, 2010).

Alberto A. Encomienda, a career Foreign Service Officer of the Republic of the Philippines, recently retired with the rank of Chief of Mission, Class I. He served as the country's ambassador to Greece, Malaysia and Singapore. His career specialization is Oceans Law and Policy with an LLM degree from the University of London in 1972, and Columbia University in 1978.

His government work in Oceans Policy and Law of the Sea, concentrated in the decade leading to his retirement, saw Mr Encomienda as head of the then Maritime and Ocean Affairs Unit (MOAU) under the Office of the Secretary of Foreign Affairs, which was at the same time the Secretariat of the high-level Cabinet Committee on Maritime and Ocean Affairs (CABCOM-MOA). The CABCOM-MOA was later abolished and at the same time the MOAU was upgraded to the Maritime and Ocean Affairs Center (MOAC) to which devolved the agenda of the CABCOM-MOA and its policy formulation and oversight functions. MOAC functions were later transferred to the Office of the President to give a higher profile and prominence to the ocean concerns of the country facing modern paradigms as an archipelagic state, through the creation of the Commission on Maritime and Ocean Affairs (CMOA) chaired by the Executive Secretary. Mr Encomienda headed the CMOA Secretariat for a year after its establishment.

Li Jianwei is director of Research Division II, National Institute for the South China Sea Studies, China. Her research interests are dispute resolution in the South China Sea, IUU fishing activities, US policies and the South China Sea. Her education includes a MMP from University of Wollongong, Australia, an MSc from the London School of Economics and a BA and MA in English Literature from Hebei University, China. Her recent publications include 'Hainan's role in the management of the South China Sea issues: a case study of the Gulf of Tonkin', in *Conflict Management and Dispute Settlement in East Asia*, edited by Ramses Amer and Keyuan Zou (Ashgate, 2011) and 'Recent practices in dispute management in the South China Sea' (co-authored with Ramses Amer), in *Maritime Energy Resources in Asia: Legal Regimes and Cooperation*, edited by Clive Schofield, Special Report No. 37 (National Bureau of Asian Research, 2012).

B. A. Hamzah is a keen student of international politics, international law and security. Currently with the Department of Strategic Studies at the National Defence University, he has extensive experience in teaching, research and consultancy. As an academician, he has served Universiti Sains Malaysia, Sultan Idris University of Education, Tg Malim and the University of Malaya.

In research, he spent 10 years at ISIS, Malaysia. He was a fellow at ISEAS in Singapore and special senior fellow at the United Nations Institute of Training and Research in Hiroshima, Japan. He was also a visiting scholar at the Lauterpacht Research Centre for International Law, Cambridge University.

B. A. Hamzah was the first head of Strategic and International Studies at the Malaysian Armed Forces Defence College. He also founded the Maritime Institute of Malaysia and became its first director-general in 1993. He has been a consultant with Petronas and Accenture.

Zou Keyuan is Harris Professor of International Law at the Lancashire Law School of the University of Central Lancashire (UCLan), UK. He specializes in international law, in particular law of the sea and international environmental law. Before joining UCLan, he worked in Dalhousie University (Canada), Peking University (China), the University of Hannover (Germany) and the National University of Singapore. He has published over 60 refereed English papers in 30 international journals. His recent books include *China-ASEAN Relations and International Law* (Chandos, 2009), and he is co-editor of *Maritime Security in the South China Sea* (Ashgate, 2009), *International Law in East Asia* (Ashgate, 2011) and *Conflict Management and Dispute Settlement in East Asia* (Ashgate, 2011). He is a member of the editorial boards of the *International Journal of Marine and Coastal Law*, *Ocean Development and International Law*, *Journal of International Wildlife Law and Policy*, *Polar Journal* and *Chinese Journal of International Law*, as well as member of the advisory board of the *China Oceans Law Review*.

Li Mingjiang is an Associate Professor at S. Rajaratnam School of International Studies (RSIS), Nanyang Technological University, Singapore. He is also the Coordinator of the China Programme and the Coordinator of the MSc in Asian Studies Programme at RSIS. He received his PhD in Political Science from Boston University. His main research interests include China's diplomatic history, the rise of China in the context of East Asian regional relations and Sino-US relations, and domestic sources of China's international strategies. He is the author (including editor and co-editor) of nine books. His recent books are *Mao's China and the Sino-Soviet Split* (Routledge, 2012) and *Soft Power: China's Emerging Strategy in International Politics* (Rowman & Littlefield, 2009). He has published papers in various peer-reviewed journals including *Global Governance*, *Cold War History*, *Journal of Contemporary China*, *Chinese Journal of International Politics*, *China: An International Journal*, *China Security*, *Security Challenges*, *International Spectator* and *Panorama* (Konrad Adenauer Stiftung). He frequently participates in various track-two forums in East Asia.

Nong Hong is a director at the Research Center for Oceans Law and Policy, National Institute for South China Sea Studies. Nong Hong received her PhD for interdisciplinary study of international law and international relations from the University of Alberta, Canada and held a postdoctoral fellowship with the China Institute, University of Alberta. She was ITLOS-Nippon Fellow for International Dispute Settlement (2008–2009), visiting fellow at the Center of Oceans Law and Policy, University of Virginia (2009) and at the Max Planck Institute for Comparative Public Law and International Law (2007). She is also a research fellow with the China Institute, University of Alberta. Her most recent publications include *UNCLOS and Ocean Dispute Settlement: Law and Politics in the South China Sea* (Abingdon, New York: Routledge, 2012); *Maritime Security Issues in the South China Sea and the Arctic: Sharpened Competition or Collaboration?* Co-edited with Gordon Houlden (Beijing: China Democracy and Legal System Publishing House, 2012).

David M. Ong is Professor of International and Environmental Law at the Nottingham Law School, Nottingham Trent University, UK. His main research interests are in the International Law of the Sea, particularly on offshore joint development, published in the *American Journal of International Law* (1999) and the *Netherlands Yearbook of International Law*, 2000 (2001); and International Environmental Law, published in the *European Journal of International Law* (2001), the *Irish Yearbook of International Law*, 2006 (2008), the *Yearbook of International Environmental Law*, 2006 (2008), the *Nordic Journal of International Law* (2010), and the *Netherlands International Law Review* (2011); as well as numerous edited volumes of essays, three of which he has co-edited. He has also served as a consultant on offshore joint development issues to the Guyana legal team in the Guyana-Suriname maritime boundary delimitation arbitration (2007); and as a technical resource expert on Joint Development at the Second United Nations Development Programme (UNDP) South-South High Level Meeting on Oil and Gas Producing Developing Countries held in Nairobi, Kenya, 12-15 October, 2009.'

Clive Schofield is professor and director of research at the Australian Centre for Ocean Resource and Security (ANCORS), University of Wollongong, Australia. ANCORS is Australia's sole academic centre devoted to multidisciplinary research on national and international ocean law, policy, management and maritime security. Dr Schofield currently holds an Australian Research Council Future Fellowship. He previously served as director of research at the International Boundaries Research Unit, University of Durham, UK. Dr Schofield is a political geographer and international legal scholar whose research interests relate to international boundaries and particularly maritime boundary delimitation. He holds a PhD (geography) from the University of Durham, UK and an LLM from the University of British Columbia, Canada. He has researched and published primarily on issues related to the delimitation of maritime boundaries, geo-technical issues in the law of the sea, maritime security and regarding maritime boundary disputes and their resolution. He has published over 100 book chapters and scholarly articles and is co-author (with Professor Victor Prescott, Emeritus Professor of Geography, University of Melbourne) of *The Maritime Political Boundaries of the World* (Martinus Nijhoff, 2005). He has also been involved in the peaceful settlement of boundary and territory disputes, for example through the provision of technical advice and research support to governments engaged in boundary negotiations and in dispute settlement cases before the International Court of Justice.

Wu Shicun has a PhD in history and is president and senior research fellow of the National Institute for South China Sea Studies, and deputy director of the Collaborative Innovation Center of South China Sea Studies, Nanjing University. Dr Wu's research interests cover the history and geography of the South China Sea, maritime delimitation, maritime economy, international relations and regional security strategy. His main single-authored books include *Solving Disputes for Regional Cooperation and Development in the South China Sea: A Chinese Perspective* (Woodhead, 2013), *A Study on the South China Sea Disputes* (Hainan Publishing House, 2005) and *The Origin and Development of the Nansha Disputes* (Ocean Press, 1999). His main edited books include *Securing the Safety of Navigation in East Asia: Legal and Political Dimensions* (UK: Woodhead Publishing Limited, 2013), *Maritime Security in the South China Sea* (Ashgate, 2009), *Selective Studies on World Famous Island Economic Bodies* (World Knowledge, 2006) and *Collection of Documents Relating to South China Sea Issues* (Hainan Publishing House, 2001). Dr Wu is published widely in academic journals. He has also received frequent media interviews as a senior commentator on South China Sea issues.

Stein Tønnesson is research professor at the Peace Research Institute Oslo, adjunct professor at the Department of Peace and Conflict Research, Uppsala University where he leads a six-year research programme on East Asian Peace, associate editor for Asia in the *Journal of Peace Research*, board member of Norfund, a Norwegian development finance institution and member of the editorial board of *Global Asia*. His research interests include decolonization, revolution, war and nation-building in Southeast Asia, and the disputes in the South China Sea. His most recent book is *Vietnam 1946: How the War Began* (University of California Press, 2010), a Vietnamese translation of which was published by the Su That publishing house in Hanoi 2013. His publications on maritime questions include 'China and the South China Sea: a peace proposal', *Security Dialogue,* 31(3), September 2000: 307–326; 'The South China Sea in the Age of European decline', *Modern Asian Studies* 40(1), 2006: 1–57; (with Song Yann-huei), 'The Impact of the Law of the Sea Convention on Conflict and Conflict Management in the South China Sea', *Ocean Development and International Law* 44(3), 2013: 235–269, and 'Could China and Vietnam Resolve the Conflicts in the South China Sea?' in Song Yann-huei and Zou Keyuan, eds, *Major Law and Policy Issues in the South China Sea,* London: Ashgate, 2014: 207–241.

Mark J. Valencia is an internationally known maritime policy analyst, political commentator and consultant focused on Asia. He is an Adjunct Visiting Professor, National Institute for South China Sea Studies. Most recently he was a research associate with the National Asia Research Programme. Previously he was a visiting senior fellow at the Maritime Institute of Malaysia and a Visiting Senior Scholar at Japan's Ocean Policy Research Foundation. From 1979 to 2004, Dr Valencia was a senior fellow with the East-West Center where he originated, developed and managed international, interdisciplinary projects on maritime policy and international relations in Asia. Before joining the East-West Center, he was a lecturer at the Universiti Sains Malaysia and a Technical Expert with the UNDP Regional Project on Offshore Prospecting based in Bangkok. He has a PhD in Oceanography from the University of Hawaii and an MA in Marine Affairs from the University of Rhode Island.

Dr Valencia has published some 15 books and more than 150 articles and is a frequent contributor to publications such as the *Far Eastern Economic Review*, *International Herald Tribune*, *Asia Wall Street Journal*, *Japan Times* and *Washington Times*. Selected major policy relevant works include 'The proliferation security initiative: making waves in Asia', *Adelphi Paper* 376 (International Institute for Strategic Studies, 2005), 'Military and intelligence gathering activities in the exclusive economic zone: consensus and disagreement' (co-edited), *Marine Policy Special Issues* (March 2005 and January 2004) and 'Pacific Ocean boundary problems: status and solutions' (with Douglas Johnston, Martinus Nijhoff, 1991).

Preface

Wu Shicun

The South China Sea is one of the most important economic assets in the eastern hemisphere. Not only is it the main economic lifeline between the Pacific and the Indian oceans, but its rich natural resources are strategically significant to all surrounding nations. Its underlying reserve of petroleum and natural gas is so enormous that the South China Sea has been dubbed 'the second Persian Gulf,' drawing the attention of countries beyond its immediate area.

But this abundance and the attention it brings to the South China Sea can also bring problems. Past incidents in similar areas have demonstrated that exploring and using disputed areas can sometimes trigger friction and conflicts. Because of the escalating arms trade and an increase in military activity in surrounding countries, including the purchase of advanced weapons systems, worries and unnecessary mistrust abound in the South China Sea region. Instead of complicating the matter by throwing mud and bickering, the surrounding countries should resolve this dispute through civilized dialogue and consultation. A peaceful resolution is in the best interest of all countries involved. Ongoing confrontations will not resolve the current problems; dialogue and cooperation are the only way forward. Among all the proposed solutions, joint development is the proven, feasible route.

There are many international examples of successful joint development of resources. Take the North Sea oil field in Europe – joint development turned a disputed resource-rich area into an important sea oil and gas production base, benefiting the countries concerned. From this and similar cases, we derive two obvious solutions: to embed the establishment of joint development zones, or benefit sharing mechanisms, into border agreements or, in the absence of a border agreement, to strike a consensus on joint development, beginning with the overlapping claims.

The concept of joint development was put forward by the then Chinese Vice Chairman Deng Xiaoping as a solution to the dispute between China and Japan concerning Diaoyu Island. On a visit to Japan in 1978 he suggested that they shelve the dispute and instead pursue joint development. In the 1980s he again raised the concept of joint development in the South China Sea. China has been working toward this end ever since. In 2004, China and Vietnam signed an agreement for establishing a joint fishing zone in the Gulf of Tonkin (Beibu). In 2005, China, the Philippines and Vietnam signed a proposal known as the Joint Marine

Seismic Undertaking. Though this agreement was halted for political reasons, it was still considered a concrete, historic step forward because it showed how China's proposal of 'shelving differences, and going for joint development' could be taken from paper to practice.

However, due to diverging political ideologies, varying levels of economic development, cultural differences and other constraints, consensus has yet to be reached. If we add to this international stew the influences within and beyond the region, it is easy to see why this consensus remains but a hope. Complicated work must be done, but it is hindered by difficulties while a consensus remains undetermined. This indecision places the peace and stability of the area under shadow. Developing a plan to build trust and promote cooperation so as to realize joint development in the South China Sea becomes an urgent task.

Given the complexities and difficulties of finding solutions for similar territorial disputes, the dispute over the South China Sea islands and their adjacent waters is unlikely to go away in the near future. The issue might even get worse before it gets better. Therefore, 'putting aside disagreements, and seeking joint development' would be a wise move toward downplaying disputes and realizing mutually beneficial cooperation. In the long term, particularly, this policy would be the best choice. Building mutual trust and increasing consensus through joint development will promote communication among involved countries and help countries in the area avoid conflict escalation and strategic misjudgment. The endeavor is important to the common interests and the wellbeing of all people around the South China Sea.

Joint development requires that all parties put aside differences, make compromises and seek mutually beneficial results. All nations should act in a spirit of cooperation and understanding to break the stalemate in maritime disputes and geo-political competition. They should explore and exercise institutional arrangements for joint development and promote cooperation through consultation and hotline mechanisms. Only in this way is it possible to effectively control conflicts and disagreements, to avoid further complicating and escalating the disputes.

The drafting of a feasible joint development plan should be discussed by all nations, so that through their cooperation they may ensure the plan's sustainability and consistency and choose reasonable and agreeable fields of cooperation. It is imperative to balance and bridle the rights and obligations of all parties and to carefully address the legal and economic issues involved. Since there are already some successful examples of joint development, it is useful to explore existing cooperation models and experiences to see whether and how they could be applied to the disputed areas in South China Sea region.

Against the new backdrop of the evolving South China Sea, those searching for the proper solution to the South China Sea disputes face great challenges as well as opportunities. We must honor the spirit of the Declaration on the Conduct of Parties in the South China Sea (DOC). We must press ahead seriously with direct negotiations and consultations among the countries involved. We must promote cooperation and joint development in a concrete manner, and only address the disputes through peaceful means. Only then can we transform the South China Sea into a sea of friendship and cooperation.

Introduction

Wu Shicun and Nong Hong

This edited volume analyzes the most recent developments in the South China Sea dispute, tests the applicability of the joint development regime in this region and explores the prospects of joint development as a way to manage the increasingly escalating conflict among the disputant states and the conflicting interests of claimant states and user states.

The conference on 'Recent Development of the South China Sea Dispute and Prospects of Joint Development Regime' was held in December 2012 in Haikou, organized by the National Institute for South China Sea Studies. Eminent scholars in the field of South China Sea studies were invited to contribute papers on such topics as 'Recent developments of the South China Sea dispute', 'Legal context of joint development in the South China Sea: legal framework, key issues and case studies', 'Practice of joint development in disputed waters: experiences and lessons', 'Joint development in the South China Sea: challenge and prospects', and 'Prospect of joint development'.

Part I of this volume comprises three papers on the recent development of the South China Sea dispute. In Chapter 1, Mark Valencia shares his observation of the South China Sea situation as sliding from order to disorder. He proposes several interim measures to manage the situation, such as a moratorium on drilling in disputed areas, a moratorium on military and intelligence gathering activities in disputed areas, ad hoc mechanisms or an understanding to deal with fishery incidents and INCSEA agreements.

B. A. Hamzah, in Chapter 2, observes the South China Sea policies of China and the US. He considers China's policy to be more assertive, supported by actions of increasing civilian and military assets in the region. The US policy of pivoting to the region is viewed as a deliberate policy of containing China's rise. Having considered the internal challenges within the Association of Southeast Asian Nations (ASEAN), Hamzah expresses confidence in the resilience of ASEAN.

In Chapter 3, which examines China–Vietnam and China–Philippine relations, Ramses Amer and Li Jianwei list the major incidents that have occurred in the South China Sea related to China, Vietnam and the Philippines. Having analyzed the possible causes of the incidents, they make proposals on how to improve the bilateral relationships between China and Vietnam and between China and the Philippines. Amer and Li believe that the three parties possess the potential to stimulate dialogues between China and ASEAN countries.

Part II is composed of four papers that address the legal context of joint development in the South China Sea and the practice of joint development in disputed waters with the aim to share experiences and lessons. In Chapter 4, Robert Beckman encourages the countries concerned to enter into provisional arrangements of a practical nature without prejudice to the final delimitation. With regard to the way forward in the South China Sea, Beckman identifies several areas, including increasing knowledge of features in the Spratly Islands, clarifying claims, increasing knowledge of hydrocarbon resources through joint seismic surveys, implementing the DOC and enhancing understanding of the nature and importance of joint development arrangements.

Zou Keyuan, in Chapter 5, establishes a link between joint development and historic rights. He suggests that both of the concepts have been well recognized by international law. The character of flexibility shared by the two concepts along with their respective application to the South China Sea has demonstrated the potential of their union. Zou believes the concept of historic rights could potentially stimulate regional cooperation in the South China Sea region.

In Chapter 6, Clive Schofield points out that the definition of the precise geographical area within which joint development is to proceed is a key consideration in the negotiation and establishment of maritime joint development arrangements. Schofield explores past experiences of how this delicate issue has been dealt with, suggests lessons that can be derived from past practice and concludes with prospects for their application to the South China Sea.

In Chapter 7, David Ong suggests that the Chinese U-shaped line is not in fact a sovereignty claim or even a putative maritime boundary claim. He argues that the Chinese position is understandable notwithstanding the serious and continuing questions over the legality of the claim itself under the international law. He addresses the international legal framework providing procedural obligations for cooperation. Ultimately, the application of these specific procedural obligations by claimant states in the South China Sea may lead to the adoption of joint development agreements, several models of which are now in evidence throughout the world.

Part III comprises five papers on the challenges and prospects of joint development in the South China Sea. Alberto Encomienda, in Chapter 8, introduces two instances of joint cooperation that the Philippines was involved in, one of which was subsequently aborted while the other led to a successful conclusion. The joint development aspect of the Joint Marine Seismic Undertaking failed, not because of any issue related to the validity and applicability of the concept to disputed waters, but because of issues internal to the Philippines. Encomienda draws the conclusion that, in the case of the Philippines, an important lesson is to ensure that projects are insulated from domestic politics.

In Chapter 9, Hasjim Djalal expresses support for joint development in overcoming territorial problems. Djalal argues that the concept of joint development cannot be very meaningful unless the relevant countries are able to formulate and agree on at least five points: the 'zone', the 'nature', the 'subject' or the 'topics', the 'mechanism' for such joint development, and the 'who' that will participate in such joint development or joint cooperation activities.

Ralf Emmers, in Chapter 10, discusses the significance of natural resources as a source of inter-state cooperation and competition in the South China Sea. He argues that due to the high economic costs and interests at stake, little progress has been made toward the joint development of resources in the South China Sea. Furthermore, a joint development scenario is not risk-free, especially for the weaker claimant states. Thus, the joint development of resources is an unlikely scenario in the coming years.

In Chapter 11, Vannarith Chheang discusses some challenges and determines some prospects for joint development in the South China Sea. He argues that in order to contain and manage the disputes in the area, the situation requires trust and confidence, and then the parties concerned could move to joint development of some areas without taking into consideration which islands and water belong to whom.

Irene Chan and Li Mingjiang, in Chapter 12, examine the political will and domestic receptiveness of the five rival claimants to the South China Sea toward negotiation for joint development. They conclude that joint development between the five rival claimants, while not impossible, is unlikely in the foreseeable future.

Part IV comprises three papers that examine the prospect of the joint development of the South China from a broader perspective. Stein Tønnesson, in Chapter 13, looks at Chinese national interests in the South China Sea from a foreign scholar's perspective. He observes that when dealing with the South China Sea issue, China should consider its grand strategy: its good neighbor policy; market access in the USA and the EU, access to technology and avoidance of trade war; continuing rapprochement with Taiwan; delimitation of maritime boundaries (while shelving island disputes) as well as establishment of joint fishery management and joint ventures to explore for oil and gas – under clear, national jurisdiction regimes.

In Chapter 14, Rommel C. Banlaoi observes that although joint development is something that all claimants hope to pursue in order to peacefully manage the maritime territorial conflict in the South China Sea, that hope is battered by differences between claimants on definitional issues of joint development and on procedural concerns on how to implement it. A functional approach to the management of conflicts in the South China Sea could reduce, if not totally remove, substantive barriers to cooperation. Banlaoi concludes that functionalism could also facilitate eventual collaboration among political elites in the littoral states of the South China Sea.

Nong Hong, in the final chapter, observes that given the complex nature of the territorial and maritime disputes in the South China Sea, a temporary arrangement is the most practical solution pending the final dispute settlement. However, due to legal, economic and political considerations, as well as the new developments, it is hard to foresee any joint development of oil and gas resources in the South China Sea. Hong offers some alternative thoughts on promoting the concept of joint development in the South China Sea.

Part I

Recent developments in the South China Sea

1 The South China Sea disputes

Recent developments

Mark J. Valencia

A diplomatic Rubik's cube

In November 2012 there were two important summit meetings in Phnom Penh – the 21st ASEAN Summit, followed by the East Asia Summit – involving China, the U.S. and six other invited countries with interests in East Asia. It was clearly hoped by ASEAN and the U.S. that there would be agreement on a code of conduct (COC) for the South China Sea between ASEAN and China at this East Asia Summit. But this was not to be, despite extraordinary diplomatic efforts led by Indonesia's Foreign Minister Marty Natalegawa. This development – or lack thereof – puts a spotlight on why the South China Sea disputes are so difficult to resolve or even manage.

The main reason an agreement has evaded the best efforts of seasoned negotiators is its political complexity – it is like a diplomatic Rubik's cube – six sides, each with three layers. To paraphrase Winston Churchill's immortal description of Russia in 1939, the solution 'is a riddle wrapped in a mystery inside an enigma.'

At its core are disputes between several key ASEAN members – Malaysia, the Philippines and Vietnam. These disputes should be resolved or formally placed aside before moving on to the next layer of the puzzle. They involve both territory (islands) and maritime space. The good news is that Malaysia and Brunei – a claimant to maritime space and resources in the southern part of the South China Sea – have apparently resolved their differences regarding their overlapping maritime claims in a still secret pact. Rumor has it that Malaysia relinquished its claim in exchange for a guaranteed share of petroleum in the former area of overlap. Malaysia has also reached agreement with Vietnam regarding their overlapping continental shelf and exclusive economic zone (EEZ) claims. They also made a joint submission to the UN claiming an extended continental shelf.

The bad news is that the dispute between Malaysia and the Philippines over maritime space derives in part from a territorial dispute over the present Malaysian state of Sabah. The Philippines claims Sabah as part of its sovereign territory and has incorporated its claim in its constitution. Malaysia claims a territorial sea, EEZ, continental shelf and extended continental shelf from Sabah. Malaysia, the Philippines and Vietnam also claim several of the same features in the Spratly Islands.

The second layer of the 'cube' involves the ASEAN claimants and their fellow ASEAN members. These issues are the enigma – veiled and subtle – but just as real and difficult as the first layer of the puzzle. Singapore, Thailand and supposedly Indonesia have no claims to the disputed area but are nevertheless significant players in the attempt to negotiate a COC for national behavior in the disputed areas for all of ASEAN as well as between ASEAN and China. Why are these non-claimants so intimately involved in trying to negotiate a COC, and why should China have to negotiate with non-claimants?

These are the questions asked by China, which is the prominent factor in the third layer of the 'cube'. China claims all of the features and apparently most of the maritime space in the South China Sea. The mystery is what exactly China claims – as well as Taiwan, its alter ego in this dispute and a sixth side of the 'cube'. What specifically is the meaning of the historic nine-dashed line? This is important to the negotiating process because until or unless this claim is specific, it must be assumed that it includes part of Indonesia's EEZ. This means that in China's eyes Indonesia is neither neutral nor credible as a mediator in the dispute or in its attempt to lead negotiations for a COC. The additional bad news is that China (and Taiwan) and Vietnam claim all the features. That means that some of them are claimed by five governments (China, Taiwan, Malaysia, the Philippines, and Vietnam).

As if matters are not complicated enough, these disputes – concerning both territory and maritime space – are infused with domestic nationalism that is putting pressure on leadership during a key transition in China. China has intensified the imbroglio by essentially putting on a 'full court press' – verbally threatening its rival claimants, enforcing a ban on fishing in its claimed waters, offering oil blocks for lease on Vietnam's claimed continental shelf, designating a new administrative headquarters and garrison for the South China Sea, confronting the Philippines over the Scarborough Shoal, challenging petroleum exploration in waters claimed by the Philippines, Vietnam and Malaysia, and publicly thanking Cambodia for supporting China's interests at the failed ASEAN meeting – all the while telling the U.S. to 'butt out.' China is apparently trying to establish its 'effective control' of the area and essentially establish a new status quo. To back up its claims, China is using its 'civilian' vessels such as maritime surveillance and fisheries enforcement ships in step by step progressive assertions that some call 'salami tactics.'

Basically China sees itself as a victim – previously of colonial powers and currently of their successors – small Southeast Asian countries who are stealing its maritime resources and are backed by the U.S. The sense of victimization feeds its nationalist discourse and underpins its moral outrage and righteousness in foreign policy. Most importantly, it reinforces public demand for tough uncompromising positions that make management of the conflicts difficult and compromising on or resolving them near impossible.

ASEAN realized that its credibility might be severely damaged if it did not address the problem, and the ASEAN and East Asia summits were thus 'the most critical gathering of regional leaders in years.'[1] ASEAN had to take a position which is neutral, forward-looking and encourages the peaceful resolution of the issues. Otherwise, according to Indonesian Foreign Minister Marty Natalegawa, deeper divisions could open between Southeast Asian claimants and China.

There is actually a fourth layer to this conundrum – a U.S.–China struggle for the 'hearts and minds' of Southeast Asians and ASEAN members. The U.S. is pressuring both China and ASEAN to negotiate a binding COC and is even prepared to accept a period of higher tensions no matter what progress is made. Indeed the U.S. thinks that tensions in the South China Sea are now the new 'normal.'

Just before the contentious July 2012 ASEAN meeting, the U.S. stated its position on the issues and essentially encouraged ASEAN to stand up to China. Much to China's chagrin, the U.S. administration also increased its activity behind the scenes, pressing some countries on the issue and trying to influence the content of the COC. China responded by accusing the U.S. of 'meddling' in the South China Sea disputes.

This diplomatic Rubik's cube is why the disputes are so hard to resolve and why a robust COC will be so difficult to achieve. This issue will certainly continue to challenge ASEAN's diplomatic skills as the organization strives to maintain its 'centrality' in the security of the region and maneuver between China and the U.S.

Recent developments: increasing entropy

In physics, in isolated systems, order tends toward disorder i.e. increased entropy. This is what appears to be happening politically in Southeast Asia as the U.S. and China have increased their roles in the regional security 'system.' Indeed, there is an ongoing action–reaction cycle of escalation as well as considerable maneuvering both in front of and behind the scenes regarding the South China Sea disputes that threatens to destabilize the region.

Moreover, the South China Sea situation is becoming a bellwether of the nature, style and tone of China's rise. The U.S. presence and 'rebalancing' feeds and reinforces a hedging strategy by Southeast Asian countries should China become more 'aggressive.' Because the U.S. is a formal military ally of one of the claimants (the Philippines), it feels that China and others cannot assert that events in the South China Sea are 'none of its business.' Nevertheless, China argues that the U.S. is not naturally a western Pacific power and that beefing up its naval and intelligence presence in the South China Sea is provocative and unjustified by its public explanations.[2] In private, American officials admit that the planning for Air-Sea Battle 'is designed for a possible conflict involving Taiwan or a dispute in the South China Sea.'[3] In late September 2012, Chinese and U.S. military officials held their annual consultations under the Sino-U.S. military Maritime Consultative Agreement but not surprisingly no significant progress on core issues was reported.[4] The U.S. has been encouraging the claimants to stand up to China. Moreover U.S. Secretary of State Clinton's tour of the region reasserting American interests, and the late October cruise of a U.S. aircraft carrier group through the South China Sea[5] have only confirmed Beijing's worst fears. The George Washington Carrier Strike Group undertook joint operations with Malaysia, conducted live fire exercises off Vietnam, and made a port call in the Philippines. The U.S. is clearly determined to manage China's rise in a manner that does not diminish vital American interests.[6] But there continues to be some doubt that the U.S. can actually bear the economic and political cost of the containment of China.[7]

The U.S. intensified its attempts to influence the negotiations between ASEAN and China on a COC. Indeed, Clinton publicly 'urged all parties to make "meaningful progress"'[8] by the November East Asia Summit in Phnom Penh. It reportedly tried to influence the content as well. On 3 August 2012 the U.S. State Department issued a statement criticizing China's 'upgrading of the administrative level of Sansha City and its establishment of a new military garrison there covering disputed areas of the South China Sea.'[9] China's Ministry of Foreign Affairs responded the next day by reiterating its sovereignty over the South China Sea islands and adjacent waters as well as its right to administer them as it sees fit. More significantly, it criticized other countries for violating the Declaration on the Conduct of Parties in the South China Sea (DOC) and warned that 'while being open to discussing a COC with ASEAN countries, China believes that all parties concerned must act in strict accordance with the DOC to create the necessary conditions and atmosphere for the discussion of a COC.'[10] This indicated that China was having second thoughts about negotiating a COC, especially if the U.S. continues to 'meddle.'

Nevertheless, the U.S. is likely to continue pressuring both China and ASEAN to negotiate a binding agreement. 'We are not going to be able to go back to situations in which things were easy and that decisions were made without a certain amount of strain. All this requires hard work, heavy lifting and very challenging discussion. ASEAN has generally been content to sort of skate on the surface and to avoid debates. These issues are going to be much more difficult to deal with.'[11]

The U.S. wants to maintain the existing status quo in Southeast Asia – a status quo in which it is the dominant actor and patron.[12] This is essentially a continuation of its Cold War policy and posture in the region – a substantial forward deployed military presence and a hub-and-spoke alliance structure.[13] The U.S. also has tactical objectives in mind to support this strategic goal. For example, it would like to place a high-tech radar system somewhere in Southeast Asia. More generally it would also like to improve its 'maritime domain awareness' by integrating Southeast Asian countries like the Philippines into a regional system. Further it wants to enhance the military power of allies like the Philippines and potential allies like Indonesia.[14] In sum, the U.S. apparently expects Southeast Asian states to fear China and welcome U.S. power. This is not happening as quickly, broadly, or as clearly as hoped.[15] Indeed American dominance may be beginning to reach its strategic limits.

Meanwhile, the Chinese leadership has shown no sign of complying with U.S. wishes or being more flexible regarding the maritime disputes. Moreover some think the issue touches on existential strategies in that China needs the South China Sea to hide and protect its new generation of nuclear powered nuclear armed submarines based at Sanya.[16] China clearly does not think the U.S. is neutral in the disputes.[17] Nor does it believe the U.S. rhetoric that claims it wants China to share responsibility and power to maintain stability in the region. In fact, China is not interested in 'stability' if it means the status quo with the U.S. being dominant in the security arena.

China has sought to simultaneously consolidate its regional claims and manage resulting tensions.[18] Most recently and most worrying, China's naval exercises with civilian maritime patrol vessels in the East China Sea were clearly intended to 'warn regional rivals against escalating territorial disputes.'[19] Similar exercises in the South China Sea cannot be far behind. Whether intended to or not, these actions can create incidents involving U.S. maritime surveillance forces and at least give the appearance of enhancing the chance of clashes. Indeed 'China may be escalating risk in the belief that US risk aversion will cause self-restraint.'[20]

Since 2006, China has been warning international oil companies not to sign exploration contracts with Vietnam for areas claimed by China.[21] Nevertheless, SOCO International of the U.K. announced it may take concessions from Vietnam in an area claimed by China.[22] China has also acted against other claimants but they have chosen not to publicize it. For example, on 19 August 2012 Chinese patrol vessels confronted a seismic survey vessel in Malaysia's Block SR 318 undertaking work under contract to Shell Sarawak. They ordered the vessel to cease and desist and it complied. But it renewed its work after a 'protective buffer' was put in place.[23] Malaysia did not publicly protest because it does not want its disputes with China in the South China Sea to affect their economic relationship.[24]

Chinese strategists feel China is 'trapped' and vulnerable and must break out of any strategic 'containment.' Of course its actions to 'break out' create anxieties in its neighbors, who feel threatened. When asked to explain why China will not clarify its claims, Chinese analysts' response is 'to do so would require difficult political and bureaucratic compromises that would provoke domestic nationalists.'[25]

Unfortunately in the world of physics – and international relations – for every action there is a reaction. The U.S. reaction is to meet China's new assertiveness in kind – what David Shambaugh calls 'meeting Chinese realism with American realism.'[26] This in turn feeds the China threat thesis and if not mitigated will transform Asia into a cockpit of competition and conflict between China and the U.S. This is in neither country's interest nor in that of Southeast Asian nations.

China obviously does not want to be told 'what to do,' especially by the U.S., or to necessarily abide by a U.S. dominated 'international order.' If China rejects a 'rules-based framework' for activities in disputed areas in the South China Sea it would be an indication that it wants to change that order and that as its power grows, time is on its side. It maintains that ASEAN is not the place to resolve the disputes because they are between China and only some ASEAN members. As Chinese Foreign Minister Yang Jiechi told Hilary Clinton,

> as for the dispute over the sovereignty of some islands and reefs of the Nansha Islands and the overlapping rights, interests, and claims over some waters of the South China Sea, these should be discussed by the directly concerned countries on the basis of historical fact and international law, and handled and settled through direct negotiations and friendly consultation.

The U.S. response is that while the territorial issues should be resolved between claimants, broader questions about conduct in disputed areas and methods of resolving disputes should be addressed in multilateral settings. China also argues that its historical claim and rights in the South China Sea is not superseded by its ratification of the United Nations Convention on the Law of the Sea (UNCLOS).[27] ASEAN and the U.S. argue that such rights were discussed in the UNCLOS negotiations process and are therefore superseded by the convention, and that according to the Vienna Law of Treaties, China must bring its domestic law into conformity with UNCLOS.

The issues were further complicated when China was immersed in its own leadership transition. After the leadership transition China was expected to put a Politburo member in charge of diplomatic affairs policy making and to co-ordinate and reduce discordance among domestic agencies.[28] It was hoped this would help China avoid its foreign policy being characterized by disagreements with others and the backlash that inevitably followed – rather than by its ability to propose and build consensus.[29] Nevertheless, some analysts fear that China's regional strategy will inevitably clash with 'America's alliance focused approach [and] produce an unstable and increasingly uncertain region in which conflicts over relatively marginal matters of strategic significance will become more frequent.'[30]

Southeast Asian countries are clearly concerned that the South China Sea situation may get 'out of hand.'

Vietnam continued to protest China's actions, including its naval exercises in the Paracels, establishment of the Sansha City administration headquarters, and use of drones to monitor disputed waters.[31] Vietnam maintains that these acts violate Vietnam's sovereignty, international law, the agreement on basic principles between Vietnam and China, and the DOC. Meanwhile China continued to tighten its grip on Philippine-claimed features like Mischief Reef and the Scarborough Shoal,[32] and the Philippines continued to rail at China. Even though the U.S. quietly brokered an arrangement under which both Filipino and Chinese vessels were to leave the Scarborough Shoal, some Chinese vessels remained and China blocked the entrance channel with a cable. This created a new status quo. Philippine Foreign Minister Albert del Rosario warned that the Philippines will respond to the situation accordingly.[33] He also renewed his appeal for a united ASEAN stand on the South China Sea.[34] He went on to criticize China's statement 'that freedom and safety of navigation in the South China Sea is assured.'

The Philippines argues that China indirectly asserted its nine-dashed line claim by implying that it is the sole guarantor of freedom of navigation in the South China Sea and can thus withdraw that assurance if it so chooses.[35] President Aquino also directed the National Mapping and Resource Information Authority to 'produce and publish charts and maps of the Philippines reflecting the West Philippine Sea.' But the Philippine administration began to crack under the pressure when the President at China's recommendation selected Senator Antonio Trillanes as a backchannel negotiator between Manila and Beijing. This was apparently done without del Rosario's knowledge and caused China and a significant portion of the Philippine people to lose confidence in him as foreign minister.[36] The Aquino administration seemed determined to push forward with its attempt to bring the issue before an international body.

Progress on a COC

An unofficial outline of the elements of an ASEAN COC has been circulated.[37] According to then ASEAN Secretary General Surin Pitsuwan an ASEAN–China COC would *not* be signed at the November ASEAN and East Asia summits.[38] Nevertheless, Indonesian Foreign Minister Marty Natalegawa continued to pursue a viable COC. Indonesia produced a draft with provisions for confidence building, conflict prevention and conflict management based on the DOC and the COC 'elements' previously agreed by ASEAN. This draft was discussed by ASEAN foreign ministers on the sidelines of the U.N. General Assembly meeting in late September. Negotiations continue.

Once ASEAN has agreed on the draft, the next step is to formally discuss it with China. It was hoped that it would be like 'the rules of the road', expected behavior to maintain stability – but comprehensively binding. The principle objective was to obtain an ASEAN–China accord on the COC before the November East Asia Summit in Phnom Penh,[39] and to finalize and formalize it there. But this was looking ever more unlikely as of the date of writing.

Natalegawa has cautioned that the process should proceed 'naturally without any pressure.'[40] But many observers are skeptical that China will ever agree to a robust COC with dispute-resolution mechanisms.[41] China has made clear that progress on a COC will be inhibited by any U.S. involvement – either directly or indirectly. This has or could become a sticking point in the negotiations.[42] And some 'wicked' problems may remain unresolved such as agreement on the area to be covered by the COC. This lack of agreement resulted in the attempt to negotiate a COC in 2002 being downgraded to agreement only on a non-binding DOC. Another more fundamental problem facing Natalegawa and Indonesia is that China does not really believe Indonesia is neutral in this affair. In fact Indonesia and China probably have overlapping jurisdictional claims in the South China Sea – depending on the meaning of China's nine-dashed historic line[43] which Indonesia has formally criticized to the United Nations. Natalegawa has warned that 'Absent a code of conduct, absent a diplomatic process, we can be certain of more incidents and more tension for our region.'[44]

Nevertheless, Natalegawa was optimistic that China recognizes the need for diplomatic progress including implementing the non-binding DOC.[45] In this regard, Chinese Foreign Minister Yang Jiechi made a diplomatic tour of three Southeast Asian countries in July 2012 to try to move dispute management forward. Thailand – the country co-ordinator for ASEAN–China relations – hosted a Senior Officials Meeting on 25 October to discuss the South China Sea disputes. The meeting tabled guidelines for negotiations between ASEAN and China for the coming year and urged China to return to discussions on a COC. Moreover, ASEAN 'concerned think tanks' have held several brainstorming sessions with their Chinese counterparts regarding the key principles and elements of a COC.[46] The participants reaffirmed the benefit of concluding a binding COC and in the meantime fully observing and implementing the DOC. They also agreed that a COC should be drafted based on the DOC but that it should be more 'comprehensive and effective than the DOC.' The meetings further suggested that 'experts and eminent' persons should be utilized to support the official track to develop a COC 'if and when called upon.' Such meetings could be funded by the ASEAN-China Maritime Fund.

On another more technical front the Philippines hosted the third ASEAN Maritime Forum (AMF) and the first Expanded Maritime Forum (3–5 October 2012).[47] The AMF seeks to promote maritime cooperation under the ASEAN political security community framework with a key element being the maintenance of ASEAN centrality in addressing maritime issues in the region. However, the South China Sea security issues per se were not on the agenda.

Looking forward: alternative futures

> There are known knowns, there are things we know we know. We also know there are known unknowns, that is to say we know there are some things we do not know. *But there are also unknown unknowns, the ones we don't know we don't know.*
>
> Donald Rumsfeld

There are several ways the South China Sea political drama could unfold. In perhaps the worst scenario from an ASEAN perspective the U.S.–China rivalry will feed upon itself, becoming a serious ideological and political struggle dominating the issues, splitting ASEAN on this issue, and subordinating its 'centrality' in security. This would leave the South China Sea disputes to fester and tensions would wax and wane in action/reaction dynamics. International oil companies would shy away and exploration would remain in limbo. Proxy domestic and interstate political conflict would be the new 'normal.' Another consequence of China's rise and the South China Sea issues is the role of the Chinese diaspora in Southeast Asia. In some countries the national loyalty of Chinese is still questioned by suspicious majority ethnic governments and citizenry. These suspicious could be exacerbated by the China–ASEAN contretemps.[48]

An ASEAN preferred scenario would be one in which a robust binding COC is agreed and implemented – not only by ASEAN but by China as well. This would diminish one opportunity for U.S.–China conflict and reaffirm ASEAN political competence and centrality in regional security. The U.S. and other powers active in the region would accede to the COC. Not only would this lead to an era of peace and stability in the South China Sea but the claimants would find a way to encourage hydrocarbon exploration and exploitation in the area – perhaps through joint development. A non-mutually exclusive alternative proposed by the Philippines is to jointly declare at least the islands as international marine reserves. In this ASEAN preferred scenario, everyone lives happily ever after – or at least until the next political imbroglio draws in outside powers.

Neither of these scenarios are likely and the reality will be somewhere in between these extremes. The disputes can be managed but probably not resolved – at least not in the foreseeable future. Talks are likely to drag on both within ASEAN and between it and China – and diplomatic vitriol and tensions will ebb and flow.

ASEAN can try to ensure the reality is closer to its preferred scenario by trying to manage the U.S.–China rivalry without obviously siding with either protagonist. This will not be easy but it may be key to preserving ASEAN unity on this issue. As China's military might grows and the U.S. steps up its political and military involvement in the region, hard choices need to be made and the window of opportunity for a peaceful settlement of the South China Sea disputes is closing. ASEAN should 'seize the bull by the horns' and be proactive, take a coherent and balanced approach,[49] and prepare for crisis management.

ASEAN could also help manage the conflict by establishing a moratorium on drilling and agreeing to jointly determine the quantity and quality of petroleum in disputed areas. If the potential is low and/or too costly to exploit then it may be easier to agree to refrain from unilateral drilling. It should also reassure China that it does not – as a body – seek the assistance of the U.S. against China nor will it do its bidding in this regard. The U.S. for its part should strike a balance between reassuring its allies, continuing to support a 'rules based' order, and reassuring China that it is not trying to contain it – a neat diplomatic maneuver if it can do so.

Perhaps, as Hasjim Djalal has put it,

> the six ASEAN non-claimants (Indonesia, Singapore, Laos, Cambodia, Thailand and Myanmar) can take a joint initiative, informally or formally, to offer their good offices to bring the four ASEAN claimants (Brunei, Malaysia, the Philippines and Vietnam) to the negotiating table with the other two non-ASEAN claimants or 'South China Sea entities' (China and Taiwan), perhaps first informally, in order to achieve understanding and, if possible to reach general agreement.[50]

Hot spots

There are several situations in the South China Sea that could result in violent conflict.

- *Chinese interference with exploration, particularly drilling, by Vietnam-licensed contractors operating on the Vietnamese-claimed continental shelf.* Other countries may bark but Vietnam has proven it can and will bite as well, no matter how powerful the opponent.
- *Chinese interference with exploration, particularly drilling by Philippine-licensed contractors on the Reed Bank.* Although the Philippines has little military capability, its potential backing by the U.S. and domestic political pressure could force it to make a dangerous miscalculation. While Chinese use of non-military vessels for such 'interference' will mitigate such situations, it has its limits. The continuing 'stand-off' at the Scarborough Shoal could also still trigger conflict.
- *Another confrontation between U.S. intelligence gathering vessels and Chinese vessels in China's EEZ.* Although the two have apparently worked out a modus operandi that has prevented further incidents, deteriorating relations could result in another incident that could spiral out of control.

In the meantime

It would appear that agreement on and effective implementation of a robust COC will take quite some time. Meanwhile the situation cries out for interim conflict management measures to calm the situation. Perhaps a dispute forum would serve as a safety valve or at least a temperature gauge for the region. Other interim measures might include a moratorium on drilling or maritime military activities in disputed areas, including provocative intelligence gathering activities, demilitarization of the features, and some ad hoc mechanism to resolve fisheries disputes or at least agreement on mutually expected behavior when a country is faced with what it deems violations of its laws in a disputed area. Given the rapid modernization and expansion of navies and air forces in the region, it is also well past time to begin discussing INCSEA (Incidents at Sea) agreements among the claimants.

The establishment of a strong COC and its successful implementation are a significant challenge for the region. But the situation also provides a great opportunity. ASEAN unity has its back against the wall, and China's preferred image of a 'peaceful' rise is also at stake. The parties can demonstrate to the world that they can resolve their problems by themselves – without involving outside powers or mechanisms. Not only would this preserve at least a semblance of ASEAN centrality in regional security management but it would also be some proof of China's 'good intentions' toward its neighbors. Needed now is a regional solution to a regional problem, at a high diplomatic level.

Notes

1 Mark Valencia, 'A political Rubik's cube,' *The Straits Times*/Asia News Network, Singapore, Opinion, Saturday 10 November 2012, at http://www.thejakartapost.com/news/2012/11/10/a-political-rubik-s-cube.html.
2 Dylan Welch, 'US blueprint for war with China flawed and could spark nuclear strikes, says expert,' *Sydney Morning Herald*, 9 August 2012.
3 'Between the US and Asia the best defense is dialogue,' *New York Times*, 9 August 2012.
4 Wang Yuanyuan, 'China, U.S. militaries hold annual maritime security meeting,' *English.news.cn*, 28 September 2012.
5 'US Carrier force supports Asean,' *cross.com*, 21 October 2012.
6 Douglas H. Paal, 'Why the South China Sea is not a "Sudetenland Moment",' *The Diplomat*, 18 August 2012.
7 'US, China clash on key issues,' *SFGate*, 9 September 2012.
8 'US expect South China Sea tension to rise,' *Associated Press*, 6 September 2012; Matthew Lee, 'Clinton seeks Chinese accord on South China Sea,' *Associated Press*, 4 September 2012.
9 Patrick Ventrell, 'South China Sea,' Office of Press Relations, Washington DC, 3 August 2012.
10 Qin Gang, 'Statement of the Ministry of Foreign Affairs of China on the US State Department issuing a so-called Press Statement of the South China Sea,' 4 August 2012.
11 'China says no questioning its sovereignty over South China Sea,' *State of Affairs*, 6 September 2012, available at http://www.voafanti.com/gate/big5/blogs.voanews.com/state-department-news/2012/09/06/china-says-no-questioning-its-sovereignty-over-south-china-sea/ (accessed 26 October 2012).
12 John R. Deni, 'US Pacific policy,' *Los Angeles Times*, 6 September 2012.
13 Nick Bisley, 'Biding and hiding no longer: a more assertive China rattles the region,' *Global Asia*, 6(4), Winter 2011.
14 Jim Wolf, 'US plans $1.4 billion arms-package for Indonesia,' *Reuters*, 21 September 2012.
15 David C. Kang, 'Is America listening to its East Asian allies,' Pacific Forum, CSIS, *PacNet*, 4, 19 October 2012.
16 Michael Richardson, 'Nuclear edge to sea disputes,' *Japan Times*, 7 September 2012.
17 'Clinton, in Beijing, seeks Chinese accord on resolving South China Sea issues,' *Washington Post*, September 2012.
18 'CMSI Conference on China's Far Seas Operations 9–10 May, 2012, Executive Summary,' U.S. Naval War College.
19 'China holding maritime drills in East China Sea in bid to warn "regional rivals" against escalating,' *News Track India*, 22 October 2012.
20 'CMSI Conference on China's Far Seas Operations.'
21 'Alarm bells over South China Sea,' *AFP*, 3 August 2011; Huy Dong, 'Negotiating the South China Sea,' *The Diplomat*, ASEAN Beat, 20 July 2011.
22 R. Jennings, 'Why won't China sign the South China Sea code of conduct?,' *Christian Science Monitor*, 12 July 2012; 'China ready to join talks in South China Sea,' *Voice of America*, 19 September 2012.
23 Personal communication to Mark J. Valencia, September 2012.
24 Leslean Arshad, 'Malaysia, China boost ties, overlapping claims in South China Sea not a factor,' *Bernama*, 21 September 2012.
25 Joseph Nye, 'Asian nationalism rising at sea,' *International Herald Tribune*, 3 September 2012.

26 David Shambaugh, 'Coping with a conflict China,' *Washington Quarterly*, 34(1), Winter 2011, pp. 7–27, at p. 24.
27 Article 14 of China's EEZ and Continental Shelf Act of 26 June 1998 provides that 'the provisions of this Act shall not affect the historical rights of the People's Republic of China.'
28 Teddy Ng, vice premier for foreign affairs will co-ordinate foreign policy.
29 *National Bureau of Asian Research*, 6 September 2012.
30 Bisley, 'Biding and hiding no longer.'
31 'Vietnam requires China to respect sovereignty,' *DiploNews*, 11 October 2012.
32 Alexis Romero, 'China expanding Mischief structures,' *Philippine Star*, 3 September 2012.
33 Delon Porcallo and Jose Katigbak, 'Phl also wants sea row settled peacefully,' *Philippine Star*, 28 September 2012.
34 *Philippine Daily Inquirer*, 4 September 2012.
35 Philippines Department of Foreign Affairs' statement on Freedom of Navigation in the West Philippine Sea, *DiploNews*, 6 September 2012: 'No state can arrogate under itself the unilateral right to determine or assure the existence or non-existence of the freedom of navigation in the West Philippine,' DFA, Philippines.
36 'China handpicked Trillanes – Aquino,' *Standard Today*, 22 September 2012; Richard Javad Heydarian, 'China splits Philippine politics,' *Asia Times*, 10 October 2012.
37 Carlyle A. Thayer, 'ASEAN's Code of Conduct (Unofficial),' *Thayer Consultancy Background Brief*, 11 July 2012. This document was apparently approved at the 45th AMM in July. But it has not been officially released and remains an unofficial draft document. Indonesia has also circulated a 'zero draft' of a COC presumably based on these elements but this is unavailable to me. Other versions of a COC or a summary of what it should contain that have been prepared and circulated include those by the Philippines, by ASEAN ISIS, and by myself.
38 'ASEAN Sec-Gen rules out early signing of Code of conduct treaty,' *ABC Australia*, 25 October 2012.
39 'China mends fences in sea dispute,' www.rfa.org/english/east-asia-beat/sea, 22 September 2012.
40 Yohanna Rivihena, 'RI circulates draft code of conduct on South China Sea,' *Jakarta Post*, 29 September 2012.
41 Ian Storey, Interview, nbr.org/research activity.aspx?id=262 (accessed 22 November 2012).
42 'China mends fences in sea dispute,' www.rfa.org/english/east-asia-beat/sea, 22 September 2012.
43 I Made Andi Arsana, 'Watch out, the ocean might "shrink",' *Jakarta Post*, 6 April 2011.
44 'Clinton meets ASEAN leaders about South China Sea,' *Voice of America*, 8 September 2012.
45 Matthew Pennington, 'Indonesia seeks rule of road for South China Sea,' *Associated Press*, 26 September 2012.
46 'Memorandum, on approaches towards building a Code of Conduct on the South China Sea to better protect peace and stability in the region,' ASEAN-ISIS, 3 August 2012.
47 'PHL to host ASEAN maritime forum Oct. 3–5,' *GMA News*, 2 October 2012; 'Phl proposes Asean info-sharing to better watch disputed areas,' *Philippine Star*, 5 October 2012.
48 'GOP outlines tough stance on China,' *Voanews*, 29 August 2012.

49 Simon Tay, 'America's "return" to Asia, poses challenge for ASEAN,' *Malaysian Insider*, 19 March 2012.

50 Hasjim Djalal, 'Taiwan desperately wants to be involved in shaping a COC, Taiwan wants part in shaping West PHL Sea code of conduct,' 12 September 2012, personal communication.

2 US-Sino relations: impact on security in the South China Sea

B. A. Hamzah[1]

Where elephants fight the grass is trampled.

Swahili proverb

The background of a renewed US-Sino competition in Asian waters is well documented. However, in the South China Sea, the competition became more intense following the decision of the Obama regime to return to the region in 2010; pivoting to the East has become President Barrack Obama's signature defense policy during his first term as President. Despite budgetary constraint, he is likely to stay on course with this policy in his second term as President.

Many Chinese scholars claim the US policy to pivot to the Asia-Pacific is a deliberate effort to rebalance its worldwide military deployment with an eye *mainly* on China. Of course, Washington has denied these charges. Despite denials to the contrary by various policy makers, every step that the US has taken bears the mark of a deliberate policy to contain China's rise, which appears to be inevitable. Kissinger has elaborated on why China fears encirclement and he has advised against such policy.[2] He maintains that the competitive relations between China and the US 'need not – and should not – become a zero-sum game.'

This chapter examines the impact of US-Sino relations on regional maritime security within the context of recent developments in the South China Sea. Some of the recent events that could pose a challenge to the maritime security include:

- the impact of the continuing standoff between China and the Philippines at the Scarborough Shoal (April 2012);
- the passage of Vietnamese maritime law[3] (known as the Law on Vietnam's Sea) in June 2012;
- the ASEAN foreign ministers' failure to issue a joint communiqué at their 45th meeting at Phnom Penh in July 2012;
- China's formal establishment of the Shansha garrison[4] in July 2012;
- President Aquino's decision to sign an administrative order on 5 September 2012 to rename part of the South China Sea as 'the Western Sea of the Republic of the Philippines' as well as the order to publish a new map to include Kalayaan and the Scarborough Shoal as part of the Western Sea.[5]

At a strategic level, there are more worrying signs too. They include:

- Beijing's increasingly assertive policy in the South China Sea and in the East China Sea;
- the growing US–Vietnam and US–Philippines military ties and their impact on China's threat perception in the South China Sea;
- US perception of an increase in China's military capacity for anti-access and anti-denial (A2/AD) has led to the deployment of littoral combat ships and anti-ballistic missile systems as part of its Air-Sea Battle operational strategy in the region;
- Beijing's policy of resisting the US-inspired containment policy has worsened US-Sino political relations.

The above events are a harbinger of an uncertain future in the regional maritime security environment. Overall, the outlook for regional maritime security in the South China Sea is one of ambivalence, bordering uncertainty.

The US encirclement policy will harden China's options

In seeking greater access to the region, since 2012 the US has deployed some 2,500 marines to Darwin on a six-month rotation basis; it has conducted military exercises with some ASEAN states, including those at odds with China in the South China Sea. Within the context of rebalancing its forces for power projection purposes, Washington has also agreed to deploy initially four littoral combat ships to Singapore,[6] presumably to protect its interests in the South China Sea and in the Straits of Malacca. This deployment is very much in line with Obama's speech at the Australian Parliament (November 2011) which reassured 'friends and allies' that America remains a Pacific power.[7] Of course, more recently, in the third week of October 2012, the US sent its aircraft carrier group (the nuclear powered *USS George Washington*) to the South China Sea, a day after the PLA navy staged a joint exercise with the civilian maritime agencies off the Diayou/Senkaku Islands.

The powers that are likely to have significant influence in the region are the US, China, Japan, India,[8] and ASEAN. Russia is slowly rebuilding influence in the region.[9] The four Great Powers in Asia and ASEAN are redefining their strategic interests as they interact with each other and other states in the region.

These powers compete for pre-eminent positions in the region more intensely than others do. Some compete for different strategic reasons; some objectives are identical. For example, Japan and the US tend to view the rise of China as a threat to their security in the region. Hence, their policies towards China's military rise tend to be identical. Both Japan and the US are understandably very skeptical of China's anti-access and anti-denial (A2/AD) capabilities at sea. The proposed anti-missile defense system under the aegis of the current Air-Sea Battle concept reflects their coordinated stand.

Although India and the US do not share common strategic interests in the Asian sub-continent, both tend to view China's overall political rise with suspicion.

China and India have unresolved territorial problems[10] that go back to the days of the British Raj and could spill over into the Indian Ocean as both build large navies to secure their growing interests. India views China's increasing maritime influence in the Indian Ocean as alarming. So does the US. In 2004, President George Bush offered India a special deal on nuclear energy cooperation to strengthen the global strategic partnership of the two countries. According to Washington, this special deal has nothing to do with Pakistan or China.

Events in Africa and Latin America, where China has established a very strong economic presence in the last decade or so, have also shaped US-Sino relations.

Viewed from Beijing,[11] the three big powers (India, Japan and the US), separately or together, have ulterior designs, which in the case of the US includes a policy of containment or encirclement. Although there is no evidence of a 'conspiracy' between Japan and India to curb China's rise, despite their limited resources to openly challenge China, they separately view China's rise with suspicion. Where their interests converge, they work together and often with the US to undermine China. In my view, China is too vast, too complex, and too costly for any single power to contain it.

In the long run, it will be difficult for the US to manage China's rise in ways that do not diminish US interests in the region. Many consider the US policy of containment against the Soviet Union during the Cold War era (1949–1990) as overwhelmingly successful. In challenging the US, the Soviets were seduced into an arms race against an economically strong US. The arms race with the US undermined the Soviet economy and it caused the state to break up.[12]

Unlike the case of the Soviet Union, there is no evidence to suggest that China has entered into an arms race with the US. On the contrary, China has scoffed at the arms race and continued to develop its PLA at its own pace. Currently, by World Bank estimates in 2011, China spends 2 percent of its GDP on defense compared with 4.7 percent for the US.[13] The International Monetary Fund forecast in 2012 that despite the global economic slowdown (estimated at 3.3 percent), China's economy is expected to grow by 7.8 percent, the highest growth rate in the world.[14] In other words, its economic foundation remains strong enough to weather some future turbulence, although its growth figures for the third quarter of 2012 fell to 7.4 percent.[15]

Against the background of slower growth rates in China and coupled with rising anger against those states nibbling at its maritime territories, the US encirclement policy will further harden China's foreign policy options.

The following are among the reasons offered for the hardening of Beijing's policy options:

- Rising nationalism in China. For example, in September 2012, there were consumer boycotts of Japanese products, and the Chinese government did not restrain those who took to the streets protesting against Japanese policy towards the Senkaku/Dioyou Islands.[16] More recently, senior Chinese Bank officials boycotted the IMF and World Bank meeting at Tokyo in October 2012. This policy of snubbing Japan came after the spats at sea.

- China views the US economy as no longer robust and believes that the US will not be able to support extensive military campaigns as it did during the Cold War era against the Soviet Union. Various writers have alluded to this inevitability – that is, that the US is in a strategic decline mode. Johan Galtung, who forecast the breakup of the Soviet Union, predicted in 2004 that the US would fall apart in 2020.[17] Although Norman Davies did not make any forecast on the US decline his statement that 'All states and nations, however great, bloom for a season and are replaced'[18] is prophetic and applicable to any power, the US included. However, in my opinion, the US is not about to commit pre-emptive suicide as suggested by some .[19]
- China views US foreign policy as becoming hostage to its economy.
- The US strategic overreach has taken an economic toll. Today the US is the most indebted nation in the world, estimated at US$16 trillion and despite Ben Bernanke's recent quantitative easing, announced in September 2012, the numbers are not encouraging.[20]
- The US economic malaise has caused Washington to cut its military spending by more than US$100 billion over a decade. This cut will strain the US ability to project power beyond its shores on a sustainable basis.[21]
- Beijing believes that the current downturn in the world economy has affected the US and Japan more than it affects China, although the latter has experienced a slower growth rate.[22]
- Many in and outside of China believe that geography is on its side. Hawaii, the homeport of the 7th Fleet, for example, is 8,000 nautical miles away. China has certain geographical advantages over the US in this region. According to Hugh White, 'in Asia where Chinese and American power meet, China enjoys many asymmetric advantages.'[23] All military operations have to factor in resources, technology, distance, and geography.

US-Sino competition in the South China Sea[24]

US-Sino competition has caused temperatures to rise in the South China Sea. The *Nation* of Thailand warns in a recent editorial that:

> If the current tension continues in South China Sea, especially between the Philippines and China, it could lead to an all-out war. This is not an alarmist's warning but a real concern. With poisonous rhetoric and growing tension, there is a possibility that conflicting parties would cross the line. This could be a result of miscalculation.[25]

This editorial refers to the impasse over the Scarborough Shoal. While the impasse would not lead to an 'all-out war,' the likelihood of a miscalculation is scary. In the opinion of the *Nation*, it (war) 'can be the most dangerous game in town.'

China has been accused of stoking tensions in the South China Sea.[26] Beijing has been heavily criticized over the Scarborough Shoal standoff and over the establishment of a military garrison city on Woody Island in July 2012.[27]

In my view, the hype over Sansha City and the military garrison is unnecessary. The decision to establish the Sansha City was formalized in 2007. The PLA has occupied the Paracels archipelago since 1974.

Many have accused China of behind the scene maneuvers during the 45th ASEAN Foreign Ministers Meeting at Phnom Penh. When the ministers failed to issue a joint communiqué, the blame was put on China for putting pressure on Cambodia not to agree to any communiqué that would mention the Scarborough Shoal, as requested by the Philippines.[28]

No one denies that China has been assertive in the South China Sea since it removed the South Vietnamese troops from the Paracels (including Woody Island) on 19 January 1974. In April 1988, it fought a brief naval war with Vietnam and in 1995 it occupied the Mischief Reef, which the Philippines has claimed since 1978 as part of its Kalayaan territory.

Like China, Vietnam, Malaysia and the Philippines have garrisoned their territories in the South China Sea from the time of their occupation. Taiwan has had the largest military garrison on Itu Aba since 1953. Brunei is the only claimant that has not sent troops to occupy any island/rock feature.

What actually happened at Scarborough in April 2012?

On 10 April 2012, Manila sent its largest warship, *BRP Gregorio del Pilar* (former US Coast Guard Cutter *USS Hamilton*), to arrest Chinese fishermen at the Scarborough Shoal for 'breaching Philippines sovereignty and maritime jurisdiction'[29] – a euphemism for illegal entry, illegal fishing, and poaching. Two Chinese civilian vessels from the Bureau of Fisheries Administration rushed to the scene just in time to stop the seizure of eight fishing vessels; however, the catch was impounded.

Of course, this was not the first arrest of Chinese fishing vessels for illegal fishing and poaching in the area.[30] For example, in July 1997 the Philippine navy arrested 21 Chinese fishermen for alleged illegal entry in the vicinity of the Scarborough Shoal. The fishermen were arraigned before the Regional Trial Court of Olongapo in Zambales District, which administers the Scarborough Shoal on behalf of the Philippines. Presiding Judge Elioboro Ubiadas dismissed the case on the ground that the accused were apprehended in 'in a place over which there is yet agreement between the Chinese and the Philippine governments.'[31] He further opined that there can be no legal basis to conclude that 'the accused entered the Philippine territory illegally.'

This decision is likely to dent Manila's claim. Historically, the Scarborough Shoal has always been outside the boundary limit of the 1898 Spanish–US treaty of cession, a point that Manila does not deny. However, since 2009 the Philippines has redrawn its boundary to include the Scarborough Shoal and the Kalayaan Island group in its maritime territory. In September 2012, President Benigno Aquino passed an administrative order (AO29)[32] placing Kalayaan and Scarborough in the part of South China Sea that he has renamed the West Philippines Sea.

Many parties in the region have protested against the 2009 Presidential Decree to incorporate the Scarborough Shoal into the Regime of Islands under the

United Nations Convention on the Law of the Sea (UNCLOS).[33] Although the Shoal is in its claimed exclusive economic zone, it is not part of the Philippines baseline system.

Manila has based its claim to the Scarborough Shoal on 'effective occupation and effective jurisdiction since independence.' Manila has discounted proximity as the basis of its claim. On 18 April 2012, the Department of Foreign Affairs admitted that its sovereignty and jurisdiction over the Scarborough Shoal (Bajo de Monsiloc) is *not* premised on proximity or 'the fact that the rocks are within its 200 nautical miles or continental shelf under UNCLOS.'

ASEAN must not allow indecisiveness over a phrase to undermine the peaceful process that it has assiduously developed over the years with China. The code of conduct negotiations should not become hostage to some inflexible internal politics. ASEAN has more pressing, larger geo-strategic issues to worry about.

The US-Sino competition involving proxies in the South China Sea may complicate the regional maritime security dynamics. The involvement of external powers in regional conflicts may raise the stakes. Driven by strategic considerations and the prospects for maritime resources, all claimants have been expanding their military and enforcement capabilities in the disputed South China Sea. Buoyed by nationalist sentiments, some claimants (notably the Philippines) have sought outside help. The presence of external forces could undermine the military power equilibrium in the region.

Without some confidence-building mechanisms like the Incidents at Sea Agreements or joint development projects between the claimants, the maritime security situation in the South China Sea may take a turn for the worst.

Therein lies the real danger.

While neighbors should solve their territorial disputes by themselves, claimant states bordering the South China Sea must also seek fresh solutions to their divergent interests.

The Scarborough Shoal incident and ASEAN unity[34]

ASEAN is divided on the Scarborough Shoal. Writing in the *Wall Street Journal* in June 2012, Ian Storey criticized ASEAN's failure to close ranks over the Scarborough Shoal incident.[35] He pointed out that the incident at Scarborough had caused division due 'to differing national interests, including the value they place on their relationships with China.' This division, according to Storey, has resulted from a lack of cohesion and from inaction in dealing with China in the South China Sea.

It is true that the ASEAN countries do not have a common position on how to deal with China; for that matter, ASEAN states do not have a common policy or position vis-à-vis any large or small power.

Singling out China for the impasse does not explain the entire story. Before May 2010, the security situation in the South China Sea was bearable despite China's assertive policy. In 1995, for example, following the Mischief incident, Manila and Beijing signed a code of conduct pledging to solve their dispute by peaceful means. A year later (November 1996), President Ramos agreed with President Jiang Zemin that both parties would settle their disputes in the South China Sea, including the Scarborough Shoal, via joint development.

The tipping point was June 2010 in Singapore. Robert Gates' statement in Singapore in June 2010 and Hillary Clinton's reaffirmation, at the ASEAN Regional Forum in Hanoi on 23 July 2010, of the US policy of returning to the region after a long period of neglect introduced a new element in regional security dynamics. Beijing has viewed the US return to the Asia-Pacific and military engagement in the South China Sea as an integral part of US containment per se. Partly in response to the US containment policy, China has become more assertive in the South China Sea. Although Beijing has deployed more military assets in the South China Sea to show its presence, its enforcement activities are primarily conducted by civilian enforcement agencies.[36]

How does the US-Sino 'rivalry' affect ASEAN unity?

The US-Sino rivalry has caused some states to take sides. This action will have long-term consequences on the power equilibrium in Southeast Asia. The impasse at Scarborough has ramifications beyond China and the Philippines; it has brought non-claimant parties into the fray. The conflict will be more difficult to resolve with the involvement of those whose interests are not focused on the South China Sea problem but are using the South China Sea conflict to undermine China's security interests. Claimant states could become pawns in US-Sino relations. The competition could ultimately undermine ASEAN security and cohesiveness if the matter is not handled properly. However, for the time being, the situation is under control and the fall-out have not scarred ASEAN unity.

It would appear that the 45th ASEAN Foreign Ministers Meeting at Phnom Penh has put ASEAN credibility on line. In my opinion, the skeptics are too quick to pass judgment. Some say ASEAN has lost its centrality, others think ASEAN will sink after the foreign ministers' failure to issue a joint communiqué, for the first time in 45 years. Many have ridiculed ASEAN's credibility.

So what if ASEAN cannot cobble together a consensus? Does it mean ASEAN will close shop after the failure to agree on a communiqué? Is the communiqué so vital that without it, the entire ASEAN cooperative mechanism will fall apart?

It is puzzling how critics can ignore the record of ASEAN accomplishments, including forging a security community by 2015. It is true that intra-ASEAN trade remains sluggish at 26 percent, but as a region, it has a vibrant market. Its vibrancy does not occur by chance.

I beg to differ with the skeptics.[37]

Everything must be seen in the proper context. A small window makes sense only in the context of the overall architectural design. On its own, a small window looks misplaced. Looking at the Scarborough Shoal without the benefit of the larger geo-strategic design and landscape, including US-Sino rivalry, distorts the story.

The apprehension of ASEAN is misplaced. ASEAN is not a single-issue organization. The Scarborough Shoal impasse between China and the Philippines will resolve itself and it will not dent ASEAN unity. The Philippines and China will soon patch up their relationship if third parties stop interfering.

ASEAN has weathered worst storms in its existence and it gets stronger after each crisis. I have watched events unfold since its difficult birth in 1967. Philippine–Malaysian relations were bedeviled by the former's claim to part of Sabah as soon as Malaysia was formed in 1963. But the lingering claim has not caused ASEAN to collapse.

In 1968, for example, critics cried foul when Singapore hanged two Indonesian marines for the bombing of the MacDonald House in 1965. The nationalists in Indonesia demanded retribution. Diplomatic relations were ruffled. In hindsight, Singapore's decision to execute the decision of the court was wise.

In 1991, the Philippines recalled its ambassador from Singapore for hanging a maid who confessed to a crime. When the situation cooled down, diplomatic relations resumed. I hope that the recall of the Cambodian Ambassador Hos Sereythonh from Manila in August 2012 will not permanently damage diplomatic relations between the two ASEAN states.

In 1979, Vietnam reoccupied Amboyna Cay, which Malaysia included in its 1979 continental shelf map. In the same year, Philippine troops also reclaimed Commodore Reef in the South China Sea from Malaysia.

None of these incidents caused ASEAN to collapse.

ASEAN states have overcome more serious territorial disputes between themselves mainly through negotiation and by judicial means. For example, Indonesia and Malaysia went to the International Court of Justice (ICJ) to determine who owns the islands of Sipadan and Ligitan. The ICJ in 2002 decided that Malaysia had better title and awarded the two islands to Malaysia.

Singapore and Malaysia have taken their territorial disputes to litigation twice. In September 2003, for example, Malaysia sought and received provisional measures from the International Tribunal on Law of the Sea (ITLOS) at Hamburg on Singapore's land reclamation in and around the Straits of Johor. In May 2008, the ICJ rendered a decision on the status of Pedra Branca/Pulau Batu Putih.

ASEAN has moved on.

None of these territorial disputes has undermined ASEAN unity. On the contrary, ASEAN wisdom has reigned. In February 1979, Thailand and Malaysia agreed to jointly develop a disputed area in the Gulf of Thailand; similarly, in 1992, Vietnam and Malaysia signed a memorandum of understanding to jointly exploit for mineral resources in an overlapping maritime area. Both joint development agreements have withstood time and now all parties are reaping the returns from their commercial ventures.

In March 2009, Malaysia and Brunei agreed to vide the letters of exchange (LOE) to resolve their overlapping maritime boundaries and through the LOE, Brunei agreed to allow Malaysia to jointly develop oil and gas resources in a defined concession area (known as Block L and Block M), on commercial basis, for a period of 40 years. The agreement was reached amicably and it removed an irritant in the relations between Brunei and Malaysia.

Because territories are sacrosanct, many would have thought that claimant parties in the South China Sea would come to blows. Malaysia maintains cordial relations with the Philippines despite the Sabah claim and the occupation of the Commodore Reef. Likewise, Malaysia and Vietnam have opted for a joint development project and agreed to shelve their territorial disputes in the South China Sea.

The Scarborough Shoal incident is insignificant compared with the territorial problems. The Scarborough Shoal impasse is between China and the Philippines and it could be amicably resolved. In 1996, in Manila, President Ramos and Jang Zemin agreed to shelve their dispute in favor of joint development. In 1992, Manila signed the ASEAN Declaration on the South China Sea and gave the undertaking that it would resolve all sovereignty and jurisdictional issues in the South China Sea by peaceful means, without resort to force. In 2005, China and the Philippines (and later Vietnam) agreed to undertake a short-lived joint maritime seismic undertaking in the Palawan maritime area. One authority on the South China Sea even hailed the Arroyo presidency as the 'golden era' in Manila–Beijing relations.

Those were the good days.

Failure to agree on the wording of a joint communiqué is equally insignificant if we view ASEAN in the larger geo-strategic and geo-economic context. Surely, ASEAN is much bigger than the wording in a diplomatic communiqué. In the light of a new consensus on the six-point principles announced by the ASEAN foreign ministers following the Phnom Penh impasse, I think we should close the Cambodian chapter and move on as ASEAN states have usually done in the past. There is no point crying over spilt milk.

We all can and should savour the good days.

Few have recalled how ASEAN overcome the difficult days. One of the most difficult times in ASEAN history was in 1986 when the ASEAN heads of state summoned their moral strength to attend the third ASEAN summit at Manila after a lapse of 10 years. Credit for reinvigorating the Bangkok declaration at Manila must go to ASEAN leaders, in particular President Corazon Aquino for her tenacity in getting ASEAN back on track. She went to great lengths to please many ASEAN leaders, agreeing to limited control of the airspace over Manila during the summit. She permitted some states to send warships to Manila Bay in case something went wrong during the summit. Looking back, the 1986 summit at Manila was ASEAN's turning point; it renewed the spirit of regionalism. In hindsight, the summit was held partly because of President Corazon Aquino's tenacity and continuing support for regionalism.

Let us hope that President Corazon's son, President Benigno 'Ninoy' Aquino Junior III, will not let ASEAN down in difficult times like this. He holds the key to the Scarborough Shoal and his actions can have an impact on ASEAN cooperation. Hopefully, the 21st ASEAN Summit in November 2012 at Phnom Penh will not become bogged down by another insignificant event.

For the time being, ASEAN unity is stronger than the sum of its parts. It remains intact. Closing ranks will reinforce ASEAN unity as in 1986. I see no reason why ASEAN cannot unite over some protruding rocks in the Scarborough Shoal when it has survived ordeals and tribulations without a summit for a decade.

Concluding remarks

Relations between China and the US are expected to enter some stormy areas. As David Shambaugh explains, '[US-Sino] relations now operate on the basis of a number of systemic factors' beyond the control of personalities.[38] It will take a far greater display of pragmatism and realism on both sides to rebuild trust and steer away from a collision course.

New geo-economic dynamics in the Asia-Pacific region present opportunities for countries in the region to redefine their relationship with China and the US, especially in the maritime sector.

The factors that are likely to hinder closer relations between China and the US are geopolitical and domestic in nature. From the geopolitical perspective, the military power in-equilibrium in the Asia-Pacific region has been complicated by Barrack Obama's signature policy to pivot to the East. Many in China view this as a deliberate policy to contain an emerging China, which wants to exercise more control in its own maritime backyard now that it has the means to enforce the control.

Of course, this Chinese single-handed attempt to convert the South China Sea, for example, into an internal lake, similar to what the US did in the nineteenth century in the Caribbean, has caused some uneasiness among the claimant ASEAN states in the absence of well-established regional mechanisms for dispute settlement. Of late, their relations with China over the overlapping claims have been made more complex by the decision of some claimants to involve external powers inimical to China's interest to resolve their territorial problems. Beijing has resented efforts to multi-lateralize what it views as bilateral problems.

On the domestic front, rising nationalism can be a spoiler or a game changer. Whether it is in China, Japan, India, the Philippines, or Vietnam, unbridled pressure from nationalist groups can make it difficult for states to manage their foreign policies on an even keel. In the South China Sea and in the East China Sea where China has territorial claims, we have seen how nationalist pressures on the respective political leaderships have complicated diplomatic efforts to resolve their differences. Such pressures could trigger strategic miscalculations by the conflicting parties, for example when maritime commanders act in an overzealous manner.

While I remain bullish concerning ASEAN as a regional security and economic organization, the US-Sino relations that come on the heels of a declining Pax Americana and a resurgent China may spell danger for the region. History is replete with stories of powers in transition misbehaving. As it struggles to retain dominance, in transition the US may engage in dangerous policies to prove critics wrong.

Likewise, in transition to becoming an influential major power, China may miscalculate its strength and motivations by taking offensive, adventurist, and hostile policies. Likely to be hostage to US-Sino competition for more space is the deliberate policy to confuse national jurisdictional issues (like sovereign rights and territorial claims) with rights under international law to use the sea (for example, the freedom of navigation).

This danger may manifest in the South China Sea in the form of a proxy war/crisis. What begins as a bilateral issue may metamorphose into a larger crisis, when rival powers engage in proxy wars. The danger is when in their eagerness to buttress strength they seek alliances with another rival party. The ASEAN states, especially those with territorial claims in the South China Sea, for example, must not to be sucked into the maelstrom of the big power games –in this case, US-Sino rivalry.

The Philippines, which has been putting pressure on the US to support its quarrel with China over the Scarborough Shoal, for example, is a likely pawn in the political game. Although Washington has formally declared its neutrality over the territorial claims, since 2010 it has expanded its military presence in the area, for example in the Subic Bay and Clark Air Force Base.[39] President Obama will be in the region visiting Burma, Thailand, and Cambodia to attend the Seventh East Asia Summit on 20 November 2012. Washington is reportedly mending fences with Vietnam, with an eye on the former Russian Naval Base at Cam Ranh Bay, and reinvigorating military ties with Bangkok too. All this will certainly heighten anxieties in Beijing.

ASEAN states must not become pawns in or held hostage to this big power rivalry game.

> Where elephants make love the grass is *also* trampled.
>
> Anonymous

Notes

1 This revised paper was completed on 1 December 2012. The original paper was presented at the 1st Roundtable Conference on Malaysia-Cambodia/Laos/Myanmar Relations towards Strengthening ASEAN through Multi-channel Dialogue, Institute of Diplomacy and Foreign Relations (IDFR), Kuala Lumpur, 27 & 28 August 2012. The views are personal.

2 Henry Kissinger, *On China*, New York: Penguin, 2011.

3 This Law was adopted by the National Assembly of the Socialist Republic of Viet Nam at the 3rd Session on 21 June 2012. It will come into force on 1 January 2013.

4 For an alternative view, see Dennis Blasko and Taylor Fravel, 'Much ado about the Sansha garrison,' *The Diplomat*, 23 August 2012. According to both writers, the Sansha military garrison is 'more of an administrative move than an arms build-up in the South China Sea.'

5 President Aquino said in Administrative Order No. 29 of 5 September 2012 that 'By virtue of the powers vested in me by the Constitution and by law, do hereby order … [that the] maritime areas on the western side of the Philippine archipelago are hereby named as the West Philippine Sea.' President Aquino also ordered all government

agencies to 'employ the name West Philippine Sea' in all documents, messages and communications.

6 According to some sources, the Pentagon will deploy 10 littoral combat ships to Singapore by 2013.

7 The world will judge its actions: whether it is going to be a pacific power, a benign power, or a destructive power.

8 The ability of India to influence events in the South China Sea is constrained by geography and trade.

9 At the 20th Asia-Pacific Economic Cooperation (APEC) Heads of State meeting at Vladivostok (7–10 September 2012) President Vladimir Putin announced that Russia and Japan would build a US$7 billion liquefied natural gas (LNG) plant. According to some media reports Russia spent more than US$22 billion to build the infrastructure for the APEC meeting as well as laying the groundwork to transform Siberia and the Far East with Vladivostok as the its gateway to Asia-Pacific.

10 For example, the Aksai Chin and Arunachal Pradesh over which India and China fought a brief war in 1962.

11 For an American view of Chinese perception of the US, see Andrew Nathan and Andrew Scobell, 'How China sees America,' *Foreign Affairs*, 91(5), Sept./Oct. 2012. See also David Shambaugh, 'The rocky road ahead in US-China relations,' *Foreign Policy*, 23 October 2012, available at http://www.chinausfocus.com/foreign-policy/the-rocky-road-ahead-in-u-s-china-relations/ (accessed 5 November 2012).

12 According to Globalsecurity.org (http://www.globalsecurity.org/military/world/russia/mo-budget.htm; accessed 22 October 2012) by the mid-1980s, the Soviet Union had devoted between 15 and 17 percent of its GDP to military spending. In 1988, Soviets spent 21 million roubles on defence for operations and maintenance. Western analysts believed that Moscow has deflated the defense expenses by a factor of 10. According to James Dobbins 'China shows no interest in matching US military expenditure' ('War with China,' *Survival*, 54(4), Aug.–Sept. 2012). See also David Adams, 'The collapse of the Soviet Economy,' *Political Affairs*, Sept./Oct. 1991.

13 See 'Military Expenditure (% of GDP),' World Bank Report, 2011, at http://data.worldbank.org/indicator/MS.MIL.XPND.GD.ZS (accessed 20 October 2012).

14 International Monetary Fund, 'World Economic Report,' Washington, April 2012, at http://www.imf.org/external/pubs/ft/weo/2012/01/index.htm (accessed 5 April 2012).

15 See Bob Davis and Tom Orlik, 'China sees its growth slow further,' *Wall Street Journal*, Asia edition, xxxvii, 19–21 October 2012.

16 It has been reported that the demonstrations had caused many Japanese companies in Japan to suspend their operations (see BBC Report on 'China protests: fears over Japan-China trade ties', 18 September 2012). See also Nicholas Clement, 'The economic costs of China's anti-Japanese sentiment,' posted on 12 September 2012 by 2point6billion.com (accessed 12 October 2012).

17 Johan Galtung, *The Fall of the US Empire – And Then What?*,' Transcend University Press, 2009. See also Galtung's interview with Russia Today Radio (Moscow), 27 February 2011, available at http://blog.hiddenharmonies.org/2011/02/27/in-2020-the-u-s-empire-will-come-crumbling-down/ (accessed October 2011).

18 Norman Davies, *Vanished Kingdoms: The History of Half-Forgotten Europe*, London: Penguin, 2011.

19 Robert Kagan, *The World America Made*, New York: Knopf, 2012. See also Robert Kagan's interview with Christiane Amanpour, 'Is the US committing pre-emptive superpower suicide?,' *Brookings*, 22 February 2012, available at http://www.brookings.edu/research/interviews/2012/02/22-us-china-kagan; Robert Kagan, 'The myth of American decline,' *New Republic*, 11 January 2012.

20 'Bernanke Unleashes "QE 3",' *Equities Weekly*, 17 September 2012, available at http://

www.fundsupermart.com.my/main/articleFiles/webarticles/2733/MY/Weekly%20Commentary%20on%2009172012_merged.pdf. Christine Lagarde, Managing Director of the IMF, has suggested that that the policy of quantitative easing (an accommodative monetary policy) could cause overheating and asset bubbles in emerging economies. See statement by Lagarde attributed to AFB/Reuters in *theSun* (Malaysia), 15 October 2012, *Sunbiz*, p. 17.

21 See Peter W. Singer, 'Separating sequestration facts from fiction: sequestration and what it would do to U.S. military power, Asia, and the flashpoint of Korea,' *Brookings Center for Northeast Asian Policy Studies*, 9 October 2012.

22 President Hu Jintao's Statement at the 20th APEC meeting, Vladivostok, 6–9 September 2012.

23 Hugh White, *The China Choice: Why America Should Share Power*, Collingwood, Australia: Black, 2012. See also Robert Kaplan, 'The geography of Chinese power,' *Foreign Affairs*, 89(3), May/June 2010.

24 For an overview of the US role in the South China Sea, see Taylor Fravel, 'The United States in the South China Sea disputes,' paper presented at 9th Berlin Conference on Asian Security, Berlin, 18–19 June 2012; See also B. A. Hamzah, 'Overhyping the South China Sea,' *New Straits Times*, 21 August 2012.

25 'Temperatures rising in the South China Sea,' *The Nation*, 28 May 2012.

26 See Hamzah, 'Overhyping the South China Sea.'

27 See Blasko and Fravel, 'Much ado about the Sansha garrison.'

28 Carl Thayer provides an insight into different ASEAN positions at the 45th ASEAN Foreign Ministers Conference at Phnom Penh in April 2012. See Carl Thayer, 'ASEAN's Code of Conduct in the South China Sea: a litmus test for community building?,' *Asia Pacific Journal: Japan Focus*, 10, Issue 34, No. 4, 20 August 2012.

29 See Department of Foreign Affairs, 'Philippine Position on Bajo de Monsiloc and the Waters within its Vicinity', Manila, 28 April 2012.

30 According to the Philippine Coast Guard Report on Apprehension of Foreign Fishing Vessels conducting Illegal Fishing in Selected Philippine Waters (unpublished, 2012), there were 17 incidents of arrest between 2001 and 2012; 16 Chinese vessels and 1 from Vietnam.

31 Quoted from Domingo Siazon press statement in the *Philippines Inquirer,* 13 July 1997, p. 5.

32 'Renaming of South China sea draws flak,' *China Daily*, 22 September 2012. See http://europe.chinadaily.com.cn/china/2012-09/19/content_15769140.htm (accessed 22 September 2012).

33 Vietnam, China, and Taiwan were among many who protested.

34 See B. A. Hamzah, 'ASEAN Unity remains paramount,' *Sundaily*, 17 August 2012.

35 Ian Storey, 'ASEAN is a house divided,' *Asia Wall Street Journal*, 14 June 2012. See http://online.wsj.com/article/SB10001424052702303734204577465861459787498.html (accessed 22 September 2012). See also Ann Jung, 'Asean and the South China Sea,' *National Bureau of Asian Research*, 16 July 2012.

36 'Stirring up the South China Sea (I),' Asia Report No 223, International Crisis Group, Brussels, 23 April 2012, available at http://www.crisisgroup.org/en/regions/asia/north-east-asia/china/223-stirring-up-the-south-china-sea-i.aspx.

37 Hamzah, 'ASEAN Unity remains paramount.'

38 Shambaugh, 'Rocky road ahead.' This article was written before Barrack Obama was re-elected US President for the second term and before Xi Jinping was confirmed Paramount ruler of China in November 2012.

39 See Reuters Report, 'The U.S. military pivot to Asia when bases are not bases,' *Asahi Shimbun*, 14 November 2012, available at http://ajw.asahi.com/article/asia/china/AJ201211140085 (accessed 15 November 2012).

3 Recent developments in the South China Sea

Assessing the China–Vietnam and China–Philippines relationships

Ramses Amer and Li Jianwei

The main aim of this chapter is to examine recent developments in the South China Sea through two bilateral relationships – China–Vietnam and China–Philippines, respectively. The chapter first outlines recent developments in both bilateral relationships relating to the South China Sea. The nature of the events causing tension is identified and the way in which the events have been managed is examined. Particular attention is given to the management or lack of management mechanisms in the two bilateral relationships. Possible differences between the two relationships are explored with the aim of assessing whether relevant variations in management mechanisms can be explained by such differences. The chapter concludes with a summary of the main findings and some observations.

The first section deals with China–Vietnam relations and developments in relation to the South China Sea issues. The next section outlines China–Philippines relations and developments in relation to the South China Sea issues. In the final section the two relationships are compared and assessed by offering our observations.

Developments relating to the China–Vietnam relationship in the South China Sea[1]

Background[2]

Since full normalization of relations in late 1991 tension in bilateral relations has primarily been caused by differences relating to territorial disputes. Sharp differences relating to all the territorial disputes – that is, overlapping claims to the Paracel and Spratly archipelagos, to water and continental shelf areas in the South China Sea and in the Gulf of Tonkin, and to areas along the land border – were prevalent from May to November 1992. Differences relating to oil exploration in the South China Sea and the signing of contracts with foreign companies for exploration were prevalent during the periods April–June 1994, April–May 1996 and March–April 1997. In 1998 there was no extended period of tension relating to the border disputes but shorter periods can be noted such as in January along the land border and in the South China Sea in April, May, July and September 1998.[3]

In 1999 the focus was on reaching a settlement of the land border dispute and this resulted in the signing of a Land Border Treaty on 30 December 1999. In 2000 focus was on settling the Gulf of Tonkin disputes and this resulted in the signing of the Agreement on the Demarcation of Waters, Exclusive Economic Zones and Continental Shelves in the Gulf of Tonkin on 25 December 2000. During both years there was no noticeable tension relating to the disputes in the South China Sea.[4]

From 2001 to 2008 this pattern of interaction relating to the disputes in the South China Sea continued to prevail with continued dialogue and only limited periods of tension caused by the disputes in the area.[5] After the ratification of the Land Border Treaty in 2000 the Gulf of Tonkin agreement was ratified in 2004.[6] The demarcation process of the land border was completed at the end of 2008.[7] During the period 2009–2011 there were periodic increases in the level of tension relating to the disputes in the South China Sea.[8] In response bilateral contacts increased and in October 2011 China and Vietnam reached an Agreement on Basic Principles Guiding the Settlement of Sea-related Issues (hereafter Agreement on basic principles).[9]

In order to manage their territorial disputes China and Vietnam initiated a system of talks and discussions which was both highly structured and extensive. From bottom to top it looked as follows: expert-level talks; government-level talks – deputy/vice-minister, foreign minister-level talks; and high-level talks – presidents, prime ministers and secretary-generals of the Communist Party of China (CPC) and the Communist Party of Vietnam (CPV).[10]

The talks at the expert and government levels deserve further attention. Talks at the expert level were initiated in October 1992; up to late 1995 the talks focused mainly on the land border and the Gulf of Tonkin issues. Talks at the government level began in August 1993 and the thirteenth round of talks was held in January 2007. There have also been meetings and talks that have not been included in the official rounds. The first achievement was the signing of an agreement on 19 October 1993 on the principles for handling the land border and the Gulf of Tonkin disputes. It was further agreed to set up joint working groups at the expert level to deal with the two issues. The joint working group on the land border held 16 rounds of talks from February 1994 to December 1999 when the Land Border Treaty was signed. The joint working group on the Gulf of Tonkin met 17 times from March 1994 to December 2000 when the Agreement on the Demarcation of Waters, Exclusive Economic Zones and Continental Shelves in the Gulf of Tonkin was signed. Talks at the expert level on the disputes in the South China Sea proper, the so-called 'sea issues', were initiated in November 1995 and the eleventh round of talks was held in July 2006.

The negotiation process resulting in the signing of a treaty relating to the land border on 30 December 1999 reflected the substantially higher degree of progress made in negotiations on the land border compared with talks on other border disputes up to the end of 1999. In 2000 the negotiations on the Gulf of Tonkin issue were stepped up with the aim of reaching an agreement within that year. This goal was reached on 25 December 2000. Thus, the deadlines for resolving the land border and the Gulf of Tonkin issues were met in 1999 and 2000 respectively.

Less progress has been achieved with regard to the disputes in the South China Sea proper – that is, the competing sovereignty claims to the Paracel and Spratly archipelagos as well as the overlapping claims to water and continental shelf areas to the east of the Vietnamese coast. Talks have been initiated but the parties have yet to agree on which disputes to be included on the agenda. Vietnam pushes for the inclusion of the Paracels as an issue alongside that of the Spratlys, whereas China only wants to discuss the latter issue. To further complicate matters, China seems to view the disputes over water and continental shelf areas as part of the Spratly conflict whereas Vietnam seems to see them as separate issues. It would appear that Vietnam does not want to initiate talks relating to the areas of overlapping claims in the South China Sea proper as this could be interpreted as giving legitimacy to China's claims to those areas. Thus, of the three South China Sea issues to be addressed by the two countries there is only agreement on putting one on the agenda for talks, namely the Spratly archipelago, which is a multilateral conflict situation involving other claimants as well.

Developments since 2009[11]

Differences between China and Vietnam increased in 2009. In early May 2009 Vietnam submitted a 'Partial Submission' relating to Vietnam's extended continental shelf in the 'North Area' of the South China Sea as well as a 'Joint Submission' together with Malaysia relating to the 'southern part' of the South China Sea to the Commission on the Limits of the Continental Shelf (CLCS). Both submissions prompted China to protest and to reiterate its claims in the South China Sea. On a more positive note the government-level delegations dealing with territorial issues met on two occasions in 2009, in August and in November. Vietnam also protested about the arrest of Vietnamese fishermen by China on several occasions in 2009 and also in 2010. Furthermore, Chinese fishing bans led to Vietnamese protest in 2009 and 2010.

In response to the heightened tension the prime ministers of the two countries held talks in Hanoi on 28 October 2010 and decided to 'seek satisfactory solutions to existing issues relating to' the South China Sea. According to the official Vietnamese report the two sides also 'reached consensus on speeding up negotiations on basic principles to settle sea issues, and satisfactorily settling fishermen and fishing boat issues'. However, the official Chinese report did not mention anything about fishermen and fishing boats.

Open differences relating to activities in the South China Sea continued during the first half of 2011 and the most serious incidents occurred in late May and early June. Two incidents, on 26 May and 9 June, respectively, were related to Vietnamese oil exploration activities in areas that Vietnam considers to be within its exclusive economic zone (EEZ) and continental shelf to the east of the Vietnamese coast and Chinese reactions to and actions against these activities, which China considers to be within areas under China's 'jurisdiction'. Vietnam accused China of cutting the cables of the exploration ships operated by Vietnam, while China accused Vietnam of illegal activities within an area under its 'jurisdiction'. During the 9 June incident China also accused Vietnam of chasing away Chinese fishing boats. In connection with the incidents Vietnam explicitly rejected China's claim within the so-called 'nine-dashed line' in the South China Sea.

After this public display of differences and tension relating to activities in the South China Sea the two countries took action to ease the situation. Vietnam dispatched a Special Envoy to Beijing for discussions with the Chinese leaders. The two sides agreed to 'speed up the tempo of negotiations so as to early sign an "Agreement on basic principles guiding the settlement of sea issues between Vietnam and China"' as well as to 'boost the implementation' of the Declaration on the Conduct of Parties in the South China Sea (DOC) and of 'follow-up activities so that substantial progress will soon be achieved'.

Two significant developments took place in October 2011: the Agreement on basic principles was signed in Beijing on 11 October and the first high-level summit between the two countries since 2008 took place on 11–15 October when the Secretary-General of the CPV, Nguyen Phu Tong, visited China.

The Agreement on basic principles stated that the government-level delegations of both countries 'agree that the satisfactory settlement of sea-related issues between Vietnam and China is suitable for the basic interests and common aspirations of the two countries' people and helpful for regional peace, stability, co-operation and development'. They also agreed that on the basis of 'common perceptions of the Vietnamese and Chinese leaders reached on sea-related issues' to 'solve sea-related issues pursuant to' a set of 'principles' divided into six points.[12]

During his visit to China the Secretary-General of the CPV met with China's then President and Secretary-General of the CPC Hu Jintao and other Chinese leaders. In the joint statement issued in connection with the high-level summit considerable attention was devoted to maritime issues. It was stated that the two sides 'exchanged views in a sincere and straightforward manner on the sea issue, stressing their political will and determination to settle disputes via friendship, negotiation and talks in order to maintain peace and stability' in the South China Sea. The two sides agreed to 'speed up negotiations on the sea issue, seek basic and long-term solutions acceptable to both sides'. The two sides also stated that they 'will firmly speed up negotiations on the demarcation of areas beyond the mouth of the Tonkin Gulf and actively discuss co-operation for mutual development on this area'.[13]

China's then Vice-President Xi Jinping made an official visit to Vietnam on 20–22 December 2011. He held meetings with Vietnamese leaders. The two sides reviewed the overall collaboration between the two countries, including territorial issues.

In February 2012 Vietnam's Foreign Minister, Pham Binh Minh, made an official visit to China. In talks with his Chinese counterpart, Yang Jiechi, the two reviewed the bilateral relationship, including territorial issues, and reiterated the two sides' commitment to settle their differences by peaceful means. In late February Vietnam's Deputy Foreign Minister, Ho Xuan Son, held talks with his

Chinese counterpart, Zhang Zhijun, in Beijing. They agreed to establish working groups at the 'department level to negotiate on the delineation of the sea area outside the Bac Bo (Tonkin) Gulf mouth and cooperate in jointly developing this area'. They also agreed to set up working groups to cooperate in 'less sensitive sea domains, including sea environment protection, scientific research out at sea, search and rescue activities and mitigation of damage caused by natural calamities'. Finally, they agreed to launch a 'hotline between the two foreign ministries'. The hotline was opened on 2 March.

On 21–22 May, the 'first-round of talks at the departmental level' was held in Hanoi on the 'demarcation of areas outside the mouth of' the Gulf of Tonkin. This signalled the resumption of talks relating to this area. The second round of talks was held in Beijing on 26–27 September. The third round of talks was held in Hanoi on 29–30 May 2013.

On 29–30 May 2012, the first round of talks on 'co-operation in less sensitive fields at sea' was held in Beijing. The second round of talks was held in Hanoi on 6–8 November. The third round of talks was held in Beijing on 22–24 April 2013.

On 19–21 June 2013, Vietnam's President made a state visit to China. In connection with the visit an agreement was made between Vietnam's Ministry of Agriculture and Rural Development and China's Ministry of Agriculture on 'the establishment of a hot line on unexpected incidences in fishing operations at sea'. In the Joint Statement from the state visit it was stated that the two sides had reached 'consensus that the two Parties and States should maintain regular exchanges and dialogues'. They will 'persistently seek fundamental and long-term solutions acceptable to both sides through consultations and friendly negotiations'. It was agreed to 'intensify negotiations of the Working Group on the sea off' the Gulf of Tonkin as well as to 'increase negotiations of the Working Group on Viet Nam–China cooperation in less sensitive issues at sea'. The two sides also agreed to 'properly settling emerging issues with a constructive attitude, not letting the issue affect the overall situation of their relationship as well as peace and stability in the South China Sea.' Finally, the two sides 'reached consensus on the comprehensive and effective implementation' of the DOC.[14]

Despite these positive developments some incidents reveal that differences relating to the South China Sea still prevail. This can be seen from official Vietnamese complaints in 2012 in response to China's fishing ban, to the arrest of Vietnamese fishermen, to the opening up of blocks for oil concessions in the South China Sea, to Chinese activities relating to the establishment of the city of Sansha, and to an incident in late November in which Vietnam claimed that Chinese fishing boats had 'blocked' and 'severed' the cable of a Vietnamese seismic survey vessel in the vicinity of Con Co Island in an area located within Vietnam's continental shelf and EEZ. China's main complaint was in response to the adoption of Vietnam's 'Law of the sea', also referred to as 'Maritime Law'.

There have also been some incidents in 2013 that led to Vietnamese complaints in response to China's activities in the South China Sea, for example legislative decisions and developments plans affecting the Paracel and Spratly archipelagos, activities in two archipelagos and harassment of Vietnamese fishing boats.

Developments relating to the China–Philippines relationship in the South China Sea

Background[15]

Since diplomatic relations were established in 1975, the China–Philippines relationship has in general developed smoothly. Although rows emerged due to the overlapping claims in the South China Sea, they were prevented from escalating out of control. The most serious disputes before 2000 were the 1995 Mischief Reef (Meiji Jiao in Chinese) and 1997 Scarborough Reef (Huangyan Dao in Chinese) incidents. Realizing the potential negative impacts on bilateral relations of these incidents, the governments of both countries have practised measures to manage them at bilateral and regional levels.

After the Mischief incident, the dialogue between China and the Philippines led to an eight-point code of conduct in the Joint Statement of the Republic of Philippines and the People's Republic of China Consultations on the South China Sea and on other Areas of Cooperation of August 1995. This works as a model to initiate a more active role of the Association of Southeast Asian Nations (ASEAN) in the South China Sea. Active consultation and negotiation resulted in the DOC signed between the 10 ASEAN countries and China in November 2002.[16] In 1996, China and the Philippines issued a joint press release in which both sides agreed to set up bilateral consultation mechanisms, including three working groups in charge of fishery, marine environmental protection and confidence-building respectively. In particular practical cooperation in the fields of search and rescue, anti-piracy and counter-smuggling were encouraged to promote bilateral confidence. In the 2000 joint communiqué issued by the two foreign ministers, both reaffirmed the positive work of the confidence-building working groups and agreed to promote practical cooperation between the two militaries in fields such as information sharing and disaster relief to promote maritime security.[17] Therefore, during the period from 1995 to 2000 the two countries moved to initiate mechanisms for confidence-building through practical measures rather than directly managing conflicts that may have resulted from the disputes.[18]

Such cooperative an environment was further promoted under the Arroyo administration. In 2004, Arroyo paid a state visit to China. During the visit the countries signed a joint communiqué, in which an agreement was reached on the principles relating to managing the South China Sea issues. First, both reiterated their continuous efforts in promoting peace and stability in the region. Second, pending the final resolution of the territorial disputes and disputes over maritime rights, both would continue exploring cooperation measures, including joint development. Furthermore, both agreed to push ahead for peaceful settlement of the disputes on the basis of international law, including the 1982 United Nations Convention on the Law of the Sea (UNCLOS). The last point was that it was beneficial to build the South China Sea into a sea of cooperation through active and early implementations of the DOC.[19] Under these principles, both countries agreed to carry out joint marine seismic survey in November 2004. Later, in

March 2005, together with the PetroVietnam, oil companies from China and the Philippines signed an agreement on the Joint Marine Seismic Undertaking (JMSU), which was highlighted during Hu Jingtao's state visit to the Philippines in 2005. In the joint statement issued during Hu's visit the two countries agreed to 'continuously make efforts to maintain peace and stability in the South China Sea region and extend the welcome to the China–Philippines–Vietnam JMSU'.[20] The joint statement signed during Wen Jiabao's 2007 visit to the Philippines re-emphasized the similar cooperative spirits. Both countries promised to 'understand and support each other in issues relating to state sovereignty and territorial integrity'. Meanwhile, it was reaffirmed that 'China and ASEAN will implement the DOC through practical activities and projects' and that 'the trilateral JMSU could be a cooperation model in the region'. Also in this joint statement both countries agreed to 'further explore to promote the trilateral cooperation to a new stage to promote confidence in the region'.[21] However, this wishful thinking has not become reality. At the end of the first stage of work in 2008 the project came to an end as a result of domestic politics in the Philippines.[22]

Exchange of visits between leaders of the countries plays an important role in setting the tone for both countries to manage their maritime disputes. Worth noting here is that it was between the top leaders of China and the Philippines that the concept of joint development was first raised in regard to managing the disputes in the South China Sea. At the meeting between Deng Xiaoping and his Filipino counterpart Aquino on 16 April 1988, Deng was quoted as saying, 'after many years of consideration, we think that to solve the issue [of Nansha/ the Spratlys], all parties concerned could explore joint development under the premise of admitting China's sovereignty over them'.[23]

Developments since 2009

Pushed by active communication between the top leadership of both countries, bilateral relations entered a new stage. However, the maritime disputes persisted and developments since 2009 display a downward trend away from positive dispute management.

A Revitalized legal spat over maritime claims

In February–March 2009, the interpretation and application of Article 7 of UNCLOS regarding straight baselines became an issue in the South China Sea. Bill 3216, adopted by the House of Representatives of the Philippines on 2 February 2009, aimed to define the archipelagic baselines of the Philippine archipelago and reportedly both the Kalayaan Islands group[24] and the Scarborough Reef were enclosed within the said baselines. China responded by reiterating its sovereignty claim to Huangyan Island, the Nansha Islands and to 'their adjacent waters'. China also expressed 'hope that the relevant country can earnestly abide by' the DOC and 'refrain from taking actions that may complicate and increase disputes' in the South China Sea. A further development relating to the baselines of the Philippines is that on 10 March 2009 President Arroyo signed the Republic Act No. 9522 which did not include the Kalayaans and the Scarborough Reef within its archipelagic baselines, but the baselines there 'shall be determined as "regime of islands" under the Republic of the Philippines consistent with Article 121' of UNCLOS.[25] China responded by reiterating its statement of 3 February and by protesting against the Republic Act No. 9522 after it was submitted by the Philippines to the United Nations.[26]

To fulfil the obligation set by UNCLOS, by 13 May 2009 all relevant parties of the South China Sea dispute submitted their cases to the CLCS. In 2009 no immediate communication had been made by either China or the Philippines in relation to their separate notes to the United Nations in response to the joint submission by Malaysia and Vietnam of May 2009. Nearly two years later, on 5 April 2011, the Philippines sent a note to the Secretary-General of the United Nations in response to China's May 2009 notes with the attached maps displaying the U-shaped lines. In this note, the Philippines stated that 'under the international law principle of "la terre domine la mer" … the extent of the waters that are adjacent to the relevant geographical features are definite and determinable under UNCLOS, specifically under Article 121 (Regime of Islands) of this said Convention'.[27] Furthermore, in this note the Philippines seems to suggest that there is 'no legal basis for claiming sovereign rights and jurisdiction over any resources in or under the waters within the nine-dashed line outside the waters adjacent to the islands'. In response to the note of the Philippines, China sent a note to the Secretary-General of the United Nations on 14 April 2011. China stated that 'China's Nansha Islands is fully entitled to Territorial Sea, Exclusive Economic Zone (EEZ) and Continental Shelf.' China did not mention or attach any map to this note.[28] Also in this note, China pointed out that prior to the 1970s the Philippines 'had never made any claims to Nansha Islands or any of its components' and it was since 1970s that the Philippines had 'started to invade and occupy some islands and reefs of China's Nansha Islands'. The note further stated that the Philippines' occupation 'constitutes infringement upon China's territorial sovereignty'.[29]

At the ASEAN Ministerial Meeting Retreat in Bali on 19 July 2011, the Philippines' Foreign Minister Albert F. del Rosario openly criticized China by saying that 'the new introduction of China of the 9-dash in 2009, becomes the core of the problem'.[30] In August a forum entitled 'The Spratly Islands Issue: Perspective and Policy Responses' was held in Manila. At the forum Rosario again stated that 'China's claims in relation to the U-shaped line are baseless.'[31] On 22 January 2013 the Philippines initiated arbitral proceedings against China, calling on the Arbitral Tribunal for a ruling that:

> [d]eclares that China's rights in regard to maritime areas in the South China Sea, like the rights of the Philippines, are those that are established by UNCLOS, and consist of its rights to a Territorial Sea and Contiguous Zone under Part II of UNCLOS, to an EEZ under Part V, and to a Continental Shelf under Part VI; [and d]eclares that China's maritime

> claims in the SCS based on its so-called nine-dash line are contrary to UNCLOS and invalid.[32]

On 19 February, China returned the Philippines' notification in regard to the case, stating that China would not accept it and hoped that the Philippines would keep its promise and not take any actions that would make things more complicated. In the meantime, China expressed its wish that the Philippines would respond positively to China's suggestion on setting up a China–Philippine consultation mechanism on sea-related issues as well as revitalizing their bilateral confidence-building measures.[33] The Arbitral Tribunal was formed on 21 June when Judge Thomas Mensah of Ghana was appointed to replace Judge Chris Pinto of Sri Lanka, who resigned from the arbitration panel in May shortly after his appointment because his wife is Filipino.[34] The procedure has been initiated to deal with the China–Philippine arbitration case.

An administrative spat over attempts to exploit resources

Revitalizing the domestic economy is one of the targets for Aquino III's government. The potential oil and gas resources in the sea area around the Spratlys are important to the Philippine economy. In regard to the 2005 trilateral JMSU agreement, Aquino III commented at a ceremony on 4 January 2011 that the Philippines should not have gone into the JMSU with China and Vietnam and it had started oil exploration in offshore area off Palawan.[35] Oil and gas exploration in the disputed sea area around the Spratlys re-appeared as a source of tension.

In early 2011, the Philippine government endowed a UK-based company, Energy Forum, with a two-year contract to explore the oil and gas resources in the disputed area in the South China Sea. On 2 March, the Philippines claimed that the seismic survey vessels of the Forum Energy Philippines Corporation (FEPC) were harassed by Chinese marine surveillance vessels.[36] On 23 March, the FEPC completed the work programme for Service Contract 72 (SC 72) located in the Reed Bank (Lile Tan in Chinese) and announced on its website that it would immediately 'begin processing the data with the aim of further evaluating the commercial potential of the block, and to help identify the best location for possible appraisal wells to be drilled'.[37] When responding to a question regarding this announcement, the spokesperson for the Chinese Foreign Ministry responded:

> China has indisputable sovereignty over the Nansha Islands and its adjacent waters. Oil and gas exploration and exploitation by any country or company without the permission of the Chinese Government constitute infringement on China's sovereignty and sovereign rights, which is invalid.[38]

Three of the 15 oil blocks listed for bidding by the Philippines on 30 June are located to the north-west of Palawan.[39] The Philippines deny China's claim over this sea area. At the above-mentioned forum in August 2011, Rosario declared that the Reed Bank, located 85 nautical miles from the nearest coast of Palawan, 'is part of the continental shelf of the western coast of Palawan Province in the Philippines'. He further stated, 'The Reed Bank can only be exclusively developed by the Philippines and foreign investors could be invited to assist in developing the area in accordance with Philippine laws.'[40]

Unilateral resources development in the overlapping sea area tends to increase the danger of clashes between relevant parties.

Besides oil and gas exploration, fishing also became a source of tension in 2011. On 25 February Philippine fishing vessels found at the vicinity of Jackson Atoll in the Spratlys were warned by Chinese law enforcement vessels.[41] On 25 March six Chinese fishermen were arrested by the Philippines in the Spratlys sea area.[42] Again, on 18 October, a Chinese fishing vessel was 'harassed by a Philippine warship when it was carrying out normal fishing activities'.[43]

An incident resurfaces[44]

On 10 April 2012, the Philippines' biggest naval vessel, *BRP Gregorio Del Pilar*, attempted to intercept Chinese fishing boats which were reported to be taking shelter from a storm in the lagoon of Scarborough Reef. The incident over the Scarborough Reef resurfaced. Similar incidents first emerged on 30 April 1997, when Philippine naval vessels prevented three Chinese boats from approaching the reef and hoisted the Philippine flag, but this time the incident dragged on for much longer.

The tensions over the Scarborough Reef had been fluctuating and reached a peak on 7 May when Chinese Vice Foreign Minister Fu Ying met with the Philippines' chargé d'affaires in Beijing and criticized the Philippines for having made serious mistakes by escalating tensions. He stated that 'China has made all preparations to respond.'[45] Diplomatic negotiations resumed on 9 May and both countries stated their desire to find a solution to the situation. At the same time both sides maintained their tough stance. With the incident dragging on the negative impacts spilled over to other areas of bilateral relations. First, it aroused strong nationalistic feelings from both countries. In the Philippines protesters shouted slogans such as 'China, back off the Panatag Shoal, stop poaching'. In China protesters responded with 'Get out of Huangyan Island'. Second, bilateral trade and tourism slowed down. China is the fourth largest market for tourists to the Philippines and the number of tourists from China had increased by 77 per cent during the first three months of 2012. However, since 16 May no Chinese tourist groups had visited the Philippines. Third, the existence of tensions in the water area of the Scarborough Reef had prevented fishermen from undertaking normal fishing activities.

As long as the sovereignty dispute over the Scarborough Reef remains unsettled, incidents such as the present stand-off may occur again. It is necessary for both countries to manage the situation peacefully and to prevent tension from re-occurring in the future. Political wisdom is needed to find creative means to address the situation and to create mechanisms to reduce the re-emergence of tension in the future.

Positive developments

In the light of the global financial crisis both countries realized the importance of a peaceful environment if they were to achieve total economic recovery. Aquino III paid a state visit to China in September 2011. During the visit both governments reached consensus relating to the dispute settlement in the South China Sea. In a joint statement, both agreed that maritime disputes should never negatively affect bilateral friendly and cooperative relations. It was also reiterated that their disputes should be solved by peaceful means in order to continuously maintain peace, security and stability in the region.[46]

Before Aquino III's visit, Rosario paid an official visit to China in July 2011. During the meeting between Rosario and his Chinese counterpart Yang Jiechi, bilateral cooperation was emphasized. Rosario and Yang agreed not to let the maritime disputes affect the broader picture of friendship and cooperation between the two countries. The two sides reaffirmed their commitments to respect and abide by the DOC.[47]

Emerging divergence of approaches to dispute management

Regarding resolving the South China Sea issues both countries have emphasized the importance of peaceful settlement. They have agreed that direct communication would help ease tensions. However, there appears to be a divergence of approaches to dispute settlement in recent developments. China wants to resolve the disputes through direct diplomatic means, that is, bilaterally. At the same time China has been promoting its coordination with ASEAN to manage the overall situation in relation to the South China Sea.[48] According to China, the DOC, as well as the future code of conduct (COC), is not for dispute settlement but for conflict management to maintain peace, security and stability in the region.

On the other hand, the Philippines has turned to practices beyond bilateral means. It has tried to get a unified voice within ASEAN, to get support from its treaty ally the United States and to secure international jurisprudence. First, the Philippines has been promoting one voice within ASEAN to deal with China using two approaches. The first is to push for a legally binding COC. In the first half of 2011, leaders and officials of the Philippine government travelled through the key countries of ASEAN for such a purpose. In April, during his visit to Vietnam, Rosario agreed with his Vietnamese counterpart to mutually push ahead for the COC. In May Aquino III visited Thailand and Brunei. During the visit, he tried to persuade the two countries to press China to reach a COC.[49] The second approach is to promote the ASEAN–China Zone of Peace, Freedom, Friendship and Cooperation (ZoPFFC). At an August forum, Rosario promoted the concept of ZoPFFC. He explained that under ZoPFFC, the relevant disputed features in the South China Sea would be segregated from the undisputed waters in accordance with international law, specifically UNCLOS.[50] In the joint communiqué of the ASEAN Foreign Ministers Meeting on 19 July 2011, the ASEAN

Senior Officials' Meeting was asked, with the assistance of maritime legal experts, to seriously study the proposal of ZoPFFC.[51]

Second, more clearly than before, the Philippines has turned to the US for security reassurance in dealing with a larger neighbouring country, China. The US–Philippine alliance relationship was considered as the basis of Aquino III's government. Since Aquino took office the US has provided economic and military assistance to the Philippines, openly expressing its plan to improve the Philippines' capability in protecting sovereignty over the islands by providing the Philippines with new military equipment and strengthening bilateral military cooperation.[52] In February 2011, Rosario stated that the US was the only strategic partner of the Philippines. In March, then US secretary of State Clinton exchanged views over the phone with her Filipino counterpart Rosario. Both emphasized the need to ensure maritime security in the Asia-Pacific and agreed that a way forward was the conclusion of a binding regional code of conduct in the South China Sea.[53] Also in June, the Philippines and the US carried out one bilateral and one multilateral military exercise in or near the South China Sea area.[54] During the Scarborough Reef incident the Philippine Department of Foreign Affairs posted a message on its official website stating that Clinton had firmly reiterated that the US would honour its treaty obligations under its mutual defence treaty with the Philippines and urged claimant countries to clarify and settle their claims legally in accordance with international law, including UNCLOS.[55] At the ASEAN–US Ministerial Meeting held on 11 July 2012, Clinton echoed the Philippine position in promoting one common ASEAN voice by saying, '[w]hat might be a challenge today for some of ASEAN's members, if left unaddressed by all of ASEAN, could lead tomorrow to issues that may become problems for (the rest of) other ASEAN members.' This was interpreted in reference to the tensions in the South China Sea.[56]

Third, the possibility of international jurisprudence has been explored and put into practice. In Aquino III's Nation Address of 25 July 2011, it was raised that '[w]e are also studying the possibility of elevating the case on the West Philippine Sea[57] to the International Tribunal for the Law of the Sea, to make certain that all involved nations approach the dispute with calm and forbearance.'[58] On 22 January 2013 the Philippines brought China to arbitration 'under Article 287 and Annex VII of UNCLOS' to challenge 'the validity of China's nine-dash line claim' and to 'desist from unlawful activities that violate the sovereign rights and jurisdiction of the Philippines under the 1982 UNCLOS'.[59] From the perspective of the Philippines, it 'has exhausted almost all political and diplomatic avenues for a peaceful negotiated settlement of its maritime dispute with China'.[60] It is the first time that international jurisprudence has been invoked in relation to the South China Sea issues.

Conclusions[61]

The most evident feature of this empirical overview of the developments relating to the South China Sea situation in the relationships between China and Vietnam and between China and the Philippines is that between China and Vietnam there are established forms of dialogue and talks from high level down to expert level to address differences and tensions while China and the Philippines have no such established forms of dialogue. In fact the structure of talks between China and Vietnam has developed continuously since the early 1990s and the two sides have agreed on mechanisms and principles to better handle and manage their differences. In relation to China and the Philippines the current lack of both established forms of dialogue and mechanisms can be contrasted with the mid-1990s when the two sides agreed on a bilateral 'code of conduct' to be observed in the South China Sea.

The differences between the two relationships in terms of management approaches towards tension in recent years can be observed when comparing China and Vietnam's response in 2011 with the response by China and the Philippines in both 2011 and 2012. China and Vietnam reached the Agreement on basic principles in October 2011 and took steps to implement the agreement in 2012 and 2013. In addition the two countries held the first high-level summit for three years in October 2011 and directly addressed the South China Sea issues at the summit. The high-level summit of June 2013 confirmed this trend. Between China and the Philippines no equivalent progress has been made. Both countries depend on ad hoc diplomatic negotiations to reduce the tensions in relation to their maritime disputes. This is illustrated very clearly in the Scarborough Reef incident of 2012. Even at the peak of the tensions the Philippines failed to appoint its ambassador to China. In the end two envoys were chosen to go to Beijing to handle the negotiations. The eighteenth Foreign Ministry Consultations were held in Manila on 19 October 2012. However, this regular bilateral foreign-minister-level mechanism is not meant to deal with maritime dispute issues, but is a venue for the two countries to discuss bilateral, regional and multilateral issues of mutual concern, including promoting areas of cooperation in various fields, such as trade and investment, tourism, culture and education, defence and security, agriculture and fisheries, transportation and communication, and consular matters.[62] The Philippines' recent move to apply for arbitration is an obvious divergence from bilateral mechanisms. It is a new approach for handling issues in relation to the South China Sea dispute. At the moment it is hard to predict its impact on bilateral relations. However, China's lack of participation indicates a failure of bilateral dispute management. Clearly the failure to agree on a bilateral mechanism to deal with their maritime disputes has negatively impacted the effectiveness of bilaterally handling such issues and opened the door to other options.

A summary of the main achievements of China and Vietnam displays that the demarcation of the land border has been completed. In the Gulf of Tonkin both the boundary agreement and the fishery agreement have entered into force. On-going talks and discussions on the remaining territorial disputes in the South China Sea are a further indication of the importance placed by both countries on managing and avoiding tensions.

However, continued efforts are needed. In the Gulf of Tonkin successful completion of the negotiations on the delimitation of the so-called 'mouth' of the

Gulf is important. An interim approach could be a bilateral joint development arrangement in relevant agreed waters in the mouth area. The continued implementation of the fishery agreement is essential. The collaboration relating to the maintenance of order in the Gulf through joint patrols needs to be expanded. In the South China Sea it is essential to avoid future confrontation, not only for bilateral relations but also for the stability of the region. It is also necessary to move both the bilateral and the multilateral conflict management processes forward. Although formal settlements of the disputes are unlikely in the current climate there is room for further progress both bilaterally and multilaterally in managing both the disputes and the broader security situation in the South China Sea.

At the bilateral level, the October 2011 Agreement on basic principles has enhanced the mechanisms for management of sea-related issues and disputes through a de facto bilateral ‘code of conduct’, and the high-level summit of October 2011 signalled a renewed high-level push for better management of the sea-related issues. This high-level push continues, as displayed by the June 2013 high-level summit. The combination of these two factors has created conditions more conducive to managing disputes and to reducing tension between China and Vietnam in the South China Sea. This addresses the need to enhance and expand the bilateral management approach relating to the South China Sea issues that was highlighted by the incidents in late May and early June 2011 and by the periodically increased tension relating to developments in the region during the period 2009–2011.

As has been the case since full normalization of the bilateral relations between China and Vietnam, overlapping claims to maritime zones in the South China Sea to the east of the Vietnamese coastline – where Vietnam’s claims to EEZ and continental shelf overlap with China’s claims within the so-called ‘nine-dashed line’ – will most likely be the subject of continued differences between the two countries and the risk of incidents causing periodic tension in bilateral relations is likely to persist. Developments in 2012 and 2013 support this prediction. On a more positive note the initiation of ‘department-level’ talks on the mouth of the Gulf of Tonkin and the initiation of talks on ‘co-operation in less sensitive fields at sea’ show that the two sides are making progress in implementing the Agreement on basic principles.

One issue that remains to be addressed is the lack of mutual agreement on the scope of talks on the South China Sea. Only the Spratlys are on the agenda. China opposes the inclusion of the Paracels. Vietnam opposes the inclusion of areas to the east of the Vietnamese coast where Vietnam claims to continental shelf and EEZ areas extend beyond the limit of the so-called ‘nine-dashed line’ claim by China. If China and Vietnam could agree on the scope and the issues that are disputed it would be an important step forward as this would create a realistic agenda for expert-level talks and it would also contribute to the multilateral efforts. This should not be interpreted as an argument that either side should abandon their sovereignty claims to the Paracel and Spratly archipelagos, but rather that they should recognize that they have overlapping claims and that such situations need to be addressed.

In the history of China–Philippines relations relating to the South China Sea issues the period from 1995 to 2000 seems to have been more proactive in promoting bilateral mechanisms to manage issues that could otherwise lead to tensions. In August 1995 the first bilateral code of conduct in the South China Sea region was reached between the two countries. In 1996 it was agreed to set up some bilateral consultation mechanisms, including three working groups on fishery, marine environmental protection and confidence-building. This was the result of mutual political will which recognized the need for dispute management mechanisms. Such a cooperative interaction positively affected other disputant parties as well as ASEAN as a whole, leading to the DOC. Partially due to the ASEAN–China confidence-building mechanism and in particular strong political will from both countries in relation to the China–Philippine management of disputes, the South China Sea remained reasonably calm up until 2009. Before then tensions did appear but were normally brought under control quickly. The improvement in the overall bilateral cooperative relations contributed positively to the bilateral success in handling differences and promoting cooperation in the disputed sea area, including the trilateral 2005–2008 JMSU. However, it seems unfortunate that under such positive relations no bilateral mechanisms were formally established in relation to managing the South China Sea issues. China–Philippine relations have been negatively affected by the recent management of their maritime disputes, as clearly seen in the 2012 Scarborough Reef incident. The obvious lack of some mechanism to coordinate or manage their differences in relation to South China Sea disputes could easily turn the situation out of control. This would be detrimental to bilateral relations and confidence-building. In view of the countries' consensus on not letting their maritime issues affect their generally friendly relations there is an urgent need for such a mechanism to target management of their bilateral disputes in the South China Sea.

At the regional level all three countries are parties to the DOC. China, the Philippines and Vietnam can positively contribute to the successful implementation of the DOC and also to the process of further developing the conflict management mechanisms needed to maintain stability and avoid tension and confrontation in the South China Sea. A possible future regional 'code of conduct' applicable to the South China Sea within the framework of the ASEAN–China dialogue could contribute to such a development. The impact of a new form of dispute settlement practice – international jurisprudence – brought up unilaterally by the Philippines in January 2013, remains to be seen.

Notes

1 The information relating to border and territorial issues in China–Vietnam relations is derived from earlier studies: see R. Amer, *The Sino-Vietnamese Approach to Managing Boundary Disputes*, Maritime Briefing, vol. 3, no. 5, Durham: International Boundaries Research Unit, University of Durham, 2002 (hereafter Amer, *Sino-Vietnamese Approach*); R. Amer, 'The Sino-Vietnamese approach to managing border disputes – lessons, relevance and implications for the South China Sea situation', in Tran Truong Thuy (ed.), *The South China Sea: Cooperation for Regional Security and Developments, Proceedings of the*

International Workshop, co-organized by the Diplomatic Academy of Vietnam and the Vietnam Lawyers' Association, 26–27 November 2009, Hanoi, Vietnam, Hanoi: Gioi and Diplomatic Academy of Vietnam, 2010, pp. 251–271 (hereafter Amer, 'Sino-Vietnamese'); R. Amer, 'Sino-Vietnamese border disputes', in B. Elleman, S. Kotkin and C. Schofield (eds), *Beijing's Power and China's Borders: Twenty Neighbors in Asia*, Armonk, NY and London: M. E. Sharpe, 2012, pp. 295–309 (hereafter Amer, 'Sino-Vietnamese border'); and R. Amer and J. Li, 'Recent developments in the South China Sea – an assessment of the core bilateral relationship between China and Vietnam', in G. Houlden and N. Hong (eds), *Maritime Security Issues in the South China Sea and the Arctic: Sharpened Competition or Collaboration?*, Beijing: China Democracy and Legal System Publishing House, 2012, pp. 41–75.

2 For a broad overview on the border issues in China-Vietnam relations, see Amer, 'Sino-Vietnamese border', pp. 295–309.

3 Amer, *Sino-Vietnamese Approach*, pp. 8–26.

4 Ibid., pp. 26–34.

5 For an overview of incidents during this period, see Amer, 'Sino-Vietnamese', pp. 264–267.

6 Information derived from R. Amer and H. T. Nguyen, 'Vietnam's border disputes: legal and conflict management dimensions', in B. S. Chimni, M. Masahiro and L.-a. Thio (eds), *The Asian Yearbook of International Law*, vol. 12 (2005–2006), Leiden and Boston, MA: Martinus Nijhoff, 2007, pp. 117–121 (hereafter Amer and Nguyen, 'Vietnam's border disputes').

7 Amer, 'Sino-Vietnamese', pp. 256–257.

8 For an overview of key incidents in 2009 and 2010, see R. Amer, 'Vietnam in 2009 – facing the global recession', *Asian Survey*, 50(1), 2010, pp. 215–216; R. Amer, 'Vietnam in 2010 – regional leadership', *Asian Survey*, 51(1), 2011, pp. 196–201, at p. 200; and R. Amer, 'Dispute settlement and conflict management in the South China Sea – assessing progress and challenges', in Tran Truong Thuy (ed.), *The South China Sea: Towards A Region of Peace, Security and Cooperation*, Hanoi: Gioi and Diplomatic Academy of Vietnam, 2011, pp. 245–268, at p. 266. For details about developments in 2011, see Amer and Li, 'Recent developments in the South China Sea', pp. 43–58. For developments from 2009 to 2011, see also R. Amer, 'China, Vietnam and the South China Sea – disputes and dispute management', *Ocean Development and International Law*, 45(1), 2014 (forthcoming).

9 See Amer and Li, 'Recent developments in the South China Sea', pp. 53–56.

10 Amer, *Sino-Vietnamese Approach*, pp. 9–14, 50–58; R. Amer, 'Assessing Sino-Vietnamese relations through the management of contentious issues', *Contemporary Southeast Asia*, 26(2), 2004, pp. 329–331; Amer and Nguyen, 'Vietnam's border disputes', pp. 118–122; R. Amer and H. T. Nguyen, 'The management of Vietnam's border disputes: what impact on its sovereignty and regional integration?', *Contemporary Southeast Asia*, 27(3), 2005, pp. 433–434; and R. Amer and H. T. Nguyen, 'Vietnam's border disputes – assessing the impact on its regional integration', in Stéphanie Balme and Mark Sidel (eds), *Vietnam's New Order: International Perspectives on the State and Reform in Vietnam*, Basingstoke and New York: Palgrave Macmillan, 2007, pp. 71–87, at pp. 74–76.

11 For an overview of key incidents in 2009 and 2010, see Amer, 'Vietnam in 2009', pp. 215–216; Amer, 'Vietnam in 2010', p. 200; and Amer, *Dispute Settlement*, p. 266. For details about developments in 2011 and into early 2012, see Amer and Li, 'Recent developments in the South China Sea', pp. 43–58. For developments up to 2013, see Amer, 'China, Vietnam'.

12 For a detailed overview, see Amer and Li, 'Recent developments in the South China Sea', pp. 53–56. The text of the Agreement is reproduced as an annex in Amer, 'China, Vietnam'.

13 'Vietnam-China joint statement', 16 October 2011, from the website of the *Communist Party of Vietnam Online Newspaper*, at http://www.cpv.org.vn/cpv/Modules/News/NewsDetail.aspx?co_id=30107&cn_id=484891 (accessed 14 August 2013).
14 'Viet Nam, China issue joint statement', 22 June 2013, from the website of Viet Nam Ministry of Foreign Affairs, at http://www.mofa.gov.vn/en/nr040807104143/nr040807105001/ns130624152141/newsitem_print_preview (accessed 28 June 2013).
15 For background reading, the following articles have been referred to: R. Marlay, 'China, the Philippines, and the Spratly Islands', *Asian Affairs, an American Review*, 23(4), 1997, pp. 195–209; I. Storey, 'Creeping assertiveness: China, the Philippines and the South China Sea dispute', *Contemporary Southeast Asia*, 21(1), 1999, pp. 95–118; U. Granados, 'Ocean frontier expansion and the Kalayaan Islands Group claim: Philippines' postwar pragmatism in the South China Sea', *International Relations of the Asia-Pacific*, 9, 2008, pp. 267–294; A. Baviera, 'The influence of domestic politics on Philippine foreign policy: the case of Philippines–China relations since 2004', *The S. Rajaranam School of International Studies Working Paper Series*, No. 241, 2012; and R. Castro, 'Probing into the legality of the People's Republic of China's (PRC) claim to sovereignty over the Spratly Islands', *Philippine Political Science Journal*, 21(44), 2012, pp. 27–56.
16 J. Li and R. Amer, 'Recent practices in dispute management in the South China Sea', in C. Schofield (ed.), *Maritime Energy Resources in Asia: Legal Regimes and Cooperation*, Special Report, no. 37, Seattle: National Bureau of Asian Research, 2012, pp. 79–103, at p. 90.
17 F. Zhong, 'Domestic politics and the institutionalization of the South China Sea issue: bilateral policy coordination in Sino-Vietnamese and Sino-Philippines relations', *Journal of Contemporary Asia-Pacific Studies*, 3, 2012, pp. 94–115, at p. 102.
18 Ibid., p. 101.
19 'Joint Press Release between the People's Republic of China and the Republic of the Philippines', 3 September 2004, from the website of Ministry of Foreign Affairs of the People's Republic of China, at http://www.fmprc.gov.cn/chn/gxh/zlb/smgg/t155753.htm (accessed 28 November 2012).
20 'Joint Statement between China and the Philippines', 28 April 2005, from the website of Ministry of Foreign Affairs of the People's Republic of China, at http://www.fmprc.gov.cn/chn/gxh/zlb/smgg/t193789.htm (accessed 28 November 2012).
21 'Joint Statement between the People's Republic of China and the Republic of the Philippines', 16 January 2007, from the website of Ministry of Foreign Affairs of the People's Republic of China, at http://www.fmprc.gov.cn/chn/gxh/zlb/smgg/t289365.htm (accessed 28 November 2012).
22 T. Davenport, 'Joint development in Asia: some valuable lessons learned', in C. Schofield (ed.), *Maritime Energy Resources in Asia: Legal Regimes and Cooperation*, Special Report, no. 37, Seattle: National Bureau of Asian Research, 2012, pp. 129–160, at p. 145.
23 Li and Amer, 'Recent practices', p. 94.
24 Part of the Spratlys (Nansha Islands in Chinese).
25 The text of the Republic Act No. 9522 can be found as one of the documents submitted by the Philippines to the United Nations as part of the 'Deposit of the list of geographical coordinates of points as contained in Republic Act No. 9522: An Act to Amend Certain Provisions of Republic Act No. 3046, as Amended by Republic Act No. 5446, to Define the Archipelagic Baselines of the Philippines, and for Other Purposes', M.Z.N.69.2009.LOS (Maritime Zone Notification, 21 April 2009, available at http://www.un.org/Depts/los/LEGISLATIONANDTREATIES/PDFFILES/phl_2008_act9522.pdf (accessed 1 December 2013).
26 H. T. Nguyen and R. Amer, 'A new legal arrangement for the South China Sea?', *Ocean Development and International Law*, 40(4), 2009, pp. 333–349, at p. 340.

27 H. T. Nguyen and R. Amer, 'Coastal states in the South China Sea and submissions on the outer limits of the continental shelf', *Ocean Development and International Law*, 42(3), 2011, pp. 245–263, at p. 257.
28 Ibid., pp. 257–258; and H. Ju, 'South China Sea policy of the Philippines: interest driven policy choice', *Journal of Contemporary Asia-Pacific Studies*, 3, 2012, pp. 78–93, at p. 90.
29 Ibid., p. 86; and China, 'Note verbale dated 21 May 2009 from the Permanent Mission of China to the United Nations addressed to the Secretary-General', from the website of the United Nations, at daccess-ddsny.un.org/doc/UNDOC/GEN/N09/346/61/PDF/N0934661.pdf (accessed 28 October 2010).
30 'Secretary del Rosario to pursue PHL key initiatives in ASEAN Foreign Ministers' meeting on July 19', 5 August 2011, from the website of Department of Foreign Affairs of the Republic of the Philippines, at http://www.gov.ph/section/briefing-room/department-of-foreign-affairs-briefing-room/page/68/ (accessed 26 January 2013).
31 Q. Chen, 'Adjustment of its policies over the South China Sea by the Philippines and the reasons behind', *International Sources and Information*, 10, 2011, pp. 15–20, at p. 18.
32 'Statement: The Secretary of Foreign Affairs on the UNCLOS Arbitral Proceedings against China, January 22, 2013', from the website of Department of Foreign Affairs of the Republic of the Philippines, at http://www.gov.ph/2013/01/22/statement-the-secretary-of-foreign-affairs-on-the-unclos-arbitral-proceedings-against-china-january-22-2013/ (accessed 26 January 2013).
33 'Press Conference Hosted by Hong Lei, Spokesperson for China's Foreign Ministry', from the website of Ministry of Foreign Affairs of the People's Republic of China, at http://www.fmprc.gov.cn/mfa_chn/fyrbt_602243/jzhsl_602247/t1014798.shtml (accessed 9 May 2013).
34 T. Quismundo, 'Panel to hear PH case vs China now complete', http://globalnation.inquirer.net/78663/panel-to-hear-ph-case-vs-china-now-complete (accessed 28 June 2013).
35 Chen, 'Adjustment of its policies', p. 17.
36 'The Philippine Oil Company was warned by China of its oil exploitation', 25 March 2011, from the website of *Huanqiu Shibao* (*Global Times* in Chinese), at http://world.huanqiu.com/roll/2011-03/1587256.html (accessed 23 March 2011); and A. Rosario, 'Philippine policy response and action', 5 August 2011, from the website of Department of Foreign Affairs of the Republic of the Philippines, at http://dfa.gov.ph/main/index.php/newsroom/dfa-releases/3531-philippine-policy-response-and-action-by-the-hon-albert-f-del-rosario-secretary-of-foreign-affairs (accessed 25 September 2011).
37 C. Jia, 'Philippines seeks oil exploration in South China Sea inside China waters', 24 March 2011, from the website of *Global Times*, at http://world.globaltimes.cn/asia-pacific/2011-04/637562.html (accessed 3 May 2011).
38 'Press conference by Spokesperson Jiang Yu of 24 March 2011', from the website of Ministry of Foreign Affairs of the People's Republic of China, at http://www.fmprc.gov.cn/chn/gxh/tyb/fyrbt/t809390.htm (accessed 24 March 2011).
39 Ju, 'South China Sea policy of the Philippines', p. 86.
40 Rosario, 'Philippine policy response and action'.
41 Ibid.
42 Chen, 'Adjustments of its policies', p. 17.
43 'Press conference by Spokesperson Jiang Yu of 20 October 2012', from the website of Ministry of Foreign Affairs of the People's Republic of China, at http://www.fmprc.gov.cn/chn/gxh/tyb/fyrbt/jzhsl/t869317.htm (accessed 26 October 2012).
44 This section is partly derived from J. Li and R. Amer, 'Will the China–Philippine standoff over Huangyan Island lead to cooperation?', 30 May 2012, from the website of *China-US Focus*, at http://www.chinausfocus.com/foreign-policy/will-

the-china-philippine-standoff-over-huangyan-island-lead-to-cooperation/ (accessed 1 June 2012).

45 'Vice Foreign Minister Fu Ying met with Charge D'affaires of the Philippine Embassy in China again over the incident at Huangyan Island', 8 May 2012, from the website of the Ministry of Foreign Affairs of the People's Republic of China, at http://www.fmprc.gov.cn/eng/wjdt/wshd/t929748.htm (accessed on 12 May 2012).

46 'Joint Statement between the People's Republic of China and the Republic of the Philippines', 1 September 2011, from the website of Ministry of Foreign Affairs of the People's Republic of China, at http://www.fmprc.gov.cn/chn/pds/ziliao/1179/t854349.htm (accessed 2 December 2012); and Zhong, 'Domestic politics and the institutionalization', p. 104.

47 'China-Philippines Joint Press Release', from the website of Ministry of Foreign Affairs of the People's Republic of China, at http://www.fmprc.gov.cn/eng/wjdt/wshd/t837952.htm (accessed 24 August 2011).

48 Li and Amer, 'China-Philippine standoff'.

49 Ju, 'South China Sea policy of the Philippines', p. 90.

50 Rosario, 'Philippine policy response and action'.

51 'Statement of Secretary Albert F. Del Rosario at the ASEAN Foreign Ministers' Meeting (AMM) 15 November 2011, Bali, Indonesia', 15 November 2011, from the website of Department of Foreign Affairs of the Republic of the Philippines, at http://www.dfa.gov.ph/index.php/newsroom/dfa-releases/4141-statement-of-secretary-albert-f-del-rosario-at-the-asean-foreign-ministers-meeting-amm-15-november-2011-bali-indonesia (accessed 2 December 2012).

52 Ju, 'South China Sea policy of the Philippines', p. 85.

53 'Secretary Del Rosario receives call from US Secretary of State Clinton', 14 March 2011, from the website of Department of Foreign Affairs of the Republic of the Philippines, at http://dfa.gov.ph/main/index.php/newsroom/dfa-releases/2698-secretary-del-rosario-receives-call-from-us-secretary-of-state-clinton (accessed 24 March 2011).

54 Ju, 'South China Sea policy of the Philippines', p. 86.

55 'US reiterates it will honor obligations under MDT amid standoff in Bajo de Masinloc, urges claimant states to the WPS to clarify claims under UNCLOS', 3 May 2012, from the website of Department of Foreign Affairs of the Republic of the Philippines, at http://dfa.gov.ph/main/index.php/newsroom/dfa-releases/5317-us-reiterates-it-will-honor-obligations-under-mdt-amid-standoff-in-bajo-de-masinloc-urges-claimant-states-to-the-wps-to-clarify-claims-under-unclos (accessed 25 September 2011).

56 'Clinton and Del Rosario urge ASEAN to take a common position on Scarborough Reef', 12 July 2012, from the website of Department of Foreign Affairs of the Republic of the Philippines, at http://dfa.gov.ph/main/index.php/newsroom/dfa-releases?start=8 (accessed 17 July 2012).

57 On 5 September 2012, Aquino III announced renaming the South China Sea as 'the West Philippine Sea'. 'Administrative Order No. 29, s 2012', *Official Gazette*, at http://www.gov.ph/2012/09/05/administrative-order-no-29-s-2012/ (accessed 26 September 2012); and 'The Philippines named so-called "the West Philippine Sea" and intend to make new maps', 12 September 2012, from the website of *Zhongguo Xinwen Wang* (*Chinanews* in Chinese), at http://www.chinanews.com/gj/2012/09-12/4179172.shtml (accessed 18 September 2012).

58 Ju, 'South China Sea policy of the Philippines', p. 86; and 'Benigno S. Aquino III Second State of the Nation Address', 25 July 2011, from the website of Official Gazette by the Office of the President of the Philippines, at http://www.gov.ph/2011/07/25/benigno-s-aquino-iii-second-state-of-the-nation-address-july-25-2011-en/ (accessed 28 November 2012).

59 Note 32, 'Statement: The Secretary of Foreign Affairs on the UNCLOS Arbitral Proceedings against China, January 22, 2013'.
60 Ibid.
61 Some of the observations relating to the China–Vietnam relationship are derived from Amer and Li 'Recent developments in the South China Sea'; and from Amer, 'China, Vietnam'.
62 'Philippines, China to hold 18th Foreign Ministry Consultations', 19 October 2012, from the website of Department of Foreign Affairs of the Republic of the Philippines, at http://www.dfa.gov.ph/index.php/newsroom/dfa-releases/6585-philippines-china-to-hold-18th-foreign-ministry-consultations (accessed 30 November 2012).

Part II

The legal context of joint development in the South China Sea: legal frameworks, key issues, case studies, experiences and lessons

4 The legal framework for joint development in the South China Sea

Robert Beckman

The features in the South China Sea, especially those in the Spratly Islands, have been a source of tension and potential conflict in the region for many years. Some or all of the features in the Spratly Islands are claimed by Brunei Darussalam, China, Malaysia, the Philippines, Vietnam and Taiwan.

It is generally assumed that given the number of claimants and the sensitivity of the disputes on sovereignty over the islands, it will not be possible for the claimants to resolve the disputes through negotiation for the foreseeable future. Further, it is assumed that the claimants will not be willing to agree to refer the sovereignty disputes to an arbitral or judicial tribunal.

Since the 1980s it has been suggested that the best way to defuse tension in the Spratly Islands is to set aside the sovereignty disputes and jointly develop the resources in and under the waters surrounding the islands. Deng Xiaoping, the late paramount leader of China, promoted the principle of 'setting aside disputes and pursuing joint development'. This concept was first openly advanced by Deng on 11 May 1979 in relation to China's dispute with Japan over the Diaoyu (Senkaku) Islands.[1] He stated that consideration may be given to joint development of the resources adjacent to the Diaoyu Islands without touching upon their territorial sovereignty.[2]

When China entered into diplomatic relations with Southeast Asian countries in the 1970s and 1980s, Deng Xiaoping made the same proposal for resolving disputes over the Nansha (Spratly) Islands, stating:

> The Nansha Islands have been an integral part of China's territory since the ancient times. But disputes have occurred over the islands since the 1970s. Considering the fact that China has good relations with the countries concerned, we would like to set aside this issue now and explore later a solution acceptable to both sides. We should avoid military conflict over this and should pursue an approach of joint development.[3]

China and ASEAN have also taken steps which could lead to setting aside the sovereignty and maritime boundary disputes and jointly developing the resources. The 2002 Declaration on the Conduct of Parties in the South China Sea (2002 DOC) was adopted by the Foreign Ministers of ASEAN and the People's Republic of China at the 8th ASEAN Summit in Phnom Penh on 4 November 2002.[4] The 2002 DOC contains provisions on the following: (a) peaceful resolution of the territorial and jurisdictional disputes; (b) self-restraint in the conduct of activities that would complicate or escalate disputes and affect peace and stability; (c) confidence-building measures; and (d) cooperative activities.

In 2011 China and ASEAN agreed on Guidelines for the Implementation of the 2002 DOC.[5] Despite this, little discussion has taken place on setting aside the disputes and jointly developing the resources in the disputed areas.

UNCLOS as a legal basis for joint development arrangements

The 1982 United Nations Convention on the Law of the Sea (UNCLOS)[6] establishes a legal framework to govern all uses of the oceans. UNCLOS was adopted in 1982 after nine years of negotiations. It entered into force in November 1994 and has been almost universally accepted. The States making claims to sovereignty over all or some of the islands in the South China Sea – Brunei, China, Malaysia, Philippines and Vietnam – are all parties to UNCLOS.[7] Taiwan is not able to ratify UNCLOS because it is not recognized as a State by the United Nations, but it has taken steps to bring its domestic legislation into conformity with UNCLOS.[8]

UNCLOS has no provisions on how to resolve sovereignty disputes over offshore features. However, it does have provisions on maritime boundary delimitation. The UNCLOS provisions on the delimitation of the exclusive economic zone (EEZ) and continental shelf boundaries assume that it will not always be possible to negotiate boundary agreements in overlapping claim areas because of sovereignty disputes or for other historical reasons.

UNCLOS provisions of maritime boundary delimitation

The UNCLOS provisions on boundary delimitation purport to provide a solution to the fact that it may be extremely difficult for States to reach agreement in areas of overlapping EEZ and continental shelf claims. This solution is found in paragraph 3 of Articles 74 and 83, which provide that if delimitation cannot be effected by agreement:

> [T]he States concerned, in a spirit of understanding and cooperation, shall make every effort to enter into provisional arrangements of a practical nature and, during the transitional period, not to jeopardize or hamper the reaching of the final agreement. Such arrangements shall be without prejudice to the final delimitation.

This provision is designed to 'promote interim regimes and practical measures that could pave the way for provisional utilization of disputed areas pending delimitation' and 'constitutes an implicit acknowledgement of the importance of avoiding the suspension of economic development in a disputed maritime area'.[9]

Obligations regarding 'provisional arrangements of a practical nature'

The use of the word 'provisional' implies that the arrangements are interim measures pending the final delimitation of maritime boundaries.[10] It is commonly observed that the use of the term 'arrangements' implies that the arrangement can include both informal documents such as notes verbales, exchange of notes, agreed minutes, memoranda of understanding and so forth[11] as well as more formal agreements such as treaties.[12] With regard to the meaning of 'practical nature', the article itself does not give much guidance, but has been interpreted to mean that such arrangements 'are to provide practical solutions to actual problems regarding the use of an area and are not to touch upon either the delimitation issue itself or the territorial questions underlying this issue'.[13]

It is clear that there are two aspects to the obligation in Articles 74(3) and 83(3). First, States concerned shall make every effort to enter into provisional arrangements of a practical nature. Second, States, in good faith, shall make every effort not to jeopardize or hamper the reaching of the final delimitation agreement.

The obligation of States to make every effort to enter into provisional arrangements of a practical nature has been succinctly summarized by scholars, based on judicial precedents such as the *North Sea Continental Shelf Cases*:

> The states concerned are obliged 'to enter into negotiations with a view to arriving at an agreement' to establish provisional arrangements of a practical nature and … 'not merely to go through a formal process of negotiation.' The negotiations are to be 'meaningful, which will not be the case when either [state] insists upon its own position without contemplating any modification of it.' However, the obligation to negotiate does not imply an obligation to reach agreement.[14]

This view was endorsed in the 2007 arbitration between Guyana and Suriname by an Arbitral Tribunal constituted under Annex VII of UNCLOS.[15] While it was acknowledged that the language 'every effort' leaves 'some room for interpretation by the States concerned, or by any dispute settlement body', it imposes on the parties 'a duty to negotiate in good faith'. This requires the parties to take 'a conciliatory approach to negotiations, pursuant to which they would be prepared to make concessions in the pursuit of a provisional arrangement'.[16] Further, the obligation to negotiate in good faith 'is not merely a nonbinding recommendation or encouragement, but a mandatory rule whose breach would represent a violation of international law'.[17]

However, it is clear that States are under no obligation to enter into any provisional arrangement but must only 'make every effort' to negotiate in good faith. Articles 74(3) and 83(3) also leave States with significant discretion as to the type of provisional measures that should be taken.[18]

The obligation to negotiate in good faith appears to include an obligation for States to consult with each other if they intend to carry out unilateral activities in a disputed area and to continue to negotiate even after such unilateral activities take place. In the *Guyana v Suriname* arbitration, it was found that the parties had breached their obligation to negotiate provisional arrangements of a practical nature pending maritime delimitation of their territorial sea, EEZ and continental shelf boundary. This stemmed from an incident in 2000 where an oil rig and drill ship engaged in seismic testing under a Guyanese concession was ordered to leave the disputed area by two Surinamese vessels. It was found that Guyana had violated its obligation under Article 83(3) as it should have, in a spirit of cooperation, informed Suriname of its exploratory plans, given Suriname official and detailed notice of the planned activities, offered to share the results of the exploration, given Suriname an opportunity to observe the activities and offered to share all the financial benefits received from the exploratory activities.[19] Similarly, the Tribunal found that when Suriname became aware of Guyana's exploratory efforts in disputed waters, 'instead of attempting to engage it in a dialogue which may have led to a satisfactory solution for both Parties, Suriname resorted to self-help in threatening the oil rig and drill ship in violation of [UNCLOS]'.[20]

The second part of the obligation provides that during this transitional period States are obliged not to jeopardize or hamper the reaching of a final agreement on delimitation. It is said that a court or tribunal's interpretation of this obligation must reflect the delicate balance between preventing unilateral activities that affect the other party's rights in a permanent manner but at the same time, not stifling the parties' ability to pursue economic development in a disputed area during a time-consuming boundary dispute.[21]

International courts and tribunals have found that 'any activity which represents an irreparable prejudice to the final delimitation agreement'[22] is a breach of this obligation and that 'a distinction is therefore to be made between activities of the kind that lead to a permanent physical change, such as exploitation of oil and gas reserves, and those that do not, such as seismic exploration.'[23] For example, in the *Guyana v Suriname* arbitration it was found that allowing exploratory drilling in disputed waters was a breach of the obligation to make every effort not to hamper or jeopardize the reaching of a final agreement, as this could result in a physical change to the marine environment and engender a 'perceived change to the status quo'.[24] This was in contrast to seismic testing, which did not cause a physical change to the marine environment.

Notably, it was also found that Suriname's actions in using the threat of force in getting the Guyana-licensed vessel to leave was not only a breach of its obligation not to jeopardize the final agreement, but also a breach of its obligation not to use force under UNCLOS, the UN Charter and general international law.[25]

Provisional arrangements are 'without prejudice' to the final delimitation of boundaries

The key aspect of provisional arrangements of a practical nature is that they are 'without prejudice' to the final delimitation. The effect of such a feature is that:[26]

- nothing in the arrangement can be interpreted as a unilateral renunciation of the claim of either party or as mutual recognition of either party's claim;
- the arrangement itself does not create any legal basis for either party to claim title over the area and its resources;
- the States concerned cannot claim any acquired rights from the interim arrangement;
- final delimitation does not have to take into account either any such preceding arrangement or any activities undertaken pursuant to such arrangement.

Essentially, parties are preserving their claims either to sovereignty over disputed territory or to sovereign rights over the waters surrounding such territory and, at the same time, shelving the sovereignty disputes and the final boundary delimitation.[27]

It is debatable whether it is necessary to have an express 'without prejudice clause' in a provisional arrangement because there is a general 'without prejudice clause' in the final sentence of Articles 74(3) and 83(3). Arguably, 'simply referring to the provisions of Articles 74(3) and 83(3) in an arrangement would be sufficient for preserving the positions of each party on final delimitation, if the parties to the arrangement are also parties to the LOS Convention'.[28] However, it is of course preferable in terms of legal certainty to have an express 'without prejudice' clause. The 'without prejudice' clause in the 1959 Antarctic Treaty is a good example of a 'without prejudice' clause:

> 1. Nothing contained in the present Treaty shall be interpreted as:
> a) a renunciation by any Contracting Party of previously asserted rights of or claims to territorial sovereignty in Antarctica;
> b) a renunciation or diminution by any Contracting Party of any basis of claim to territorial sovereignty in Antarctica which it may have whether as a result of its activities or those of its nationals in Antarctica, or otherwise;
> c) prejudicing the position of any Contracting Party as regards its recognition or non-recognition of any other State's rights of or claim or basis of claim to territorial sovereignty in Antarctica.
> 2. No acts or activities taking place while the present Treaty is in force shall constitute a basis for asserting, supporting or denying a claim to territorial sovereignty in Antarctica or create any rights of sovereignty in Antarctica. No new claim, or enlargement of an existing claim, to territorial sovereignty in Antarctica shall be asserted while the present Treaty is in force.

The area to which provisional arrangements apply

Articles 74(3) and 83(4) do not specify the area to which the provisional arrangements apply, although some suggestions and proposals raised during the negotiations of UNCLOS contained references to specific geographical lines or areas.[29]

Ranier Lagoni opines that the obligation to negotiate provisional arrangements has a geographical connotation:

> In accordance with the above-mentioned object and purpose of paragraph 3, the obligation applies only to those areas about which the governments hold opposing views. These views must be expressed formally, for example by declarations, or may be implied, for example through protests filed against the acts of other states or foreign nationals, by acts of the national legislator, or by the granting of licenses and concessions.[30]

Types of provisional arrangements

As discussed above, Articles 74(3) and 83(3) do not mandate the type of provisional arrangements States can enter into, but leave it to the discretion of the States concerned. State practice shows that provisional arrangements can include a wide variety of arrangements, such as mutually agreed moratoriums on all activities in overlapping areas, joint development or cooperation on fisheries, joint development of hydrocarbon resources, agreements on environmental cooperation and agreements on allocation of criminal and civil jurisdiction. The next section will explore one type of provisional arrangement, namely, the joint development of hydrocarbon resources.

Provisional arrangements involving joint development in the Spratly Islands

Arguably, the claimant States have an obligation under Articles 74(3) and 83(4) of UNCLOS to make every effort to negotiate, in good faith, provisional arrangements of a practical nature. The claimant States also have an obligation not to undertake unilateral activities which would irreparably damage resources or the interests of other claimants. Such obligations would apply even though negotiations on maritime delimitation have not begun and even though the overlapping claim area has not been defined due to the lack of clarity in both the sovereignty and maritime zone claims of the claimant States.[31]

One type of provisional arrangement which could be agreed upon in the South China Sea is the joint development of hydrocarbon resources and fisheries resources.

Rationale for joint development in the South China Sea

There are good reasons why the claimants should make an effort to enter into joint development arrangements in the South China Sea. First, there is unlikely to be a resolution of the sovereignty disputes and maritime delimitation disputes in the immediate or near future.

Second, there are considerable economic incentives for claimants to enter into joint development arrangements. Admittedly, the exact amount of hydrocarbon resources in the South China Sea is unknown and may not be as much as estimated in some accounts. However, the cost of oil is rising and coupled with shortage in supply, the claimants will want to and may need to exploit every resource possible. The claimants will face considerable difficulties in exploiting any oil in areas which are subject to competing claims, particularly if the exploration and exploitation is done in areas near the disputed features.

Third, joint development arrangements in the South China Sea have the potential to reduce tension and facilitate cooperation between claimants. The disputes relating to the Spratly Islands have been a major irritant which spills over to other aspects of bilateral and multilateral relations.

Identifying the area subject to joint development arrangements

One practical obstacle to any joint development arrangements being negotiated in the South China Sea is that there will have to be agreement on the geographic area or areas which will be subject to joint development and in which claimants will participate in joint development arrangements.

The Philippines and Vietnam have maintained that certain areas of their EEZs are not in dispute because they are close to the coast of their mainland territory or main archipelago and far from any of the disputed islands. Their position is that joint development arrangements must be limited to those maritime areas that are in dispute.

It will be difficult to agree on the areas in dispute and subject to joint development in the Spratly Islands unless agreement can be reached on the status of the geographic features and the maritime zones to which such features are entitled. There is no agreement on which features in the Spratly Islands are 'islands' entitled to maritime zones of their own because they are naturally formed areas of land above water at high tide, as set out in Article 121(1) of UNCLOS. Scholars have estimated that less than one-third of the features in the Spratly Islands are naturally formed areas of land above water at high tide. Furthermore, many of the features which do meet the definition of an island in Article 121(1) are very tiny and might be classified as 'rocks' which cannot sustain human habitation or economic life of their own, as provided in Article 121(3) of UNCLOS. If so, such features would not be entitled to an EEZ or continental shelf of their own, but only a 12 nautical mile (nm) territorial sea.

Uncertainty as to the status of the features and the maritime zones they generate could be a serious obstacle to the claimants reaching agreement on the areas in dispute which are subject to joint development. The Philippines maintains that Reed Bank is not an area in dispute because it is a submerged bank which is part of its continental shelf and which is outside the maritime zone that can be measured from any disputed island. Its position seems to be that the disputed features near Reed Bank either do not meet the definition of an island in Article 121 or, if they are islands, they are rocks within Article 121(3) which are not entitled to an EEZ or continental shelf of their own. Therefore, its position is that the Reed Bank area is not an area in dispute and is not to be subject to joint development.

Currently, the only areas clearly 'in dispute' in the Spratly Islands are the features which are islands because they are naturally formed areas of land above water at high tide, and the 12 nm territorial sea adjacent to such islands.

One approach to reaching agreement on the area in dispute in the Spratly Islands is to determine the status of every geographic feature and the maritime zones to which they are entitled. However, this would be exceedingly difficult to negotiate because the claimants are likely to take positions on the features that favour their national interest. One possible way this could be done is for the claimants to agree to have a neutral third party conduct a study on the status of the various features. However, it would still be difficult to reach agreement because of the ambiguity of the definition of a rock in Article 121(3).

A more fruitful way to reach agreement on the area for joint development arrangements might be for the claimants concerned to enter into serious negotiations to try to reach agreement on the area for joint development. Discussions could begin by focusing on the area where most of the larger islands are located, which is in the northern part of the Kalayaan Island group claimed by the Philippines. All of these islands are claimed by China, the Philippines, Vietnam and Taiwan, and all of the larger features in this area are occupied by one of those claimants. Therefore, the islands and the 12 nm territorial waters adjacent to them are areas in dispute. In addition, some of these islands are arguably large enough to be entitled to an EEZ of their own, at least in principle. Therefore, the claimants concerned may be able to agree that the maritime zones measured from these disputed islands will overlap with the EEZ claims and extended continental shelf claims of the ASEAN claimants. This area of overlap could be the agreed area in dispute. Vietnam and the Philippines may be amenable to such an approach as it would exclude areas close to their mainland coasts. Such an approach would also be advantageous to China as it could be done without any reference to the nine-dashed line map.

A more cautious approach might be to first attempt to negotiate joint development arrangements in the areas where there are only two claimants. It might be possible for China and the Philippines to agree on a joint development area surrounding the Scarborough Shoal. It might also be possible for China and Vietnam to agree on a joint development area in the Gulf of Tonkin, especially since they have been able to negotiate part of the maritime boundary in this area.[32]

Recommendations for moving forward on joint development

On 16–17 June 2011 the Centre for International Law at the National University of Singapore organized a Conference on Joint Development and the South China Sea. The Conference brought together international legal experts on joint development, representatives from the oil and gas industry and government officials from the region to examine the law and policy issues relating to the joint development of oil and gas resources in areas of overlapping claims in the South China Sea.

The Report of the Conference makes several recommendations for moving towards joint development in the South China Sea.[33] Although these recommendations are focused on the Spratly Islands, many of them could be equally applicable to the other areas in dispute in the South China Sea. These recommendations are summarized below.

Encourage claimants to clarify claims in conformity with UNCLOS

At present, there is a significant lack of clarity on the basis, nature and extent of the maritime claims surrounding the Spratly features. It is not clear what maritime zones, if any, are being claimed from the Spratly features by the various claimants. The ASEAN claimants, at least for now, appear to be treating the Spratly features as either 'rocks' entitled only to a 12 nm territorial sea or low-tide elevations that are not entitled to any maritime zone, but they have not expressly stated this.

China's claim from the Spratlys remains ambiguous. While it has recently confirmed that it believes the Spratly Islands are entitled to a territorial sea, EEZ and continental shelf, its nine-dashed line map surrounding the Spratly Islands and covering a large part of the waters of the South China Sea continues to raise suspicions that China is claiming 'historic rights' to explore and exploit the natural resources inside the nine-dashed line.

Clarification of the claims would help the claimants move towards joint development in two ways. First, it would be a step towards clarifying the areas that could be subject to joint development. Until agreement can be reached on which marine spaces in the South China Sea are in dispute and subject to joint development, and which marine areas are not in dispute and will not be subject to joint development, it will be impossible to begin discussions on joint development.

Second, a clarification of the claims would foster an atmosphere of trust and confidence which is necessary for joint development. Once the nine-dashed line is clarified and the prospect of claims based on historic rights is put to rest, the necessary trust and confidence to pursue joint development will be present.

Increase knowledge of features in the Spratly Islands

The number and nature of the features in the Spratlys remain shrouded in mystery. While there are accounts of physical descriptions of some of the features made by geographers and academics they are not up to date and the accounts are not consistent with each other. The lack of definitive information on the number and nature of the features contributes to the uncertainty and lack of clarity of the claims made by the claimants. It also makes it difficult to identify disputed areas in which joint development can take place. Therefore, there should be further research on the features in the Spratly Islands.

Increase knowledge of hydrocarbon resources through joint seismic surveys

While the Spratlys are often referred to as 'oil rich', estimates of hydrocarbon resources differ widely and there is an absence of reliable publicly available data regarding hydrocarbon reserves. Actual knowledge of hydrocarbon resources will enable the claimants to know where the hydrocarbons are and, hence, assist in identifying areas that could be suitable for joint development.

Joint seismic surveys between some or all of the claimants conducted on a 'without prejudice' basis in areas that are clearly in dispute would be a tremendous step towards joint development. The parties to the joint seismic survey should be the claimants that have bona fide claims made in good faith to the area in which the survey will be taking place. It should also involve all claimants that have claims in that area so as to avoid protests and persistent challenges. The agreement for the joint seismic survey should have robust 'without prejudice' clauses to allay concerns of States and their national populations.

Implement the 2002 ASEAN–China Declaration on the Code of Conduct in the South China Sea

The 2002 ASEAN–China Declaration on the Code of Conduct in the South China Sea was an important milestone as it set down a series of conflict avoidance mechanisms, such as mutual restraint and cooperative activities designed to build confidence between parties. The cooperative activities the parties are encouraged to undertake are marine environmental protection, marine scientific research, safety of navigation and communication at sea, search and rescue operations and combating transnational crime. These are arguably less controversial than joint development of hydrocarbon resources and, hence, may be easier to reach agreement on. Small incremental steps such as these will help foster the goodwill and trust necessary for discussions on joint development.

Enhance understanding on nature and importance of joint development arrangements

There appears to be a lack of understanding in some countries on the nature of joint development arrangements, particularly that joint development can be done without compromising the sovereignty claims of the claimants. Seminars, workshops and meetings can be organized by think tanks and research institutes on a Track 2 basis so as to enhance understanding of joint development arrangements. Given the role of the media in fanning the flames of nationalism, some of the sessions should include members of the media.

Better management of domestic politics and nationalistic rhetoric

The Spratly Islands have become a potent symbol of nationalism for the populations of the claimants. Accordingly, the public often perceives its government as weak if it fails to aggressively assert its claims over the Spratlys. This makes it difficult for the claimants to make reasonable compromises in negotiations without being accused of surrendering their sovereignty. This is a major obstacle to any joint development agreement in the South China Sea (and any peaceful settlement of the disputes for that matter).

Accordingly, the governments of the claimants and the media have a significant role to play in managing domestic politics and nationalist rhetoric associated with the Spratlys. First, the governments and the media can refrain from stoking national sentiments when incidents occur which are perceived as a threat to national sovereignty. Second, the governments can avoid taking extreme positions which are difficult to back down from. Third, the governments can educate the public on the benefits and importance of joint development and the fact that it does not involve a surrender of sovereignty. Last, the governments should be as transparent as possible or, at the very least, give the appearance of transparency, in any negotiations relating to joint development.

Greater discussion on appropriate institutional framework for discussion and negotiations

There is a lack of agreement on the appropriate institutional framework for discussion and negotiations on joint development. There appears to be a lack of agreement between claimants on the forum where such issues should be discussed and on who should be included in the discussions. The confusion on the proper forum is exacerbated by China's insistence that sovereignty disputes and competing claims be discussed bilaterally between individual claimants and by the actions of some ASEAN claimants in organizing conferences and workshops which appear to be intended to internationalize the issues. There also seems to be some confusion on the role of ASEAN in the Spratly disputes.

ASEAN can provide a forum for discussion between the claimants without it becoming a dispute between the ASEAN claimants and China. In fact, there is little likelihood that ASEAN will have a common position since the non-claimant members view the issues differently than the claimants. Once the claims of all of the claimant States have been clarified, all of the claimants should be able to agree that there are areas in the EEZs of the ASEAN claimant States which are not in dispute and which are not subject to joint development. While it may be difficult to reach a formal agreement clarifying the areas not in dispute, such a consensus can be achieved by State practice. For example, if the Philippines licenses a company to do a seismic survey in an area of its EEZ and none of the other claimants protest when the survey is done, they will have impliedly agreed that the area in question is solely within the EEZ of the Philippines.

Involve oil companies in the discussions

Oil companies (both state-owned and privately owned) have a significant role to play in facilitating joint development in the South China Sea. They are the contractors who will ultimately be carrying out exploration and exploitation and will be providing considerable capital input. They have the potential to exert influence on States to enter into a joint development arrangement in order to ensure political and legal certainty for their investment.

A more indirect way for oil companies to facilitate joint development is through education and dialogue with the claimants on the benefits of joint development and on technical matters related to joint development (such as licensing regimes, petroleum laws, safety of installations and so on). This would not only enhance understanding on joint development but also improve the lines of communication between the claimants and oil companies.

Do research on joint development regimes suitable for the South China Sea

While examining common provisions in existing joint development arrangements in Asia was useful for setting out the issues and considerations that need to be addressed in any joint development arrangement, it also demonstrated that each situation is unique and that the terms of any joint development agreement will depend on the needs and circumstances of the States at the time. Accordingly, it would greatly move forward joint development if more research was done on joint development regimes that would specifically be suitable for the South China Sea.

If the claimants were to actually see *how* and/or *on what terms* joint development can be done in real terms (as opposed to the abstract way joint development has been discussed to date), it would significantly increase the chances of them coming to an agreement on joint development. While the joint development regime put forward would not bind the claimants in any manner, it would provide an excellent starting point for negotiations.

Conclusions

The sovereignty disputes in the Spratly Islands are intractable and are unlikely to be resolved in the foreseeable future. Another extremely difficult problem is the status of the features in the Spratly Islands and the maritime zones those features can generate. Given these obstacles it is unlikely that the States concerned will be able to reach agreement on the maritime boundaries in the Spratly Islands.

Nevertheless, the claimant States have obligations under UNCLOS to make every effort to enter into provisional arrangements of a practical nature pending final agreement on maritime boundaries. Furthermore, until the sovereignty and boundary issues are finally resolved, the claimants have an obligation not to take any measures in the areas of overlapping claims that would jeopardize or hamper the reaching of a final agreement on the boundaries. The provisional arrangements of a practical nature include the cooperative measures called for in the 2002 China–ASEAN DOC. More importantly, they include the measure called for by the late Deng Xiaoping of 'setting aside disputes and pursuing joint development'.

It is in the interests of all of the claimants to begin discussion on provisional arrangements of a practical nature concerning joint development of the resources in the Spratly Islands. Such arrangements would be without prejudice to the sovereignty claims or the final determination of the maritime boundaries. They would be in the common economic interests of the claimants and would further mutual trust and confidence in the region.

One major obstacle to agreement of provisional arrangements concerning joint development in the Spratly Islands is the lack of consensus on the precise geographic areas that would be subject to joint development. This problem is exacerbated by the fact that the claimants have fundamental differences over the appropriate forum for addressing these issues. China argues for bilateral negotiations and the ASEAN claimants argue for negotiations between China and ASEAN.

There may be a 'middle way' of going forward to define the areas in dispute. As stated earlier, the area that seems to be the most obvious candidate for joint development is centred in the Kalayaan Island group where the largest islands (with the exception of Taiwan-occupied Itu Aba) are claimed and occupied by China, the Philippines and Vietnam. If these three claimants could begin serious discussions on defining the areas in dispute, it would be a major step forward. If the focus of the negotiations was to reach a consensus on the area of overlapping claims surrounding the larger islands, and define it as the area in dispute which is subject to joint development by the three States (and possibly Taiwan), it would go a long way towards finding an amicable solution. An advantage to such an approach is that it would enable the parties to completely avoid discussing the nine-dashed line map or China's right to undertake activities in certain areas in the EEZ of the other two claimants.

Another approach would be to first attempt to negotiate joint development arrangements in the areas where there are only two claimants. It might be possible for China and the Philippines to agree on a joint development area surrounding the Scarborough Shoal. It might also be possible for China and Vietnam to agree on a joint development area in the Gulf of Tonkin, especially since they have been able to negotiate part of the maritime boundary in this area.

If the claimant States are able to generate the necessary political will to take the steps required to move towards joint development, it will be a major step in managing potential conflicts in the region.

Notes

1 'Set aside dispute and pursue joint development', Statement of Ministry of Foreign Affairs of the People's Republic of China, 17 November 2000, available at http://www.fmprc.gov.cn/eng/ziliao/3602/3604/t18023.htm (accessed 16 November 2012).
2 Ibid.
3 Ibid.
4 2002 Declaration on the Conduct of Parties in the South China Sea signed at the 8th ASEAN Summit on 4 November 2002 in Phnom Penh, Cambodia, by the Foreign Ministers of ASEAN and the People's Republic of China. CIL Documents Database, available at http://cil.nus.edu.sg/2002/2002-declaration-on-the-conduct-of-parties-in-the-south-china-sea-signed-on-4-november-2002-in-phnom-penh-cambodia-by-the-foreign-ministers/; and from the ASEAN website at http://www.asean.org/asean/external-relations/china/item/declaration-on-the-conduct-of-parties-in-the-south-china-sea (accessed 16 November 2012).

5 Guidelines for the Implementation of the DOC, available at http://biengioilanhtho.gov.vn/eng/TempFiles/Guidelines%20on%20the%20implementation%20of%20the%20DOC.pdf (accessed 16 November 2012).

6 United Nations Convention on the Law of the Sea, 1833 U.N.T.S. 397, adopted in Montego Bay, Jamaica, on 10 December 1982, entered into force on 16 November 1994. As of 12 November 2012, there are 164 parties, including the European Union.

7 The dates of ratification of the five claimant States are Brunei Darussalam, 5 November 1996; China, 7 June 1996; Malaysia, 14 October 1996; Philippines, 8 May 1984; and Viet Nam, 25 July 1994. UN Treaties Collection, Status of Treaties, available at http://treaties.un.org/ (accessed 16 November 2012).

8 For the action taken by Taiwan to pass legislation claiming maritime zones as provided in UNCLOS, as well as a comparison of the positions of China and Taiwan, see Y. H. Song and Z. Keyuan, 'Maritime legislation of mainland China and Taiwan: developments, comparison, implications, and potential challenges for the United States', *Ocean Development and International Law*, 31, 2000, pp. 310–312.

9 *Guyana v Suriname*, Award of the Arbitral Tribunal, 17 September 2007, p. 153, para. 460, available at http://www.pca-cpa.org/showpage.asp?pag_id=1147 (accessed 16 November 2012).

10 R. Lagoni, 'Interim measures pending maritime delimitation agreements', *American Journal of International Law*, 78, 1984, pp. 345–368, at p. 356.

11 S. P. Kim, *Maritime Delimitation and Interim Arrangements in North East Asia*, Leiden: Martinus Nijhoff, 2004, p. 47. Kim notes that 'some States may prefer MOUs to formal agreements for provisional arrangements because these have some advantages in several aspects: no need to publish them as these are not treaties: no need for elaborate final clauses or the formalities surrounding treaty-making: easy amendment; and no need to be submitted for an approval of the parliament.' See also Lagoni, 'Interim measures pending maritime delimitation agreements', p. 358.

12 See Kim, *Maritime Delimitation*.

13 Lagoni, 'Interim measures pending maritime delimitation agreements', p. 358.

14 Ibid., p. 356.

15 See *Guyana v Suriname*.

16 Ibid., p. 153, para. 461.

17 Lagoni, 'Interim measures pending maritime delimitation agreements', p. 354.

18 N. Klein, 'Provisional measures and provisional arrangements in maritime boundary disputes', *International Journal of Marine and Coastal Law*, 21(4), 2006, pp. 423–460, at p. 444.

19 *Guyana v Suriname*, para. 477.

20 Ibid., para. 476.

21 Ibid., para. 470.

22 Lagoni, 'Interim measures pending maritime delimitation agreements', p. 366.

23 *Guyana v Suriname*, para. 467.

24 Ibid., para. 480.

25 Ibid., para. 445.

26 As succinctly summarized by Dr Gao Zhiguo in G. Zhiguo, 'Legal aspects of joint development in international law', in M. Kusuma-Atmadja, T. A. Mensah and B. H. Oxman (eds), *Sustainable Development and Preservation of the Oceans: The Challenges of UNCLOS and Agenda 21*, Honolulu: Law of the Sea Institute, 1997, pp. 629–644, at p. 639.

27 H. Fox et al., *Joint Development of Offshore Oil and Gas: A Model Agreement for States with Explanatory Commentary*, London: British Institute of International and Comparative Law, 1989, p. 378.

28 Kim, *Maritime Delimitation*, p. 53.

29 Lagoni, 'Interim measures pending maritime delimitation agreements', p. 356.

30 Ibid.

31 As mentioned above, R. Lagoni observed that the obligations in Articles 74(3) and 83(3) may arise 'in exceptional situations if no definite claim can be asserted because the principles of delimitation are at issue, or if the delimitation is contingent on the resolution of a dispute over sovereignty of an island.' See Lagoni, 'Interim measures pending maritime delimitation agreements', p. 357.

32 2000 Agreement between Vietnam and China on the Delimitation of the Territorial Seas, Exclusive Economic Zones and Continental Shelves of the Two Countries in the Beibu Gulf / Bac Bo Gulf. Article VII 'If any single petroleum or natural gas structure or field, or other mineral deposit of whatever character, extends across the delimitation line defined in Article II of this Agreement, the two Contracting Parties shall, through friendly consultations, reach agreement as to the manner in which the structure, field or deposit will be most effectively exploited as well as on the equitable sharing of the benefits arising from such exploitation.' The 2000 Agreement between Vietnam and China is available at http://biengioilanhtho.gov.vn/eng/TempFiles/Bac%20Bo%20Gulf%20Agreement.pdf (accessed 16 November 2012).

33 The Conference Report for the CIL Conference on Joint Development and the South China Sea is available at http://cil.nus.edu.sg/wp/wp-content/uploads/2011/06/Report-of-CIL-Conference-on-Joint-Development-and-the-South-China-Sea-2011-04.08.2011.pdf (accessed 22 November 2012).

5 Historic rights and joint development with special reference to the South China Sea

Zou Keyuan

What are historic rights in international law?

There is no established definition of the term 'historic rights' under international law. However, some scholars have attempted to explain it in their own ways. For example, according to Blum, 'the term "historic rights" denotes the possession by a State, over certain land or maritime areas, of rights that would not normally accrue to it under the general rules of international law, such rights having been acquired by that State through a process of historical consolidation'.[1] Blum further explains that 'historic rights are a product of a lengthy process comprising a long series of acts, omissions and patterns of behaviors which, in their entirety, and through their cumulative effect, bring such rights into being and consolidate them into rights valid in international law'.[2] Other scholars use the term 'historic rights' to indicate 'those rights which a state has acquired vis-à-vis one or more other states by effectively exercising those rights, with the acquiescence of the state or states concerned'.[3]

The United Nations International Law Commission (ILC) had discussed the concept of historic waters, and in 1962 the UN Secretariat, upon the request of the ILC, prepared a study on the juridical regime of historic waters, including historic bays. The study examined the elements of title to historic waters, the issues of burden of proof, the legal status of waters regarded as historic waters and the settlement of disputes. However, it did not give a conclusive concept of historic waters and the standard according to which this concept could be applied.[4] Thus the theoretical problem in regard to the concept of historic waters has not yet been resolved. Because of the controversy around this concept, the Third UN Conference on the Law of the Sea (UNCLOS III) dropped the issue for discussion and only left it as some wordings in the 1982 United Nations Convention on the Law of the Sea (UNCLOS 1982).[5] Generally speaking, there should be three conditions to be fulfilled to sustain a historic water claim. They are (1) the exercise of authority over the area; (2) the continuity over time of this exercise of authority; and (3) the attitude of foreign States to the claim.[6]

UNCLOS III did not discuss the issue of 'historic rights' or 'historic waters'.[7] However, a variant term of historic bay and/or historic title is mentioned in UNCLOS 1982 relating to bays, delimitation of the territorial sea between States with opposite or adjacent coasts, and limitations and exceptions in the settlement of disputes. It is obvious that UNCLOS 1982 deliberately avoids the issue of 'historic rights' or 'historic waters', and leaves it to be governed by customary international law as reaffirmed by its preamble.[8] On the other hand, the Convention bears some implications for the concept of 'historic waters' in that those waters are related to the territorial seas or internal waters since the mentioning in the Convention only appears in the sections of the rules for the territorial sea regime and the settlement of territorial disputes.

Historic rights in state practice

In state practice, historic rights or waters are reflected in domestic legislation and bilateral agreements. In September 1976 Sri Lanka enacted a Law to Provide for the Declaration of the Territorial Sea and Other Maritime Zones of Sri Lanka, and All Other Matters Connected Therewith or Incidental Thereto, in which Article 9 expressly stipulates that '(1) The President may by Proclamation published in the Gazette, declare the limits of the historic waters of Sri Lanka. (2) The Republic of Sri Lanka shall exercise sovereignty, exclusive jurisdiction and control in and over the historic waters, as well as in and over the islands and the continental shelf and the sea-bed and sub-soil thereof within such historic waters.'[9] The Law on the State Boundary of the former Soviet Union, entered into force on 1 March 1983, provides that the waters of bays, inlets, coves and estuaries, seas and straits historically belonging to the USSR are relegated to internal waters of the USSR.[10] More relevant to historic rights is the Portuguese law of August 1966, which provides that 'without prejudice to historic rights [claims?], conventions, and other international agreements, the Portuguese State exercises exclusive fishing rights, and exclusive control over fishing activities in the high sea zones adjacent to its territorial sea, up to twelve miles measured from the base line of said sea'.[11]As for bilateral agreements, an example can be found in the agreement between India and Sri Lanka on the Boundary in Historic Waters between the Two Countries on 26 June 1974, in which the vessels of India and Sri Lanka will enjoy in each other's waters such rights as they have traditionally enjoyed therein.[12]

It is inevitable to mention the practice exercised by the Kingdom of Tonga. As early as 1887, Tonga issued a Royal Proclamation claiming its historic title to 'all islands, rocks, reefs, foreshore and waters lying between the fifteenth and twenty-third and a half degrees of south latitude and between the one hundred and seventy-third and the one hundred and seventy-seventh degrees of west longitude from the Meridian of Greenwich'.[13] It is further emphasized in its Submission to the Commission on the Limits of the Continental Shelf in May 2009. According to Tonga, it is 'proud to have the longest legal claim of historic title to maritime domain in the world' and has exercised continuous jurisdiction and authority over the land territory and maritime spaces in accordance with the Proclamation for over 120 years.[14] According to Tonga, there is no contradiction between historic title and UNCLOS 1982 and on the contrary the latter recognizes historic title in its relevant provisions. Therefore, Tonga asserts in its submission consistency between its claim of historic title made by means of the Royal Proclamation of 24 August 1887 and its maritime jurisdiction as established in UNCLOS 1982.[15]

The case most relevant to historic rights rather than historic waters and historic bays is Tunisia's historical claims, which were assessed in the 1980s by an Italian scholar.[16] In addition to its historic claim to the Gulf of Tunis[17] and the Gulf of Gabès,[18] Tunisia also claimed 'historic rights' beyond its territorial sea, particularly historic fishing rights. In its reply to Libya's objections against Tunisia's claim, Tunisia stated that 'historic rights' acquired in bygone ages could extend over areas of sea or seabed which could today qualify as internal waters, territorial waters, a fishing zone or the continental shelf.[19] But this view was contested by the following arguments that 'a state cannot claim a vast area of sea as internal waters on the sole basis of "historic rights" previously acquired for fishing purposes, unless it is possible to consider that those "historic rights" were in fact indicative of a right of full sovereignty'.[20] As for Tunisia's historic rights beyond its territorial sea, those rights are essentially concerned with the exploitation of 'sedentary fisheries', such as sponge fisheries. Tunisia claimed exclusive jurisdiction over those so-called 'fixed fisheries' whatever their distance from the coast.[21] The claimed historic fishing rights were not disputable; even the contestant State Libya recognized those rights: '[e]vidence of the general recognition of Tunisian proprietary rights and ancillary rights to protection and control over the sedentary species asserted is not the issue. For the fact is that such rights existed.'[22] On the other hand, it should be stressed that such 'historic rights' did not exclude foreigners from the exploitation of sponge and octopus fisheries. Therefore, it is argued that the fishery zone created by the 1951 Tunisian decree on the sole basis of the 'historic rights' previously acquired is not justified, and the 1951 decree put forward a completely new and different claim since for the first time, the established fishery zone included all biological resources of the sea.[23]

In the case of the continental shelf between Libya and Tunisia in 1982, the ICJ observed Tunisia's unilateral line at 45°ZV (Zenith Vertical) north-east, starting from RasAjdir, as the eastern limit of its 'exclusive fishery zone' under the 1951 Decree, and found that although no State may unilaterally establish international maritime boundary lines, the line adopted by Tunisia which was 'originally intended only as a limit of an area of surveillance in the context of specific fishery regulations, constitutes a unilateral claim, but was never a line plotted for the purpose of lateral maritime delimitation, either in the seas or in the continental shelf'.[24] The court found instead that the line perpendicular to the coast was the only lateral boundary opposable to Libya of the area claimed by Tunisia as being subject to 'historic rights'.[25]

Meanwhile, Tunisia stressed the importance of its 'historic rights' with a view to the future delimitation of the exclusive economic zone (EEZ) by arguing that its claim was supported either by the new law of the sea or by the historic rights acquired through its immemorial exercise of jurisdiction. Libya questioned the nature and extent of Tunisia's 'historic rights' asserting that they did not amount to sovereignty over the seabed and that they had never been exercised throughout the area claimed by Tunisia. In addition, Libya stressed that these rights could not 'deprive a neighboring State of a shelf area which, according to the law, appertains to it *de jure* and *ab initio*'.[26] The court avoided the question of whether Tunisia's historic rights were relevant for the purpose of delimiting its continental shelf, but the court did make some important remarks that 'historic rights' must enjoy respect and be preserved as they had always been by long usage.[27] On the other hand, the court seemed to have denied any relevance of 'historic rights' to the delimitation of continental shelf as it found that 'basically, the notion of historic rights or waters and that of the continental shelf are governed by distinct legal regimes in customary international law. The first regime is based on acquisition and occupation, while the second is based on the existence of rights "*ipso facto*" and "*ab initio*".'[28] Thus in the view of the court, the 'historic rights' would perhaps have been relevant for the purpose of delimiting Tunisia's EEZ, but not for the purpose of delimiting its continental shelf.[29] Nevertheless, as concluded by Gioia, 'Tunisia could not unilaterally claim the whole area over which her "historic rights" extended as part of her exclusive economic zone', but 'Tunisia's "historic rights" could operate as an important factor when negotiating delimitation agreements with the interested states.'[30]

Case of **Eritrea–Yemen** *arbitration*

Another international judicial case relating to historic rights is that of *Eritrea–Yemen* arbitration in 1998.[31] The two contesting parties – Eritrea and Yemen – requested the specially established Arbitral Tribunal to decide on questions of territorial sovereignty over disputed islands in the Red Sea 'in accordance with principles, rules and practices of international law applicable to the matter, and on the basis, in particular, of *historic titles*' (original emphasis).[32] Eritrea based its claim to territorial sovereignty over the disputed 'Red Sea Islands' on a chain of title extending over more than 100 years, and on international law of 'effective occupation'. Eritrea traced this chain of title through the relevant historical records, beginning with the Italian colonization of the Eritrean mainland in the latter part of the nineteenth century.[33] Yemen based its claim to the disputed islands on 'original, historic or traditional Yemeni title, which could be traced to the *Bilad el-Yemen*, or realm of Yemen, which was said to have existed as early as the 6th Century AD'. Yemen contended that its incorporation into the Ottoman Empire, from 1538 to c.1635, and again from 1872 to 1918, did not deprive it of historic title to its territory. Yemen also contended that the Treaty of Lausanne had no effect on Yemeni title, because Yemen was not a party to the treaty, and because Turkey's renunciation of rights could not prejudice the interests of third parties. Yemen took the view that the effect of Article 16 was not to make the 'islands' *terra nullius*, but rather, territory 'the title to which was undetermined'. Yemen provided a historical review of alleged Yemeni acts of administration and control to supplement and confirm Yemen's historic title to the 'islands'.[34] It is clear that both sides presented their arguments based on historic rights in addition to evidence, in particular the Yemeni side. The Tribunal reviewed those arguments and held that 'there can be no doubt that the concept of historic title has special resonance in situations that may exist even in the contemporary world'. 'A different situation exists with regard to uninhabited islands which are not claimed to be falling within the limits of historic waters.'[35] The Tribunal then pointed out that 'in the present case, neither party has formulated any claim to the effect that the disputed islands are located within historic waters'. It further confirmed that

> the conditions that prevailed during many centuries with regard to the traditional openness of southern Red Sea marine resources for fishing, its role as means for unrestricted traffic from one side to the other, together with the common use of the islands by the populations of both coasts, are all important elements capable of creating certain 'historic rights' which accrued in favour of both parties through a process of historical consideration as a sort of '*servitude internationale*' falling short of territorial sovereignty. Such historic rights provide a sufficient legal basis for maintaining certain aspects of a *res communis* that has existed for centuries for the benefit of populations on both sides of the Red Sea.[36]

Here it seems that the Tribunal recognized the historic rights of both sides. That makes it difficult for the Tribunal to render its decision based on historic title and rights in favor of either party. Finally, despite great efforts made by the Tribunal to investigate both claims to historic titles, the Tribunal held that 'neither Party has been able to persuade the Tribunal that the history of the matter reveals the juridical existence of an historic title, or of historic titles, of such long-established, continuous and definitive lineage to these particular islands, islets and rocks as would be a sufficient basis for the Tribunal's decision'.[37] On the other hand, the Tribunal held that 'Yemen shall ensure that the traditional fishing regime of free access and enjoyment for the fishermen of both Eritrea and Yemen shall be preserved.'[38]

What is the concept of joint development?

The concept of joint development first appeared in international law in the 1970s. There are various definitions of joint development in the relevant legal literature. The British Institute of International and Comparative Law, having compared different definitions, defines joint development as 'an agreement between two States to develop so as to share jointly in agreed proportions by inter-State cooperation and national measures the offshore oil and gas in a designated zone of the seabed and subsoil of the continental shelf to which both or either of the participating States are entitled in international law'.[39] This definition is broad enough to cover all relevant situations in which joint development is needed and/or required. Generally speaking, the concept of joint development contains several characteristics: (a) it is an arrangement between two countries; (b) it is usually concerned with an overlapping maritime area; (c) it can be used as a provisional arrangement pending the settlement of the boundary delimitation disputes between the countries concerned; and (d) it is designed to jointly develop the mineral resources in the disputed area or a defined area shared by two countries. In this sense, joint development is a most feasible mechanism to shelve the dispute so as to pave the way for cooperation pending the settlement of territorial and/or maritime disputes over a certain sea area due to overlapping claims.

It is necessary to differentiate the concept of joint development from similar concepts such as unitization, which straddles the same structure licensed to two oil companies, or joint venture, which is established between, say, a Chinese enterprise and a foreign investor, though the detailed implementation of joint development will incorporate features of unitization and/or joint venture agreements. Furthermore, joint development carries special meaning and should not be misunderstood simply as something equivalent to joint cooperation. Finally, while joint development is mainly applicable to the use of mineral resources, it is not excluded in the area of marine living resources management, as manifested in some existing cases, such as the Colombia–Jamaica Treaty of 12 November 1993, which set up a 'Joint Regime Area' for joint management, control, exploration and exploitation of the living and non-living resources,[40] and the Guinea–Bissau–Senegal Agreement of 14 October 1993 which covers not only oil and gas but also living marine resources.[41]

In state practice, there are many precedents setting forth joint development arrangements. The earliest example of a joint development regime was that made between Kuwait and Saudi Arabia in 1922. Based on the 1922 Aqeer Agreement, the two countries were co-tenants in the Neutral Zone, holding shares equally and jointly in condominium and later on they consented to joint development by their concessionaires.[42] It is summarized that there are generally three types of joint development schemes: (1) to be devised with the maritime boundary delimited, such as the Bahrain–Saudi Arabia Agreement concerning the Delimitation of the Continental Shelf of 22 February 1958, the France–Spain Convention on the Delimitation of the Continental Shelves of the Two States in the Bay of Biscay of 29 January 1974, the Sudan–Saudi Arabia Agreement Relating to the Joint Exploration and Exploitation of the Natural Resources of the Seabed and Subsoil of the Red Sea in a Defined Area of the Two Countries in the Red Sea of 16 May 1974, and the Iceland–Norway Agreement on the Continental Shelf between Iceland and Jan Mayen of 22 October 1981; (2) for the purpose of unitizing hydrocarbon deposits that straddle the boundary line, such as the Norway–United Kingdom Agreement Relating to the Delimitation of the Continental Shelf between the Two Countries of 10 March 1965 and its subsequent agreements for the exploitation of Frigg Field gas and Statfjord Field and Murchison Field petroleum respectively; and (3) to be worked out with the issue of boundary delimitation shelved or kept unresolved, such as the Japan–Korea Agreement Concerning Joint Development of the Southern Part of the Continental Shelf Adjacent to the Two Countries of 30 January 1974, the Malaysia–Thailand Memorandum of Understanding on the Establishment of a Joint Authority for the Exploitation of Resources of the Seabed in a Defined Area of the Two Countries in the Gulf of Thailand of 21 February 1979 (followed by the 1990 Malaysia–Thailand Joint Development Agreement) and the Australia–Indonesia Treaty on the Zone of Cooperation in an Area between the Indonesian Province of East Timor and Northern Australia of 11 December 1989 (now superseded by the 2002 Australia–Timor Leste Agreement).[43] The third type is linked to the provisional arrangements stipulations under UNCLOS 1982.

How do the two legal concepts apply together?

Both are valid concepts recognized by international law

Though not expressly provided for in UNCLOS 1982, the essence of the two concepts is embodied in the Convention.

UNCLOS 1982 recognizes historic title and historic rights of coastal states. Article 10(6) provides that '[t]he foregoing provisions [on bays] do not apply to so-called "historic" bays'.[44] Article 15 does not allow the median line to apply to special circumstances such as 'by reason of historic title' for the delimitation of the territorial seas of the two States.[45] Article 298 permits the contracting States to exclude the compulsory procedure provided for in the Convention from applying to the disputes 'involving historic bays or titles'.[46] Furthermore, Article 51 provides that

> an archipelagic State shall respect existing agreements with other States and shall recognize traditional fishing rights and other legitimate activities of the immediately adjacent neighbouring States in certain areas falling within archipelagic waters. The terms and conditions for the exercise of such rights and activities, including the nature, the extent and the areas to which they apply, shall, at the request of any of the States concerned, be regulated by bilateral agreements between them.

On the other hand, UNCLOS 1982 provides a legal basis for joint development in disputed maritime areas pending the settlement of the maritime boundary delimitation. Articles 74(3) and 83(3) provide that pending agreement reached between them on the delimitation of the EEZ and continental shelf, the states concerned, in a spirit of understanding and cooperation, are required to 'make every effort to enter into provisional arrangements of a practical nature and, during this transitional period, not to jeopardize or hamper the reaching of the final agreement'. Joint development is obviously one of the most welcome options to enter into provisional arrangements before a maritime dispute or a maritime boundary issue is finally settled.

Both are non-exclusive and open to collaboration

We have to realize that the term 'historic rights' is not equivalent to 'historic waters' or 'historic bays', though 'historic rights' may carry a broader meaning and may include historic waters and bays. The term 'historic rights' also covers certain special rights without involving a claim of full sovereignty, such as historic fishing rights which a State might have acquired in particular areas of the high seas. The South China Sea is generally a traditional fishing ground of its littoral States.

This type of non-exclusive historic rights may also be extended to cooperation in the development of non-living resources, such as oil and gas, which is directly related to the concept of joint development. It is remembered that the State-owned oil companies of China, the Philippines and Vietnam (CNOOC, PetroVietnam and the Philippine National Oil Company) did sign an agreement on joint seismic exploration in a designated area (143,000 km^2) of the South China Sea in March 2005. It is imperative therefore that the three countries resume the collaboration in this regard and deepen it further.

The concept of joint development has been formulated for the purpose of international cooperation, particularly in a disputed area, as a provisional measure in accordance with international law.

Both concepts are reflected in the practice of the littoral states of the South China Sea

In practice, China treats Bohai Bay and the Qiongzhou Straits as its historic waters. China supported the former USSR's historic claim to the Peter the Great Bay in the Sea of Japan (East Sea).[47] On 26 June 1998, China officially promulgated the Law on the Exclusive Economic Zone and the Continental Shelf in which Article 14 provides that 'the provisions of this Law shall not affect the historic rights enjoyed by the People's Republic of China'.[48] It is generally agreed that this clause is connected to China's claim to the South China Sea within the U-shaped line. However, instead of using the term 'historic waters', China wisely chose a less strong term, 'historic rights'. As for Vietnam, it once declared the Gulf of Tonkin as historic waters. Vietnam also concluded an agreement on historic waters with Cambodia in July 1982, placing an area of over 8,000 km^2 in the Gulf of Thailand under the status of historic internal waters. The two countries agreed to use the Brévie Line, a line adopted by Governor Brévie in 1939, as the dividing line of sovereignty over islands between the two countries.[49] In the Scarborough Reef stand-off, both China and the Philippines claimed that the surrounding areas of the reef were traditional fishing grounds for their fishermen, and such statements clearly indicate the enjoyment of historic fishing rights by both sides. According to Ambassador Tong Xiaoling, the waters adjacent to the Huangyan Islands are China's traditional fishing grounds.[50] In the Philippine position paper on the Scarborough Reef, it states that 'Filipino fishermen have always considered it as their fishing grounds, owing to their proximity to the coastal towns and areas of Southwest Luzon.'[51]

As for joint development, in addition to the 2005 agreement mentioned above, China reached a principled consensus with Japan in 2008 on joint development in the East China Sea.[52] China has called for joint development in the South China Sea since the late 1980s. Vietnam has concluded joint development agreements with Indonesia, Malaysia and Thailand, such as the Vietnam–Malaysia

Agreement on the Joint Petroleum Exploitation of 5 June 1992.[53] It is reported that Brunei and Malaysia have also reached an agreement on joint development in the South China Sea.

Obligation under international law

The UN Charter encourages UN Member States to implement the principle of good neighborliness and international cooperation. Article 74 of the UN Charter embodies this general principle and requires Member States to apply it to the consideration of 'the interests and well-being of the rest of the world, in social, economic, and commercial matters'.[54] Cooperation implies the taking into account of the interests of others and a share of certain authority, competence or power.[55] Cooperation can be reflected in international relations in various ways and forms.

UNCLOS 1982 requires coastal States adjacent to a semi-enclosed sea to cooperate, in particular in the areas of the management, conservation, exploration and exploitation of the living resources of the sea, the protection and preservation of the marine environment, and marine scientific research.[56] According to UNCLOS Article 123, the States adjacent to a semi-enclosed sea like the South China Sea have the obligation of cooperation:

> (a) to coordinate the management, conservation, exploration and exploitation of the living resources of the sea; (b) to coordinate the implementation of their rights and duties with respect to the protection and preservation of the marine environment; (c) to coordinate their scientific research policies and undertake where appropriate joint programmes of scientific research in the area; (d) to invite, as appropriate, other interested States or international organizations to cooperate with them in furtherance of the provisions of this article.[57]

It is to be noted that cooperation between the South China Sea States and other States is clearly stated in this provision. It is suggested that experiences and lessons from the Mediterranean Sea and the Caribbean Sea can be learnt by the South China Sea States.[58]

The 2002 Declaration on the Conduct of Parties in the South China Sea (DOC) certainly serves as a basis to formulate the legal regime for the South China Sea. As pledged in the 2002 DOC, all signatories 'reaffirm their commitment to the purposes and principles of the Charter of the United Nations, the 1982 UN Convention on the Law of the Sea, the Treaty of Amity and Cooperation in Southeast Asia, the Five Principles of Peaceful Coexistence, and other universally recognized principles of international law which shall serve as the basic norms governing state-to-state relations'.[59] Therefore the guiding principles can be found in the UN Charter as well as in general international law, including UNCLOS 1982. In September 2011, ASEAN countries and China adopted the Guidelines for the Implementation of the DOC, in which the parties pledge to conduct possible joint cooperative activities, measures and projects as provided for in the DOC with a step-by-step approach.[60]

The negotiations between ASEAN countries and China on the adoption of a code of conduct (COC) have clearly shown that the parties concerned have taken the right direction and made an essential step forward. Personally, I do not like the terms DOC or COC as such terms contain implications of mutual distrust as these documents are mainly designed to curb the behavior of the parties towards each other. The more preferable term is TAC, Treaty on Amity and Cooperation.

Conclusions

From the above observations, we can reach a preliminary conclusion that the concepts of historic rights and joint development are not contradictory, rather they are co-existent. The concept of historic rights can play a complementary role in promoting the implementation of the concept of joint development in the South China Sea.

We remain mindful that the nations and peoples surrounding the South China Sea have maintained friendly and peaceful interactions throughout history and part of such interactions are demonstrated and explained by Wang Gungwu in his book *The Nanhai Trade*.[61] It is important and also essential for the littoral States of the South China Sea to respect history, rationally deal with reality and look forward to further cooperation in the future so that a win-win solution can be achieved for the prosperity, peace and security of and around the South China Sea.

Notes

1 Yehuda Z. Blum, 'Historic rights', in Rudolf Bernhardt (ed.), *Encyclopaedia of Public International Law*, Instalment 7, Amsterdam: North-Holland, 1984, at p. 120.
2 Ibid., p. 121.
3 G. Sperduti, 'Sul Regime Giuridico dei Mari', *Rivista di Diritto Internazionale*, 43, pp. 58–76, at p. 72; cited in Andrea Gioia, 'Tunisia's claims over adjacent seas and the doctrine of "historic rights"', *Syr. J. Int'l L. & Com.*, 11, 1984, pp. 327–376, at p. 328.
4 See UN Doc. A/CN.4/143, p. 6.
5 Some scholars assume that there are two possible reasons for this. First, the 12-mile territorial sea had generally been accepted by most coastal states, which made it possible to place the waters concerned under a state's sovereignty and jurisdiction. Second, the development of the legal regimes of the continental shelf, EEZ and archipelagic waters may bring about a gradual phasing out and eventual elimination of the phenomenon of 'historic' claims. See Yann-huei Song and Peter Kien-hong Yu, 'China's "historic waters" in the South China Sea: an analysis from Taiwan, R.O.C.', *American Asian Review*, 12(4), 1994, at p. 91.
6 UN Doc. A/CN.4/143, p. 13.
7 During the conference, the proposal advanced in 1976 by Colombia regarding the standards of claiming historic waters was discarded. See UNCLOS III, *Official Records* (1977), vol. 5, p. 202.
8 The preamble of the LOS Convention affirms that 'matters not regulated by this Convention continue to be governed by the rules and principles of general international law'.
9 Sri Lanka Law, No. 22 of 1976.
10 Article 6 of the Law on the State Boundary of the USSR; reprinted in 22 *ILM* 1055 (1983).

11 Portugal: Law on Territorial Waters, Law No. 2130, 5 *ILM* 1094 (1966).
12 See Article 6 of the Agreement, reprinted in 13 *ILM* 1441(1974).
13 The full text is available at http://faolex.fao.org/docs/pdf/ton28403.pdf (accessed 19 October 2012).
14 See Executive Summary: A Partial Submission of Data and Information on the Outer Limits of the Continental Shelf of the Kingdom of Tonga Pursuant to part VI and Annex II to the United Nations Convention on the Law of the Sea, 11 May 2009, available at http://www.un.org/Depts/los/clcs_new/submissions_files/ton46_09/ton2009executive_summary.pdf (accessed 19 October 2012).
15 Ibid., p. 2.
16 See Gioia, 'Tunisia's claims over adjacent seas'.
17 The Gulf was claimed as territorial sea by Laws Nos. 62–35 of 16 October 1962 and Nos. 63–49 of 30 December 1963. The texts of the Laws are reprinted in *Journal Officiel de la RépubliqueTunisienne*, 12–16 October 1962, p. 1224 and 31 December 1963, p. 1870.
18 Tunisia made its claim in 1973 by a decree.
19 See Gioia, 'Tunisia's claims over adjacent seas', p. 346.
20 Ibid., p. 347.
21 Ibid., p. 359.
22 See the Libyan Counter-Memorial, 1980 ICJ Pleadings, p. 53.
23 Gioia, 'Tunisia's claims over adjacent seas', p. 365.
24 See *Case Concerning the Continental Shelf* (Tunisia v. Libyan Arab Jamahiriya), 1982 ICJ, Vol.18 (Judgement of Feb. 24), p. 68.
25 Gioia, 'Tunisia's claims over adjacent seas', p. 369.
26 Ibid., p. 370.
27 *Case concerning the Continental Shelf*, p. 73.
28 Ibid., p. 74.
29 Gioia, 'Tunisia's claims over adjacent seas', p. 371.
30 Ibid., p. 373.
31 For a thorough assessment of the case, see Barbara Kwiatkowska, 'The Eritrea/Yemen Arbitration: landmark progress in the acquisition of territorial sovereignty and equitable maritime boundary delimitation', *IBRU Boundary and Security Bulletin*, 8(1), 2000, pp. 66–86.
32 Eritrea-Yemen Arbitration Award, Phase I: Territorial Sovereignty and Scope of Dispute, 9 October 1998, para. 2, available at http://www.pca-cpa.org/ER-YE AwardTOC.htm (accessed 17 May 2000).
33 Ibid., paras 13–14.
34 Ibid., paras 31–41.
35 Ibid., para. 123.
36 Ibid., para. 126.
37 Ibid., para. 449.
38 Ibid., para. 526.
39 British Institute of International and Comparative Law, *Joint Development of Offshore Oil and Gas: A Model Agreement for States for Joint Development with Explanatory Commentary*, London: British Institute of International and Comparative Law, 1989, p. 45.
40 See Masahiro Miyoshi, *The Joint Development of Offshore Oil and Gas in Relation to Maritime Boundary Delimitation*, Maritime Briefing, vol. 2, no. 5, Durham: International Boundaries Research Unit, University of Durham 1999, p. 23.
41 Ibid., p. 37.
42 See Ibrahim F. I. Shihata and William T. Onorato, 'Joint development of international petroleum resources in undefined and disputed areas', in G. H. Blake, M. A. Pratt and C. H. Schofield (eds), *Boundaries and Energy: Problems and Prospects*, London: Kluwer Law International, 1998, pp. 436–437.

43 Masahiro Miyoshi, 'Is joint development possible in the South China Sea?', in Mochtar Kusuma-Atmadja, Thomas A. Mensah and Bernard H. Oxman (eds), *Sustainable Development and Preservation of the Oceans: The Challenges of UNCLOS and Agenda 21*, Honolulu: Law of the Sea Institute, University of Hawaii, 1997, pp. 610–624, at pp. 613–614.
44 Articles 10(6), 15, and 298(1)(a)(i) of the LOS Convention. United Nations, *The Law of the Sea: United Nations Convention on the Law of the Sea with Index and Final Act of the Third United Nations Conference on the Law of the Sea*, New York: United Nations, 1983, p. 5.
45 United Nations, *The Law of the Sea*, p. 6.
46 Ibid., p. 103.
47 For details, see Zou Keyuan, 'Historic rights in international law and in China's practice', *Ocean Development and International Law*, 32, 2001, pp. 149–168.
48 See *People's Daily* (in Chinese), 30 June 1998. An unofficial English version translated and published by this author is reprinted in Zou Keyuan, *China's Marine Legal System and the Law of the Sea*, Leiden: Martinus Nijhoff, 2005, pp. 342–345. Another variant English translation is available in *Law of the Sea Bulletin*, 38, 1998, pp. 28–31.
49 See Manh Dong, 'Maritime delimitation between Vietnam and her neighboring countries', UN-Nippon Foundation Alumni Meeting, Tokyo, 13–16 April 2009, available at http://www.un.org/Depts/los/nippon/unnff_programme_home/alumni/tokyo_alumni_presents_files/alum_tokyo_dong.pdf (accessed 12 November 2012).
50 For the Chinese position, see 'Chinese Ambassador to ASEAN: stop the Philippines from illegal fishing in Huangyan Islands', 15 May 2012, available at http://www.nanhai.org.cn/news_detail.asp?newsid=2337 (accessed 12 December 2012). For the Philippine position, see Department of Foreign Affairs, 'Philippine position on Bajo de Masinloc (Scarborough Shoal) and the waters within its vicinity', 18 April 2012, available at http://www.gov.ph/2012/04/18/philippine-position-on-bajo-de-masinloc-and-the-waters-within-its-vicinity/ (accessed 12 December 2012). In the position paper, it states that 'Filipino fishermen have always considered it as their fishing grounds, owing to their proximity to the coastal towns and areas of Southwest Luzon.'
51 See Department of Foreign Affairs, 'Philippine position on Bajo de Masinloc'.
52 The text is available at http://news.xinhuanet.com/english/2008-06/18/content_8394206.htm (accessed 12 December 2012). For relevant commentaries, see Gao Jianjun, 'A note on the 2008 cooperation consensus between China and Japan in the East China Sea', *Ocean Development and International Law*, 40, 2009, pp. 291–303.
53 See Nguyen Hong Thao, 'Vietnam and joint development in the Gulf of Thailand', *Asian Yearbook of International Law*, vol. 8, 1998–99, pp. 137–150.
54 Article 74 of the UN Charter, available at http://www.un.org/aboutun/charter/index.html (accessed 13 November 2012).
55 Franz Xaver Perrez, *Cooperative Sovereignty: From Independence to Interdependence in the Structure of International Environmental Law*, The Hague: Kluwer Law International, 2000, p. 260.
56 See Article 123 of the LOS Convention.
57 See Article 123 of the LOS Convention.
58 See Nien-Tsu Alfred Hu, 'Semi-enclosed troubled waters: a new thinking on the application of the 1982 UNCLOS Article 123 to the South China Sea', *Ocean Development and International Law*, 41, 2011, pp. 281–314.
59 The text is available at http://www.asean.org/13163.htm (accessed 29 September 2012).
60 An English version of the document is available at http://biendong.net/en/documents/law/306-guidelines-for-the-implementation-of-the-doc.html (accessed 28 November 2012).
61 Wang Gungwu, *The Nanhai Trade: Early Chinese Trade in the South China Sea*, Singapore: Eastern Universities Press, 2003.

6 Defining areas for joint development in disputed waters

Clive Schofield

In recent years maritime joint development zones have emerged as an important means to overcome deadlock in relation to maritime jurisdictional claims. A key consideration in the negotiation and establishment of maritime joint development arrangements is the definition of the precise geographical area within which joint development is to proceed. This chapter reviews joint development practice with particular reference to the spatial definition of joint zones.

This experience can be broadly divided into joint zones that have been agreed in addition to a maritime boundary line and those that have been defined in the absence of a boundary line, which have proved a more popular alternative. With respect to the latter type of joint zone, many such joint areas are determined by the limits of competing maritime claims and thus involve the joint development of disputed waters.

The definition of joint zones in this manner is often a sensitive and challenging issue. This is the case because, without prejudice clauses notwithstanding, the use of unilateral maritime claims as the limits of a joint area to an extent validates such claims, giving them practical impact and thereby a degree of endorsement and legitimacy which they may not, in fact, warrant. This has led to reluctance on the part of some States to, in a sense, recognise and accept what are regarded as excessive claims through their use in the definition of the limits of a maritime joint development zone. This chapter explores past experience of how this delicate issue has been dealt with. Some observations drawn from this inventory and assessment of past practice are offered, together with some preliminary considerations on the applicability of these observations to overlapping claims in the South China Sea.

The rationale for joint development

Where overlapping claims exist and the parties have reached a deadlock in maritime boundary delimitation negotiations, the alternative of a shared rather than a unilateral management regime may prove attractive. Although a number of these cooperative mechanisms predate the United Nations Convention on the Law of the Sea (UNCLOS),[1] such joint maritime zones have predominantly been concluded since the Convention was opened for signature. The key provisions within

UNCLOS in this respect are Articles 74(3) and 83(3) which provide, in identical terms, that:

> Pending agreement as provided for in paragraph 1, the States concerned, in a spirit of understanding and cooperation, shall make every effort to enter into provisional arrangements of a practical nature and, during this transitional period, not to jeopardize or hamper the reaching of the final agreement. Such arrangements shall be without prejudice to the final delimitation.

State practice in maritime joint development, reviewed below, can be broadly divided into joint zones that have been agreed in addition to a maritime boundary line and those that have been defined in the absence of a boundary line, which have proved a more popular alternative. Six examples of joint zones concluded in conjunction with the delimitation of a maritime boundary line and 16 where no boundary line has yet been drawn are reviewed below.

The spatial definition of joint development zones

Brief outlines of the key attributes of each of the maritime joint developments considered are provided below. Greater emphasis has, however, been devoted to those joint zones in the Asia-Pacific region, reflecting the focus of the present volume. It is worth noting that the joint development arrangements reviewed do not comprise an exhaustive list of all such mechanisms. For example, a number of joint arrangements that are now defunct, such as that which existed offshore the, now divided, Kuwait–Saudi Arabia Neutral Zone, are not considered here.[2]

Joint development agreements in addition to a boundary line

A number of joint zones have been defined in conjunction with the delimitation of a maritime boundary between the parties concerned. In these circumstances, the joint zone may act as a catalyst for reaching agreement on the delimitation line, for example providing both parties with some rights in the maritime area of interest. This serves to counter the potential drawback of defining a boundary line and subsequently discovering that the bulk, or all, of the resources in the area subject to overlapping maritime claims fall on the 'wrong side of the line' as it were. It can be observed that many of the joint zones so defined bear little relation to the original area of overlapping maritime claims.

Bahrain–Saudi Arabia

Signed in January 1958, this agreement arguably represents the first maritime joint development agreement worldwide.[3] In a sense, however, it is not a joint zone at all in that it is wholly located on one side (Saudi Arabia's) of the agreed Bahrain–Saudi Arabia line. This is in distinction to other joint zones defined in conjunction with maritime boundary agreements which tend to straddle the agreed line. Nonetheless, the Bahrain–Saudi arrangement is joint in the sense that the revenue derived from the oil resources exploited within the defined area are shared between the parties. The agreement provides that the exploitation of the oil resources in this area will be carried out in the way chosen by the King of Saudi Arabia 'on the condition that he grants to the Kingdom of Bahrain one half of the net revenue accruing to the Government of Saudi Arabia and arising from this exploitation'.[4] The zone defined is hexagonal and encompasses the Fasht Abu-Sa'fah oilfield which had previously been contested between the parties.

Argentina–Uruguay

Argentina and Uruguay established a 'common fishing zone' as well as a joint Administrative Commission in conjunction with the delimitation of their boundary in the estuary of the Rio de la Plata (River Plate) and seawards into the South Atlantic Ocean.[5] The common fishing zone is defined as the area seaward of the parties' 12 nm territorial sea limits. The outer limit of the joint area is expansive as it is described in Article 73 of the agreement as being defined 'by two arcs of circles with radii of 200 nautical miles whose centre points are, respectively, Punta del Este (Uruguay) and Punta del Cabo San Antonio (Argentina)'. While being primarily concerned with fishing issues, the joint Administrative Commission is also tasked, through Article 66 of the accord, with promoting joint scientific research, particularly that relating to marine living resources and the prevention and elimination of pollution as well as aiding navigation.

Australia–Papua New Guinea

Australia and Papua New Guinea (PNG) reached a particularly innovative, as well as highly complex, agreement relating to the Torres Strait in 1978.[6] The agreement delimits separate continental shelf and fisheries boundaries. This recognised the geographically complex character of the Torres Strait including numerous islands. Many of these islands, including ones in close proximity to the mainland coast of PNG are under Australian sovereignty. In order to achieve an equitable outcome, a continental shelf boundary was defined centrally in the Strait, midway between the mainland coasts of both States, while a fisheries boundary, passing close to the PNG coast, was defined around the Australian islands in the northern part of the Torres Strait. Thus, in this area PNG seabed underlies Australian water column.

Rather than creating a joint development zone as such, the Torres Strait Treaty instead established a broad protected zone encompassing the Torres Strait. The objective of the protected zone is to safeguard traditional fishing activities and the free movement of traditional inhabitants, to regulate commercial fisheries and to protect the marine environment. In keeping with these objectives a moratorium on oil and gas exploration within the protected zone was agreed. The Torres Strait Treaty provided for the establishment of a joint advisory council set up to promote cooperation,[7] and also provides for a detailed regulatory regime designed to protect traditional rights while promoting cooperative development of commercial fisheries.[8]

Iceland–Norway (Jan Mayen Island)

In 1980 Iceland and Norway reached agreement on a maritime boundary relating to the exclusive economic zone (EEZ), to be based on 200 nm arcs measured from base points on Iceland.[9] In addition to the boundary line a joint zone was also to be established. A particularly notable feature of this 45,470 km^2 joint zone is that while in common with many other joint zones established in addition to a boundary line it straddles the agreed boundary, the Iceland–Norway zone does so in uneven fashion.[10] Overall, 61 per cent of the joint zone lies on the Norwegian side and 39 per cent on the Icelandic side of the boundary line. While each State is entitled to 25 per cent of revenues deriving from the exploitation of oil and gas on the other side of the boundary,[11] hydrocarbon fields straddling the joint zone and Icelandic waters are considered wholly Icelandic.[12] This boundary agreement and joint zone were negotiated between the parties on the basis of the recommendations of a Conciliation Commission. The uneven distribution of the joint zone across the delimitation line, in favour of Iceland, took the disparities between Iceland and Jan Mayen, particularly in terms of population, into account. Additionally, Iceland's lack of mineral resources as compared with Norway was a factor in the recommendations of the Conciliation Commission.[13]

Denmark–United Kingdom

In May 1999 Denmark and the United Kingdom concluded a maritime boundary agreement for the area between the Faroe Islands and Scotland.[14] While seabed and water column boundaries are coincident for most of the line, in the central part of the boundary a 'Special Area' was defined, providing for joint fisheries jurisdiction. The Special Area covers an area of 2,337 nm^2 or approximately 8,000 km^2.[15] It straddles the continental shelf boundary but does so in unequal manner, the majority of it being located on the UK side of the seabed boundary line. This reflects the overwhelming dependence of the Faroe Islands economy on fisheries.[16] Within the Special Area each party has the right to continue to conduct fishery operations, including the issuing of licences, and the parties also agreed not to interdict fishing vessels operating in the joint zone under a licence issued by the other party.[17] Denmark and UK also agreed to take 'all possible steps to prevent and eliminate pollution' resulting from their offshore activities, including exploration activities related to seabed hydrocarbon resources,[18] and also agreed to cooperate on measures to protect the marine environment.[19]

China–Vietnam

China and Vietnam concluded a maritime boundary agreement in the Gulf of Tonkin (Beibu Gulf to China and Bac Bo Gulf to Vietnam) in December 2000 and simultaneously created no less than three joint fishing zones.[20] In conjunction with the boundary treaty an Agreement on Fishery Cooperation in the Gulf of Tonkin was concluded. Through the fisheries cooperation agreement a joint

Common Fishery Zone of approximately 30,000 km^2 (around 8,747 nm^2) was defined which straddles the maritime delimitation line and extends 30.5 nm on either side of it, from the 20°N parallel of latitude to the closing line of the Gulf.[21] Additionally, a transitional arrangement zone north of 20°N was established where the parties aim to gradually reduce the number of fishing vessels operating. A buffer zone either side of the parties' territorial sea boundary in the immediate vicinity of the terminus of the land boundary on the coast in the north of the Gulf was defined in order to minimise disputes involving for small fishing vessels that may have trespassed across the boundary line.[22] While the setting of fishing quotas and the number of fishing vessels allowed in the Common Fishery Zone is established jointly through a Joint Fisheries Committee, it is important to note that enforcement is conducted on the basis of coastal State authority, that is, on the basis of which side of the defined boundary line the activity takes place, rather than on the basis of flag State control.

Joint development agreements in lieu of a boundary agreement

Cambodia–Vietnam

Cambodia and Vietnam reached agreement in 1982 on the establishment of a joint area of 'historic waters' in the Gulf of Thailand.[23] The primary purpose of the agreement was the resolution of the parties' dispute over several islands, sovereignty over which had previously been contested. Rather than reflecting the area of overlapping claims, therefore, the oblong-shaped joint historic waters area created through the 1982 agreement is instead essentially framed by, though does not include, the formerly disputed islands.

The joint historic waters area extends seawards from the mainland coastlines of the two countries out to the vicinity of the Poulo Wei group of islands, which were specified as Cambodian, and the Tho Chu (Poulo Panjang) Islands, which according to the agreement were determined to be Vietnamese, as was the large island of Phu Quoc. No maritime boundary was defined through the joint area, though it was stated that negotiations on this issue would take place 'at a suitable time'.[24] It appears that a suitable time has yet to eventuate as, as far as can be established, such negotiations have yet to take place. Additionally, the agreement served to integrate Cambodia and Vietnam's straight baseline systems which meet at 'Point O', whose precise location is unspecified, on the south-western limit of the historic waters area.[25]

While not a joint arrangement overtly targeted at the cooperative development or management of marine resources or activities, the agreement does include some maritime joint development provisions. For example, Cambodia and Vietnam agreed to undertake the exploitation of natural resources within the joint historic waters area on the basis of 'common agreement', and to carry out joint surveillance and patrols in the joint area.[26] The fishing activities of both parties were specified as being set to continue within the joint historic waters area 'according to the habits that have existed so far'. Cambodia and Vietnam's claim to the establishment of this unconventional joint historic waters area, and to joining their respective straight baseline systems at an apparently 'floating' point out to sea proved controversial and resulted in international protests, notably from Thailand[27] and the United States. In a note to the UN Secretary General dated 17 June 1987, the United States government protested against the Cambodian–Vietnamese agreement, stating that the claim was made known internationally 'less than five years ago' and that as a result there was 'insufficient' evidence to demonstrate the required effective exercise of authority for such a historic claim. Additionally, the US note stated that 'the United States has not acquiesced in this claim, nor can the community of States be said to have done so'.[28]

Japan–Korea

Although Japan and the Republic of Korea were able to delimit a maritime boundary between their respective territories in the southern part of the Sea of Japan (East Sea to Korea) and through the Korea Strait,[29] they adopted radically different positions on the principles and methods of delimitation applicable to the southern part of their potential continental shelf boundary extending into the East China Sea. On the one hand, Japan favoured delimitation on the basis of an equidistance or median line. On the other, Korea asserted that the boundary line should be influenced by geophysical factors on the basis of natural prolongation arguments. These contrasting approaches resulted in a broad area of overlapping maritime claims. The parties' dispute over sovereignty concerning the islands of Dok-do (to Korea) or Takeshima (to Japan) also frustrated progress towards the delimitation of a maritime boundary further north.

In order to overcome the deadlock in maritime boundary delimitation negotiations, in 1974 Japan and Korea reached agreement on joint development with respect to the broad area (29,092 nm^2) encompassed by their overlapping claims to maritime jurisdiction in the East China Sea.[30] The Japan–Korea joint development zone shelved the issue of boundary delimitation. Indeed, Article 28 of the Japan–Korea treaty states that: 'Nothing in the Agreement shall be regarded as determining the question of sovereign rights over all or any portion of the Joint Development Zone or as prejudicing the positions of the respective Parties with respect to the delimitation of the continental shelf.' The agreement is specifically designed to facilitate the exploration for and exploitation of seabed oil and gas resources over a 50-year period (from entry into force in 1978) although, to date, without success. The agreement may, however, be extended if no maritime boundary is delimited, although it can be terminated by either side with three years' notice.[31] The joint zone is divided into sub-zones (originally nine, subsequently reduced to six) and innovatively side-stepped concerns over the application of laws and regulations within each sub-zone by establishing an 'operator formula' approach. That is, within each sub-zone, concessionaires, authorised by each of the parties, have an undivided interest and one operator is chosen from among the two concessionaires to conduct activities in a particular sub-zone. Thus, Japanese law applies to a Japanese operator within a particular sub-zone and Korean law similarly applies to a Korean operator within another sub-zone.[32] The costs incurred by the parties in the exploration and exploitation phases are to be shared equally between the concessionaires of the two countries, as are the proceeds from the natural resources extracted in a sub-zone. The parties also established a Joint Commission[33] in order to facilitate liaison between the governments concerned, though they stopped short of setting up a more powerful joint authority. Had Japan and Korea in fact discovered oil and gas within the joint zone, a potentially major additional complication and disincentive to development is the fact that a third party, China, also claims as yet not clearly defined parts of the joint zone and has refused to recognise its creation.[34]

Saudi Arabia–Sudan

The joint zone defined between Saudi Arabia and Sudan in 1974[35] stands apart from other maritime joint development zones as its area of application is not defined by a series of geographic coordinates joined by lines, nor by the overlap in competing maritime claims. Instead, the joint zone applies to that part of the central part of the Red Sea between the two countries' respective coasts which is greater than 1,000 metres in depth. The northern and southern limits of the joint zone have not, however, been defined. Although the agreement covers all natural resources, its primary objective was to allow for the joint exploration for and exploitation of seabed mineral resources, notably metalliferous sediments rich in heavy metals such as copper, manganese, zinc, iron and silver, known to exist in the Red Sea deeps.[36] Although a Saudi–Sudanese Red Sea Commission was established in 1975, it is understood that little exploration activity has in fact taken place and no commercial discoveries or developments have eventuated.[37]

Australia–Indonesia

Australia's seabed boundaries with Indonesia in the Timor Sea of 1972 were negotiated prior to Indonesia's 1975 occupation and subsequent annexation of East Timor, creating a discontinuity in the line which became commonly referred to as the 'Timor Gap'. Following Indonesia's invasion of East Timor and Canberra's subsequent acceptance of Indonesian sovereignty over East Timor, boundary negotiations for the Timor Gap were initiated in order to, essentially "join up" the separate sections of their existing maritime boundary agreements to the east and west. However, largely as a consequence of subsequent evolutions in the international law of ocean boundary-making, Indonesia refused to simply "close the gap" on the same basis as its earlier agreements with Australia. As a result no boundary agreement could be reached regarding the Timor Gap which was, instead, filled with a joint development zone – the Timor Gap Zone of Cooperation.[38]

The Timor Gap cooperative arrangement covers an area of 60,500 km^2 and is in large part based on the overlapping claims of the parties. The joint zone was, however, divided into three sub-zones – a large central, 'sovereignty neutral' Zone A, where revenues were to be shared on a 50:50 basis, and two smaller 'national' zones, Zone B to the south, where the ratio was 90:10 in favour of Australia, and a narrow Zone C, where the ratio was 90:10 in favour of Indonesia.

The treaty itself was signed in December 1989 with additional detailed regulations being added in 1991, and was widely regarded as the most sophisticated and comprehensive maritime joint development zone in the world. Indeed, the Timor Gap Treaty, together with its annexed model production sharing agreement and Petroleum Mining Code, runs to in excess of 100 pages. The initial duration of the agreement was to be 40 years, to be followed by successive terms of 20 years. The Timor Gap Treaty is, however, no longer in force having been replaced by agreements concluded between Australia and East Timor (see below).

Malaysia–Thailand

Although Malaysia and Thailand were able to agree on the alignment of their territorial sea boundary without undue difficulty,[39] they were only able to delimit their continental shelf boundary out to a point approximately 29 nm offshore.[40] Seaward of that point, a dispute over the validity of a small Thai island as a base point led to a roughly wedge-shaped overlap in continental shelf claims. This overlap in maritime claims provided the basis for the Thai–Malaysian joint development area (JDA).

The agreement on joint development between Thailand and Malaysia took a considerable time to reach fruition, however. Although a Memorandum of Understanding (MoU) was concluded between the two States in February 1979, which established broad principles for the joint development of 'non-living-resources, in particular petroleum',[41] a further agreement to deal with complex issues such as the detailed regulations to govern activities in the JDA and on the establishment of a Joint Authority was not signed until May 1990.[42] As commercially viable oil and gas fields have been discovered and development is underway, the joint arrangement can be viewed, in principle, as a successful one.

That said, significant difficulties have emerged in relation to bringing the gas extracted from within the JDA onshore via the Thai–Malaysian Pipeline project. These issues relate to potential impacts of the project on local stakeholders, including fishing communities. It is also worth noting that Vietnam also claims the most seaward part of the Thai–Malaysian JDA. However, in the Thai–Vietnamese maritime boundary treaty of 7 August 1997 there exists a specific indication that the parties, together with Malaysia 'shall enter into negotiations … in order to settle the tripartite overlapping continental shelf claim area'.[43] At the time of writing a tripartite agreement arising from these negotiations has yet to emerge.[44]

Malaysia–Vietnam

The agreement concluded by Malaysia and Vietnam in 1992 establishes a long, narrow 'Defined Area' in the south-eastern part of the Gulf of Thailand for the exploration for and exploitation of seabed petroleum deposits.[45] The Defined Area corresponds with the two States' overlapping claims to continental shelf and was prompted by oil discoveries made by Malaysian contractors within the disputed zone. The joint arrangement was established for 40 years, subject to reviews and extensions and with costs and benefits to be shared equally. The agreement offers a framework under which nominees of the two governments can enter into agreements for exploring and exploiting petroleum reserves once the area has been delimited. The joint mechanism is therefore a relatively straightforward commercial arrangement whereby each country's rights are managed by their respective national oil companies (Petronas of Malaysia and PetroVietnam of Vietnam). That said, it can be observed that the two governments retain a right of veto with regard to any agreements their national oil companies might reach.

Colombia–Jamaica

The 1993 Maritime Delimitation Treaty between Colombia and Jamaica[46] established a 'Joint Regime Area' (JRA) to the west of an agreed maritime boundary. The JRA was defined as being a 'zone of joint management, control, exploration and exploitation of the living and non-living resources … pending the determination of the jurisdictional limits of each Party'. Within this area, however, two 12 nm-radius areas around the Colombian Seranilla Bank and Bajo Nuevo Cays were excluded. The total area of the JRA is approximately 4,500 nm^2.[47] Within the JRA the parties agreed that they could explore for and exploit the natural resources therein, whether living or non-living, establish and use artificial islands, installations and structures, conduct marine scientific research, and take action to protect and preserve the marine environment and conserve living resources.[48] With regard to activities relating to the exploration and exploitation of non-living resources, as well as those in respect of marine scientific research and on the protection and preservation of the marine environment, however, the parties are to carry out activities 'on a joint basis' reached through agreement between them.[49] Colombia and Jamaica furthermore agreed that within the JRA each State would have jurisdiction over its own nationals and vessels flying its own flag and they agreed to adopt measures to ensure that the nationals and vessels of third-party States would comply with any regulations and measures the parties were to adopt.[50] The parties also agreed to establish a Joint Commission to 'elaborate the modalities for the implementation and carrying out of' activities within the JRA.[51]

Argentina–United Kingdom

Despite the long-standing sovereignty dispute between Argentina and the United Kingdom over the Falkland Islands (Islas Malvinas to Argentina), South Georgia and the South Sandwich Islands, the parties have, following their 1982 conflict, sought to improve bilateral relations and this has yielded some maritime cooperative initiatives in the South Atlantic. On 2 November 1990 the two countries issued a Joint Statement on the Conservation of Fisheries,[52] established a South Atlantic Fisheries Commission and announced the cooperation of the two governments over the conservation of fish stocks between 45°S and

60°S. Additionally, on 27 September 1995 Argentina and the UK issued a Joint Declaration on Cooperation over Offshore Activities in the South West Atlantic.[53] The Joint Declaration 'coordinated activities' in relation to a 'sedimentary structure' in an area defined to the south-west of the disputed islands within which the two governments would cooperate to encourage the exploration and production of hydrocarbons. The area in question covers approximately 20,000 km^2 (around 5,831 nm^2). Unfortunately, although these joint arrangements still exist in principle, at the time of writing bilateral relations have deteriorated markedly and no active cooperation is taking place.

Nigeria–São Tomé and Príncipe

Nigeria and Sao Tomé and Príncipe concluded a treaty in 2001 establishing a joint zone between them.[54] The joint zone is the largest such arrangement established to date with an area of 34,540 km^2 (around 10,070 nm^2). The geographical scope of the joint zone in large part reflects the parties' overlapping claims – the zone's north-western limit is based on an equidistance line between opposite coasts, its north-eastern limit is defined by an equidistance line with neighbouring Equatorial Guinea, its south-western limit by 200 nm arcs from Nigeria, while the south-eastern limit approximately reflects a one-third effect line for Sao Tomé and Príncipe versus Nigeria. The objective of the joint arrangement is to exploit and share the natural resources of the joint zone, especially seabed hydrocarbons. Revenues to be derived from the exploitation of the resources within the joint zone are to be shared on the basis of 60 per cent to Nigeria and 40 per cent to Sao Tomé and Príncipe.[55] The agreement establishes a Joint Ministerial Council and a Joint Authority (since renamed the Joint Development Authority).

Australia–Timor Leste (East Timor) in the Timor Sea

Prior to achieving independence, the East Timorese government in waiting, together with the United Nations Transitional Authority for East Timor (UNTAET) had made it clear that East Timor would not be bound by any of the agreements relating to East Timor's territory entered into by Jakarta – including the Timor Gap joint development zone mentioned above. In order to safeguard ongoing seabed resource developments in the Timor Sea, a new agreement, the Timor Sea Treaty (TST), was signed between Australia and East Timor on the day that East Timor became independent.[56] The TST established a Joint Petroleum Development Area (JPDA), which coincides with the central part of the old Australia–Indonesia joint zone (Zone A). Whereas in the past revenues from Zone A had been shared between Australia and Indonesia on an equal basis, under the TST revenues from seabed resources exploited within the JPDA are split 90:10 in East Timor's favour.

Complications then arose, especially in relation to the Greater Sunrise complex of fields straddling the north-eastern limit of the JPDA.[57] Unitisation agreements between Australia and East Timor were signed but East Timor opted to delay ratification.[58] It became clear that according to the unitisation agreements that 20.1 per cent of Greater Sunrise lies within the JPDA with the remaining 79.9 per cent falling on what Australia regards as its side of the line. Consequently, East Timor was set to benefit from only marginally over 18 per cent of the proceeds from Greater Sunrise (90 per cent share of the 20.1 per cent of the field falling within the JPDA). East Timor subsequently argued that it was not bound by the dimensions of the 'Timor Gap' defined by previous Australia–Indonesia boundary agreements and claimed areas adjacent to the JPDA. The delimitation negotiations that ensued proved complex and contentious.[59]

Australia and East Timor were eventually able to overcome the barriers to agreement and the Treaty on Certain Maritime Arrangements in the Timor Sea (CMATS) was signed in 2006.[60] The treaty establishes a further interim resource sharing agreement whose area of application is coincident with the 'Unit Area' defined in the previously negotiated unitisation agreement and therefore encompasses the Greater Sunrise complex of fields. The agreement provides for the equal sharing of revenues deriving from the upstream exploitation of petroleum resources within this zone. Consequently, rather than an 18.1 per cent share in Greater Sunrise as would have been the case under the earlier accords, East Timor stands to gain a full 50 per cent share in the revenues deriving from the development of those fields.

CMATS is without prejudice to either side's claims to maritime delimitation[61] and includes stringent requirements for a moratorium on claims while the treaty is in force. In particular, the parties are restricted from the direct or indirect initiation of, or participation in, any proceedings relating to maritime boundary delimitation in the Timor Sea before 'any court, tribunal or other dispute resolution mechanism' or even raising such issues in 'any international organisation'.[62] The parties agreed to defer their claims to maritime jurisdiction and boundaries in the Timor Sea for up to 50 years or, 'until the date five years after the exploitation' of the area covered by the treaty ceases, 'whichever occurs earlier'.[63] The treaty will, however, lapse if either a development plan for Greater Sunrise has not been approved within six years or production has not started within 10 years from the agreement entering into force.[64]

CMATS also provides for East Timorese jurisdiction over the water column above the JPDA. Specifically, CMATS Article 8 refers to a line defined by means of a list of coordinates of latitude and longitude, referred to World Geodetic System 84 and joined by geodesic lines, contained in a treaty annex. The line so defined is consistent with the southern boundary of the JPDA, with Australia to exercise jurisdiction to the south and East Timor to the north. The agreement also serves to establish a bilateral joint Maritime Commission to 'constitute a focal point for bilateral consultations with regard to maritime matters of interest to the Parties'.[65] Unfortunately, however, it is understood that the Maritime Commission has yet to meet.

While the arrangements between Australia and Timor Leste appear to offer considerable benefits to both parties and hold significant potential to transform Timor Leste's developing economy and reduce or even eliminate its dependence on aid, it is worth noting that serious complications have subsequently arisen. In particular, disputes have emerged over downstream activities especially with respect to the destination of any pipeline onshore, that is, will the resources be landed in Australia or Timor Leste, and thus location of downstream processing infrastructure.[66] Moreover, in April 2013 Timor Laste initiated arbitration proceedings under the terms of the Timor Sea Treaty which call into question the validity of CMATS and could ultimately result in that arrangement unravelling.[67]

Joint fishing zones in East Asia

Four joint fisheries agreements that emerged following the ratification of UNCLOS, the declaration of EEZs by China, Japan and the Republic of Korea and the resulting overlapping maritime claims may be considered together. The agreements in question are the China–Japan agreement of 11 November 1997 relating to part of the East China Sea, the Japan–Korea agreement of January 2000 in respect of parts of both the East China Sea and the Sea of Japan (East Sea to Korea), and the China–Korea agreement of 30 June 2001 dealing with parts of the Yellow Sea.[68] These joint agreements cover only part of China, Korea and Japan's substantial areas of overlapping maritime claims. They are of a provisional nature and are without prejudice to final maritime boundary delimitation.

These joint arrangements have drawbacks, notably that they provide for enforcement on a flag State basis with minimal joint enforcement envisaged and include no provisions for enforcement against third parties. Thus, none of the above-mentioned agreements provide for enforcement against vessels from, for example, Taiwan, which is a significant fishing entity in the waters concerned.

More recently the issue of fishing on the part of vessels from Taiwan was at least partially addressed through the conclusion of a further joint fishery agreement in the East China Sea, this time between Japan and Taiwan on 10 April 2013. The agreement covers the southern part of the East China Sea. The agreement does, however, exclude the 12 nm breadth territorial waters of the disputed Senkaku/Diaoyutai Islands and its conclusion is without prejudice to the parties' positions concerning that dispute.[69]

Furthermore, the agreements encompass only part of the picture and substantial 'current fishing patterns' zones where fishing is at the least uncoordinated and at the worst largely unregulated. Nonetheless, they represent a positive step towards cooperative, joint solutions to shared problems and a potentially useful application of maritime joint development concepts, frequently focused on seabed hydrocarbons, to living resources.[70]

Cambodia–Thailand

On 18 June 2001, Cambodia and Thailand signed a Memorandum of Understanding regarding the Area of their Overlapping Claims to the Continental Shelf in the Gulf of Thailand.[71] The area covered by the MoU appears to coincide with the parties' large overlapping claims area – an area believed to offer high prospects with respect to seabed hydrocarbon resources. It can be inferred that the area of overlap between the parties has been reduced following the resolution of Cambodia and Vietnam's sovereignty dispute over islands. Uncertainty does, however, persist in relation to the southern limit of the area covered by the MoU.[72]

Cambodia and Thailand have been engaged in negotiations over this area of overlap since the early 1990s without realising an agreement. Indeed, the MoU signed in 2001 has been aptly described as merely 'an agreement-to-agree'.[73] It does, however, mark potentially significant progress as it separates delimitation of a lateral maritime boundary in the vicinity of the terminus of the land boundary on the coast in the north from joint development of the area of overlapping claims towards the centre of the Gulf, south of the 11°N parallel of latitude. The negotiations towards delimitation and joint development are to be conducted 'simultaneously' and represent 'an indivisible package'.[74] Although the MoU mentioned 'accelerated negotiation',[75] no agreement has yet been realised. Indeed, in 2009 the Thai government reportedly intended to unilaterally revoke the MoU, although this does not appear to have formally occurred.[76] This turn of events was attributable in part to sporadic clashes along their land border in the vicinity of the Preah Vihear Temple as well as Cambodia's appointment of ousted Thai Prime Minister Thaksin Shinawatra as an economic adviser. Nonetheless, the conclusion of the MoU and the ensuing negotiations must be considered a broadly positive step forward towards resolution of this long-standing maritime dispute even if final resolution of it remains elusive.

China–Japan

It was reported on 16 June 2008 that China and Japan had reached 'principled consensus' on cooperation in the East China Sea.[77] The broad area of overlap between the parties' claim in the East China Sea results from their radically different views on the method of maritime delimitation to be applied – Japan basing its claim on equidistance and China basing its claim on natural prolongation principles which would see a boundary line coincident with the Okinawa Trough, leaving much of the East China Sea on the Chinese side of the line. As a 'first step' towards making the East China Sea a 'sea of peace cooperation and friendship', China and Japan agreed to joint development of a specified block of seabed. The joint area to be explored 'under the principle of mutual benefit' straddles the median line between the parties' coasts and has an area of approximately 2,700 km^2.[78] Additionally, the two countries agreed to allow a Japanese corporation to invest in the Chinese entity already engaged in development activities in relation to the Chunxiao gas field (called the Shirakaba gas field by Japan), located on the Chinese side but in close proximity to the theoretical median line. The June 2008 agreement makes it clear that cooperation will be entered into 'in the transitional period prior to delimitation without prejudicing their respective legal positions'.[79] Further negotiations were anticipated regarding converting this agreement in principle into a formal treaty and with regard to other disputed gas fields in close proximity to the median line in the East China Sea. Progress towards such a formal agreement on implementing the joint development arrangement has been slow, however.[80] This is arguably unsurprising when set against the backdrop of worsening disputes between the parties in the East China Sea, especially with respect to sovereignty over the Senkaku/Diaoyutai Islands and in relation to maritime delimitation in the East China Sea.

Observations and opportunities

What commonalities and lessons can be gleaned from the above inventory and assessment of State practice in maritime joint development? Further, what does this practice suggest with respect to the potential application of maritime joint development in the South China Sea?

With respect to joint zones defined in addition to maritime boundary agreements, the spatial dimensions of such joint arrangements are generally not confined or defined by the limits of overlapping maritime claims. The delimitation of a boundary line in essence appears to have freed negotiators of joint zones defined in conjunction with them of the limitations of national maritime claims. Concerning joint zones in lieu of boundary agreements, however, there is a much stronger tendency to define the dimensions of the joint zone according to the limits of areas of overlapping claims. As noted at the beginning of this chapter, this is often a sensitive and challenging issue.

The key reason why this is the case is that to accept unilateral maritime claims as the limits of a joint area invests those unilateral claims with a degree of practical impact and thus, superficially at least, some legitimacy. This is particularly problematic where such unilateral maritime claims are excessive in character. Indeed, if the scope of maritime joint development areas is to be defined on the basis of unilateral maritime claims, this provides a strong rationale for coastal States to advance maximalist and manifestly excessive claims to maritime jurisdiction.

A notable example in this context is provided by the overlapping claims area between Cambodia and Thailand in the Gulf of Thailand. Cambodia's lateral maritime claim is a clearly excessive one, proceeding from the terminus of the land boundary on the coast straight over a Thai island before proceeding to the central part of the Gulf.[81] Given the excessive nature of Cambodia's claim line, it was inconceivable that Thailand could accept it as the limit of a maritime joint development area. Thailand and Cambodia were able to side-step this issue in the negotiation of their 2001 MoU by separating the northern part of their overlapping area, where delimitation discussions would proceed, from the southern part of the overlap, where joint development was the objective of negotiations.

An analogous example, though not so extreme, is provided by the Thai–Malaysian experience in defining their joint development area, also in the Gulf of Thailand. As noted above, the key reason for an overlap in the maritime claims of the parties related to the status of a particular Thai offshore feature and its potential capacity to generate maritime claims and thus its role in maritime delimitation. Thailand claimed that the small islet in question, Ko Losin, is an island capable of generating continental shelf and EEZ rights and consequently represented a valid base point for maritime delimitation with Malaysia. Malaysia in contrast argued that Ko Losin is no more than a 'rock' within the meaning of UNCLOS Article 121(3) and as such is only capable of generating claims to a 12 nm breadth territorial sea and contiguous zones.[82] As Ko Losin is a mere 1.5 m (5 ft) high and steep all round it would seem that Malaysia had a point. Arguably this represents a case of Thailand seeking to maximise its maritime claims with a view to securing the best outcome, either in maritime delimitation negotiations or through widening the geographical scope of the area subject to joint development, with the latter proving to be the outcome.

These examples demonstrate how unilateral maritime claims may not, in fact, necessarily provide an appropriate basis for the definition of a joint development zone, notwithstanding the apparent success of, for example, the Thai–Malaysia joint zone in terms of the discovery and development of seabed oil and gas resources. In this context it is also worth noting that States are under an obligation to formulate their maritime claims in 'good faith' under both customary international law and UNCLOS.[83] Further, maritime claims need to be clearly defined if they are to be used for this purpose.

It can also be remarked that an important purpose of establishing maritime joint development areas is to provide jurisdictional certainty and thus a sound basis for offshore resource development and management activities. In the case of the development of seabed hydrocarbons, for instance, exploration and exploitation costs run in the billions of dollars and activities stretch over decades, so providing a secure investment framework to international oil companies is crucial. In this context, the existence of a claim on the part of a third State to a bilaterally defined maritime cooperative arrangement can be regarded as a major complication. For example, as noted above, while Japan and Korea reached agreement on their joint zone, China objected. These objections had a direct bearing on US oil companies ceasing their operations in the joint zone. Similarly, in the Thai–Malaysian case, Vietnam's claims to part of the Thai–Malaysian joint development area have led to no activities being undertaken within that part of the joint zone though there are prospects that a trilateral arrangement may emerge for this area.

Arguably the key factors mentioned above that provide a basis for the spatial definition of maritime joint development zones are presently lacking in the South China Sea and this serves as a significant impediment to the definition of joint development zones therein. That is, a number of maritime jurisdictional claims are excessive in character and it is therefore questionable whether they have been made in good faith. Moreover, the basis and meaning of some of the claims made in the South China Sea, notably but not exclusively China's so-called "nine-dashed line" claim line, are vague and ill-defined. Consequently, maritime claims in the South China Sea have yet to be articulated in a clear enough fashion, as well as justified in international law, such that maritime zone arrangements based on areas of overlapping claims advanced in keeping with UNCLOS can be properly defined. Additionally, the multitude of overlapping maritime claims for which the South China Sea is renowned not only adds considerable complexity to the equation but raises ample potential concerns over third-party claims that are likely to undermine efforts to enter into joint development arrangements on a bilateral basis.

Taken together, these factors severely undermine the prospects for the definition of maritime joint development areas within the South China Sea generally. That said, hope of applying joint development arrangements to the South China Sea remain. It is notable, for example, that the South China Sea, and particularly its Gulf of Thailand extension, already hosts multiple joint development zones, especially towards its periphery. There may therefore be some scope for bilateral joint development arrangements to be pursued in selected parts of the South China Sea. Potential opportunities of this nature arise, for example, in the north-west of the South China Sea where China and Vietnam have sovereignty disputes (concerning the Paracel Islands) and overlapping maritime claims seaward of the Gulf of Tonkin and also in the north-east where China/Taiwan and the Philippines similarly have a dispute concerning the Scarborough Shoal and associated waters plus overlapping maritime claims further to the north-east which are unrelated to that contested feature. Additionally, there is possibility of bi- or trilateral arrangements being realised in the south-western South China Sea between Indonesia and both Malaysia and Vietnam, although China's apparent claims to at least part of this area via the nine-dashed line map would seem to render this scenario problematic.

Elsewhere, the complexities associated with the multilateral character of the South China Sea disputes would seem to undermine the chances of the conclusion of "traditional" maritime joint development arrangements either defined together with a maritime boundary, something that must be considered highly unlikely under present circumstances, or encompassing the entirety of the marine area subject to overlapping claims. Further, while as an alternative there might be a possibility of arriving at a joint arrangement not overtly tied to areas of overlapping claims, there appears to be little prospect of this at present. Overall, not only would a multilateral joint development arrangement be likely to prove fiendishly complicated to negotiate, but the very substantial degree of political will crucial to achieving such an outcome appears to be decidedly lacking. Nonetheless, the clearer definition of claims to maritime jurisdiction and their definition in good faith in keeping with UNCLOS would be significant steps forward. Indeed, these factors remain critical, and sadly presently missing, ingredients to the successful realisation of maritime joint development in the South China Sea. As this contribution has sought to demonstrate, there exist many, frequently innovative, maritime joint development models that could prove useful in definition for a joint development arrangement applicable to parts of the South China Sea. The clear definition of maritime claims on the basis of UNCLOS remains a critical prerequisitve, however.

Notes

1 United Nations Convention on the Law of the Sea, 10 Dec. 1982, 1833 U.N.T.S. 397.
2 The present review of joint development practice draws on the author's earlier

published work though with a spatial emphasis, notably, C. H. Schofield, 'Blurring the lines: maritime joint development and the cooperative management of ocean resources', *Issues in Legal Scholarship*, 8(1) (Frontier Issues in Ocean Law: Marine Resources, Maritime Boundaries, and the Law of the Sea), Berkeley Electronic Press, 2009, Article 3.

3 Bahrain–Saudi Arabia Boundary Agreement dated 22 February 1959 (signed 22 February 1958, entered into force 26 February 1958). Treaty text available from the United Nations Division on the Law of the Seas (DOALOS) 'Maritime Space' database at http://www.un.org/Depts/los/LEGISLATIONANDTREATIES/index.htm (hereafter DOALOS website). See also J. I. Charney and L. M. Alexander (eds), *International Maritime Boundaries*, vol. II, Dordrecht: Martinus Nijhoff, 1993, pp. 1489–1497.

4 Bahrain–Saudi Arabia Boundary Agreement, Second Clause.

5 Agreement between the Government of Argentina and the Government of Uruguay Relating to the Delimitation of the River Plate and the Maritime Boundary Between Argentina and Uruguay (signed 19 November 1973, entered into force 12 February 1974). Treaty text available at the DOALOS website. See also J. I. Charney and L. M. Alexander (eds), *International Maritime Boundaries*, vol. I, Dordrecht: Martinus Nijhoff, 1993, pp. 757–766.

6 Treaty between Australia and the Independent State of Papua New Guinea concerning sovereignty and maritime boundaries in the area between the two countries, including the area known as Torres Strait, and related matters, 18 December 1978 (entry into force, 15 February 1985). Treaty text available at [1985] ATS 4 and the DOALOS website. See also Charney and Alexander, *International Maritime Boundaries*, vol. I, pp. 929–975.

7 See, for example, S. B. Kaye, *Australia's Maritime Boundaries*, 2nd edn, Wollongong Papers on Maritime Policy, 12, Wollongong: Centre for Maritime Policy, 2001, pp. 104–105; and D. Renton, 'The Torres Strait Treaty after 15 years: some observations from a Papua New Guinean perspective', in J. R. Crawford and D. R. Rothwell (eds), *The Law of the Sea in the Asian Pacific Region*, Dordrecht: Martinus Nijhoff, 1995, pp. 171–180.

8 In accordance with Article 23 of the treaty, revenues are split 75:25 according to whose jurisdictional sector of the zone the fish are caught in.

9 Agreement between Norway and Iceland on Fishery and Continental Shelf Questions, 28 May 1980 (entered into force 13 June 1980). Treaty text available at the DOALOS website.

10 Agreement on the Continental Shelf between Iceland and Jan Mayen, 22 October 1981 (entered into force 2 June 1982). Treaty text available at the DOALOS website. See also Charney and Alexander, *International Maritime Boundaries*, vol. II, pp. 1755–1765.

11 Agreement on the Continental Shelf between Iceland and Jan Mayen, Articles 5 and 6.

12 Ibid., Article 8.

13 Charney and Alexander, *International Maritime Boundaries*, vol. II, p. 1757.

14 Agreement between the Government of the Kingdom of Denmark together with the Home Government of the Faroe Islands on the one hand and the Government of the United Kingdom of Great Britain and Northern Ireland on the other hand relating to the Maritime Delimitation in the area between the Faroe Islands and the United Kingdom, 18 May 1999 (entered into force 21 July 1999). Treaty text available at the DOALOS website. See also J. I. Charney and R. W. Smith (eds), *International Maritime Boundaries*, vol. IV, Dordrecht: Martinus Nijhoff, 2002, pp. 2955–2977.

15 Charney and Smith, *International Maritime Boundaries*, pp. 2955–2977.

16 Ibid., 2959–2960.

17 Denmark–UK Agreement, Article 5.
18 Ibid., Article 6.
19 Ibid., Article 7.
20 Agreement between the People's Republic of China and the Socialist Republic of Viet Nam on the Delimitation of the Territorial Sea, the Exclusive Economic Zone and Continental Shelf in Beibu Bay/Gulf of Tonkin (25 December 2000) and Agreement between the People's Republic of China and the Socialist Republic of Viet Nam on Fisheries Cooperation for the Gulf of Tonkin. Treaty text available at the DOALOS website. See also D. A. Colson and R. W. Smith (eds), *International Maritime Boundaries*, vol. V, Leiden: Martinus Nijhoff, 2005, pp. 3745–3758.
21 Z. Keyuan, 'The Sino-Vietnamese agreement on maritime boundary delimitation in the Gulf of Tonkin', *Ocean Development and International Law*, 36, 2005, pp. 13–24, at p. 16.
22 Colson and Smith, *International Maritime Boundaries*, p. 3749. See also N. H. Thao, 'maritime delimitation and fishery cooperation in the Tonkin Gulf', *Ocean Development and International Law*, 36, 2005, pp. 25–44.
23 Agreement on Historic Waters of Vietnam and Kampuchea, 7 July 1982 (entered into force 7 July 1982). See J. I. Charney and L. M. Alexander (eds), *International Maritime Boundaries*, vol. III, Dordrecht: Martinus Nijhoff, 1998, pp. 2364–2365.
24 Agreement on Historic Waters of Vietnam and Kampuchea, Article 2.
25 Ibid., Article 3.
26 Ibid.
27 Thailand protested against the agreement in a note to the UN Secretary General dated 9 December 1985. See *United Nations Law of the Sea Bulletin*, 7, April 1986, p. 111.
28 See *United Nations Law of the Sea Bulletin*, 10, November 1987, p. 23. See also J. A. Roach and R. W. Smith, *United States Responses to Excessive Maritime Claims*, 2nd edn, The Hague: Martinus Nijhoff, 1996, pp. 39–40; and C. H. Schofield and M. Tan-Mullins, 'Claims, conflicts and cooperation in the Gulf of Thailand', *Ocean Yearbook*, 22, Leiden/Boston: Martinus Nijhoff, 2008, pp. 75–116, at pp. 91–92.
29 Agreement between Japan and the Republic of Korea Concerning the Establishment of Boundary in the Northern Part of the Continental Shelf Adjacent to the Two Countries, 30 January 1974 (entered into force 22 June 1978). Treaty text available at the DOALOS website. See also Charney and Alexander, *International Maritime Boundaries*, vol. I, pp. 1057–1089.
30 Agreement between Japan and the Republic of Korea Concerning Joint Development of the Southern Part of the Continental Shelf Adjacent to the Two Countries, 30 January 1974 (entered into force 22 June 1978). Treaty text available at the DOALOS website.
31 Japan–Korea treaty, Article 31(2).
32 Ibid., Article 19.
33 Ibid., Article 24.
34 Charney and Alexander, *International Maritime Boundaries*, vol. I, p. 1058.
35 Agreement Relating to the Joint Exploration of the Natural Resources of the Seabed and Subsoil of the Red Sea in the Common Zone, 16 May 1974.
36 J. R. V. Prescott and C. H. Schofield, *The Maritime Political Boundaries of the World*, Leiden/Boston: Martinus Nijhoff, 2005, p. 488.
37 D. J. Dzurek, *Parting the Red Sea: Boundaries, Offshore Resources and Transit*, Maritime Briefing, vol. 3, no. 2, Durham: International Boundaries Research Unit, University of Durham, 2001, p. 16.
38 Treaty between Australia and the Republic of Indonesia on the Zone of Cooperation in an Area between the Indonesian Province of East Timor and Northern Australia, 11 December 1989. Treaty text available at the DOALOS website. See also Charney and Alexander, *International Maritime Boundaries*, vol. II, pp. 1245–1328.

39 Treaty between the Kingdom of Thailand and Malaysia Relating to the Delimitation of the Territorial Seas of the Two Countries, 24 October 1979 (entered into force 15 July 1982). Treaty text available at the DOALOS website. See also Charney and Alexander, *International Maritime Boundaries*, vol. I, pp. 1091–1098.

40 Memorandum of Understanding between the Kingdom of Thailand and Malaysia on Delimitation of the Continental Shelf Boundary between the Two Countries in the Gulf of Thailand, 24 October 1979 (entered into force 15 July 1982). Treaty text available at the DOALOS website. See also Charney and Alexander, *International Maritime Boundaries*, vol. I, pp. 1099–1123.

41 Memorandum of Understanding between the Kingdom of Thailand and Malaysia on the Establishment of a Joint Authority for the Exploitation of the Resources of the Sea-Bed in a Defined Area of the Continental Shelf of the Two Countries in the Gulf of Thailand, done on 21 February 1979. Treaty text available at the DOALOS website. See also Charney and Alexander, *International Maritime Boundaries*, vol. I, pp. 1107–1123.

42 Agreement between the Government of Malaysia and the Government of the Kingdom of Thailand on the Constitution and Other Matters Relating to the Establishment of the Malaysia–Thailand Joint Authority. See Charney and Alexander, *International Maritime Boundaries*, vol. I, pp. 1111–1123. On the reasons for the long hiatus between the MoU and implementing agreement, see C. H. Schofield, 'Unlocking the seabed resources of the Gulf of Thailand', *Contemporary Southeast Asia*, 29(2), August 2007, pp. 286–308, at pp. 292–293; and Schofield and Tan-Mullins 'Claims, conflicts and cooperation', pp. 108–111.

43 Agreement between the Government of the Kingdom of Thailand and the Government of the Socialist Republic of Vietnam on the Delimitation of the Maritime Boundaries between the Two Countries in the Gulf of Thailand, 9 August 1997 (entered into force 28 February 1998), Article 2. Treaty text available at the DOALOS website. See also Charney and Smith, *International Maritime Boundaries*, pp. 2692–2694.

44 Schofield, 'Unlocking the seabed resources of the Gulf of Thailand', p. 300 and Schofield and Tan-Mullins, 'Claims, conflicts and cooperation', pp. 112–113.

45 Memorandum of Understanding between Malaysia and the Socialist Republic of Vietnam for the Exploration and Exploitation of Petroleum in a Defined Area of the Continental Shelf Involving the Two Countries was signed on 5 June 1992 and entered into force on 4 June 1993. See Charney and Alexander, *International Maritime Boundaries*, vol. III, pp. 2335–2344.

46 The treaty was signed on 12 November 1993 (entered into force 14 March 1994). Treaty text available at the DOALOS website. See also Charney and Alexander, *International Maritime Boundaries*, vol. III, pp. 2179–2204.

47 Charney and Alexander, *International Maritime Boundaries*, vol. III, p. 2181.

48 Colombia–Jamaica Treaty, Article 3(2).

49 Ibid., Article 3(3).

50 Ibid., Article 3(5 and 6).

51 Ibid., Article 4.

52 See R. R. Churchill, 'Falkland Islands – maritime jurisdiction and cooperative arrangements with Argentina', *International and Comparative Law Quarterly*, 46(2), 1997, pp. 463–477, at pp. 463–467.

53 Ibid., pp. 468–471.

54 Treaty between the Federal Republic of Nigeria and the Democratic Republic of Sao Tomé and Príncipe on the Joint Development of Petroleum and other Resources, in Respect of Areas of the Exclusive Economic Zone of the Two States, 21 February 2001 (entered into force 16 January 2003), Article 4. Treaty text available at the DOALOS website. See also Colson and Smith, *International Maritime Boundaries*, pp. 3638–3682.

55 Nigeria-Sao Tomé and Príncipe Treaty, Articles 3 and 18 and Colson and Smith, *International Maritime Boundaries*, p. 3638. See also H. Groves, 'Offshore oil and gas

resources: economics, politics and the rule of law in the Nigeria-Sao Tomé e Príncipe joint development zone', *Journal of International Affairs*, 59(1), Fall/Winter 2005, pp. 81–96.
56 Timor Sea Treaty (Dili, 20 May 2002, entry into force 2 April 2003). Treaty text available at the DOALOS website.
57 C. H. Schofield, 'Dividing the resources of the Timor Sea: a matter of life and death for East Timor', *Contemporary Southeast Asia*, 27(2), August 2005, pp. 255–280.
58 This agreement is often referred to as the Greater Sunrise International Unitisation Agreement, or Sunrise IUA. Memorandum of Understanding between the Government of the Democratic Republic of East Timor and the Government of Australia concerning an International Unitization Agreement for the Greater Sunrise field, Dili, 20 May 2002; and Agreement between the Government of Australia and the Government of the Democratic Republic of Timor-Leste relating to the Unitization of the Sunrise and Troubadour fields, Dili, 6 March 2003. Treaty texts available at the DOALOS website.
59 See, for example, C. H. Schofield, 'Minding the gap: the Australia–East Timor Treaty on Certain Maritime Arrangements in the Timor Sea', *International Journal of Marine and Coastal Law*, 22(2), 2007, pp. 189–234.
60 See Transcript of the Prime Minister, the Hon John Howard, MP, Joint Press Conference, Philip Street, Sydney, 12 January 2006, at www.pm.gov.au/news/interviews/Interview1744.html. For a copy of the treaty text, see www.laohamutuk.org/Oil/Boundary/CMATS per cent20text.htm or Schofield, 'Minding the gap'.
61 CMATS, Article 2.
62 CMATS, Article 4.
63 CMATS, Article 12.
64 Ibid.
65 CMATS, Article 9. For a more in-depth analysis of the CMATS Treaty, see Schofield, 'Minding the gap'.
66 D. Kingsbury, 'Impasse on deal to plunder Timor's gas riches', *Sydney Morning Herald*, 10 May 2010, available at http://www.smh.com.au/opinion/politics/impasse-on-deal-to-plunder-timors-gas-riches-20100510-uo2c.html.
67 The Permanent Court of Arbitration (PCA) in the Hague serves as the Registry for the arbitration. See the PCA website at http://www.oca-cpa.org/showpage.asp?pag_id=1403 (accessed 20 February 2014).
68 The China–Japan agreement was signed on 11 November 1997 and entered into force on 1 June 2000; the South Korea–Japan agreement entered into force in January 1999; and the China–South Korea agreement entered into force on 30 June 2001. See S. P. Kim, 'The UN Convention on the Law of the Sea and new fisheries agreements in North East Asia', *Marine Policy*, 27, 2003, pp. 97–109.
69 Shih Hsiu-chuan, 'Taiwan, Japan Ink Fisheries Agreement', *Taipei Times*, 11 April 2013, available at http://www.taipeitimes.com/News/front/archives/2013/04/11/2003559323/2.
70 See C. H. Schofield, 'Cooperative mechanisms and maritime security in areas of overlapping claims to maritime jurisdiction', in P. Cozens and J. Mossop (eds), *Capacity Building for Maritime Security Cooperation in the Asia-Pacific*, Wellington: Centre for Strategic Studies, New Zealand, 2005, pp. 99–115.
71 Colson and Smith, *International Maritime Boundaries*, pp. 3743–3744.
72 See T. L. McDorman, 'Maritime boundary delimitation in the Gulf of Thailand', *Hogaku Shimpo* [The Chuo Law Review], CIX(5–6), March 2003, pp. 253–280, at pp. 278–279. See also Schofield, 'Unlocking the seabed resources of the Gulf of Thailand', pp. 301-303 and Schofield and Tan-Mullins, 'Claims, conflicts and cooperation', pp. 113–115.
73 McDorman, 'Maritime boundary delimitation in the Gulf of Thailand', p. 277.
74 Cambodia-Thailand MoU, Article 2.

75 Ibid.

76 T. Davenport, 'Joint development in Asia: some valuable lessons learned', in C. H. Schofield (ed.), *Maritime Energy Resources in Asia: Legal Regimes and Cooperation*, NBR Special Report no. 37, Seattle: National Bureau of Asian Research, 2012, pp. 129–160; *Energy-pedia News*, 'Thailand terminates maritime pact with Cambodia', 9 November 2009, available at http://www.energy-pedia.com/article. aspx?articleid=137744; *Maritime Updates*, 'Thailand to cancel Thai-Cambodian maritime deal', 16 November 2009, available at http://www. maritimeupdates.com.

77 'China, Japan reach principled consensus on East China Sea issue', Xinhua News Agency, 18 June 2008, available at www.chinadaily.com.cn/china/2008-06/18/content_6774860.htm.

78 Ibid. See also 'Japan, China agree on investment, joint gas project in E. China Sea', Kyodo News Agency, 18 June 2008, available at http://home.kyodo.co.jp/modules/fstStory/index.php?storyid=384582.

79 Ibid.

80 See, for example, C. H. Schofield and I. Townsend-Gault, 'Choppy waters ahead in a "sea of peace, cooperation and friendship?" Slow progress towards the application of maritime joint development to the East China Sea', *Marine Policy*, 35, 2011, pp. 25–33.

81 Cambodia's 1972 continental shelf claim uses the Franco-Siamese Treaty of 23 March 1907 as a justification to define its claims in this manner. However, the 1907 treaty was concerned with the allocation of certain islands and territories and is predominantly concerned with the land boundary. However, it did refer to the use of the summit of Thailand's Koh Kut Island as a reference point for the position of the terminus of the land boundary on the coast. Cambodia has made use of this reference as a basis to project its continental shelf claim from the terminus of the land boundary on the coast in a line projecting westwards in line with the summit of Koh Kut – a highly dubious interpretation to say the least.

82 Charney and Alexander, *International Maritime Boundaries*, vol. I, p. 1101. See also Schofield and Tan-Mullins, 'Claims, conflict and cooperation'.

83 See UNCLOS Article 300.

7 Specifying procedural obligations for joint development and alternative joint development models for the South China Sea

David M. Ong

This chapter begins with an exploration of the suggestion that the Chinese U-shaped, nine-dashed or nine-dotted line drawn on the South China Sea map is not in fact a sovereignty claim or even a putative maritime boundary claim. It is in fact no more than an entitlement claim to the sovereign rights over resources and jurisdiction over other types of activity (for example, marine scientific research) provided to the coastal States under the 1982 UN Convention on the Law of the Sea (UNCLOS). In the face of the competing territorial claims over the island/rock features in the South China Sea, it is understandable that China wishes to ensure that its own entitlement to sovereign rights over natural resources and jurisdiction over activities such as fishing, hydrocarbon exploration/exploitation and marine scientific research are thus preserved. The legal nature of coastal State sovereign rights over the continental shelf is inherent and does not require any further action to confirm the *entitlement* of the adjacent coastal State under normal circumstances.[1] It is the geographical limits of this continental shelf entitlement that must then be delimited either vis-à-vis other, neighbouring coastal/island States[2] or when it extends beyond 200 nm – the deep seabed 'Area' subject to Part XI of UNCLOS.[3] However, given the extraordinarily complex geopolitical situation in which China finds itself within the South China Sea, China has arguably had little option but to attempt to re-establish its *entitlement* to maritime jurisdiction and thereby confirm the Chinese 'presence' within this semi-enclosed sea. The U-shaped Chinese nine-dashed line is the embodiment of its *entitlement* claim to the sovereign rights and jurisdiction over the relevant activities and should be perceived accordingly. Previous State practice in the form of the 'Patrimonial Sea' claims going back to the early 1970s, as well as the more recent Chilean claim to a 'Mar Presencial' going beyond the 200 nm limit of its coastline, along with recent international tribunal jurisprudence on the legality of seabed entitlement claims, notably the *Bangladesh/Myanmar* case (2012) before the International Tribunal for the Law of the Sea (ITLOS),[4] arguably lend support for the Chinese right to make its *entitlement* claim for sovereign rights and jurisdiction within the South China Sea, as delimited by the U-shaped, nine-dashed line on the map.

The implications of this finding for the relationships between China and the other claimant States in the South China Sea will need careful examination. In particular, while this argument may justify the Chinese nine-dashed line as an *entitlement* claim on the South China Sea map, this does not mean that this Chinese claim is legitimate until and unless it is accepted by all the affected States or legally certified by an international tribunal. This chapter argues that the Chinese position is understandable, notwithstanding the serious and continuing questions over the legality of the claim itself under international law, especially beyond 200 nm. As ITLOS put it in the *Bay of Bengal* case: 'Not every coast generates entitlements to a continental shelf extending beyond 200-nm.'[5] Based on the international jurisprudence presented (see below) and assuming that all claimant States to islands/rocks in the South China Sea have at the very least an entitlement to make such claims due to the geomorphologic similarities of the South China Sea seabed to that of the Bay of Bengal, the next section addresses the international legal framework providing for procedural obligations for cooperation. It is submitted that the applicable framework now provides for general obligations to notify, inform and consult, as well as to conduct appropriate environmental assessments in relation to 'shared natural resources' such as international river basins and specific obligations in relation to common hydrocarbon resources – whether situated in overlapping claims areas or transboundary in nature.

Coastal State entitlement to continental shelf beyond 200 nm: State practice and international case law

Previous State practice in the form of the 'Patrimonial Sea' concept of the early 1970s, the more recent Chilean claim (from 1991) to a 'Mar Presencial' going beyond the 200 nm exclusive economic zone (EEZ) limit from its coastline, as well as recent international tribunal jurisprudence on the legality of seabed entitlement claims in the ITLOS *Bangladesh/Myanmar* and ICJ *Nicaragua/Colombia* cases arguably lend support for the Chinese nine-dashed claim line on its South China Sea map.

The 'Patrimonial Sea' concept and State practice in the 1970s

Following the 1945 Truman Proclamation on the US Continental Shelf, Nelson observed that 'certain States, particularly some Latin American republics, went further than the United States in that they claimed sovereignty not only over the continental shelf but also over the waters above the continental shelf – the so-called epicontinental sea'.[6] Specifically, Chile, Ecuador and Peru adopted the Declaration of Santiago, including the Declaration on the Maritime Zone (Annex I) on 18 August 1952, at the First Conference on the Exploitation and Conservation of the Maritime Resources of the South Pacific in Santiago, Chile. This declaration was subsequently ratified by the parties and later acceded to by Costa Rica on 9 October 1955. The three most important provisions of this (initially) tripartite declaration were Articles II, III and V. Article II stated that 'The Governments of Chile, Ecuador and Peru [therefore] proclaim as a principle of their international maritime policy that each of them possesses sole sovereignty and jurisdiction over the area of sea adjacent to the coast of its own country and extending not less than 200 nautical miles from the said coast.' Article III then appears to extend full and complete national sovereignty over this newly declared maritime zone, as follows: 'Their sole jurisdiction and sovereignty over the zone thus described includes sole sovereignty and jurisdiction over the sea floor and subsoil thereof.' However, Article V then proceeds to qualitatively circumscribe this initial claim of absolute sovereignty by providing that: 'This declaration shall not be construed as disregarding the necessary restrictions on the exercise of sovereignty and jurisdiction imposed by international law to permit the innocent and inoffensive passage of vessels of all nations through the zone aforesaid.' While still problematic from the perspective of maritime powers that claimed high seas freedom of navigation, as opposed to mere 'innocent passage' for all types of ships, including warships, beyond the confines of the territorial sea, the Santiago Declaration can nevertheless be seen to ultimately fall short of claiming complete national sovereignty over both the seabed and adjacent waters up to the 200 nm limit that initially appeared to be the case. Similar implicit limitations and restrictions can therefore be placed on Chinese claims to sovereignty over the South China Sea islands/rocks, as well as its sovereign rights and jurisdiction over the adjacent seabed and subsoil and superjacent waters to these insular features.[7]

The Chilean 'Mar Presencial' claim

Writing on the evolution of this concept, Kibel initially observes that Chile has long been at the forefront of international efforts to extend the ocean jurisdiction of the coastal State.[8] Its 1947 unilateral declaration of a 200 mile fisher/whaling zone eventually led to the internationally recognised concept of an EEZ now contained in the 1982 UNCLOS. More recently, Chile has been promoting a new concept, the Presencial Sea, encompassing a vast triangular area of approximately 19,967,337 km^2 in the Pacific Ocean. According to Dalton, the Chilean Mar Presencial consists of a precise physical description, but also a very broad doctrinal content.[9] This would give coastal States special interests in the high seas adjacent to EEZs, and the right to take certain unilateral actions in respect of these interests. The specifics of such a concept are still in a state of development, but Chile's own claim, contained in a 1991 national law, represents a 500 per cent increase over the area covered by the country's existing EEZ. Justification of the need for the concept was in part based on problems with fisheries straddling the EEZ and high seas boundaries, but the 1995 UN Straddling Fish Stocks Agreement now provides an answer to some of those issues. Thus, according to Kibel, the concept of a Presencial Sea would in practice create chaos rather than stability in international law, and would result in the unravelling rather than the evolution of ocean governance.[10]

Implications of the **Bay of Bengal** *case for the South China Sea disputes*

To begin with, ITLOS reiterated the legal basis and inherent quality of coastal States' sovereign rights within their continental shelves, as follows:

> A coastal State's entitlement to the continental shelf exists by the sole fact that the basis of entitlement, namely, sovereignty over the land territory, is present. It does not require the establishment of outer limits. Article 77, paragraph 3, of the Convention, confirms that the existence of entitlement does not depend on the establishment of the outer limits of the continental shelf by the coastal State.[11]

Moreover, the Tribunal determined that 'the fact that the outer limits of the continental shelf beyond 200 nm have not been established does not imply that the Tribunal must refrain from determining the existence of entitlement to the continental shelf and delimiting the continental shelf between the parties concerned.'[12]

The Tribunal then aligns this notion of coastal State entitlement to a (legal) continental shelf to the presence of sedimentary rock originating from the mainland adjacent to its coastline, previously encompassed by the term 'natural prolongation'. Within this context, it should be noted that the Bay of Bengal and the South China Sea display geomorphological similarities in respect of sedimentary deposit originating from mainland sources in the northern portions of their respective basins. For example, citing the experts' reports presented by Bangladesh during the proceedings in the *Bay of Bengal* case, ITLOS noted, *inter alia*, that 'the sea floor of the Bay of Bengal is covered by a thick layer of sediments some 14 to 22 kilometres deep originating in the Himalayas and the Tibetan Plateau, having accumulated in the Bay of Bengal over several thousands of years'.[13] Similarly, Bridges had previously described the geomorphology underlying the South China Sea as follows. The south-east extremity of Asia comprises the states of Thailand, Vietnam, Cambodia, Indonesia and the Malay peninsula. These countries lie adjacent to the South China Sea, the southern part of which is shallow, less than 150 m deep. Although a diverse area, it forms a major morphological unit, because it is underlain by a stable crystalline Pre-Cambrian nucleus. Like other areas of basement complex, it is mostly covered by later sedimentary rocks but in this case it is also partly submerged below the sea. The area is known as the Sunda Shelf and its upland areas form the peninsulas and islands of this region. Bridges then describes the Sunda Shelf more specifically. This shallow sea enclosed by Cambodia, Malaysia and Borneo is everywhere less than 200 m deep, and the southern part less than 150 m deep. The crystalline basement is gently folded into several basins and wells. The surface is thought to be a late Cretaceous peneplain and in the basins up to 800 m of Tertiary sediment has accumulated.[14]

More recently, high-resolution 3-D seismic data has allowed for a detailed study of the seismic geomorphology and deep-water gravity flow depositional process in the South China Sea. The South China Sea geomorphology, especially in terms of its sedimentary characteristics, has been analysed as follows:

> The Quaternary continental slope of the Baiyun Sag in northern South China Sea is characterized by a complex topography and abundant gravity flow sedimentation. The Quaternary continental slope in the northern South China Sea is an above-graded slope … The deep-water gravity flow

> depositional process and the distribution of gravity flow sediments are greatly influenced by the continental slope topography, while the continental slope topography at the same time is reshaped by deep-water gravity flow depositional process and its products. The study of the interplay between the continental slope and gravity flow is helpful in predicting the distribution of the deep-water gravity flow sediments and the variation of sediment quality.[15]

Returning to the *Bay of Bengal* case, it is pertinent to highlight the significance with which the Tribunal considered that 'the thick layer of sedimentary rocks covers practically the entire floor of the Bay of Bengal, including areas appertaining to Bangladesh and Myanmar … [thus] indicating that the entitlement [of both Bangladesh and Myanmar] to the continental margin extending beyond 200 nm is based to a great extent on the thickness of sedimentary rocks pursuant to the formula contained in article 76, paragraph 4(a)(i), of the Convention'. This in turn led the Tribunal to arrive at the following conclusion: 'In view of uncontested scientific evidence regarding the unique nature of the Bay of Bengal and information submitted during the proceedings, the Tribunal is satisfied that there is a continuous and substantial layer of sedimentary rocks extending from Myanmar's coast to the area beyond 200 nm.'[16]

Thus, in the view of the Tribunal, the delimitation method to be employed in the present case for the continental shelf beyond 200 nm should not differ from that within 200 nm. Accordingly, the equidistance/relevant circumstances method continues to apply for the delimitation of the continental shelf beyond 200 nm. This method is rooted in the recognition that sovereignty over the land territory is the basis for the sovereign rights and jurisdiction of the coastal State with respect to both the EEZ and the continental shelf. This should be distinguished from the question of the object and extent of those rights, be it the nature of the areas to which those rights apply or the maximum seaward limits specified in Articles 57 and 76 of the Convention. The Tribunal notes in this respect that this method can, and does in this case, permit resolution also beyond 200 nm of the problem of the cut-off effect that can be created by an equidistance line where the coast of one party is markedly concave.[17] Finally, the Tribunal determined that both parties have entitlements to a continental shelf beyond 200 nm in accordance with Article 76 and has decided that those entitlements overlap.[18]

The ITLOS position on the relationship between legal entitlement to a continental shelf beyond 200 nm and its delimitation is arguably confirmed by the ICJ in the *Territorial and Maritime Dispute (Nicaragua v. Colombia)* case.[19] Here, the ICJ noted that ITLOS did not actually determine the outer limit of the continental shelf beyond 200 nm but in fact merely emphasised first, that a thick layer of sedimentary rocks covers the Bay of Bengal floor – thereby entitling both States in this case to continental shelves beyond 200 nm; and second, that both these States are UNCLOS state parties and had made full submissions to the Commission on the Limits of the Continental Shelf (CLCS). The ICJ then found that the above factors distinguished the previous case from the present one before it, between Nicaragua (an UNCLOS party which had not yet made a submission to the

CLCS) and Colombia (a non-party to UNCLOS). Adjudicating on Nicaragua's claim for continental shelf entitlement beyond 200 nm, the Court first observed that in a previous case concerning *Territorial and Maritime Dispute between Nicaragua and Honduras in the Caribbean Sea (Nicaragua v. Honduras)* it stated that 'any claim of continental shelf rights beyond 200 miles [by a State party to UNCLOS] must be in accordance with Article 76 of UNCLOS and reviewed by the Commission on the Limits of the Continental Shelf established there under'. Given the object and purpose of UNCLOS, as stipulated in its Preamble, the fact that Colombia is not a party thereto does not relieve Nicaragua of its obligations under Article 76.[20] In this regard, the Court noted that Nicaragua submitted to the Commission only 'Preliminary Information' which, by its own admission, falls short of meeting the requirements for the Commission to be able to make a recommendation relating to the establishment of the outer limits of the continental shelf.[21] As the Court was not presented with any further information, it ultimately held that Nicaragua has not established that it has a continental margin that extends far enough to overlap with Colombia's 200 nm entitlement to the continental shelf, measured from Colombia's mainland coast. The Court was therefore not in a position to delimit the maritime boundary as requested by Nicaragua,[22] and concluded that Nicaragua's claim could not be upheld.[23]

Legal implications of the Chinese nine-dashed line as an entitlement claim for maritime jurisdiction beyond 200 nm

Despite its existence on the Chinese maps for more than six decades, the nine-dash, U-shaped line, as a traditional maritime boundary line of China in the South China Sea, has never received wide recognition in the world community, much less by the other claimant states in the South China Sea. According to Zou, the U-shaped line is a legal conundrum not only for China but also for the world community, particularly after the map with the U-shaped line, together with China's notes verbales with respect to the claims to the outer continental shelves made by Malaysia and Vietnam were submitted to the UN Commission on the Limits of Continental Shelf in May 2009.[24]

Important events relating to the sovereignty dispute over the Spratly Islands have arisen by fits and starts since 2009, marking the start of a new phase in the legal battle over territorial and maritime claims in the South China Sea. While the exchange of legal arguments between the parties has gradually laid bare their maritime claims, much still remains shrouded in uncertainty. Among the obscure claims needing clarification is China's infamous nine-dashed line map, which in 2011 elicited a response and counter-response between the Philippines and China.[25]

Thus, assuming that a case can be made for the nine-dash/dot U-shaped line being an international legal entitlement claim by China from both mainland China and the rocks/islands within the South China Sea that it asserts sovereignty over – which is a questionable proposition[26] – what then are the general and specific procedural obligations that China must abide by and what are the alternative transboundary unitisation/joint development agreements that can be relied upon as models for future cooperation between China and its neighbours in this regional sea? Addressing these questions will occupy the rest of this chapter.

From general to specific procedural obligations for cooperation towards joint development

Shared natural resources

Pulp Mills (Argentina v. Uruguay) case before the ICJ (2010)

Turning to the international jurisprudence on this trend, the ICJ has also rendered a decision in the *Pulp Mills* case between Argentina and Uruguay that is at least in part about the extent of an international duty between neighbouring States across a common river boundary to notify, inform and consult each other about proposed activities that have potentially serious transboundary impacts.[27] In this case, concerning an objection by Argentina over the building of two pulp mills by Uruguay across the water from a shared river boundary between these two States, the ICJ first noted that 'the obligation to notify is intended to create the conditions for successful co-operation between the parties, enabling them to assess the plan's impact on the river on the basis of the fullest possible information and, if necessary, to negotiate the adjustments needed to avoid the potential damage that it might cause'.[28] The Court therefore concluded that 'the obligation to notify is therefore an essential part of the process leading the parties to consult in order to assess the risks of the plan and to negotiate possible changes which may eliminate those risks or minimize their effects'.[29]

Having established that Uruguay breached its procedural obligations to inform, notify and negotiate,[30] the Court turned to the relationship between the need for an environmental impact assessment, where the planned activity is liable to cause harm to a shared resource and transboundary harm.[31] Here, the ICJ ruled that 'it may now be considered a requirement under general international law to undertake an environmental impact assessment (EIA) where there is a risk that the proposed industrial activity may have a significant risk in a transboundary context, in particular, on a shared resource'.[32] The Court noted that 'the environmental impact assessments which are necessary to reach a decision on any plan that is liable to cause significant transboundary harm to another State must be notified by the party concerned to the other party … to enable the notified party to participate in the process of ensuring that the assessment is complete, so that it can then consider the plan and its effects with a full knowledge of the facts'.[33] The Court observed that this notification must take place before the State concerned decides on the environmental viability of the plan, taking due account of the EIA submitted to it.[34]

The Court concluded that Uruguay had failed to fulfil its procedural obligation to notify and allow Argentina to participate in the transboundary EIA exercise prior to approving the proposed projects.[35] It was the opinion of the Court that the parties must, for the purposes of protecting and preserving the aquatic environment with respect to activities which may be liable to cause transboundary harm, carry out an EIA, stating that: 'In this sense, the obligation to protect and preserve has to be interpreted in accordance with a practice, which in recent years has gained so much acceptance among States that it may now be considered a requirement under general international law to undertake an environmental impact assessment where there is a risk that the proposed industrial activity may have a significant adverse impact in a transboundary context, in particular, on a shared resource.'[36] Moreover, in the opinion of the Court, as long as the procedural mechanism for cooperation between the parties to prevent significant damage to one of them is taking its course, the State initiating the planned activity is obliged not to authorise such work and, *a fortiori*, not to carry it out.[37] Consequently, due diligence, and the duty of vigilance and prevention which it implies, would not be considered to have been exercised, if a State party planning works liable to affect the regime of the river or the quality of its waters did not undertake an environmental impact assessment on the potential effects of such works.[38]

On the other hand, the Court agreed with the Uruguayan assertion that one party did not have a 'right of veto' over the projects initiated by the other, such that there was a 'no construction obligation' borne by the State initiating the projects until such time as the Court has ruled on the dispute.[39] Uruguay pointed out that the existence of such an obligation would enable one party to block a project that was essential for the sustainable development of the other, something that would be incompatible with the 'optimum and rational utilization of the River' – the shared natural resource in question here. For Uruguay, reference should be made to general international law, as reflected in the 2001 draft Articles of the International Law Commission on Prevention of Transboundary Harm from Hazardous Activities (*Yearbook of the International Law Commission,* 2001, Vol. II, Part Two); in particular, draft Article 9, paragraph 3, concerning 'Consultations on preventive measures', states that 'If the consultations … fail to produce an agreed solution, the State of origin shall nevertheless take into account the interests of the State likely to be affected in case it decides to authorize the activity to be pursued.'[40]

However, on the specific requirements and standard of protection of the obligation to conduct a transboundary EIA, the Court also observed that general international law does not specify the scope and content of an EIA. Moreover, it pointed out that Argentina and Uruguay are not parties to the Espoo Convention. Consequently, it is the view of the Court that it is for each State to determine in its domestic legislation or in the authorisation process for the project, the specific content of the EIA required in each case, having regard to the nature and magnitude of the proposed development and its likely adverse impact on the environment as well as to the need to exercise due diligence in conducting such an assessment.[41]

Finally, the Court noted that the other instrument to which Argentina refers in support of its arguments, namely the 1987 Goals and Principles of Environmental Impact Assessment of the United Nations Environment Programme (hereafter the UNEP Goals and Principles),[42] is not binding on the parties, but, as guidelines issued by an international technical body, has to be taken into account by each party in accordance with Article 41 *(a)* in adopting measures within its domestic regulatory framework. Moreover, this instrument provides only that the 'environmental effects in an EIA should be assessed with a degree of detail commensurate with their likely environmental significance' (Principle 5) without giving any indication of minimum core components of the assessment. The Court also considered that an environmental impact assessment must be conducted prior to the implementation of a project. Moreover, once operations have started and, where necessary, throughout the life of the project, continuous monitoring of its effects on the environment shall be undertaken.[43]

As the Court had already considered the role of environmental impact assessment in the context of the procedural obligations of the parties, it then dealt with the specific points in dispute with regard to the role of this type of assessment in the fulfilment of the substantive obligations of the parties, *inter alia*, whether the populations likely to be affected, in this case both the Uruguayan and Argentine riparian populations, should have, or have in fact, been consulted in the context of EIA.[44] While both parties agree that consultation of the affected populations should form part of an EIA, Argentina asserts that international law imposes specific obligations on States in this regard. In support of this argument, Argentina points to Articles 2.6 and 3.8 of the Espoo Convention, Article 13 of the 2001 International Law Commission draft Articles on Prevention of Transboundary Harm from Hazardous Activities, and Principles 7 and 8 of the UNEP Goals and Principles. Uruguay considered that the provisions invoked by Argentina cannot serve as a legal basis for an obligation to consult the affected populations and adds that in any event the affected populations had indeed been consulted.[45] The Court agreed and was of the view that no legal obligation to consult the affected populations arises for the parties from the instruments invoked by Argentina.[46] In any case, having considered Uruguay's efforts in this regard, the Court held that consultation by Uruguay of the affected populations did indeed take place.[47]

Advisory Opinion of Seabed Disputes Chamber on state responsibility for activities in the seabed 'area' (2011)

Apart from the binding decisions (for the States involved) of the judicial decisions above, the ITLOS Seabed Disputes Chamber has also rendered an authoritative, albeit non-legally binding Advisory Opinion on the applicable international law and especially international environmental law principles applicable to the States that oversee the activities of legal persons or entities within the deep seabed area,[48] beyond the limits of national jurisdiction. Among the most important of these direct obligations incumbent on sponsoring States are as follows: the obligation to assist the Authority in the exercise of control over activities in the Area; the obligation to apply a precautionary approach; the obligation to apply best environmental practices; the obligation to take measures to ensure the provision of guarantees in the event of an emergency order by the Authority for protection of the marine environment; the obligation to ensure the availability of recourse for compensation in respect of damage caused by pollution; and the obligation to conduct EIAs.[49] The Chamber stressed that the obligation to conduct an EIA is a direct obligation under the Convention and a general obligation under customary international law.[50] The Chamber then reiterated Article 206 of the 1982 UNCLOS, which states the following:

> When States have reasonable grounds for believing that planned activities under their jurisdiction or control may cause substantial pollution of or significant and harmful changes to the marine environment, they shall, as far as practicable, assess the potential effects of such activities on the marine environment and shall communicate reports of the results of such assessments in the manner provided in article 205 (which refers to an obligation to publish reports).[51]

Then referring directly to paragraph 204 of the ICJ Judgment in the *Pulp Mills* case, the Chamber noted the assertion by the ICJ that 'it may now be considered a requirement under general international law to undertake an environmental impact assessment where there is a risk that the proposed industrial activity may have a significant adverse impact in a transboundary context, in particular, on a shared resource'.[52] Significantly for our purposes, in arguing for the application of this principle in the South China Sea, the Chamber noted that:

> Although aimed at the specific situation under discussion by the Court, the language used seems broad enough to cover activities in the Area even beyond the scope of the Regulations. *The Court's reasoning in a transboundary context may also apply to activities with an impact on the environment in an area beyond the limits of national jurisdiction; and the Court's references to 'shared resources' may also apply to resources that are the common heritage of mankind.* Thus, in light of the customary rule mentioned by the ICJ, it may be considered that environmental impact assessments should be included in the system of consultations and prior notifications set out in article 142 of the Convention with respect to 'resource deposits in the Area which lie across limits of national jurisdiction'.[53]

However, the Chamber also observed that, in the view of the ICJ, general international law does not 'specify the scope and content of an environmental impact assessment' (paragraph 205 of the Judgment in *Pulp Mills on the River Uruguay*). While Article 206 of the Convention gives only few indications of this scope and content, the indications in the Regulations, and especially in the Recommendations referred to in paragraph 144, add precision and specificity to the obligation as it applies in the context of activities in the Area.[54] In light of the above, the Chamber is of the view that the obligations of the contractors and of the sponsoring States concerning environmental impact assessments extend beyond the scope of application of specific provisions of the Regulations.[55]

Applying these general international procedural obligations to the South China Sea, it is possible to distil at least two requirements that apply *erga omnes* to all neighbouring and other States with interests in this region, whether territorial or resource- or freedom of navigation-based. These can be summarized as follows:

- the duty to inform and consult other interested States over *all* planned activities that may have implications for their sovereign rights and exercise of jurisdiction in the disputed region, whether these are marine-based research and/or exploration activities, or building activities on any insular formations;
- the duty to conduct an EIA for such activities, including addressing the possible impacts on freedom of navigation and ecological/environmental concerns.

Transboundary hydrocarbon resources

Moving from the *general* obligations for planned activities with environmental implications in the context of a shared natural resource such as a common international river or the deep seabed to the *specific* obligations relating to common, transboundary or otherwise shared hydrocarbon resources, once again we find that international tribunal jurisprudence confirms the need for adherence to certain procedural obligations. A continuing issue in the evolving international law on offshore joint development of shared hydrocarbon resources relates to the scope of the actions that States can undertake when it becomes clear that a seabed area the State regards as within its continental shelf entitlement is also part of an overlapping claims area.

Guyana/Suriname Maritime Boundary Delimitation Arbitral Award (2007): The Tribunal's interpretation of Articles 74(3) and 83(3) of the 1982 UNCLOS

Albeit within the context of shared/common/transboundary hydrocarbon resources, rather than transboundary environmental damage, an UNCLOS Annex VII arbitral tribunal award rendered between Guyana and Suriname in 2007 also prescribed a negotiation process involving detailed notification, information disclosure and consultation requirements for the State initiating offshore hydrocarbon exploration activities within an overlapping continental shelf claims area of the seabed, under Articles 74(3) and 83(3) of the 1982 UNCLOS.[56] These articles provide identically as follows:

> Pending agreement as provided for in paragraph 1, the States concerned, in a spirit of understanding and co-operation, shall make every effort to enter into provisional arrangements of a practical nature and, during this transitional period, not to jeopardize or hamper the reaching of the final agreement. Such arrangements shall be without prejudice to the final delimitation.

Generally, an ordered, even hierarchical, approach by the Tribunal can be discerned when comparing its consideration of both obligations inherent in the relevant articles, in the sense that the first, cooperative obligation is without qualification, whereas the second obligation of mutual restraint is tempered by the fact that not all types of exploration activity by an initiating State would be considered to be jeopardising or hampering the final delimitation agreement. This would seem to militate against the procedural order implied by Cameron whereby the obligation of mutual restraint is given pride of place before the twin principles of cooperation and good faith.[57] The Tribunal would appear to have clearly asserted a natural order of proceedings in the application of the first (cooperative) obligation, to be followed by the second (mutual restraint) obligation inherent within Articles 74(3) and 83(3).

The Tribunal began by reference to the first part of Articles 74(3) and 83(3), noting that Suriname's obligation to cooperate towards a provisional arrangement exists '[a]t all times' and became 'particularly pressing and relevant' when Suriname became aware of CGX's planned drilling programme. The Tribunal then criticised first, Suriname's lack of engagement with Guyana 'in a spirit of understanding and co-operation as required by the Convention' and, second, Suriname's 'resort to self-help in threatening the CGX rig, in violation of the Convention'. The Tribunal followed this up by noting that '[i]n order to satisfy its obligation to make every effort to reach provisional arrangements, Suriname would have *actively* had to attempt to bring Guyana to the negotiation, or, at a minimum, have accepted Guyana's last minute 2 June invitation and negotiated in good faith' (emphasis added). The Tribunal also noted that Suriname 'could have insisted on the immediate cessation of CGX's exploratory drilling as a condition to participating in further talks'. It concludes that since Suriname did not opt for either of these two courses of action – actively attempting to negotiate with Guyana or accepting Guyana's last minute offer of negotiations in good faith – it had failed in its duties under the relevant Articles 74(3) and 83(3) of the Convention.[58] It is submitted here that the emphasis the Tribunal placed on first, the continuing nature of the obligation to negotiate towards a provisional arrangement and, second, in accordance with this obligation, to negotiate actively and in good faith, constitutes a significant and authoritative statement of the legal standard applicable to interested States in similar disputes.

Moving to the second obligation that the Tribunal held was incumbent upon both States as a result of the application of Articles 74(3) and 83(3) – the obligation not to jeopardise or hamper the reaching of the final agreement – the Tribunal first notes that 'Suriname had a number of peaceful options to address Guyana's authorization of the exploratory drilling.'[59] Two of these options are then specifically mentioned by the Tribunal. First, in keeping with its other obligation under Articles 74(3) and 83(3), was the obligation to enter into discussions with Guyana on provisional arrangements. Second, the Tribunal continues by holding that '[I]n the event of failure of the negotiations, Suriname could have invoked compulsory dispute resolution under Part XV, Section 2 of the Convention', noting further that this course of action would have also given Suriname the possibility to request provisional measures to preserve its rights in the disputed maritime area or to prevent serious harm to the marine environment, pending the final decision.[60]

The Tribunal then turned to an assessment of Guyana's actions as the State that initiated the exploration activities in the disputed maritime area between the two parties. Here the Tribunal ruled that Guyana had also violated its obligations under the relevant articles. In relation to the first, cooperative, obligation to make every effort to enter into provisional arrangements, the Tribunal placed a specific obligation upon Guyana to inform Suriname *directly* of its plans to allow CGX to undertake exploratory drilling, noting further that 'notification in the press by way of CGX's public announcements was not sufficient for Guyana to meet its obligation under Articles 74(3) and 83(3) of the Convention'.[61] Guyana's 2 June 2000 invitation to bilateral negotiations was also held by the Tribunal to be insufficient to discharge its obligations under the Convention.

In an unprecedented move, the Tribunal then specified the precise steps that Guyana could have taken that would have been consistent with its obligations under the Convention and thus sufficient to discharge its duty to make every effort to reach a provisional agreement. These steps 'include (1) giving Suriname official and detailed notice of the planned activities, (2) seeking [the] co-operation of Suriname in undertaking the[se] activities, (3) offering to share the results of the exploration and giving Suriname an opportunity to observe the activities, and (4) offering to share all the financial benefits received from the exploratory activities'.[62] By providing this detailed exposition of the required notification, information-sharing and consultation process that the interested States must enter into, the Tribunal has clearly established the legally authoritative standards of behaviour for any State finding itself in a similar situation where it is seeking to initiate exploration activities, in respect of either a transboundary deposit or an overlapping claims area.

In doing so, the Tribunal has also clearly drawn from, and analogously applied, the prior notification requirement incumbent upon the International Seabed Authority in similar situations of mineral deposits lying across the limits of national jurisdiction and the deep seabed area, under Article 142(2) of the 1982 Convention.[63] Within this notification, information-sharing and consultation process, Step (3) is arguably unprecedented in its requirement to share the scientific information gathered from the exploration activities. Here, the Tribunal has also drawn from similar requirements in the marine scientific research regime established under Part XIII of the 1982 Convention. Article 248 of UNCLOS requires the researching State (or international organisation) to provide, *inter alia*, the following information to the coastal State in whose EEZ, or on whose continental shelf, it wants to conduct research: (a) the nature and objectives of the project; (b) the method and means to be used; (c) the precise geographical area in which the project is to be conducted; (d) the visiting dates of the vessels or the equipment being utilised; (e) the name of the sponsoring institution; and (f) the extent to which the coastal State can participate or be represented in the project.

In relation to the second obligation not to jeopardise or hamper the reaching of the final delimitation agreement, the Tribunal considered the specific question of whether Guyana's consent for its concessionaire's exploratory drilling programme to commence constituted an irreparable prejudice to Suriname's sovereign rights so as to entail a breach of the second obligation inherent in the relevant articles. As Fietta notes, '[t]he practical implications of the Award's *dicta* concerning the distinction between exploratory drilling and seismic exploration are potentially significant.'[64] However, given that the Tribunal declares that Guyana also violated this second (mutual restraint) obligation inherent in the relevant articles, it is notable that the Tribunal does not actually undertake a detailed analysis of the legal implications of Guyana's actions in allowing exploratory drilling to go ahead.

Thus, although the Tribunal reiterates its finding that unilateral acts that cause a *physical change to the marine environment* may jeopardise or hamper the reaching of a final delimitation agreement, resulting in either a perceived or genuine prejudice to the position of the other party, it does not actually proclaim the individual actions of Guyana in this respect to violate this obligation.[65] Indeed, the Tribunal also re-emphasises the view that not all exploratory activities need be frozen, with unilateral seismic testing in particular being permissible and only exploratory drilling that might cause *permanent damage to the marine environment* being potentially prejudicial to the other party's interest such that it is in breach of the relevant obligation of mutual restraint.[66] Here, the Tribunal appears to be suggesting that the higher standard of proof, that it had hitherto held applicable for interim/provisional measures applications, is also the standard to be applied for holding that a breach of Articles 73(4) and 83(3) has occurred. This is despite its earlier suggestion that a 'lower threshold' of proof applied for these two provisions.[67]

Moreover, even in this latter situation of Guyana's authorisation of such exploratory drilling, the Tribunal's view is that failing negotiations, Suriname's only legal recourse is resort to peaceful settlement of the dispute under Part XV of the Convention.[68] This is arguably the least helpful aspect of the Tribunal's findings on this vital question.[69] Nevertheless, the Tribunal unanimously and unequivocally declares in the final paragraph of its findings,[70] and again in its Dispositif for the Award,[71] that *both* Suriname and Guyana violated their cooperative and mutual restraint obligations under Articles 74(3) and 83(3) of the Convention in respect of their disputed maritime area.

In light of the present Award decision, as summarised in the procedural steps enumerated above, it is arguable that the balance of power between the initiating State and the responding State in these circumstances has shifted in favour of the former State. This is on the basis that the latter State's options, beyond coming to the negotiating table or resorting to the dispute settlement procedures available under Part XV of the 1982 Convention, are severely constrained. The Tribunal in this case has undertaken to elaborate in remarkably precise terms the notification, information-sharing and consultation process that any initiating and responding interested States within a disputed maritime area must follow.

Distilling the legal standards of behaviour required of both parties to this dispute by the Tribunal in this Award, it is now possible to establish in detail first, what is required of the State that is keen on initiating the exploration activities within the disputed maritime area and, second, what is required of the State that is responding to the initial moves of the first State. These detailed procedural steps are as follows:

1 The initiating State must notify the other interested State(s) *directly* of its intentions vis-à-vis the disputed maritime area concerned and in doing so pave the way for negotiations to begin in good faith towards a provisional arrangement pending further negotiations for a final maritime boundary agreement.
2 The responding State, being also under an obligation at all times to make every effort at securing a provisional arrangement allowing for exploration and eventually exploration to begin, must then begin to *actively* negotiate in good faith with the initiating State as to the modalities of the proposed exploration activities.
3 Once the negotiation offer is made by the initiating State, the responding State is precluded from undertaking any unilateral action that would jeopardise the chances of a provisional arrangement being concluded. This is especially pertinent in respect of any actions that could be viewed as a threat or use of force.
4 During these negotiations, any exploration activities can only proceed with an assurance by the initiating State that the results of such activities will be shared with the responding State and its appointed personnel allowed to observe the conduct of such activities.[72]
5 The initiating State must also offer to share the financial benefits from such exploration activities and presumably also any exploitation arising therefrom, although this latter aspect of the requirement is not specified as such by the Tribunal in the Award itself.

Finally, the non-performance by either State Party of any of the steps specified above for that State Party is likely to result in a finding of a failure to meet that State Party's obligations under the relevant Articles of the Convention.

Aside from the specific procedural obligations outlined by the Arbitral Tribunal in the above Award, recent examples from both offshore and onshore areas where possible transboundary hydrocarbon resources exist have also confirmed the procedural requirements for notification, information exchange, consultation and the negotiation of a transboundary 'Unitisation' Agreement as to the exploration, exploitation and apportionment of such resources.

2010 Norway–Russia Maritime Delimitation and Cooperation Agreement

Relevant provisions of the Treaty between the Kingdom of Norway and the Russian Federation concerning Maritime Delimitation and Cooperation in the Barents Sea and the Arctic Ocean[73] provide as follows:

> *Article 5*
> 1. If a hydrocarbon deposit extends across the delimitation line, the Parties shall apply the provisions in Annex II.
> 2. If the existence of a hydrocarbon deposit on the continental shelf of one of the Parties is established and the other Party is of the opinion that the said deposit extends to its continental shelf, the latter Party may

notify the former Party and shall submit the data on which it bases its opinion.

3. If such an opinion is submitted, the Parties shall initiate discussions on the extent of the hydrocarbon deposit and the possibility for exploitation of the deposit as a unit. In the course of these discussions, the Party initiating them shall support its opinion with evidence from geophysical data and/or geological data, including any existing drilling data and both Parties shall make their best efforts to ensure that all relevant information is made available for the purposes of these discussions. If the hydrocarbon deposit extends to the continental shelf of each of the Parties and the deposit on the continental shelf of one Party can be exploited wholly or in part from the continental shelf of the other Party, or the exploitation of the hydrocarbon deposit on the continental shelf of one Party would affect the possibility of exploitation of the hydrocarbon deposit on the continental shelf of the other Party, agreement on the exploitation of the hydrocarbon deposit as a unit, including its apportionment between the Parties, shall be reached at the request of one of the Parties (hereinafter 'the Unitisation Agreement') in accordance with Annex II.
4. Exploitation of any hydrocarbon deposit which extends to the continental shelf of the other Party may only begin as provided for in the Unitisation Agreement.
5. Any disagreement between the Parties concerning such deposits shall be resolved in accordance with Articles 2–4 of Annex II.

Annex II to the Treaty between the Kingdom of Norway and the Russian Federation concerning Maritime Delimitation and Cooperation in the Barents Sea and the Arctic Ocean on Transboundary Hydrocarbon Deposits

Article 1

The Unitisation Agreement between the Parties concerning exploitation of a transboundary hydrocarbon deposit, referred to in Article 5 of the present Treaty, shall provide for the following:

1. Definition of the transboundary hydrocarbon deposit to be exploited as a unit (geographical coordinates normally shown in an annex to the Agreement).
2. The geographical, geophysical and geological characteristics of the transboundary hydrocarbon deposit and the methodology used for data classification. Any geological data used as a basis for such geological characterisation shall be the joint property of the legal persons holding rights under the Joint Operating Agreement, referred to in paragraph 6 a) of the present Article.
3. A statement of the total amount of the hydrocarbon reserves in place in the transboundary hydrocarbon deposit and the methodology used for such calculation, as well as the apportionment of the hydrocarbon reserves between the Parties.

4. The right of each Party to copies of all geological data, as well as all other data of relevance for the unitised deposit, which are gathered in connection with the exploitation of the deposit.
5. The obligation of the Parties to grant individually all necessary authorisations required by their respective national laws for the development and operation of the transboundary hydrocarbon deposit as a unit in accordance with the Unitisation Agreement.
6. The obligation of each Party
   a) to require the relevant legal persons holding rights to explore for and exploit hydrocarbons on each respective side of the delimitation line to enter into a Joint Operating Agreement to regulate the exploitation of the transboundary hydrocarbon deposit as a unit in accordance with the Unitisation Agreement;
   b) to require the submission of a Joint Operating Agreement for approval by both Parties, as well as to issue such approval with no undue delay and not to unduly withhold it;
   c) to ensure that the provisions contained in the Unitisation Agreement prevail over the provisions of the Joint Operating Agreement in case of any discrepancy between them;
   d) to require the legal persons holding the rights to exploit a transboundary hydrocarbon deposit as a unit to appoint a unit operator as their joint agent in accordance with the provisions set out in the Unitisation Agreement, such an appointment of, and any change of, the unit operator being subject to prior approval by the two Parties.
7. The obligation of each Party not to withhold, subject to its national laws, a permit for the drilling of wells by, or on account of, the legal persons holding rights to explore for and produce hydrocarbons on its respective side of the delimitation line for purposes related to the determination and apportionment of the transboundary hydrocarbon deposit.
8. Unless otherwise agreed by the Parties, the obligation of each Party not to permit the commencement of production from a transboundary hydrocarbon deposit unless the Parties have jointly approved such commencement in accordance with the Unitisation Agreement.
9. The obligation of the Parties to determine by mutual agreement in due time before the production of hydrocarbons from the transboundary hydrocarbon deposit is about to cease, the timing of cessation of the production from the transboundary hydrocarbon deposit.
10. The obligation of the Parties to consult each other with respect to applicable health, safety and environmental measures that are required by the national laws and regulations of each Party.
11. The obligation of each Party to ensure inspection of hydrocarbon installations located on its continental shelf and hydrocarbon activities carried out thereon in relation to the exploitation of a transboundary deposit, the obligation of each Party to ensure inspectors of the other Party access on request to such installations, and to relevant metering systems on the

continental shelf or in the territory of either Party, as well as the obligation of each Party to ensure that relevant information is given to the other Party on a regular basis to enable it to safeguard its fundamental interests, including *inter alia* those related to health, safety, environment, hydrocarbon production and metering.

12. The obligation of each Party not to alter the right to explore for and produce hydrocarbons awarded by one Party, which applies to a field that is subject to unitisation in accordance with the Unitisation Agreement, nor to assign it to other legal persons, without prior consultation with the other Party.
13. The obligation of the Parties to establish a Joint Commission for consultations between the Parties on issues pertaining to any planned or existing unitised hydrocarbon deposits, providing a means for ensuring continuous consultation and exchange of information between the two Parties on such issues and a means for resolving issues through consultations.

Article 2

The Parties shall make every effort to resolve any disagreement as rapidly as possible. If, however, the Parties fail to agree, they shall jointly consider all options for resolving the impasse.

Article 3

1. If the Parties fail to reach the Unitisation Agreement referred to in Article 1 of the present Annex, the disagreement should as rapidly as possible be resolved by negotiations or by any other procedure agreed between the Parties. If the disagreement is not settled within six months following the date on which a Party first requested such negotiations with the other Party, either Party shall be entitled to submit the dispute to an ad hoc Arbitral Tribunal consisting of three members.
2. Each Party shall appoint one arbitrator, and the two arbitrators so appointed shall elect a third arbitrator, who shall be the Chairperson. The Chairperson shall not be a national of or habitually reside in Norway or the Russian Federation. If either Party fails to appoint an arbitrator within three months of a request to do so, either Party may request that the President of the International Court of Justice make the appointment. The same procedure shall apply if, within one month of the appointment of the second arbitrator, the third arbitrator has not been elected.
3. All decisions of the Arbitral Tribunal shall, in the absence of unanimity, be taken by a majority vote of its members. The Arbitral Tribunal shall in all other matters determine its own rules of procedure. The decisions of the Arbitral Tribunal shall be binding upon the Parties and the Unitisation Agreement referred to in Article 1 of the present Annex shall be concluded by them in accordance with these decisions.

Article 4

1. In the event that a failure to reach agreement concerns the apportionment of the hydrocarbon deposit between the Parties, they shall appoint an independent expert to decide upon such apportionment. The decision of the independent expert shall be binding upon the Parties.
2. Notwithstanding the provisions contained in paragraph 1 of this Article, the Parties may agree that the hydrocarbon deposit shall be reapportioned between them.

2012 Sudan–South Sudan Agreements on Border Issues and on Oil and Related Economic Matters

Similar procedural obligations, coupled with the establishment of common bilateral institutions, have also been agreed on disputed frontiers within land territory, as provided for in the following 2012 Sudan–South Sudan Agreements. The relevant provisions of the 2012 Agreement between the Republic of Sudan and the Republic of South Sudan on Border Issues[74] are as follows:

Part VII

Institutional Arrangements for Managing the Border

17. Joint Border Commision
    1. Within two weeks of the ratification of this Agreement, the Parties shall establish a Joint Border Comission ('JBC') to oversee the management and demarcation of the border.
    2. The Commission shall be composed of five representatives and a co-chair from each State. The co-chairs shall be ministers or persons holding an office of an equivocal level.
    3. Members of the Commission shall be persons with relevant experience and of high integrity.
18. Functions of the Joint Border Commission
    1. The Commission shall oversee the management of the border in accordance with the provisions of this Agreement.
    2. In carrying out its function, the Commission:
        a) shall develop, in accordance with national actors, detailed policies for managing the border in accordance with the principles set out in this Agreement;
        b) may make recommendations for the enactment of national legislation for the management of the border as necessary;
        c) shall coordinate its activities with the various stake holders including; national authorities, and local communities;
        d) shall develop an effective working relationship with the administrations of the border states;
        e) may solicit and coordinate, technical and financial support for its activities; and

f) may make recommendations to the heads of the two States, or to any other joint body, with regard to the management of the border.

19. Structures of the Commission
    1. In addition to the Joint Demarcation Committee, established in Part III of this Agreement, the Commission shall establish and facilitate joint committees for the effective carrying out of its specific functions including any of the following:
       a) Social and economic issues;
       b) Transboundary resources management;
       c) Border development and infrastructure;
       d) Legal and judicial cooperation;
       e) A committee established in accordance with the above sub-paragraph may set up its own subcommittees in consultation with the Commission.

Following the establishment of these joint institutional bodies, the Agreement of the Government of the Republic of South Sudan and the Government of the Republic of Sudan on Oil and Other Economic Matters,[75] provides specifically for written notification and possible unitization of cross border petroleum reservoirs as follows:

> 9.2 Future cross border petroleum reservoirs
> 9.2.1 In the event that a cross border petroleum reservoir is discovered, the State in which such discovery is identified shall immediately notify the other State in writing.
> 9.2.2 Upon receipt of such notification, both States shall in good faith discuss the joint appraisal of the discovery. In case it is deemed commercially viable, the two States shall agree on unitization and development of the discovery.

Joint development model agreements for continental shelf areas beyond 200 nm

Coincidentally and almost simultaneously – taking place only a day earlier than the above *Bay of Bengal (Bangladesh/Myanmar)* ITLOS judgment, on 13 March 2012 – two other states on the far (western) side of the Indian Ocean, namely Mauritius and the Seychelles, were adopting a quite far-reaching couple of cooperative agreements providing for the joint sovereign rights and joint management of their overlapping continental shelf areas beyond 200 nm that arguably represents the natural extension of the ITLOS findings on continental shelf entitlement and its relationship with maritime boundaries beyond 200 nm as between Bangladesh and Myanmar in this case. The next section of this chapter will therefore be devoted to the implications of these two agreements between Mauritius and the Seychelles, as well as the equally significant United States–Mexico Agreement on Transboundary Hydrocarbon Reservoirs in the Gulf of Mexico, adopted on 20 February 2012.

Prior to this exegesis, it should briefly be recounted that state practice on offshore joint development agreements currently encompasses at least three distinct types or models of agreement, summarised here as follows:

- Joint Development Model I is the earliest type of agreement, whereby two (or more) States enter into an agreement that expressly designates one State to exploit the designated area/field/deposit according to its own national hydrocarbon policy and law, with the proviso that the net profits derived from this exploitation will be shared in a pre-determined manner between the interested States.
- Joint Development Model II is also known as International Transboundary Unitisation (ITU) and represents an agreement between interested States designating nominated companies (usually their national oil companies) to enter into a Joint Operating Agreement whereby one of them is designated as the sole operator for the well/field concerned, with the resulting profits also divided according to a pre-determined way as laid down by the ITU Agreement, although these ratios may be subject to re-determinations on a regular basis.
- Joint Development Model III is the most sophisticated institutional framework establishing intergovernmentally represented bodies such as Joint Commissions/Authorities to oversee the licensing process within a designated Joint Area/Zone where all interested States are usually allowed to exert jurisdiction. The revenues accruing to the governments/Joint Authority/Commission will be shared according to a pre-determined ratio.

Mauritius–Seychelles agreement(s) for joint development of their overlapping continental shelves beyond 200 nm

Two recent agreements between the island republics of Mauritius and the Seychelles respectively herald an unprecedented example of State practice for putative joint development of natural resources within their overlapping continental shelf areas beyond 200 nm. These two States are small island nations located in the south-western corner of the Indian Ocean and both are Contracting Parties to the 1982 UNCLOS. In this regard, the two States signed the Convention when it was opened for signature on 10 December 1982. The Republic of Seychelles subsequently ratified the Convention on 16 September 1991. The Republic of Mauritius ratified the Convention on 4 November 1994. On 1 December 2008, the Republic of Mauritius and the Republic of Seychelles submitted to the CLCS, in accordance with Article 76, paragraph 8 of UNCLOS, information on the limits of the continental shelf appurtenant to the Republic of Mauritius and the Republic of Seychelles, which lie beyond 200 nm from the baselines from which the breadth of the territorial sea of the two States is measured in the region of the Mascarene Plateau.

Following their successful joint submission to the CLCS for an 'extended' continental shelf beyond 200 nm in 2008, which was the subject of favourable recommendations by the CLCS on 30 March 2011, these two island States gained an additional 396,000 km^2 of continental shelf in the Indian Ocean – an area equivalent in size to Germany.[76] They then proceeded to agree the following two treaties: the Treaty concerning the Joint Exercise of Sovereign Rights over the Continental Shelf in the Mascarene Plateau Region[77] and the Treaty concerning the Joint Management of the Continental Shelf in the Mascarene Plateau Region.[78]

The first of these two agreements is very brief indeed, comprising only four articles and should really be seen as a precursor to the more extensive and comprehensive treaty establishing the detailed joint management regime that will govern the exploration, exploitation and production of 'natural resources', as defined in Article 1(l) of the Joint Management Treaty. Following the delineation of the 'Joint Zone' in Article 2 by designated points, comprising the coordinates of latitude and longitude set out at Annex 1 to the Joint Sovereign Rights Treaty, Article 1 provides that the parties shall exercise sovereign rights jointly for the purpose of exploring the continental shelf and exploiting its natural resources in the Joint Zone. The only other substantive provision in this Treaty is Article 3, entitled 'Treaty without Prejudice' (*sic*), which provides that 'Nothing contained in this Treaty, and no act taking place whilst this Treaty is in force, shall be interpreted as prejudicing or affecting the legal position or rights of the Contracting Parties concerning any future delimitation of the continental shelf between them in the Mascarene Plateau Region.' Moving on to the Joint Management Treaty, paragraph (b) of Article 2 reiterates the non-prejudice clause previously included in Article 3 of the Joint Sovereign Rights Treaty.

On the other hand, a potentially significant aspect of this Joint Management Treaty is the clear wording in both the preamble paragraphs and Article 2 of this second bilateral instrument recognising the extent of the principle of cooperation in the exploration, exploitation and production of natural resources from the 'Joint Zone' designating their overlapping continental shelves beyond 200 nm, as well as the environmental principles that are applicable to such activities within the 'Joint Zone'. The following recitals within the preamble confirm this acceptance on the part of the two parties:

> … RECOGNISING the importance of providing an equitable and co-operative legal basis for the exercise by their two countries of their sovereign rights and jurisdiction over the continental shelf in the Mascarene Plateau Region in accordance with international law;
> REAFFIRMING the Treaty Concerning the Joint Exercise of Sovereign Rights over the Continental Shelf in the Mascarene Plateau Region of 13 March 2012, under which the Contracting Parties established the outer limits of the continental shelf in the Mascarene Plateau Region and agreed to exercise sovereign rights jointly for the purpose of exploring the continental shelf and exploiting its natural resources;
> MINDFUL of the importance of jointly managing the natural resources of the continental shelf in the Mascarene Plateau Region in a manner that is

> sustainable and consistent with the precautionary principle and the protection of the marine environment and the biological diversity of the continental shelf;
> DESIRING to enter into an international agreement to provide an effective and equitable framework to govern the joint management of the continental shelf in the Mascarene Plateau Region …

Article 2 of the Joint Management Treaty follows up the cooperative sentiments expressed in the preambular paragraphs (above) by restating the requirement under Article 83 of UNCLOS for States to enter into provisional arrangements of a practical nature and noting that, '(t)his Treaty is intended to adhere to such obligation'.[79] The provisional nature of this agreement is evident from Article 23(a) providing for this Treaty to 'remain in force until a permanent delimitation of the continental shelf is agreed between the Contracting Parties or for thirty (30) years from the date of its entry into force, whichever is sooner', with the possibility in Article 23(b) that it 'may be renewed by agreement between the Contracting Parties'. However, the Treaty also provides for the stability of ongoing projects, under paragraph (c): 'Natural resource projects commenced under this Treaty shall continue, notwithstanding that this Treaty is no longer in force, under conditions that are consistent with those that are provided for under this Treaty.' Significantly from the perspective of investors keen to protect their investments in such natural resource projects by ensuring the certainty of applicable domestic taxation regimes, sub-paragraph (b) of Article 6 of the Treaty provides that 'Neither Contracting Party may during the life of a natural resource project vary any of the provisions of the Taxation Code applicable to it except by mutual agreement.'

Moving onto the designation of the cooperative area of continental shelf beyond 200 nm, Article 3(a) denotes the Joint Zone described in Article 2 of the Joint Sovereign Rights Treaty as the 'Joint Management Area (JMA)', along with the provision in Article 3(b) that 'The Contracting Parties shall jointly control, manage and facilitate the exploration of the continental shelf within the JMA and the conservation, development and exploitation of its natural resources.' Also significant in terms of establishing the parameters for the 'natural resource projects' captured by this Treaty, Article 1 defines 'natural resources' in paragraph (l) as meaning 'the mineral, petroleum and other non-living resources of the seabed and subsoil of the continental shelf together with living organisms belonging to sedentary species that are at the harvestable stage either immobile on or under the seabed or are unable to move except in constant physical contact with the seabed or subsoil'; with paragraph (m) further providing that 'natural resource activities' means all activities authorised or contemplated under a contract, permit or licence that are undertaken to explore and exploit natural resources in the JMA including but not limited to development, initial processing, harvesting, production, transportation and marketing, as well as the planning and preparation for such activities; and under paragraph (o), a 'natural resources project' means any natural resource activity taking place with the approval of the Designated Authority in a specified area of the JMA.

However, a potentially very interesting variation of the types of 'natural resource' projects falling within the remit of this Treaty is raised by the inclusion of 'Biological Surveys and Bioprospecting' activities in Article 13. For these purposes, Article 1(b) defines 'bioprospecting' as 'the examination of biological resources for features including but not limited to chemical compounds, genes and their products and physical properties that may be of value for commercial development'. Article 13 then provides that:

> (a) Each of the Contracting Parties has the right to carry out biological surveys for the purposes of article 12 (on Protection of the Seabed Marine Environment) of this Treaty and to engage in bioprospecting to identify and examine living natural resources that may be of value for commercial development in the JMA or of conservation significance.
> (b) The Contracting Parties shall:
>   i. notify the Authority of any proposed survey;
>   ii. co-operate in the conduct of such biological surveys and bioprospecting, including the provision of necessary on-shore facilities; and
>   iii. exchange information relevant to biological surveys and bioprospecting in the JMA.

What is notable here is that the 'living natural resources' that may be subject to bioprospecting activities for commercial development in the JMA are not necessarily limited to the sedentary species identified within the definition of 'natural resources' in Article 1(l) of this Treaty. This potentially wider scope for bioprospecting of 'living natural resources' in the JMA may exceed the legal constraints on sovereign rights to 'natural resources' within the continental regime, as established under Article 77(4) of the 1982 UNCLOS. Under paragraph (c) of Article 3, 'natural resource activities in the JMA shall be carried out under the direction of the Designated Authority ... including where appropriate through the issue of licences or pursuant to contracts between the Authority and a contractor. This provision shall also apply to the successors or assignees of such contractors.' Paragraph (d) then provides that the two states shall 'make it an offence under their respective national laws for any person to conduct resource activities in the JMA otherwise than in accordance with this Treaty'.

This last point raises the issue of the exercise of the application of domestic laws and criminal jurisdiction within the JMA by the two States Parties. Article 7, entitled 'Application of Domestic Law', provides that the JMA shall be deemed to be and treated by each Contracting Party as forming part of its respective territory for the purposes of the application of the domestic laws of each Contracting Party related directly or indirectly to:

> i. the exploration of the continental shelf within the JMA and the development and exploitation of natural resources in the JMA; and
> ii. acts, matters, circumstances and things touching, concerning, arising out of or connected with, natural resource activities in the JMA.

Moreover, Article 1(g) defines 'criminal law' to mean 'any law in force in the territory of either of the Contracting Parties, whether substantive or procedural, that makes provision for, or in relation to offences, or for or in relation to the investigation or prosecution of offences or the punishment of offenders, including the carrying out of a penalty imposed by a court. For this purpose, "investigation" includes entry to an installation or structure in the JMA, the exercise of powers of search and questioning and the apprehension of a suspected offender.'

As for the actual exercise of such jurisdiction, Article 16, 'Criminal Jurisdiction', then provides as follows:

(a) The Contracting Parties shall examine different options for addressing offences committed in the JMA. Pending the completion of such exercise, the provisions of this article shall apply with respect to offences committed in the JMA.
(b) A national or resident of a Contracting Party shall be subject to the criminal law of the country of nationality or residence in respect of acts or omissions occurring in the JMA connected with or arising out of natural resource activities.
(c) Notwithstanding paragraph (e), a national of a third state, not being a resident of either Contracting Party, shall be subject to the criminal law of either Contracting Party in respect of acts or omissions occurring in the JMA connected with or arising out of natural resource activities. Such person shall not be subject to criminal proceedings under the law of either Contracting Party if he or she has already been tried and discharged or acquitted by a competent tribunal or already undergone punishment for the same act or omission under the law of the other country or where the competent authorities of one country, in accordance with its law, have decided in the public interest to refrain from prosecuting the person for that act or omission.
(d) In cases referred to in paragraph (c), the Contracting Parties shall, as and when necessary, consult each other to determine which criminal law is to be applied, taking into account the nationality of the victim and the interests of the country most affected by the alleged offence.
(e) The criminal law of the flag state shall apply in relation to acts or omissions on board vessels operating in the waters superjacent to the JMA.
(f) The Contracting Parties shall provide assistance to and co-operate with each other, including through agreements or arrangements as appropriate, for the purposes of enforcement of criminal law under this article, including the obtaining of evidence and information.
(g) The Contracting Parties each recognise the interest of the other country where a victim of an alleged offence is a national of that other country and shall keep that other country informed, to the extent permitted by its law, of action being taken with regard to the alleged offence.
(h) The Contracting Parties may make arrangements permitting officials of one country to assist in the enforcement of the criminal law of the other

> country. Where such assistance involves the detention of a person who under paragraph (b) is subject to the jurisdiction of the other country, that detention may only continue until it is practicable to hand the person over to the relevant officials of that other country.

In addition to providing both States Parties with jurisdiction in respect of acts or omissions occurring in the JMA connected with or arising out of natural resource activities, Article 19(a) also provides that: 'For the purposes of this Treaty, the Contracting Parties shall have the right to carry out surveillance activities in the JMA in relation to natural resource activities', as well as (b) '... co-operate on and co-ordinate any surveillance activities carried out in accordance with paragraph (a) and shall exchange information on likely threats to, or security incidents relating to, natural resource activities in the JMA'. Under Article 19(c), the Contracting Parties shall also 'make arrangements for responding promptly and effectively to security incidents in the JMA'.

Where petroleum fields or mineral deposits are found lying within or across the 200 nm limits of one or other of the EEZs of either State Party and the JMA, as has proved to be so problematic in the Australia–(East) Timor Leste situation, Article 10 provides for 'Unitisation', as follows:

> (a) Any reservoir of petroleum or unitary mineral deposit that extends across or straddles the boundary of the JMA into the Exclusive Economic Zone of either or both Contracting Parties shall be treated as a single entity for exploration, development and management purposes.
> (b) The Contracting Parties shall work expeditiously and in good faith to reach agreement on the manner in which the petroleum field or mineral deposit referred to in paragraph (a) will be most effectively managed and developed and on the equitable sharing of revenue arising from such development.

Moreover, to ensure this 'equitable sharing of revenue' occurs, notwithstanding the 50:50 basis for revenue-sharing in the JMA itself, Article 5(c) provides that Article 5(a) providing for the 50:50 split shall not apply to the equitable sharing of the benefits arising from unitisation under Article 10, unless mutually agreed by the Contracting Parties.

Mention of the 'Authority' (in Article 3(c) above) leads us to a consideration of the regulatory bodies established under Article 4(a) of Part 3 which provides for a 'three-tiered joint administrative structure consisting of a Ministerial Council, a Joint Commission and a Designated Authority'. Article 4(b)(i) provides for a Ministerial Council consisting of an equal number of Ministers designated by the Contracting Parties, which under Article 4(b)(ii), shall consider any matter relating to the operation of this Treaty that is referred to it by either of the Contracting Parties. It shall also consider any matter referred to it from the Joint Commission under Article 4(c)(iii). Under Article 4(b)(iv) all decisions of the Ministerial Council shall be adopted by consensus and (v): 'No decision of the Ministerial Council shall be valid unless it is recorded in writing and signed by at least one member from each Contracting Party.' Under Article 4(c)(i): 'The Joint Commission shall consist of an equal number of commissioners appointed by the Contracting Parties. The Joint Commission shall establish policies and regulations relating to petroleum and other natural resource activities in the JMA and shall oversee the work of the Authority', with sub-paragraph (ii) providing that a 'non-exhaustive list of more detailed powers and functions of the Joint Commission is set out in Annex C'. Like the Ministerial Council, Article 4(c)(iv) and (v) provide that decisions of the Joint Commission shall be made by consensus, meeting at least once a year. Article 4(d)(i) and (ii) then provide that 'the Joint Commission shall establish the Designated Authority, which shall have juridical personality and such legal capacities under the law of the Contracting Parties as are necessary for the exercise of its powers and the performance of its functions. It shall have the capacity to contract, to acquire and dispose of movable and immovable property and to institute and be party to legal proceedings.' Significantly, under sub-paragraph (iii), the Authority shall be responsible to the Joint Commission and shall carry on the day-to-day regulation and management of natural resource activities in the JMA, with sub-paragraph (iv) noting that a non-exhaustive list of more detailed powers and functions of the Authority is contained in Annex D and other annexes to this Treaty and that the Authority also has such other powers and functions as may be conferred upon it by the Commission. Article 4(d)(v) then provides that the Authority shall be financed on an equal basis by the Contracting Parties, including eventually through the remittance of fees collected under natural resource codes, established under Article 8.

The centrepiece of this set of cooperative bilateral arrangements is embodied in Article 5, 'Sharing of Revenue', which provides as follows:

> (a) The Contracting Parties shall share revenue received in respect of natural resource activities carried out in the JMA equally, whereby fifty (50) per cent of revenue received shall be remitted to Mauritius and fifty (50) per cent of revenue received shall be remitted to Seychelles.
> (b) To the extent that fees referred to in article 4(d)(v) and other income are inadequate to cover the expenditure of the Authority in relation to this Treaty, that expenditure shall be borne by each of the Contracting Parties in the same proportion as set out in paragraph (a).

A further substantive development in this evolving international legal regime for cooperation in the continental shelf beyond 200 nm are the detailed provisions for 'Protection of the Seabed Marine Environment' within the designated JMA/Joint Zone. In this respect, Article 12 provides as follows:

> (a) The Contracting Parties shall co-operate to protect natural resources in the JMA so as to secure seabed biodiversity and prevent pollution and other risks of harm to the environment arising from, or connected with, natural resource activities in the JMA.

(b) The Contracting Parties shall apply the precautionary principle in co-operating to conserve and protect the environment and biodiversity of the seabed in the JMA. This shall include measures concerning fishing activity in the waters superjacent to the seabed in the JMA where such activity is having a direct impact upon, or poses a significant risk to, the natural resources of the seabed and subsoil in the JMA.

(c) The Contracting Parties shall co-operate to protect seabed marine habitats and associated ecological communities of the seabed in the JMA. This shall include the identification of environmental benchmarks and the identification of seabed marine protected areas, having regard to the following:

  i. geographical distribution of seabed marine species and biological communities;
  ii. the structure of these communities;
  iii. their relationship with the physical and the chemical environment;
  iv. the natural ecological and genetic variability; and
  v. the nature and the effect of the anthropogenic influences including fishing and natural resource activities on these ecosystem components.

(d) Where pollution of the marine environment occurring in the JMA spreads beyond the JMA, the Contracting Parties shall co-operate in taking prompt and effective action to prevent, mitigate and eliminate such pollution in accordance with international best practices, standards and procedures.

(e) The Authority shall issue regulations to protect the living natural resources and seabed environment in the JMA. It shall establish a contingency plan for combating pollution from natural resource activities in the JMA.

(f) Contractors shall be liable for damage or expenses incurred as a result of pollution of the marine environment arising out of natural resource activities within the JMA in accordance with:

  i. their contract, licence or permit or other form of authority issued pursuant to this Treaty; and,
  ii. the law of the jurisdiction of the Contracting Party in which the claim is brought.

Particular attention should be paid to paragraphs (b), (e) and (f) of this article as, much like Article 13 on 'Bioprospecting', these provisions represent potential extensions of coastal State's prescriptive or legislative and enforcement jurisdiction beyond that allowed under Parts V, VI and VII of the 1982 UNCLOS. First, paragraph (e) of Article 12 provides the Authority with prescriptive jurisdiction to issue regulations to protect living natural resources and the seabed environment, thereby apparently including those living resources present in the superjacent high seas waters outside the jurisdiction of the coastal State Party, as well as those present on the seabed and subsoil that is within the coastal State Party's sovereign rights and jurisdiction under the continental shelf regime. The second sentence of paragraph (b) then clearly allows the relevant coastal State Party to exercise enforcement jurisdiction by undertaking 'measures concerning fishing activity', again in the high seas waters superjacent to the seabed in the JMA. Last but not least, paragraph (f) provides that contractors shall be liable for damage or expenses incurred as a result of marine environmental pollution arising from natural resource activities within the JMA, but where such damage occurs within the superjacent high seas waters rather than the underlying seabed, it will affect an area lying beyond national jurisdiction. This raises the question of whether either of the coastal State Parties can prosecute against such damage when they have technically suffered no injury themselves from it.

Finally, Article 21, 'Settlement of Disputes', provides as follows:

> (a) With the exception of disputes falling within the scope of the Taxation Code referred to in article 6 of this Treaty and which shall be settled in accordance with that Code as agreed by the Contracting Parties, any dispute concerning the interpretation or application of this Treaty shall, as far as possible, be settled amicably through mutual consultation.
>
> (b) Any dispute which is not settled in the manner set out in paragraph (a) and any unresolved matter relating to the operation of this Treaty under article 4(b)(ii) shall, at the request of either of the Contracting Parties, be submitted to an Arbitral Tribunal established in accordance with the procedure set out in Annex B.

United States–Mexico Agreement on Transboundary Hydrocarbon Reservoirs

In jurisdictional terms, most of the western Gulf of Mexico falls within the 200 nm limits of both the USA and Mexico, now delimited according to the equidistance method under a 1997 Mexico–US treaty.[80] However, according to McLaughlin, the geography of this area of the Gulf leaves a triangular-shaped area roughly the size of the US state of New Jersey (8,722 m^2) called the 'Western Gap',[81] where a further bilateral treaty was agreed in 2000 to delimit the Mexico–US maritime boundary beyond 200 nm.[82] A significant provision of this 2000 treaty relates to the possibility of overlapping hydrocarbon deposits found lying across the delimitation line. Article 4 therefore provides as follows:

> 1. Due to the possible existence of petroleum or natural gas reservoirs that may extend across the boundary set forth in article I (hereinafter referred to as 'transboundary reservoirs'), the Parties, during a period that will end ten (10) years following the entry into force of this Treaty, shall not authorize or permit petroleum or natural gas drilling or exploitation of the continental shelf within one and four-tenths (1.4) nautical miles of the boundary set forth in article I.

Moreover, paragraphs 4, 5 and 6 of Article 4 then establish the procedures for dealing with such transboundary reservoirs, as follows:

> 4. From the date of entry into force of this Treaty, with respect to the Area on its side of the boundary set forth in article I, each Party, in accordance with its national laws and regulations, shall facilitate requests from the other Party to authorize geological and geophysical studies to help determine the possible presence and distribution of transboundary reservoirs.
> 5. From the date of entry into force of this Treaty, with respect to the Area in its entirety, each Party, in accordance with its national laws and regulations, shall share geological and geophysical information in its possession in order to determine the possible existence and location of transboundary reservoirs.
> 6. From the date of entry into force of this Treaty, if a Party has knowledge of the existence or possible existence of a transboundary reservoir, it shall notify the other Party.

Finally, Article 5 of the 2000 treaty provides that:

> 1. With respect to the Area in its entirety, during the period set forth in paragraph 1 of article IV:
>   (a) as geological and geophysical information is generated that facilitates the Parties' knowledge about the possible existence of transboundary reservoirs, including notifications by Parties in accordance with paragraph 5 of article IV, the Parties shall meet periodically for the purpose of identifying, locating and determining the geological and geophysical characteristics of such reservoirs;
>   (b) the Parties shall seek to reach agreement for the efficient and equitable exploitation of such transboundary reservoirs;
>
>   and
>   (c) the Parties shall, within sixty days of receipt of a written request by a party through diplomatic channels, consult to discuss matters related to possible transboundary reservoirs.
> 2. With respect to the Area in its entirety, following the expiry of the period set forth in paragraph 1 of article IV:
>   (a) a Party shall inform the other Party of its decisions to lease, license, grant concessions, or otherwise make available, portions of the Area for petroleum or natural gas exploration or development and shall also inform the other Party when petroleum or natural gas resources are to commence production; and
>   (b) a Party shall ensure that entities it authorizes to undertake activities within the Area shall observe the terms of the Treaty.

Following the entry into force of the above 2000 treaty, the two states then decided in 2012 to enter into a further agreement on transboundary reservoirs in the Gulf, entitled 'Agreement between the United States of America and the United Mexican States Concerning Transboundary Hydrocarbon Reservoirs in the Gulf of Mexico',[83] the preamble of which accurately sums up the intentions of the parties as follows:

> Desiring to establish a legal framework to achieve safe, efficient, equitable and environmentally responsible exploitation of transboundary hydrocarbon reservoirs that may exist along the maritime boundaries established between the United Mexican States and the United States of America in the Gulf of Mexico;
> Recognizing principles that promote equitable and reasonable utilization of transboundary resources, and desiring to maximize the long term benefits from their exploitation, as well as to protect the resources of both Parties; and
> Recognizing that this framework is intended to encourage the establishment of cooperative arrangements based primarily on principles of unitization, and further recognizing that additional cooperative arrangements may be developed outside of the framework of this Agreement and that such arrangements may also promote efficient, equitable, and environmentally responsible exploitation of transboundary reservoirs ...

While not specifically requiring the adoption of a unitisation agreement following the detection and determination of a transboundary reservoir,[84] Chapter 2 of the 2012 Agreement, 'Exploration and Exploitation of a Transboundary Reservoir or Unit', and specifically, Article 6 , 'Unitization Agreement', provides as follows:

1. Any joint Exploration and/or Exploitation of a Transboundary Reservoir or Unit Area pursuant to the terms of a unitization agreement must be approved by the Parties. Such joint Exploration and/or Exploitation shall be conducted pursuant to the terms of a unitization agreement negotiated and proposed by the Licensees and approved by the Executive Agencies. The Executive Agencies should develop one or more model unitization agreements for use under this Agreement.
2. The unitization agreement shall include, *inter alia*:
   a. The identification of the limits of the Unit Area and that of any Transboundary Reservoir;
   b. The identity of the Licensees and their respective participating interests;
   c. The methodology used to calculate the allocation of production;
   d. A development plan for the Exploration or Exploitation of the Unit Area, including the estimated number and timing of wells, and a mechanism for delivery and approval of subsequent changes to such plan;
   e. The effective date and term of the unitization agreement;
   f. The identity and appointment of the unit operator, the process for resignation and removal of the unit operator, and the process for appointment of a successor unit operator;

g. Provisions regarding the transfer of interests;
h. Provisions for an accurate measurement of production;
i. Procedures for ensuring accurate payments of royalties and other proceeds;
j. Safety and environmental measures to be taken under the national laws of each Party;
k. Provisions for appropriate information sharing between the unit operator and each Party;
l. Procedures for the redetermination of the allocation of production, including a timetable or the events that trigger such redetermination.

The Mexican Ministry of Foreign Affairs published the US–Mexico Transboundary Hydrocarbon Reservoirs Agreement in the *Federal Register* on 22 May 2012. Writing from a Mexican perspective, Rogelio López-Velarde and Daniela Monroy have noted the historic nature of this treaty because it is the first in which these two countries have reached an understanding on how to exploit and share the benefits of a natural resource of which they share ownership. It does this by establishing the terms and conditions for exploring and developing the oil and gas reservoirs along the maritime border between the two countries in the Gulf of Mexico. For Mexico, the significance of this agreement is twofold: First, Pemex-Exploración y Producción – Mexico's exclusive licensee – will be allowed to sign a joint venture for the exploration and exploitation of hydrocarbon reserves (under the Mexican Constitution, Pemex is barred from making joint development, production-sharing or unitisation agreements) and, second, Pemex will be able to participate quickly in the development of deep-water and ultra-deep-water projects if any hydrocarbon reserves lie across the delimitation line (that is, the maritime boundaries in the Gulf of Mexico delimited by the 1970, 1978 and 2000 treaties ratified by both countries).

As noted above, this is a framework agreement whereby the parties have established the terms under which the two governments will allow their licensed operators to operate through the execution of a unitisation agreement (on the side of the United States, whichever company is granted a licence to explore or develop a reservoir within the delimitation line; and for Mexico, Pemex). According to an official statement of the US Department of the Interior, this agreement would, for the first time, allow leaseholders on the US side of the boundary to cooperate with the Mexican national oil company, Petroleos Mexicanos (Pemex), in the joint exploration and exploitation of hydrocarbon resources. The Mexican market has long been closed to participation by US companies, but a 2008 energy reform law in Mexico opened a window for joint exploration and exploitation with foreign entities as long as it would take place pursuant to an international agreement on transboundary reservoirs. This agreement would take advantage of that opening. It would also end the moratorium on exploitation along the boundary in the Western Gap and provide US leaseholders with legal certainty regarding the exploitation of transboundary reservoirs along the entire boundary so as to encourage investment. The agreement would allow leaseholders on the US side of the boundary and Pemex to explore and exploit a transboundary reservoir as a 'unit', as leaseholders are permitted to do on the US side of the boundary. Unitisation – where two or more leaseholders manage the exploration and exploitation of a resource as a unit through a single operator – promotes the rational, efficient production of a resource and reduces waste and the drilling of unnecessary wells (and therefore reduces the corresponding environmental risk).[85]

As such, the agreement provides for the following:

1 An annual consultation system whereby each country's government will inform the other about exploration and exploitation activities within three miles of the delimitation line, including the sharing of relevant geological information.
2 The obligation to notify the other government:
   (a) of the existence of a transboundary reservoir within 60 days of the date when such party became aware of the likely detection of hydrocarbons during drilling operations within three miles of the delimitation line;
   (b) within 60 days of the date when a party has approved or received for approval from its licensee an exploration plan; and
   (c) within 30 days of the date when a party has approved or received for approval from its licensee a plan for the collection of seismic data, to develop or produce an area or to drill a well, wellhead or borehole within three miles of the delimitation line.
3 A system for the determination of a transboundary reservoir by both countries, including the establishment of a joint commission comprising representatives of both governments to make such determination in case of deadlock or impasse.
4 The approval of the unitisation agreement proposed by the other government's licensee (such agreement will comply with the minimum terms and conditions required under the Treaty, including the designation of the unit operator, which could be a joint venture company in which Pemex or any licensee could participate) and the proposed allocation and redetermination of production, on the understanding that both governments agree to prepare model unitisation agreements.
5 Inspection rights pursuant to terms to be established by the parties.
6 A requirement that any income arising from the exploitation of a transboundary reservoir attributable to the licensee and the unit operator be taxed in accordance with each country's own legislation and the US–Mexico double taxation treaty.
7 Standard dispute settlement mechanisms for international treaties (for example independent expert, mediation, consultation and arbitration) and the right to early termination of the Treaty with 180 days' notice.

In cases where a unitisation agreement is not reached, the Agreement would ultimately allow for unilateral production by each side, up to the amount of hydrocarbons that exist on its side of the boundary. In addition, the agreement provides a carefully calibrated mechanism to resolve disputes regarding the development of specific reservoirs. Significantly, the agreement would also establish a system of joint inspections. Each side would regulate activity on its side of the boundary, but would also have the ability, under an inspection system to be developed, to inspect activity that takes place under the agreement on the other side of the boundary. In sum, the agreement provides a much needed mechanism to facilitate the safe and efficient exploration and exploitation of hydrocarbon resources along the maritime boundary and provides new opportunities for US companies.

The Treaty will become effective 60 days after the last notification of approval has been made by Mexico or the United States. In this regard, the Mexican Senate ratified the treaty in April 2012; therefore, the Treaty's effectiveness is subject to approval and publication by the United States, which to date has neither ratified nor published the treaty.[86]

The depth of bilateral cooperation that will be required to fulfil the detailed procedures and criteria for the establishment of any future transboundary unitisation agreements in the Gulf of Mexico, especially when juxtaposed against the joint sovereign rights and joint management treaties agreed between Mauritius and the Seychelles assessed above, lends credence to the view that the principle of transboundary unitization/joint development that has been argued to apply in all similar situations within the 200 nm limits of coastal state maritime jurisdiction[87] should now be regarded as being applicable to the same type of situations beyond the 200 nm limits as well.

Conclusions

International law is developing through successive international court/tribunal decisions as well as confirming State practice to suggest the following conclusions.

First, general international obligations for notification, information, consultation and negotiations are now applicable to shared natural resources and those found beyond areas of national jurisdiction, such as the deep seabed 'area'. This is evident from the survey of international jurisprudence on these issues undertaken above, encompassing both the *Pulp Mills* case before the ICJ and the ITLOS Seabed Chamber's Advisory Opinion on responsibility for seabed activities in the 'area'. Moreover, specific, detailed obligations obtain where the common or shared resources in question are hydrocarbons located in an overlapping continental shelf claim area, with special reference to the *Guyana–Suriname* Arbitral Tribunal award.

Second, offshore joint development practice has now extended to overlapping continental shelf *entitlement* areas beyond 200 nm, as evidenced by the Mauritius–Seychelles joint sovereign rights and joint management agreements, as well as the United States–Mexico Agreement on Transboundary Hydrocarbon Reservoirs. This strongly suggests that many of the same legal and practical reasons for States to cooperate apply to their continental shelf areas beyond 200 nm. A potentially complicating factor for net exporters of the shared mineral resources in these areas will be the operation of Article 82 of UNCLOS, which provides for revenue-sharing of the profits derived from the exploitation of such resources with developing, land-locked countries through the International Seabed Authority. These international legal developments carry the implication that the South China Sea in its entirety should also be regarded as a 'shared natural resource'. Thus, all the littoral States surrounding this semi-enclosed sea are subject to the self-same international obligations for notification, information, consultations and negotiations that are applicable to all such 'shared natural resources'. Moreover, where the contested resources within the South China Sea are hydrocarbon in nature, Joint Development practice has evolved to govern continental shelf *entitlement*, areas beyond 200-nm as well.

Notes

1 Article 77 of the 1982 UNCLOS.
2 Article 83 of UNCLOS.
3 According to the procedure laid down in Article 76(8) and Annex II of UNCLOS, by way of submission to the Commission on the Limits of the Continental Shelf (CLCS).
4 *Bay of Bengal (Bangladesh/Myanmar) Maritime Delimitation* case, ITLOS, 14 March 2012, available at http://www.itlos.org.
5 Ibid., para. 439.
6 L. D. M. Nelson, 'The Patrimonial Sea', *International and Comparative Law Quarterly*, 22(4), October 1973, pp. 668–686, at pp. 669–670.
7 See People's Republic of China, Letter to the Secretary-General, New York, 7 May 2009, CML/17/2009, at para. 2, in response to Joint Submission of Malaysia and Vietnam to the CLCS, Executive Summary, 6 May 2009, accessible on the CLCS website at www.un.org/Depts/los/clcs new/clcs home.htm.
8 P. S. Kibel, 'Alone at sea: Chile's presencial ocean policy', *Journal of Environmental Law*, 12(1), 2008, pp. 43–64.
9 J. G. Dalton, 'The Chilean Mar Presencial: a harmless concept or a dangerous precedent?', *International Journal of Marine and Coastal Law*, 8(3), 1993, pp. 397–418, at p. 397.
10 See also James L. Zackrison and James E. Meason, 'Chile, Mar Presencial, and the law of the sea', *Naval War College Review*, 50(3), 1997, pp. 65–83.
11 *Bay of Bengal* case, para. 409.
12 Ibid., para. 410.
13 Ibid., para. 444.
14 E. M. Bridges, *World Geomorphology*, Cambridge: Cambridge University Press, 1990, p. 141.
15 Lei Li, Ying Min Wang, Qiang Xu, Jing Zhou Zhao and Dong Li, 'Seismic geomorphology and main controls of deep-water gravity flow sedimentary process on the slope of the northern South China Sea', *Science China Earth Sciences*, 55(5), May 2012, pp. 747–757.
16 *Bay of Bengal* case, paras 445 and 446.
17 Ibid., para. 455, referring to earlier paras 290–291.
18 Ibid., para. 460.
19 *Territorial and Maritime Dispute (Nicaragua v. Colombia)* case, ICJ Reports, Judgment of 19 November 2012, available at http://www.icj-cij.org/docket/files/124/17164.pdf.
20 Ibid., para. 126.

21 Ibid., para. 127.
22 Ibid., para. 129.
23 Ibid., para. 131.
24 Zou Keyuan, 'China's u-shaped line in the South China Sea revisited', *Ocean Development & International Law*, 43(1), 2012, pp. 18–34.
25 Nguyen-Dang Thang and Nguyen Hong Thao, 'China's nine dotted lines in the South China Sea: The 2011 exchange of diplomatic notes between the Philippines and China', *Ocean Development & International Law*, 43(1), 2012, pp. 35–56.
26 Masahiro Miyoshi 'China's "u-shaped line" claim in the South China Sea: any validity under international law?', *Ocean Development & International Law*, 43(1), 2012, pp. 1–17.
27 *Case Concerning Pulp Mills on the River Uruguay (Argentina v. Uruguay)*, ICJ Judgment, 20 April 2010, available on the ICJ website at http://www.icj-cij.org/docket/files/135/15877.pdf.
28 Ibid., para.113.
29 Ibid., para. 115.
30 Ibid., para. 158.
31 Ibid., para. 203.
32 Ibid, para. 204, pp. 60–61.
33 Ibid., para. 119.
34 Ibid., para. 120.
35 Ibid., para. 122.
36 Ibid., para. 204.
37 Ibid., para. 144.
38 Ibid., para. 204.
39 Ibid., para. 154.
40 Ibid., para. 152.
41 Ibid., para. 205.
42 *UNEP/WG.152/4 Annex (1987)*, document adopted by UNEP Governing Council at its 14th Session (Dec. 14/25 (1987)).
43 *Pulp Mills* case, para. 205.
44 Ibid., para. 206.
45 Ibid., para.15.
46 Ibid., para. 216.
47 Ibid., para. 219.
48 Seabed Disputes Chamber of ITLOS, Advisory Opinion on 'Responsibilities and Obligations of States Sponsoring Persons and Entities with respect to Activities in the "Area"'. ITLOS Case List No. 17, 1 February 2011, available at http://www.itlos.org.
49 Ibid., para. 122, p. 38.
50 Ibid., para. 145, p. 44.
51 Ibid., para.146, p. 45.
52 Ibid., para. 147.
53 Ibid., para.148 (emphasis added).
54 Ibid., para. 149.
55 Ibid., para. 150, pp. 45–46.
56 See *Guyana v. Suriname*, UNCLOS Annex VII Arbitral Tribunal Award (2007), available at www.pac-cpa.org.
57 Peter D. Cameron, 'The rules of engagement: developing cross-border petroleum deposits in the North Sea and the Caribbean', *International & Comparative Law Quarterly*, 55, Part 3, July 2006, pp. 559–585, at pp. 565–568.
58 *Guyana v. Suriname* case, para. 476.
59 Ibid., para. 484, p.162 of the Award.
60 Ibid., citing Article 290 of the 1982 UNCLOS, which provides for the prescription of

provisional measures by a court or tribunal to preserve the respective rights of the parties to the dispute.

61 Ibid., para. 477, pp. 159–160.

62 Ibid., para. 477, p. 160 of the Award.

63 See David M. Ong, 'Joint development of international common offshore oil and gas deposits: "mere" state practice or customary international law?', *American Journal of International Law*, 93(4), October 1999, pp. 771–804, at p. 785, and Cameron, 'The rules of engagement', p. 567.

64 Stephen Fietta, 'International decisions: Guyana/Suriname Award', *American Journal of International Law*, 102, 2008, pp. 119–128, at p. 127.

65 *Guyana v. Suriname* case, para. 480, p. 161 of the Award.

66 Ibid., para. 481, p. 162.

67 Ibid., para. 469, p. 156. See also Fietta, 'International decisions', p. 127.

68 *Guyana v. Suriname* case, para. 482, p. 162.

69 Cf. Fietta, who suggests that 'the Tribunal thereby provided effective guidance to any coastal State that is faced with exploratory drilling by a neighbor in a disputed area'. See Fietta , 'International decisions', p. 128.

70 *Guyana v. Suriname* case, para. 486, p. 163 of the Award.

71 Ibid., para. 488, p. 166.

72 In this regard, it is also significant to note that the Maritime Boundary Working Group of the Cameroon/Nigeria Mixed Commission for the implementation of the 2006 Greentree Agreement, which was itself adopted to facilitate the implementation of the 2002 ICJ decision in a territorial dispute between these two countries which, *inter alia,* awarded the Bakassi peninsula to Cameroon, has stated that both countries concerned have a clear obligation to exchange information about their licensing decisions and exploration activities within the maritime area adjoining the previously disputed land territory. The Mixed Commission approved the Working Group recommendation that an extraordinary meeting be convened between 18 and 19 August 2009 in Abuja in order to consider a draft 'resource clause', a draft conflict resolution mechanism and a list of items to be considered for a framework agreement for cross-border cooperation on oil and gas. See paras 6, 7 and 8 of Final Communiqué from Cameroon–Nigeria Mixed Commission meeting in Abuja, 12 June 2009, available at http://www.un.org/unowa/cnmc/preleas/24thm.htm.

73 Done in duplicate in Murmansk on 15 September 2010, in Norwegian and Russian languages, both texts being equally authentic. Accessed from the Norwegian Ministry of Foreign Affairs official website at http://www.regjeringen.no/upload/UD/Vedlegg/Folkerett/avtale_engelsk.pdf.

74 Agreed at Addis Ababa, 27 September 2012. Available at http://sites.tufts.edu/reinventingpeace/files/2012/09/Agreement-on-Border-Issues-27091200001.pdf.

75 Adopted in Addis Ababa, Ethiopia on 27 September 2012. Available at http://sites.tufts.edu/reinventingpeace/files/2012/09/Oil-Agreement-between-SudanSouth-Sudan0001.pdf.

76 See 'Mauritius and Seychelles successfully claim 396,000 km of additional seabed', 6 May 2011, Commonwealth Secretariat website, at http://www.thecommonwealth.org/news/34580/34581/236405/050511unseabed.htm.

77 Hereinafter, Joint Sovereign Rights Treaty. Entry into force: 18 June 2012; registration #: 49782; registration date: 11 July 2012; see *Law of the Sea Bulletin*, No. 79.

78 Hereinafter, Joint Management Treaty. Entry into force: 18 June 2012; registration #: 49783; registration date: 11 July 2012; see *Law of the Sea Bulletin*, No. 79.

79 Article 2(a) of the Joint Management Treaty.

80 Treaty on Maritime Boundaries between the United States of America and the United Mexican States, signed 4 May 1978, 17 I.L.M. 1073 (1978). Mexico ratified this treaty a year later but the US Senate only ratified it on 23 October 1997.

81 Richard J. McLaughlin, 'Maritime boundary delimitation and co-operative management of transboundary hydrocarbons in the ultra-deep waters of the Gulf of Mexico', in Seoung-Yong Hong and Jon M. Van Dyke (eds), *Maritime Boundary Disputes, Settlement Processes and the Law of the Sea*, Leiden: Martinus Nijhoff, 2009, pp. 199–230, at pp.199 and 208–209.

82 Treaty between the Government of the United Mexican States and the Government of the United States of America on the Delimitation of the Continental Shelf in the Western Gulf of Mexico beyond 200 Nautical Miles, signed 9 June 2000; entry into force: 17 January 2001. Available at http://www.un.org/Depts/los/LEGISLATIONANDTREATIES/STATEFILES/MEX.htm.

83 Agreed at Los Cabos on 20 February 2012. Text accessible on US Department of State website at http://www.state.gov/p/wha/rls/2012/185259.htm.

84 See Articles 4 and 5 of the 2012 Agreement.

85 'Agreement between the United States of America and the United Mexican States Concerning Transboundary Hydrocarbon Reservoirs in the Gulf of Mexico', US (Federal Government) Department of the Interior (DOI) News Item, 03/09/2012. Available on the DOI website at http://www.doi.gov/news/doinews/Agreement-between-the-United-States-and-Mexico-Concerning-Transboundary-Hydrocarbon-Reservoirs-in-the-Gulf-of-Mexico.cfm.

86 See Rogelio López-Velarde and Daniela Monroy, 'International agreement on transboundary hydrocarbon reservoirs published', 15 October 2012. Available on the International Law Office website at http://www.internationallawoffice.com/newsletters/Detail.aspx?g=e4372625-c6db-4c78-a488-355578c5a64c.

87 See Ong, 'Joint development of international common offshore oil and gas deposits'; David M. Ong, 'The new Timor Sea arrangement, 2001: is joint development of common offshore oil and gas deposits mandated under international law?', *International Journal of Marine and Coastal Law*, 17(2), June 2002, pp. 79–122.

Part III

Joint development in the South China Sea: challenges and prospects

8 The practice of joint cooperation/ development in disputed waters

Mixed success so far for the Philippines

Alberto A. Encomienda

In regard to disputed waters in maritime Asia, where joint cooperation/ development is considered a non-traditional maritime security concern and not purely a commercial undertaking, the South China Sea is highlighted as a particularly acute and complicated case with multiple claimant States and the active intervention of extra-regional powers.

A close examination and serious consideration of the practice of joint cooperation/development in disputed waters would be most timely at this stage, following almost two decades of search for a peaceful solution to the territorial/ jurisdictional disputes in the South China Sea that have precluded unilateral exploitation, and even conservation, of marine and seabed resources. Moreover, taking into account the marine geological/geographical configuration of the South China Sea, it would appear that joint cooperation/development is the only route for exploration and exploitation of these resources. This would be true in the best of times in the relations among riparian States of the South China Sea, but necessarily so at these worst of times brought about by territorial/jurisdictional disputes.

Additionally, joint cooperation/development in the disputed waters of the South China Sea is not a stand-alone proposition. The South China Sea is an enclosed/ semi-enclosed sea and as such joint cooperation/development regarding its disputed waters would also impact on maritime peace and good order through the ocean governance cooperation mandated under the United Nations Convention on the Law of the Sea (UNCLOS). In turn, ocean governance cooperation could contribute to the establishment of a more benign political environment, a regional 'détente' that could lead to a peaceful resolution of territorial disputes.

Moreover and parenthetically, beyond the disputed waters in the South China Sea, a joint cooperation/development proposition for other disputed waters in maritime Asia, mainly in the East China Sea and the Yellow Sea, would be a valid and constructive proposition. In these aforementioned disputed waters, joint cooperation/development could well be an easier recourse inasmuch as the territorial/ jurisdictional disputes therein are bilateral in nature, and presumably simpler to manage granted the existence of shared goodwill and political will. These waters are also interconnected enclosed/semi-enclosed seas that, as with the South China Sea, would necessitate cooperative ocean governance arrangements. Extrapolating the constructive application of joint cooperation/development to the larger context of disputed waters in maritime Asia would hopefully invite greater attention and appreciation of the creative contribution of what otherwise would be an ordinary and usual commercial venture to the sustainable regional economic development of maritime Asia as well as maritime peace and good order.

The clear prognosis is that the absence of any movement towards joint cooperation/development, especially in energy resources in an ever-constricting world availability of oil and gas, and resulting competition for domestic sources of energy, would only exacerbate the already tense territorial dispute situation in maritime Asia. And it is now universally accepted that these territorial disputes have negative impacts on sustainable development among regional States whose economies have in so many ways already become interlinked/intertwined. While there is no going back regarding political/economic interaction among regional States, including 'contesting' States, an essential element in the regional sustainable economic development equation – joint cooperation/development – has been stymied because of the disputes. As indicated earlier, the critical importance of this element is underlined by its characterization as a 'non-traditional' maritime security concern, not associated with the seemingly intractable and long-running territorial/jurisdictional disputes, but a security matter nonetheless.

To reiterate in another circular way, the existence of territorial/jurisdictional disputes has prevented the institution of a cooperative regional governance, which would manage and conserve the complex marine environment and resources of the South China Sea as well as define safety and freedom of navigation in the region. In turn cooperative ocean governance would further establish a favourable atmosphere for joint cooperation/development, although one need not necessarily precede the other. Neither would settlement of maritime territorial/jurisdictional disputes preclude or necessarily precede joint development/cooperation or ocean governance cooperation. Finally, joint cooperation/development would be critical in the larger context of maritime Asia, but especially in the specific situation of the South China Sea, with interconnected economies sustained in no insignificant degree by shared marine and seabed resources and facilitated trade within interconnected enclosed and semi-enclosed seas and archipelagic waters. It is time to give joint cooperation/development a chance to play its value-added role in sustainable regional economic development and ocean governance, against the backdrop of the interconnected economies and seas of maritime Asia, premised on temporarily setting aside existing territorial/jurisdictional disputes.

Joint cooperation/development: concept and definition

Joint development has been defined as 'the cooperation between States with regard to the exploration for and exploitation of certain deposits, fields or accumulations of non-living resources which either extend across a boundary or lie in an area of overlapping claims'.[1] It has become accepted and common usage, however, to make a distinction between joint cooperation and joint development. The former would refer to a survey/exploration or research activity, while the latter refers to exploitation or development of resources. In the case of the Philippines, it is convenient to employ the distinction, as shall be seen later.

There are two possible situations in which joint cooperation/development could be implemented. It would be convenient and efficient and therefore desirable where resources straddle the boundaries of the concerned States, whether such boundaries are demarcated or not. It would be an attractive proposition to concerned States to avoid the possibility of losing out with regard to the exploitation of resources, especially energy resources, where deposit volume would vary. An oil and gas field in one State's jurisdictional area, for instance, might siphon off the same resources that are under the other State's jurisdiction.[2] It is economically more prudent for concerned States to jointly exploit the resources as one unit and agree on a scheme for apportionment of costs and benefits for such an undertaking. This arrangement is also called unitization. Where potential resources are located in an as yet undelimited area, an agreement to establish joint development may be made within the context of maritime delimitation[3] or where borders are as yet undemarcated or even disputed and wherein joint development could take the form of a provisional arrangement, although concerned States could later decide to make the arrangement permanent.

The focus of this chapter is joint cooperation/development in *disputed waters*. It must not be lost sight of, however, that in the South China Sea there are already successful models of joint cooperation/development in *undisputed waters* or where boundaries are demarcated. These models may provide useful insights in reference to disputed waters and may even obviate future disputes. In the case of the Philippines, for example, critical areas for possible joint cooperation/development are (1) the South China Sea disputed areas with Brunei, China, Malaysia, Vietnam (and Taiwan); (2) the tri-junction points with Indonesia and Malaysia, and that with Indonesia and Palau; and indeed, along the exclusive economic zone (EEZ) border area with these countries; and (3) the northern EEZ boundary with China (or Taiwan). A joint cooperation/development arrangement in the western maritime boundary of the Philippines could be possible with the International Seabed Authority (or its concessionaires). For the purpose of this chapter, the focus is the Philippines situation in the South China Sea as regards *disputed waters*.

Joint cooperation/development as a necessary and eventual recourse for the disputed waters of maritime Asia: the Deng Xiaoping doctrine

With regard to implementing the concept of joint cooperation/development in disputed waters, China should preferably take the lead, for the simple reason that it is the principal proponent for such a proposition. In the 1980s when maritime territorial disputes among countries in the region first came to light, Premier Deng Xiaoping suggested that territorial disputes be shelved and 'let sleeping dogs lie'. The Premier was quoted in 1984 as having told some American guests that 'in dealing with some international territorial disputes, the issue of sovereignty can be avoided and joint exploitation can be developed; that a new way must be found in accordance with reality to solve such issues'.[4] In the same year, Premier Deng proposed at a meeting of the Advisory Committee of the Central Party Committee of the CCP that shelving territorial disputes and developing joint exploitation be China's official approach in handling conflicts over the islands in the South China Sea.[5] Mentioning the Spratly Islands by their Chinese designation, Deng Xiaoping made the following proposal:

> The Nansha Islands have been an integral part of China's territory since the ancient times. But disputes have occurred over the islands since the 1970s. Considering the fact that China has good relations with the countries concerned, we would like to set aside this issue now and explore later a solution acceptable to both sides. We should avoid military conflict over this and should pursue an approach of joint development.[6]

In 1994, China officially proposed some basic principles on collective security in Asia, among which was the shelving of sovereignty disputes with other Asian nations in order 'to promote the formation of collective security among Asian nations'.[7] Note the nuanced link between territorial disputes and *collective* regional security.

The foregoing general proposition would seem to suggest that China's position calling for bilateral consultations/negotiations to resolve disputes is not a deliberate sinister 'divide and rule' policy, as has often been ascribed to it, but pragmatic and an intended constructive approach to override an impossible situation that has prevented the exploitation of mineral and seabed resources in disputed waters. The Deng Xiaoping 'doctrine', it must be noted and as earlier mentioned, also links joint cooperation/development with regional collective security, which could provide a guarantee of regional stability. Countries in the region might therefore be well advised to revisit the joint cooperation/development propositions and give them a cold, hard second look before armed hostilities overtake events and result in a lasting, poisoned, regional political environment. As for China, perhaps it can now go beyond the earlier vague 'trial balloon' proposition and start formulating more concrete proposals and initiatives as a common starting point for negotiations.

The joint cooperation/development route for the Philippines

Exercise Palawan/Exercise Luzon Sea

As stated earlier, the Philippines is surrounded by ocean, both disputed and undisputed waters, and with potential for disputes arising even in the latter case. The existence of and potential for disputes in its surrounding waters is present for the simple reason that none of its maritime boundaries has yet been demarcated or mapped jointly with neighbouring countries. The Philippines, among its other core national interests as an archipelagic State, and on account of its rich marine resources and delicate biodiversity, is therefore compelled to undertake joint cooperation initiatives in regard to maritime scientific research (MSR) and marine environmental protection (MEP) in a large marine eco-region setting. The foundation stone of these joint cooperation initiatives for ocean governance is UNCLOS Part IX on enclosed and semi-enclosed seas, which compels joint cooperation on a regional scale.

The Philippines' early venture into joint cooperation had an auspicious, albeit inadvertent, beginning. It was originally pursued under the Informal Workshop on Managing Potential Conflicts in the South China Sea (informal workshop MPC-SCS) which in essence is regional-scale joint cooperation – a thrust fully consistent with the Philippines' national oceans policy. At the time of its inception, the informal workshop MPC-SCS was also a most appropriate modality for confidence-building in a region of potential conflicts. It was also perceived by the Philippines as an excellent Track 2 lead-in to an institutionalized Track 1 regional ocean governance arrangement under UNCLOS Part IX, when the time came. The Philippines played a very active role in the informal workshop process and volunteered to shepherd the module on MEP, MSR and sea lines of communication (SLOC).

The informal workshop MPC-SCS provided an auspicious beginning for the Philippines as it coincided with its national interests as an archipelagic State and as a frontline State in the South China Sea conflict. Under this module, the first marine scientific research project was Exercise Anambas, held on Anambas Island in Indonesia in 2002 and planned to be followed by Exercise Palawan on Palawan Island in the Philippines. The technical scientific proposal for Exercise Palawan was conceptualized and approved at the 12th Workshop of the MPC-SCS in October 2002 in Jakarta, and finalized and formally adopted at the 13th Workshop in Medan, Indonesia in September 2003. It may be worth mentioning that the MSR/MEP/SLOCs module of the informal workshop was originally planned to be held in disputed waters. This, however, met with objections from certain claimant countries and Indonesia decided to offer Anambas Island as a 'neutral' venue. Exercise Palawan followed suit.

The adoption of the ASEAN–China Declaration on the Conduct of Parties in the South China Sea (DOC) on 4 November 2002 was, for the Philippines, a most significant favourable development in support of its national core interest of establishing regional maritime cooperation in the South China Sea. With the call for all parties to the DOC to give flesh to the substance of the declaration, the Philippines made representations via the informal workshop MPC-SCS to upgrade and graduate Exercise Palawan from a Track 2 project to a formal and institutionalized Track 1 undertaking. For the Philippines, the DOC provided the mandate and opportunity to progress Exercise Palawan from a confidence-building activity in the setting of an informal workshop on managing potential conflicts to an effort to fully implement UNCLOS Part IX on governance cooperation in enclosed and semi-enclosed seas; an obligatory joint cooperation arrangement built into UNCLOS. The DOC exhorts cooperation among parties in marine scientific research and marine environmental protection, and safety and freedom of navigation. This tack did not sit well with the organizers of the informal workshop MPC-SCS, and Exercise Palawan was removed from the programme. This was the inadvertent aspect of the launch of Exercise Luzon Sea, the new designation for Exercise Palawan, which was now conducted as a Philippines national initiative (although regional in scope), conforming to UNCLOS Part IX, as a joint cooperation venture, and to the DOC. Another consideration and concern for the Philippines at the time, in pushing its proposition to implement Exercise Palawan as Track 1, was that a principal sponsor of the informal workshop MPC-SCS, the Canadian International Development Agency, after ample leeway and advance notification, had withdrawn funding support for the workshop. This created serious concern for the Philippines in that the only show in town that touched on regional cooperation on ocean governance was facing impending difficulties.

The reason for the rejection of Exercise Palawan was not immediately clear, at least to the Philippines. Recently, however, at the Workshop on China–ASEAN Cooperation on 24 June 2012 held at the National Institute for South China Sea Studies (China) in Haikou, Dr Djalal revealed that China, at the time, 'objected' to converting the informal workshop into a Track 1 activity. Even such a long time after the event, this supposed reason was not easy for the Philippines to accept simply because the informal workshop, whatever its ultimate goal and purpose may have been, was essentially about joint cooperation. And as such, there could be no other possible direction for it but to somehow change, expectedly sooner rather than later because of its supposed influence in managing potential conflicts in the South China Sea, into a Track 1 undertaking or involvement.

There would indeed seem to be a confusing element in regard to the stage and direction of cooperation in the informal workshop process. Early on, in 1992, Dr Djalal, in the concluding paragraph of a paper entitled 'Fisheries Disputes and Their Impact on Contemporary International Law and Politics in South East Asia Evolution in the Law of the Sea', read at a SEAPOL International Workshop in Rayong, Thailand, categorically referring to the informal workshop, declared that 'the era of cooperation has now come to Southeast Asia, South China Sea and the West Pacific, including fisheries. The era of bickering and confrontation has passed or should have passed. It is incumbent upon all of us to move forward.'

If it was a matter of timing that was China's objection, there should have been some discussion about it within the informal workshop itself, but there was not. Much earlier, however, almost contemporaneously with the withdrawal of China, a senior official from the Embassy of China in Manila informed the Philippines side that Dr Djalal had visited Beijing and made strong representations to have the Chinese contingent withdrawn. (It was also learned from separate sources that Dr Djalal also called on Hanoi, Bangkok, Singapore and Kuala Lumpur to make the same request.) Seemingly, it was personal diplomacy rather than hard-nosed policy considerations that may have caused undue delay in instituting ocean governance joint cooperation in the disputed areas of the South China Sea. It will always be a matter of conjecture whether progress in the construction of an ocean governance cooperation in those disputed waters could have helped alleviate the current intensified conflict, or at least acted as a constructive influence in managing it. A perhaps wilder conjecture is what might have happened if Exercise Luzon Sea, which was projected to have ASEAN–China participation, the tripartite Joint Oceanographic Marine Scientific Research Expedition, which was projected to be ASEAN–China at a later stage, and the tripartite Joint Marine Seismic Undertaking (to be discussed below) had come together at this time.

In hindsight, some insights with regard to the timeliness of converting the Track 2 effort to Track 1 under the informal workshop could be gleaned from a presentation by Dr Djalal at a Conference on Joint Development and the South China Sea hosted recently by the Singapore Center for International Law.[8] First, his presentation on 'Lessons Learned at the SCS Workshop Process'[9] confirms that the ultimate direction and purpose of the informal workshop was to inject it, or at least some of its subjects/activities, into Track 1 in order to manage potential conflicts. The question remains, more than two decades after its inception, what would be the proper time to make a move along these lines. In the same presentation, Dr Djalal stated among 'basic principles for launching an informal initiative, that … at least in the initial stages, do not institutionalize the structure of the process or create a permanent mechanism … keep the process as flexible as possible'.[10] After the launch of the informal workshop, he cited among ten additional lessons learned that indicate that 'countries in the region should develop cooperative efforts so that potential conflicts can be managed by converting them into actual cooperation'.[11] Earlier in that presentation, in regards to organizing an informal workshop along the lines of an MPC-SCS model, he also enumerated some preliminary matters associated with a Track 1 setting, which must first be established, such as transparency in national policy, legislation and documentation, so that an overall assessment could be made that would 'indicate possible success … [wherein thereafter] … a more formal Track One approach can be attempted'.[12] This raises the question 'Which is the cart, which is the horse, Track 1 or Track 2?' For whatever reason, the informal workshop organizers felt it was not the time for the MSR/MEP/SLOCs module to morph from Track 2 to its ultimate destination, Track 1. A seemingly favourable prevailing regional political atmosphere (ASEAN–China DOC) that could have been furthered by a purposeful transmutation of Exercise Palawan into Track 1 was totally ignored, giving the impression that the informal workshop was operating in a vacuum isolated from the potential conflicts it is supposed to serve. The Philippines felt that it was time to transform the module on MSR/MEP/SLOCs into Track 1 since it had already attained significant progress as a confidence-building measure under the informal workshop MPC-SCS.

As already stated, the joint cooperation initiative Exercise Luzon Sea, although it is in territorial waters (as with Exercise Anambas), has already been established and is intended to fill the gap concerning scientific research and environmental protection in the South China Sea, given the connectivity of the oceans and the rationale for the need for holistic governance for enclosed and semi-enclosed seas. The lengthy discussion here on the informal workshop MPC-SCS is not meant to be a critique; it was an excellent idea at the time and is still valid and viable today.

It can stand on its own merits. Nevertheless, it was a defining episode that introduced the Philippines into its first venture in joint cooperation in ocean governance, a national core interest. The Philippines side regrets that Exercise Palawan/ Exercise Luzon Sea had to be divorced from the informal workshop MPC-SCS. It feels very strongly that the overall regional ocean governance design and possibilities could have been best fulfilled under an informal workshop. It is also worth mentioning that the ASEAN Foreign Ministers, in their joint communiqué at the 37th Ministerial Meeting (June 2004), 'noted with appreciation the initiative of the Philippines Government in carrying out Exercise Luzon Sea Phase I – Palawan Expedition as a practical application of Part IX of the 1982 Law of the Sea Convention on the cooperation of States in enclosed and semi-enclosed seas which is encouraged under Paragraph 6 of the DOC'.

Exercise Luzon Sea was participated in by three other countries upon the invitation of the Philippines under an UNCLOS Article 123(d) arrangement – Malaysia, Thailand and Vietnam – and by two international organizations, Conservation International and the World Wildlife Fund.[13] Exercise Luzon Sea Phase I, or ELS I, was conducted in the south-western territorial sea and EEZ of the Philippines. It was planned to proceed northwards in subsequent cruise tracks (Phase II and II-a and Phases III and IV) to cover the entire western maritime flank of the country. As will be seen later, Exercise Luzon Sea was planned to bridge the gap between the coastal/territorial sea and EEZs and the high seas coverage of the RP-Vietnam JOMSRE. ELS I was successfully completed with published results.

The Joint Oceanographic Marine Scientific Research Expedition in the South China Sea (JOMSRE-SCS)[14]

As with Exercise Luzon Sea, the Joint Oceanographic Marine Scientific Research Expedition (JOMSRE), which was a bilateral undertaking with Vietnam, was not conceptualized or planned at the outset as a joint cooperation arrangement. It was originally merely intended to be a bilateral confidence-building measure in the wake of mutual recognition of governments. Nevertheless, it is a *joint* cooperation arrangement in essence and structure, and, as with Exercise Luzon Sea, it was later formalized and institutionalized under UNCLOS Part IX.

In 1994, President Fidel V. Ramos and President Le Duc Anh of Vietnam agreed to cooperate in marine scientific research and environmental protection in the South China Sea with the aim of enhancing knowledge and information on the natural processes of the marine environment and resources. The first JOMSRE-SCS scientific cruise was conducted from 18 April to 9 May 1996 with the second from 27 May to 2 June 2000. The third and fourth JOMSRE-SCSs took place on 6–19 April 2005 and on 7–21 April 2007. At the 3rd Meeting of the Philippines–Vietnam Joint Commission for Bilateral Cooperation on 26–28 February 2003, it was agreed to institutionalize JOMSRE-SCS under UNCLOS Part IX, conforming also with the ASEAN–China DOC. At the 3rd Joint Permanent Working Group on Maritime and Ocean Concerns meeting of

1–4 March 2006 in Cebu City, it was agreed to expand JOMSRE participation to include scientists from other States, particularly the ASEAN States and China, again conforming to UNCLOS Part IX. (Indeed, at the 4th JOMSRE-SCS, a scientist from Laos participated in the scientific research cruise.) At the same meeting, the participating scientists agreed that the RP-Vietnam JOMSRE-SCS (JOMSRE I-IV), now designated as JOMSRE Phase I, had sufficiently covered the southern part of the disputed areas of the South China Sea and was complete, and further, that JOMSRE be reconfigured into JOMSRE Phase II with enlarged stakeholder participation and an enlarged research area. JOMSRE Phase I was concluded with a symposium (with published proceedings) among participating scientists to evaluate the overall outcome and results/findings of JOMSRE-SCS. The participating scientists recommended the establishment of a marine protected area within the disputed areas that would be formally designated as a transborder marine peace park.

It was agreed that JOMSRE Phase II would be the next enhanced level of ocean governance joint cooperation in the South China Sea and would include the participation of China and other interested ASEAN countries in keeping with and in the direction of implementing UNCLOS Part IX on enclosed and semi-enclosed seas and the ASEAN–China DOC. JOMSRE Phase II, also referred to as the Tripartite JOMSRE, proceeded with technical preparations that principally involving scientists from the three countries primarily involved, that is, China, the Philippines and Vietnam. It was agreed to hold three preparatory meetings alternately in Manila, Guangzhou and Nha Trang. Preparations were virtually completed at the Manila and Guangzhou meetings, and the Nha Trang meeting was seen only as a wrap-up meeting. At the final meeting in Nha Trang, it was nevertheless agreed that China would host a fourth preparatory meeting to discuss some unresolved pending issues, for example the research expedition route. The fourth meeting, however, did not take place. (The expedition route and other 'pending issues' were actually settled in the earlier meetings between the participating scientists. At the Nha Trang meeting, however, a participating State raised late objections and 'issues' of a political nature. The last minute agreement for another meeting in China, however, was overtaken by events – the 'window' of favourable weather conditions for the scientific cruise had closed.)

The Joint Marine Seismic Undertaking (JMSU)

The Joint Marine Seismic Undertaking (JMSU) is the first undertaking to be conceptualized as a joint cooperation/development venture participated in by the Philippines. It was to be in disputed waters in the South China Sea. To jump ahead in the story, the joint cooperation component, that is, the survey and research on seabed energy resources, was successfully completed with promising results. Under the terms of the agreement, joint cooperation would progress to joint development (exploitation) if commercially warranted. The joint development element, however, was aborted.

The JMSU is a tripartite agreement between China National Offshore Oil

Corporation, Vietnam Oil and Gas Corporation and Philippine National Oil Company to explore for seabed energy resources in a defined area in the disputed waters of the South China Sea. An earlier agreement was signed first between the Philippines and China on 1 September 2004 and later, on account of strong objections from Vietnam (another stakeholder claimant State in the disputed area covered in the China–Philippines agreement) a three-way agreement that includes the Vietnamese company was signed on 14 March 2005. The first phase of the JMSU was to conduct research on the petroleum resource potential in disputed areas of the South China Sea. This phase was completed and confirmed the presence of commercially exploitable energy deposits.

The JMSU is a Philippines initiative but not a government-to-government arrangement.[15] It is a commercial undertaking between private companies albeit with official blessing from their respective governments. The joint cooperation component of the arrangement, that is, resources survey (seismic), was carried out smoothly, although the Philippines part was dogged domestically with anticipated charges of unconstitutionality should the venture proceed to the exploitation phase. The joint cooperation component was successfully completed with promising results and steps were taken to proceed with joint development or exploitation. The exploitation phase, however, was aborted as the Philippines Government was compelled to suspend participation, not because of constitutional objections but because it was overtaken by serious allegations of corruption on the Philippines side.

Conclusions

Joint cooperation/development is an acknowledged remedy and an ongoing activity in border areas, whether or not disputes exist. In maritime Asia, which is virtually all disputed waters, the thrust towards joint cooperation/development is potentially a very important element in the sustainable economic development of the region. The idea, however, has not had an easy reception or acceptance among parties to the disputes. Nevertheless, halting steps under Track 2 or Track 1 have already been taken, steps which could provide further guidance and encouragement. Indeed, an early event that seemed to provide hope for these undertakings was a joint cooperation arrangement between China and Taiwan for energy exploration in the so-called Chaosan Block[16] north-northwest of the Philippines. This planted the seed for the Philippines initiative in regard to the tripartite JMSU. The bilateral JOMSRE joint cooperation arrangement between the Philippines and Vietnam was an unqualified success, complete with reports on scientific findings and published proceedings on the closing symposium from participating scientists. It was on the threshold of progressing towards a tripartite JOMSRE with China. In both cases, the JOMSRE-SCS and the JMSU (exploration) were successful and completed joint cooperation projects. Exercise Luzon Sea, although largely within territorial waters, is a joint cooperation in structure and mechanics that was to be placed under the umbrella of UNCLOS Part IX to close the MSR/MEP gap of JOMSRE-SCS from the coast to the EEZ and beyond. The first phase, ELS I, was successfully completed. The JOMSRE can quite easily be resumed, while there does not seem to be any serious hindrance to the joint development part of the JMSU, that is, actual resource exploitation, despite some misgivings from some quarters on the Philippines side in regard to its constitutionality.

As far as the Philippines is concerned, its experiences relating to the aforementioned ventures are clear demonstrations that the use of joint cooperation/development concept in disputed waters of the South China Sea is sound and implementable. The three areas of joint cooperation involving resources survey and research that the Philippines has thus far initiated or participated in – ELS 1, JOMSRE-SCS and JMSU (Phase 1) – were all successfully implemented and completed. The joint development aspect of the JMSU failed, not because of any issue relating to the validity and applicability of the concept for disputed waters, but because of issues internal to the Philippines. The absence of transparency on the Philippines side led to the failure of what otherwise was a promising beginning to a joint development arrangement. On the other hand, lack of sustained funding or political support caused grave prejudice to the idea of ocean governance joint cooperation. To minimize instances or the possibility of instances of internal or domestic issues creating an adverse impact at any stage of a joint cooperation/development project, whether in disputed waters or not, and to further to ensure that all participating stakeholders in such projects are on the same page in all aspects of preparation and implementation, what may be needed is a regional good practices guide for joint cooperation/development that could emphasize transparency. Dr Djalal's presentation on 'Lessons Learned at the SCS Workshop Process', albeit intended for initiatives where an informal workshop is deemed an appropriate modality for managing potential conflicts, could contain relevant points for a working paper in crafting such a guidebook. The 'Lessons Learned' is about the informal workshop process for managing potential conflicts, but the proposed undertakings for managing potential conflicts are joint cooperation arrangements. In the view of many in the Philippines, such a 'Good Practices Guidebook' would be valid and applicable for any joint cooperation/development venture in maritime Asia.

Notes

1 There are numerous definitions of joint development, but this chapter adopts Lagoni's definition since, in the author's view, it encompasses the broad meaning of joint development. See Lagoni (1989) as cited in Francisco Orrego Vicuña, 'Regional cooperation in nonliving resources: Joint management zones', in P. B. Payoyo (ed.), *Ocean Governance: Sustainable Development of the Seas*, Tokyo: United Nations University Press, 1994.

2 For example when China conducted oil drilling near the Japan-proclaimed theoretical median boundary line between China and Japan, the latter officially protested the oil drilling for fear that China would siphon off gas from Japan's side. See Mark J. Valencia, 'The East China Sea dispute: prognosis and ways forward', *Pacific Forum CSIS PacNet 47A*, Honolulu, Hawaii, 15 September 2006, available at https://csis.org/files/media/csis/pubs/pac0647a.pdf.

3 As in the case of the joint development arrangements in Bahrain–Saudi Arabia Agreement Concerning the Delimitation of the Continental Shelf of 22 February 1958, the France–Spain Convention on the Delimitation of the Continental Shelves in the Bay of Biscay of 29 January 1974, among others. See Zou Keyuan, 'Joint development in the South China Sea: a new approach', *International Journal of Marine and Coastal Law*, 21, 2006, p. 92. For a copy of the agreement between Bahrain and Saudi Arabia, see http://www.state.gov/documents/organization/62003.pdf. For a copy of the Spain–France Agreement, see http://www.state.gov/documents/organization/59579.pdf.
4 Yongnian Zheng, *Discovering Chinese Nationalism in China: Modernization, Identity and International Relations*, Cambridge Asia-Pacific Studies, Cambridge: Cambridge University Press, 1999.
5 Ibid.
6 See Ministry of Foreign Affairs, People's Republic of China, 'Set aside dispute and pursue joint development', 17 November 2000, available at http://www.fmprc.gov.cn/eng/ziliao/3602/3604/t18023.htm (accessed 2 May 2012).
7 Zheng, *Discovering Chinese Nationalism in China.*
8 The Conference on Joint Development and the South China Sea was held on 16–17 June 2011 at the Grand Copthorne Hotel, Singapore and was organized by the Centre for International Law, National University of Singapore. A Conference Report may be accessed at http://cil.nus.edu.sg/wp/wp-content/uploads/2011/06/Report-of-CIL-Conference-on-Joint-Development-and-the-South-China-Sea-2011-04.08.2011.pdf.
9 An article based on Dr Hasjim Djalal's presentation has been published by the *Jakarta Post* in three parts. See Hasjim Djalal, 'Lessons learned at the SCS Workshop process (Part 1 of 3)', *Jakarta Post*, 27 June 2011, available at http://www.thejakartapost.com/news/2011/06/27/lessons-learned-scs-workshop-process.html.
10 Hasjim Djalal, 'Lessons learned at the SCS Workshop process (Part 2 of 3)', *Jakarta Post*, 28 June 2011, available at http://www.thejakartapost.com/news/2011/06/28/lessons-learned-scs-workshop-part-2-3.html.
11 Hasjim Djalal, 'Lessons learned at the SCS Workshop process (Part 3 of 3)', *Jakarta Post*, 30 June 2011, available at http://www.thejakartapost.com/news/2011/06/30/lessons-learned-scs-workshop-process-part-3-3.html.
12 Djalal, 'Lessons learned at the SCS Workshop process (Part 1 of 3)'.
13 China participated in the organizational meetings of Exercise Luzon Sea but at the last minute and in the middle of the official launch ceremonies, presided over by no less than the Undersecretary of Foreign Affairs (Policy) of the Philippines, the Chinese contingent was unceremoniously withdrawn by the chargé d'affaires of the Chinese Embassy. The hasty manner of China's withdrawal after attending the preparatory meetings suggests that the supposed Chinese objection cited by Dr Djalal was an afterthought. Moreover, as later indicated, China participated in JOMSRE Phase II.
14 Alberto A. Encomienda, 'Introduction to JOMSRE-SCS', in *Proceedings of the Conference on the Results of the Philippines–Vietnam Joint Oceanographic and Marine Scientific Research Expedition in the South China Sea (JOMSRE-SCS I to IV)*, 26–29 March 2008, Ha Long City, Vietnam.
15 From the author's perspective, the JMSU took inspiration from a joint cooperation between the China National Offshore Oil Corporation and Taiwan's Chinese Petroleum Corporation to explore for oil in the Chaosan Block. See 'Landmark Taiwan–China oil exploration pact inked', *Manila Bulletin*, 17 May 2002, B-18.
16 In May 2002, China and Taiwan through their respective state-run national oil companies, the China National Offshore Oil Corporation and the Chinese Petroleum Corporation, entered into an agreement to jointly explore for oil in the Chaosan Block. The Chaosan Block is 140 km from the southern port city of Taiwan's Kaohsiung and has an area of 15,400 km^2. See 'Landmark Taiwan-China oil exploration pact inked'.

9 The joint development concept in the South China Sea workshop process

Hasjim Djalal

One of the most important issues in the South China Sea is the question of joint development or joint cooperation. I personally supported this approach as one way of overcoming territorial problems. The Workshop on Managing Potential Conflict in the South China Sea (SCSW) even formed a Special Technical Working Group (TWG) on Resources Assessment and Ways of Development (TWG-RAWD) to deal with this topic and the TWG met several times, including in Jakarta in July 1993 and in 1999. The TWG-RAWD also established a study group on joint development to better understand the concept, and this study group also met in various places, such as in Vientiane in June 1998 and in Tabanan, Bali in July 1999.

The TWG–RAWD, in its meeting in Jakarta in July 1993, discussed the possibility for cooperation: a) on living resources (fisheries); b) on non-living resources/ non-hydrocarbons; c) on non-living resources/hydrocarbons; and d) on non-living resources non-minerals, such as ocean energy.

Generally, the TWG-RAWD agreed on several points:

- that the joint development concept has excellent potential, being in line with the statement of Chinese Prime Minister Li Peng, in Singapore in 1991, expressing China's willingness to shelve territorial or sovereignty claims in favor of joint development;
- that we should study the various concepts or models of joint development around the world to learn from them what could be applied to the SCS area;
- that we should apply the joint development concept to a 'zone to be defined'.

In fact, the concept of joint development or joint cooperation was also basically indicated in Article 74(3) (on exclusive economic zones, EEZs) and Article 83(3) (on the continental shelf) of UNCLOS 1982. The articles stated that:

> Pending agreement as provided for in paragraph 1, the States concerned, in a spirit of understanding and co-operation, shall make every effort to enter into provisional arrangements of a practical nature and, during this transitional

> period, not to jeopardize or hamper the reaching of the final agreement. Such arrangements shall be without prejudice to the final delimitation.

These provisions were particularly important for the South China Sea as a semi-enclosed sea. Article 122 of UNCLOS defines 'enclosed or semi-enclosed seas' as 'a gulf, basin or sea surrounded by two or more States and connected to another sea or the ocean by a narrow outlet or consisting entirely or primarily of the territorial seas and exclusive economic zones of two or more coastal States'.

In addition, Article 123 of the Convention stipulates that:

> States bordering an enclosed or semi-enclosed sea should co-operate with each other in the exercise of their rights and in the performance of their duties under this Convention. To this end they shall endeavour, directly or through an appropriate regional organization:
>
> a. To co-ordinate the management, conservation, exploration and exploitation of the living resources of the sea;
> b. To co-ordinate the implementation of their rights and duties with respect to the protection and preservation of the marine environment;
> c. To co-ordinate their scientific research policies and undertake where appropriate joint programmes of scientific research in the area;
> d. To invite, as appropriate, other interested States or international organizations to co-operate with them in furtherance of the provisions of this article.

Since all the littoral countries or authorities of the South China Sea (except Chinese-Taipei and Cambodia) have ratified UNCLOS 1982, they should respect and implement their rights and obligations in the South China Sea in accordance with the provisions of UNCLOS, with Articles 73, 83, and 123 among others.

With regard to living resources, the TWG-RAWD in Manila in May 1993 to some extent also touched upon this subject. There were many discussions with regard to the need to conduct a living resources 'stock assessment'. It is generally recognized that the living resources in the South China Sea area migrate from one EEZ to another, particularly tuna and other shared stocks. Each country may already have the assessment of its living resources in its EEZ, assuming that the definition and delineation of each EEZ is clear. The problems are that many of those EEZ boundaries are not well defined or mutually agreed upon between neighbors. Moreover, there are various conflicting claims to islands and other features that complicate the determination of the EEZ boundaries. For these reasons, many experts feel the need to cooperate on the assessment of the living resources in the South China Sea area without regard to jurisdictional boundaries. The basis for this endeavor would be Article 123(a) of UNCLOS 1982 regarding enclosed and semi-enclosed seas.

It is also recognized that stock assessment as well as other cooperative efforts are taking place in the seas and waters beyond the proper boundaries of the South China Sea, particularly in the Philippines and Indonesian archipelagic waters as well as in the waters of the west and southwest Pacific. It is surmised that the resources in the South China Sea, particularly the highly migratory species, may have some relation to the resources in the Indonesian and the Philippine archipelagic waters and perhaps also with the living resources in the west and the southwest Pacific. The TWG also wished to discuss the possibility of undertaking cooperative efforts with the West Pacific Fisheries Consultative Committee, particularly with regard to tuna tagging, on which matter the Committee has had some cooperative experience.

There have also been plenty of regional organizations that have dealt with fisheries issues in the South China Sea area, such as the FAO (Food and Agricultural Organization), the IPFC (Indo-Pacific Fisheries Commission), ICLARM (International Centre for Living Aquatic Resources Management) and others. The knowledge of those organizations might also be tapped for the benefit of cooperative efforts in the South China Sea area. The TWG also wished to discuss this topic.

There may be other non-South China Sea states that may have interests in the living resources in the area, particularly Japan and Korea. Again, the TWG discussed the possibility of these countries participating in the cooperative efforts regarding the assessment of the living resources in the area.

It is surmised that a proper assessment of the resources would be essential for the proper conservation, management and exploitation of the living resources in the South China Sea area on the basis of Articles 61, 62 and 63 of UNCLOS 1982. These articles oblige the coastal states, among others, to determine their resources in accordance with scientific evidence, to determine their capacity to harvest and to provide possibilities for cooperation with other states in the exploitation of those resources, subject to the provisions of the Convention. The TWG wished to determine what would be the objectives of the conduct of those stock assessments in view of the provisions of UNCLOS 1982.

With regard to non-living mineral resources, discussions were divided into two categories: the hard minerals that may be found on the seabed, and the liquid minerals, namely, hydrocarbon resources (oil and gas), that may be found in the sub-soil of the seabed.

In this context, the treatment of the subject may be somewhat different from that of the living resources, simply for the reason that the living resources move from one area to another, while the non-living resources are static.

For that reason, the management of the resources aspects of the South China Sea area could be divided into three basic areas:

1 The seabed areas which are clearly under national jurisdiction and which are non-contested. It is surmised that the assessment of the resources in this area could be best left alone to the coastal states themselves.
2 The resources in the border area of which the boundary lines have not been clearly determined or on which conflicting claims exist, between either two or three coastal states. In that context, again, the solution or the assessment of the non-living resources could be left to the states concerned. In this

context, even though the boundary lines are clearly defined and agreed upon, cooperation between the states concerned may still be required if there are cross-boundary structures in accordance with the principles of unitization. In practice, neighboring states are already agreeing to various concepts of joint development in clearly defined areas for the exploitation of the resources of the border areas on which the demarcation lines have not yet been agreed upon.

3 Resources in the areas of multiple claims in the South China Sea particularly in the Spratly Islands group. It is surmised that in this area cooperative efforts with regard to the assessment of the non-living mineral resources in the area could be better conducted jointly by the interested South China Sea states. There have been some opinions which indicate that the cooperative efforts in the multiple claims areas should be undertaken:
   a) bilaterally between the states concerned. It is surmised that this approach would not be conducive to the development of the cooperative efforts simply because there are more than bilateral parties involved. Bilateralism in the multiple claims areas may simply create blocks among the claimants which in the end may aggravate and complicate the problems and make it more difficult to seek solutions.
   b) by the parties or claimants involved. Although this proposition looks attractive, it is not generally clear which states are the claimants and what are the nature of their claims. The attempt by the workshop on the South China Sea to seek clarification on this issue has not been very successful. Moreover, there may be a case where South China Sea states are not claimants to the Spratly Islands group, for example Brunei and Indonesia, but they are certainly affected by the possible boundary determination with whoever in the end is successful in claiming the Spratly Islands group. Furthermore, a good legal case could be advanced that the territorial claims to the Spratlys may not necessarily result in the justification of the claims to the seabed and the continental shelf in the area, simply because the islands are either so small or simply rocks and natural features that, according to Article 121 of UNCLOS 1982, 'cannot sustain human habitation or economic life of their own' and therefore cannot have their own EEZ or continental shelf, or cannot have full effects on delimitation of their EEZ or continental shelf with their adjacent or opposite neighbors. Therefore, although the approach to confine the assessment of the non-living resources in the multiple claims areas to the claimants only seems better than the bilateral approach, it does not seem to be satisfactory, because it is difficult to determine who are the claimants, which areas are being claimed and what are the nature of the claims, and so on.

Moreover, it should also be remembered that history has indicated that the multiple claims area has already developed into a regional concern to the effect that the instability that may be created as the result of the intensifying multiple claims will also affect stability, peace and cooperation in the South China Sea area as a whole. For this reason, perhaps the best approach to deal with the resources assessment in the multiple claims area would be a regional effort by the states surrounding the South China Sea area. The TWG wanted to discuss this issue in greater detail.

With regard to other resources that are non-living and non-mineral, such as the production of energy from wind, currents, waves, temperature differential, and so forth, according to Article 56(1a) of UNCLOS 1982, these resources also belong to the coastal states. In view of the conflicting claims in the multiple claims area, the TWG also wished to discuss the possibility of assessing these resources and if possible their exploitation in the future.

In discussing the assessment of the resources in the multiple claims area, four types of resources may be taken into account:

1. Stock assessment of the living resources as part of the attempt to conduct stock assessment in the SCS sea as a whole
2. Assessment of the resources of the hard minerals on the seabed
3. Assessment of the potential resources of the liquid minerals (oil and gas)
4. Assessment of the other non-living resources in the multiple claims area, such as ocean energy.

In view of the various claims as indicated above, and if the possibility for cooperation is agreed upon in the area, it is essential for the TWG to focus its attention also on the rough definition of the multiple claims area. It should be understood that the definition of this area does not prejudice the territorial claims of certain South China Sea states, but simply provides a clearly defined area which could be used as a basis to undertake joint cooperation and, at an appropriate time, the possibility for conducting joint development in the area, as many states have already indicated. The TWG focused its attention on a working definition of the multiple claims area that could be subjected to a possible cooperative effort.

Like the potential cooperation on the assessment of the living resources, the assessment of the mineral resources in the multiple claims area may also take advantage of the existing data and information outside the region. It is surmised that much knowledge on the resources of the multiple claims area exists outside the South China Sea states. Equally, the scientific and technological as well as technical capabilities to assess the resources may also exist outside the region and non-regional states may also have interests in the assessment of those resources, such as for the purpose of economic investment in the area. The TWG wished to identify those interested outsiders and discuss in what way they could be allowed or invited to participate in the cooperative efforts in accordance with Article 123(d) of UNCLOS.

There have been a number of cooperative models in the region either on living resources or on mineral resources. The TWG also wanted to look into those various models with a view to finding the best possible model for the multiple claims area or to find the best possible basis to develop a new model for the multiple claims area.

It is expected that the participants of the TWG would recommend their respective governments to conduct joint efforts in assessing the resources of the multiple claims area, including the living resources and mineral resources, as well as other non-living resources.

The experts at the TWG also wanted to define such an agreement in the form of a joint project including the suggestion regarding the area for cooperative efforts, the participants for the joint project as well as the possible financing that may be involved.

In view of the above, the TWG organized its meetings to discuss the following issues:

- the possible project proposal to conduct a non-living resources assessment in the multiple claims area or to discuss all matters relevant to this subject;
- the possible project proposal to conduct a living resources assessment in the SCS area as a whole.

For these reasons, I was asked to identify the area for joint development and joint cooperation in the South China Sea. In this context it appeared to me that joint cooperation could be devised for any of the three purposes as stated in Article 123 of UNCLOS, namely:

1 On the management, conservation, exploration and exploitation of the living resources
2 On the protection and preservation of the marine environment
3 On appropriate joint programs of scientific research in the area.

Once the area and the programs were agreed, then the workshop would be able to discuss the need for and possibility of inviting, as appropriate, other interested states or international organizations to cooperate in the furtherance of these purposes of cooperation, as indicated in Article 123(d) of UNCLOS.

Thus, in 1996 I travelled around the South China Sea capitals to discuss the 'area' for joint development or joint cooperation, making the following points:

1 We should start with the least controversial issues and then move on to more sensitive issues if the situation permits, such as the protection and preservation of the marine environment, the conduct of joint marine scientific research, the living marine resources and other non-living mineral resources, and the mineral resources.
2 I suggested that the area for joint development and cooperation could begin at the area outside the 200 mile EEZ from the undisputed land features/coastal areas or the legitimate baselines of the South China Sea countries. I discovered that there was still a sufficiently large area in the middle of the

South China Sea outside of the 200 miles distance from the undisputed coastlines, or legitimate west lines. Later, this area became known as the 'donut hole' in the South China Sea, just like the 'peanut hole' in the Okhoetsk Sea and the 'donut hole' in the Behring Sea. Through the various informal consultations, some participants accepted my approach, while others consider the area to be too large and involving too many claimants. I was asked to review the proposal and to suggest revisions to the proposed area.

3 In 1998, I revised the suggested area by dividing the 'donut hole' into two parts, namely the northern and the southern parts. The northern part concerns only those claimants in the area, namely the Philippines, China, Chinese-Taipei and perhaps Vietnam, while the southern part may also involve other claimants in the area, such as Malaysia, Brunei Darussalam and Vietnam. The boundary between the northern and the southern parts could be further discussed.

With regard to the mechanism for such joint development, I would think that it could be a joint authority as in the Timor Gap agreement and it should be open for participation by relevant companies.

In fact, the special Study Group on Zones of Cooperation in the South China Sea in its meeting in Vientiane, Lao PDR, on 15–18 June 1998, agreed that maritime cooperation, including joint development, has the potential to assist in resolving the difficulties in the South China Sea. The study group recommended, among others things, that:

1 Joint development or joint cooperation can facilitate the development of resources as well as political relations between the parties concerned.
2 Joint development arrangements can contribute to confidence-building and can promote cooperation and the avoidance of conflicts and at the same time promote good neighbor policies.
3 Joint development is provisional in nature, and does not deal with territorial or jurisdictional matters; rather, it is without prejudice to such issues and attempts to circumvent them.
4 Joint development encourages investment by creating a more certain investment climate.
5 The various models of joint development indicate that once agreement is reached on the need for this approach, it will take much time and effort to conclude the joint development agreement, because many issues need to be settled and agreed upon by the parties through consultation.
6 Although many joint development arrangements have been formulated in the form of treaties, in all cases the arrangement must be or is approved or supported by the authorities concerned.
7 It is important that the various authorities concerned be convinced of the utility of joint development arrangements, particularly in disputed areas, since this arrangement could be more beneficial to them than the continued disputes or the prolonged inability to develop the area or its resources.

8 The common objectives of any arrangement must be articulated clearly prior to agreement.
9 Joint development creates opportunities to continue efforts to seek solutions on territorial and jurisdictional issues.

In the meeting of the Study Group on Zones of Cooperation in the South China Sea in Tabanan, Bali, on 27 June–1 July 1999, I stated the following personal views:

1 The area for joint development or joint cooperation should involve the relevant parties.
2 The area should be clearly defined.
3 The agreement to establish the joint development or joint cooperation should be without prejudice to the respective territorial and jurisdictional claims.
4 The respective authorities can continue to discuss the resolution of territorial and jurisdictional issues.
5 The participants in the joint development efforts should be those that are maintaining presence in the zone.
6 The subject of joint cooperation or joint development, at least at the initial stage, should begin with the least controversial matters.
7 The joint development could be designed for a specified period.
8 The joint development concept should not prejudice the provisions of UNCLOS 1982.
9 The existing installations or structures in the area could be used for mutual benefit.
10 The establishment of a joint development or joint cooperation zone presupposes that the parties concerned should refrain from further occupation unless agreed by all parties.
11 The existing occupation in the disputed area should not be used for military purposes and that transparency with regard to activities in the area would increase the prospect for the development of an effective joint cooperation.

The Study Group participants agreed on the following:

1 The previous experience of fisheries cooperation between China and Japan in the East China Sea, which evolved from commercial links, was a highly functional and successful approach, conducive to the alleviation of tensions while providing a stable regime for resource development and conservation.
2 The joint development agreements in the Timor Gap between Australia and Indonesia (now between Timor Leste and Australia), and in the Gulf of Thailand between Malaysia and Thailand, and between Malaysia and Vietnam, were successful in that they enabled petroleum production to proceed to the satisfaction and benefit of all parties. Participants also agreed that

there were elements of these three arrangements which might have utility in the South China Sea, and which would not prejudice the position of any authority.

3 It would be beneficial to hold informal meetings in the region to exchange views over the possibility of joint cooperation, starting with the least controversial matters, in a defined zone in the area.

Finally, I would say that perhaps now the time has come to begin again the serious study of the concept of joint development/joint cooperation and its application in the South China Sea area. Hopefully, the initiative taken by the National Institute for South China Sea Studies on this matter will continue and bring about the implementation of the concept in the South China Sea area as envisaged originally by the Chinese Prime Minister in 1991 (at the beginning of the workshop process) and subsequently attempted by the later workshop process. As I have said on many occasions, we should be able to formulate and agree at least on four basic points, such as:

1 The 'zone' where we are going to cooperate or jointly develop
2 The 'nature', the 'subject' or the 'topics' that we are hoping to cooperate on (fisheries, minerals, gas, oil, environment, marine scientific research, marine parks, and so forth)
3 The 'mechanism' for such joint development, which could be an authority or a loose coordinative organization or arrangement
4 'Who' shall participate in such joint development or joint cooperative activities.

10 Natural resources and inter-state cooperation and competition in the South China Sea[1]

Ralf Emmers

Natural resources and energy needs have traditionally influenced the foreign policy objectives of states. The implications for conflict are obvious when you consider the finite nature of such resources. The increased demand coupled with a decreased availability of resources has the potential to aggravate existing tensions and instigate violent conflict. Nevertheless, one should also discuss the significance of living and non-living natural resources as a source of inter-state cooperation rather than competition. Key here is the possibility for the joint exploration and development of resources as a means to reduce tensions and improve the climate of relations.

A joint development agreement (JDA) is defined in this chapter 'as an agreement by two or more States whereby they pool their sovereign rights for the exploration and exploitation of natural resources and other purposes in a defined maritime area, which provides for the management of activities and the apportionment of production and/or resources'.[2] Joint exploration and development schemes are not intended to be boundary agreements. Instead, they are meant to temporarily set aside boundary negotiations so that the joint development of natural resources might proceed on an agreed basis within a specific period of time. The economic benefits of concluding a joint development agreement are clear. It enables claimant states to diversify their sources of energy and benefit economically from the exploitation of fisheries and hydrocarbon resources despite the existence of overlapping sovereignty claims.

The joint exploration of resources combined with the temporary shelving of the sovereignty question is generally discussed as the only feasible option to enhance cooperation and stability in the South China Sea. Beckman stresses that it would be 'necessary to first negotiate a framework document that "shelves" or "freezes" existing claims and sets out the principles upon which cooperation and joint development can proceed'.[3] The Timor Gap Treaty between Australia and Indonesia and the Gulf of Tonkin (Beibu) Treaty between the People's Republic of China (PRC) and Vietnam have been regarded as possible models on which to establish a joint exploration and exploitation scheme for the South China Sea. This chapter explores the prospect for JDAs in the South China Sea and asks whether the joint management of natural resources in the absence of a negotiated maritime delimitation constitutes a feasible strategy to de-escalate the maritime sovereignty disputes.

The Demand for natural resources

Fisheries

The littoral states of the South China Sea are increasingly dependent on fish stocks, as fish consumption provides a large percentage of total protein in-take in Asian countries. The South China Sea is said to account for 'as much as one-tenth of the fishing catch landed globally'.[4] China is currently the world's largest consumer of marine resources and consumes about 694 million tonnes of ocean resources each year.[5] As the purchasing power of the Chinese rises, their interest in a more diversified and nutritious diet also increases. Seafood consumption is no exception, with per capita consumption for urban residents at 14.85 kg in 2008.[6] Due to rising domestic consumption, China has to import additional aquatic products making it the sixth largest importer of ocean resources. Taiwan has a deep seafood culture and an annual per capita fishery consumption of 45 kg.[7]

Rising demand for food in Southeast Asia is expected to put additional pressure on natural resources in the region, including aquatic products. In the Philippines, fish consumption has steadily grown in both urban and rural areas in recent years, as the volume of fish production continues to increase and fishery products remain an important source of protein for its population. The country's per capita consumption is 53 kg annually. Meanwhile, other major fishery producers in the region such as Vietnam, Thailand and Malaysia have annual per capita consumption of 41.47 kg, 37.97 kg and 54.40 kg respectively.[8]

Fishery production and exports have been on the rise in East Asia to meet growing demand. China is the largest Asian exporter of fishery products contributing about 10 per cent to the global export value in 2008.[9] It is also the world's largest fish-producing country, as it was able to harvest approximately 54.6 million tonnes of fish and invertebrates in 2011.[10] That same year, China's total aquatic trade value stood at US$21.7 billion. The total fishery production of Taiwan reached 1.5 million tonnes in 2007.[11] The Southeast Asian nations exported approximately 14 per cent of the world's total export volume in 2008, with Thailand and Vietnam being the two largest Southeast Asian exporters of fish and fishery products. The Philippines is the second largest producer in Southeast Asia and one of the largest fish producers in the world.

Excessive and unsustainable fishing practices as well as land-based pollution, coral reef damage and other factors have exacerbated the depletion of fisheries in the East Asian seas. Over the last 40 years, it is estimated that fishery resources in Southeast Asia have been reduced to 25 per cent, or less, of their former levels.[12] Some researchers have even estimated that the region's fish stocks have declined to between 5 and 30 per cent of their unexploited levels.[13] Declining fish stocks in disputed East Asian waters have led to a further overexploitation of fisheries rather than the joint management of marine resources.[14]

It is not only traditional commercial fishing that has worsened the situation but also widespread illegal, unreported and unregulated fishing. Illegal fishing has, for example, been a rampant problem in Philippine territorial waters, which are lightly guarded by the Philippine maritime authorities. Chinese and Vietnamese fishermen have been caught fishing in the country's territorial waters.[15] Similarly, large foreign fishing vessels enter Vietnamese waters illegally to harvest tonnes of ocean resources every year. Fishermen and coast guards have often clashed violently. Finally, alleged illegal fishing has been a regular cause of diplomatic tension between the claimant states. Fisheries incidents in disputed maritime areas have often provoked a stronger community response and raised greater nationalistic sentiments than incidents involving seismic vessels.

Hydrocarbons

Besides the fisheries question, the South China Sea has become increasingly critical to the littoral states because of their growing need for hydrocarbon resources. China's economic growth is dependent on maintaining a secure energy supply. The political and economic future of the country is directly linked to its ability to meet consumer demand and the industrial requirements of an expanding modern economy.[16] Efforts to offset reliance on coal due to its negative environmental impact include a rising dependency on oil reserves. China's energy situation has, as a result, become a concern to the international community.[17] In 1990, China was able to export US$2.8 billion in oil to Japan. By 1993, the Chinese were themselves oil importers. By 2008, the PRC had to import half of its needs. Chinese oil consumption has surged at 7 to 8 per cent per annum in recent years. The situation is expected to grow even worse in the future as energy needs are projected to double from their 2000 levels by 2020.[18] By 2030, it is estimated that China will import 80 per cent of the oil it consumes.[19]

Energy is a major concern for Taipei. Taiwan is largely considered energy poor. Mineral deposits found on the island are not commercially viable. Moreover, in contrast to China, coal production is only able to meet a small proportion of the island's demands. Efforts to diversify sources have included the introduction of nuclear power, as well as increasing importation of coal, oil and natural gas from Southeast Asian and Middle Eastern countries.

With regard to hydrocarbon resources, Vietnam is not as deficient as China. The country is an exporter of both coal and crude oil, additionally producing adequate supplies of natural gas for its own consumption.[20] Yet economic development has increased demand for electricity, straining government capacity. While plans to develop an operating nuclear power plant by 2020 have also been introduced, the issue of energy security remains an important concern for the country.

A priority for the Philippines is attaining domestic stability and continued economic growth. Guaranteeing access to hydrocarbon resources remains a source of concern for Manila. For the Philippines, as for other developing countries in Southeast Asia, achieving economic growth is dependent on securing an adequate energy supply. Recent years have seen a rise in oil production, as offshore deposits have been exploited. Natural gas production has also increased of late. The Philippines additionally imports coal from Indonesia, China and Australia. Thus, the future economic strength and political stability of the Philippines will partly depend on its government's ability to ensure its energy security.

Malaysia is an important exporter of oil and natural gas. It has some of the largest proven reserves of oil and gas among the Southeast Asian states. Malaysia's production of oil alone accounts for a large percentage of the entire Southeast Asian production. The country remains Southeast Asia's largest net exporter of oil. Such an advantage has placed Malaysia in contention with a few of its neighbours, particularly as its wealth of natural resources relies partly on its off-shore claims. Finally, the national economy of the Sultanate of Brunei has been exceptionally prosperous due to its large oil and natural gas reserves.

The resource capacity of the South China Sea

Economic interests have influenced the South China Sea disputes. The semi-enclosed sea is economically important due to its fishing and hydrocarbon resources. Long-term fishing productivity in the South China Sea is declining due to over-fishing, coral reef damage and growing coastal pollution. Particular fishing techniques like dynamite and cyanide fishing, as well as bottom trawling, have all contributed to the fisheries depletion, which has become increasingly noticeable. For example, China's fish harvest in the semi-enclosed sea dropped from 5 million tonnes in 1989 to 3.4 million in 2005.[21] It is now estimated that 40 per cent of the fish stocks in the South China Sea have disappeared while 70 per cent of its coral reefs are in poor or fair condition.[22] Lyons and Davenport argue that 'the risk of overfishing and destructive fishing methods resulting in a permanent change to the marine environment is particularly acute'.[23] The declining long-term productivity of the fish stocks accentuates the need for cooperative fisheries management in the semi-enclosed sea.

Besides fisheries, the South China Sea is economically important due to its expected oil and gas reserves. Zhang Dawei, an official at China's Ministry of Land Resources, has optimistically claimed that the South China Sea might hold an estimated 23 to 40 billion tonnes in oil reserves, or 168 to 220 billion barrels.[24] This would constitute a greater amount than China's onshore resources. Additionally, the PRC has estimated the disputed areas to contain more than 2,000 trillion cubic feet (Tcf) of natural gas reserves.[25] If this were accurate, natural gas would be the most abundant resource in the South China Sea. Unsurprisingly, expectation of resource availability has encouraged the Philippines, Malaysia and Vietnam to control a number of islands and has been partly responsible for China's increased activity in the area.

The existence of vast commercially viable quantities of hydrocarbon resources has nonetheless been questioned. Despite the data circulated by some Chinese sources, a 1993/1994 US geological survey, for example, put the number of oil reserves at 28 billion barrels.[26] The US Energy Information Administration lists proven oil reserves at 960 million tonnes, or 7 billion barrels.[27] A 1995 study by the Russian Research Institute of Geology of Foreign Countries estimates that there is only 6 billion barrels worth, 70 per cent of which would be natural gas.[28]

One of the more optimistic Western estimates places total natural gas resources in the Spratlys at 35 Tcf.[29] Rowan stated in 2005 that 'this region retains proven oil reserves of seven billion barrels and a production capacity of 2.5 million barrels per day'.[30]

In short, the quantity of oil and gas reserves of the South China Sea has generally remained uncertain and initial estimations have been revised to lower figures.[31] Moreover, as mentioned above, estimates have varied greatly. While Western studies have often referred to reserves of up to 30 billion barrels of oil and 16 Tcf, similar Chinese studies have claimed that the South China Sea may hold up to 200 billion barrels and more substantial gas reserves. Roughly only 10 per cent of the resources are generally recovered from the overall reserves – the resources constituting the commercially and technically exploitable reserves found.[32] However, it should be stressed that the perception that the South China Sea is rich in oil and gas matters more than variations in reserve estimates when seeking to explain the ongoing rivalry over maritime resources.

Resource management in the South China Sea

Fisheries

No bilateral or multilateral fisheries agreement has so far been negotiated in the South China Sea, except for the Vietnam–PRC agreement for the Gulf of Tonkin (Beibu) that took effect in 2004. Beijing and Hanoi have failed to reach a similar agreement covering other parts of the South China Sea where their claims overlap. This is particularly due to their sovereignty dispute over the Paracel and Spratly Islands.[33] This makes the semi-enclosed sea one of the few East Asian seas where no cooperative agreement has been reached. The need for cooperation in the conservation and exploitation of marine resources is critical to address illegal and over-fishing, coral reef damage, coastal pollution and poor fishing practices detrimental to the marine ecosystem. Yet, the declining trends and environmental concerns have increased rather than reduced fishing activity in the South China Sea, as an attempt by countries both to exploit what they see to be their sovereign resources and to defend their claims against others. The lack of progress thus derives from the fact that the fisheries issue is woven into the sovereignty question.

The absence of a cooperative arrangement can be contrasted to the situation in the Sea of Japan and the East China Sea where successful bilateral fisheries agreements have been reached despite the sovereignty disputes involving, respectively, South Korea and Japan, and China, Japan and Taiwan. Discussing the South China Sea situation, Lyons and Davenport explain that 'the difference between the fishing capacity of the Claimants makes the reaching of a cooperation agreement particularly challenging. Claimants which rely on smaller fishing vessels and traditional and artisanal fishing methods (notably Vietnam and the Philippines) cannot compete with China's industrial fisheries.'[34] In contrast, the arrangements on fisheries cooperation established in the Sea of Japan and the East China Sea, which came into force in 1999 and 2000 respectively, can partly be explained by the fact that China, Japan and South Korea have similar commercial fishing capabilities, which eased the reaching of an agreement.

Furthermore, besides the difference in fishing capabilities, the sheer number of claimants in the South China Sea complicates the issue and hinders cooperation, as there are multiple sets of national interests competing with each other. Hence, unlike in the Sea of Japan and the East China Sea, bilateral agreements in the South China Sea may not work well since the territorial disputes affect more than two countries.

Hydrocarbons

The prospect for the joint development of hydrocarbon resources in the South China Sea has been under discussion since the early 1990s. Chinese Premier Li Peng already stated in 1990 that Beijing was ready to shelve the issue of sovereignty in favour of joint development in the semi-enclosed sea. Nonetheless, diplomatic commitment to the joint development of hydrocarbon resources has not been translated into action. On the contrary, energy considerations have repeatedly escalated the situation.

Tensions eased somewhat with the signing of the Declaration on the Conduct of Parties in the South China Sea (DOC) by the PRC and members of the Association of Southeast Asian Nations (ASEAN) in November 2002. This was followed by China, the Philippines and Vietnam concluding a three-year agreement in March 2005 designating their state-owned oil companies to conduct a joint seismic study in the South China Sea. This deal had originally been signed by China and the Philippines in 2004 before Vietnam joined in 2005.

The Joint Marine Seismic Undertaking (JMSU) took effect on 1 July 2005. It was a commercial rather than a political agreement between the Philippine National Oil Company, the China National Offshore Oil Company and the Vietnam Oil and Gas Corporation. Despite the agreement having been signed by oil companies rather than national governments, which was expected to simplify the process, no Taiwanese party was invited to take part in the undertaking. The agreement was heralded by the parties involved as a significant breakthrough. For example, Philippine President Gloria Arroyo deemed the JMSU to be a 'diplomatic breakthrough for peace and security in the region'.[35]

The signing of the JMSU was welcomed as a first attempt at de-escalating the resource question. The signing of such an agreement guaranteed that Manila and Hanoi be at least included in the exploration process in areas where they have overlapping sovereignty claims with Beijing. The JMSU was not a joint development agreement, however, but simply an initial joint seismic survey. Such surveys are meant to determine the size of the available hydrocarbon resources and thus often precede the negotiation of a JDA.

The significance of the JMSU was rapidly questioned, however. Some analysts were critical about whether the JMSU should be regarded as a step in the right direction. The JMSU did arguably weaken ASEAN solidarity on the South China Sea question by encouraging the individual Southeast Asian claimants to negotiate directly and unilaterally, rather than as a group, with the PRC. Dosch argued, for instance, that it reflected 'a new strategic setting in which the Southeast Asian claimants compete for the most favorable bilateral or multilateral agreements with China'.[36] The JMSU expired on 30 June 2008 and was never extended by the parties involved, partly due to domestic opposition in the Philippines. The failure of the JMSU was therefore a reminder that such undertakings can be undermined by domestic politics.[37]

Some progress towards the joint development of hydrocarbon resources was made in 2009. The Malaysian state-owned company Petronas and the Brunei National Petroleum Company signed a commercial agreement on the joint exploration and production of oil and gas in two deep-water blocks offshore the Brunei–Sarawak border in the South China Sea. The agreement followed the bilateral resolution of the Limbang land and maritime boundary issues. Significantly, Malaysia agreed to give up its territorial claims over the respective blocks disputed with Brunei in exchange for Petronas being allowed to take part in the joint development of their hydrocarbon resources.[38] It is too soon to say whether this commercial agreement, involving one party renouncing its sovereign rights in exchange for its participation in a joint development scheme, may constitute a new cooperative approach applicable elsewhere in the South China Sea.

During a visit by Vietnam's Communist Party Leader Nguyen PhuTrong to Beijing in October 2011, both countries signed an 'agreement on basic principles guiding the settlement of sea issues', which referred once again to the joint development of resources. Yet, after years of bilateral negotiations, the PRC and Vietnam have been unable to make progress towards the negotiation of a joint development agreement in the disputed waters.[39] This is in contrast to the settlement of their land border dispute in 1999 and the negotiation of the delimitation of their exclusive economic zones (EEZs) and continental shelves in the Gulf of Tonkin (Beibu).

In 2011, Benigno S. Aquino, Philippine president since June 2010, tabled a proposal to resolve the South China Sea disputes. The proposal, called the Zone of Peace, Freedom, Friendship and Cooperation (ZoPFFC), advocated 'a multilateral, rule-based approach to the disputes, in contrast to China's oft-stated preference for bilateral talks'.[40] Significantly, it aimed to 'segregate' disputed from non-disputed areas in the South China Sea as a starting point in negotiating joint cooperation and development zones. ZoPFFC called for the establishment of 'enclaves' of disputed areas in the Spratlys where progress could be made towards the implementation of a code of conduct as well as the demilitarization of the disputed reefs and the establishment of a joint development agency. Furthermore, under ZoPFFC, the joint exploration of resources would be excluded within non-disputed areas, as states would instead be allowed to develop resources unilaterally within their defined EEZ and continental shelf.

President Aquino therefore recommended a 'what is disputed can be shared' formula to be applied to the disputed Spratly Islands in the South China Sea. The ZoPFFC proposal was notably different from the JMSU, which had allowed for joint seismic surveys to be conducted within the Philippine 200 nm EEZ.

Illustrating this shift, Aquino rejected in February 2012 a Chinese offer to jointly explore for hydrocarbon resources in areas that the Philippines does not consider to be disputed with Beijing. One of these areas, Reed Bank off Palawan Island, is expected to hold natural gas reserves of at least 3.4 Tcf, making it possibly the Philippines' largest natural gas field. Manila offered three exploration contracts at Reed Bank in late July 2012. Yet, to avoid upsetting Beijing, none of the large oil and gas companies entered bids, as two of these areas overlapped with Chinese claims.[41]

The PRC rejected the ZoPFFC proposal, presumably because the maritime areas claimed by the Philippines to be non-disputed fall within the U-shaped line. The ASEAN members failed to reach a consensus, with only Vietnam supporting the proposal. Acting as Chair, at the ASEAN summit held in Bali in November 2011, Indonesia repeated through its Foreign Minister Marty Natalegawa that ASEAN remained committed to the adoption with Beijing of a regional code of conduct for the South China Sea.[42]

In short, over the years the PRC has developed its own capabilities to explore and exploit hydrocarbon resources in the South China Sea. China's deep-water oil and gas exploration technologies have continued to advance rapidly. China has simultaneously called for the joint development of resources in the South China Sea. The Southeast Asian states have generally supported in principle the idea of joint development in disputed areas defined in accordance with the principles of the United Nations Convention on the Law of the Sea (UNCLOS). The Malaysia–Brunei commercial agreement negotiated in 2009 constitutes a successful example of joint management of hydrocarbon resources. While all the claimants have rhetorically been committed to joint development and various proposals have been tabled, no JDA has so far been signed between the PRC and a Southeast Asian claimant state. Beckman notes that joint development agreements may only be concluded in the South China Sea once all the claimants have clarified their ambiguous claims in conformity with UNCLOS.[43]

Furthermore, since 2010, there has been an increase in the number of incidents all over the South China Sea involving the harassment of survey vessels, the cutting of cables and the repeated arrest of fishermen. The most significant escalation occurred in April 2012 with Chinese and Philippine vessels involved in a stand-off at Scarborough Shoal in the South China Sea. Significantly, these events coincided with the Philippines and the United States holding their annual military exercises on Palawan Island.[44] Philippine naval authorities had discovered several Chinese fishing vessels anchored at the Shoal disputed by both China and the Philippines. A Philippine navy ship attempted to arrest the Chinese fishermen allegedly accused of poaching and illegal fishing. Two Chinese maritime surveillance ships intervened, however, and prevented the arrest from occurring. The Scarborough Shoal incident led to a tense stand-off between the Philippine navy ship and the Chinese maritime vessels and eventually resulted in tensions between Beijing and Manila that lasted for several weeks.[45] Unsurprisingly, the escalation of the situation further complicated the negotiation of a JDA between the parties involved.

Nevertheless, it should be noted that the climate of diplomatic relations over the South China Sea issue improved somewhat in 2013. In April 2013 Beijing proposed a special meeting involving the foreign ministers from the ASEAN countries and China to hasten progress on the negotiation of a code of conduct (COC) for the South China Sea. China and the ASEAN states agreed at the 2013 ASEAN Ministerial Meeting held in Brunei to start formal consultations on a COC in September 2013. At a High-level Forum held in Bangkok on 2 August 2013, Chinese Foreign Minister Wang Yi also called for dialogue and the joint development of resources in the South China Sea. The need to prevent a further escalation of the sovereignty disputes in the South China Sea was expressed again at the ASEAN–China foreign ministers' meeting in Beijing and at the second Asian Defence Ministers' Meeting-Plus in Brunei in August 2013. The first consultations on a COC were eventually held at the 9th ASEAN–China Joint Working Group Meeting on the Implementation of the DOC held in Suzhou in September 2013. Finally, Chinese Premier Li Keqiang called for peace and cooperation in the South China Sea at the ASEAN–China Summit held in Brunei in October 2013. The signing of a legally binding COC would certainly help to build trust and confidence among the claimant states and to establish a conflict management mechanism. It is too soon to say, however, how these diplomatic developments may influence the negotiation of a JDA in the years to come.

Conclusions

Little progress has so far been made towards the joint development of resources in the South China Sea. For fisheries, the multilateral nature of the disputes and the differences in fishing capacity partly explain the absence of a cooperative agreement. Oil and gas exploration in off-shore areas is a capital-intensive activity with no guarantee of commercial success. There is also generally a 10-year gap between the discovery of hydrocarbon resources and their ultimate exploitation. Moreover, claimant states often need to rely on funds and the expertise of private oil and gas companies to exploit their seabed resources. Yet, due to the high costs of exploration and exploitation, such companies are 'reluctant to operate in disputed territory', as they prefer the disputes over maritime delimitation to be resolved first.[46]

Furthermore, a joint development scenario is not risk free, especially for the weaker claimant states. Even if the size of the oil and gas reserves is finally determined, the disputants would still have to decide on how to share these commodities. Beyond the joint exploration of resources, reaching an agreement on their common exploitation will ultimately be more complex. The asymmetry in power capabilities and the absence of an overall agreement on the sovereign rights of the coastal states could affect the negotiating position of the weaker parties as well as leaving them vulnerable if conditions were to change in the disputed areas. To prevent such a scenario from occurring, a joint development agreement should be as clearly negotiated and specific as possible.

So what explains the ongoing failure to conclude cooperative agreements in the South China Sea? The negotiation of such agreements and their potential de-escalating attributes have been undermined by rising nationalism and diplomatic tensions. Cooperative resource exploitation cannot be separated from nationalist considerations and power politics calculations. Nationalist sentiments have constituted a stumbling block towards the joint management of resources in disputed waters. Moreover, the rising perception of military power as a useful instrument to guarantee access to natural resources has led to a further escalation of the maritime territorial disputes. Collaborative resource schemes are dependent on an improvement in inter-state relations before they can be negotiated and implemented successfully. Yet, wider geopolitical considerations have transformed the dynamics of the South China Sea disputes and once again confirmed the resource question as a source of inter-state competition rather than cooperation.

Notes

1 This chapter draws from R. Emmers, *Resource Management and Contested Territories in East Asia*, Basingstoke: Palgrave Macmillan, 2013.
2 T. Davenport, I. Townsend-Gault, R. Beckman, C. Schofield, D. Ong, V. Becker-Weinberg and L. Bernard, *Conference Report*, Conference on Joint Development and the South China Sea, organized by the Centre for International Law, June 2011, p. 14.
3 R. Beckman, 'Legal regimes for cooperation in the South China Sea', in S. Bateman and R. Emmers (eds), *Security and International Politics in the South China Sea: Towards a Cooperative Management Regime*, Abingdon: Routledge, 2009, pp. 222–235, at p. 233.
4 'The devil in the deep blue detail', *The Economist*, 4 February 2012.
5 'China, Japan, US lead fish consumption-report', *Reuters*, 22 September 2010, available at www.worldfishing.net/news101/report-china,-japan,-us-lead-fish-consumption.
6 Global Agriculture Information Network, *People's Republic of China Annual Fishery Products*, Washington DC: GAIN, 2011, p. 7.
7 'Seafood to Taiwan: trends and opportunities', 21 November 2011, available at www.austrade.gov.au/Seafood-to-Taiwan/default.aspx.
8 Southeast Asian Fisheries Development Center, *The Southeast Asian State of Fisheries and Aquaculture 2012*, Bangkok: SEAFDEC, 2012, p. 100.
9 Ibid., p. 21.
10 Global Agriculture Information Network, *People's Republic of China Annual Fishery Products*, p. 4.
11 World Fishing, *Taiwan*, 1 December 2009, available at www.worldfishing.net/features101/new-horizons/taiwan.
12 Southeast Asian Fisheries Development Center, *The Southeast Asian State of Fisheries and Aquaculture 2012*, p. 66.
13 L. R. Garces, M. D. Pido and R. S. Pomeroy, 'Fisheries in Southeast Asia: challenges and opportunities', in A. Pandya and E. Laipson (eds), *Transnational Trends – Middle Eastern and Asian Views*, Washington DC: Henry L. Stimson Center, 2008, pp. 171–182, at p. 175.
14 D. Rosenberg, 'Fisheries management in the South China Sea', in S. Bateman and R. Emmers (eds), *Security and International Politics in the South China Sea: Towards a Cooperative Management Regime*, Abingdon: Routledge, 2009, pp. 61–79.
15 'Philippines arrests 122 Vietnamese fishermen', *Agence France-Presse*, 30 May 2011, available at http://globalnation.inquirer.net/2684/philippines-arrests-122-vietnamese-fishermen.
16 M. T. Klare, *Resource Wars*, New York: Henry Holt, 2001, p. 115.

17 See P. Andrews-Speed and R. Dannreuther, *China, Oil and Global Politics*, Abingdon: Routledge, 2011.
18 Klare, *Resource Wars*, p. 113.
19 P. K. Lee, 'China's quest for oil security: oil (wars) in the pipeline?', *Pacific Review*, 18(2), 2005, pp. 265–301.
20 Energy Information Administration, *Country Analysis Briefs: Vietnam*, 2006, available at http://www.eai.doe.gov/emeu/cabs/Vietnam/Full.html.
21 K. Sato, *South China Sea: China's Rise and Implications for Security Cooperation*, 2011, available at http://nghiencuubiendong.vn/en/conferences-and-seminars-/the-third-international-workshop-on-south-china-sea/645-south-china-sea-chinas-rise-and-implications-for-security-cooperation-by-koichi-sato.
22 H. L. Wang, *Joint Development of Marine Fisheries Resources*, 2011, available at http://nghiencuubiendong.vn/en/conferences-and-seminars-/second-international-workshop/598-join-development-of-marine-fisheries-resources-by-wang-hanling.
23 Y. Lyons and T. Davenport, 'South China Sea: limits to commercial fishing by claimants', *RSIS Commentaries*, No. 113, Singapore: S. Rajaratnam School of International Studies, 3 July 2012.
24 L. Buszynski and I. Sazlan, 'Maritime claims and energy cooperation in the South China Sea', *Contemporary Southeast Asia*, 29(1), 2007, pp. 143–171, at p. 156.
25 E. Kreil, 'Energy issues in the South China Sea region', in J. C. Baker and D. G. Wiencek (eds), *Cooperative Monitoring in the South China Sea*, Westport, CT: Praeger, 2002, pp. 35–48, at p. 43.
26 Ibid., p. 42.
27 Buszynski and Sazlan, 'Maritime claims and energy cooperation in the South China Sea', p. 156.
28 See S. Snyder, 'The South China Sea dispute: prospects for preventive diplomacy', *Special Report 18*, Washington DC: United States Institute of Peace, 1996.
29 Kreil, 'Energy issues in the South China Sea region', p. 43.
30 J. P. Rowan, 'The US-Japan security alliance, ASEAN, and the South China Sea dispute', *Asian Survey*, 45(3), 2005, pp. 414–436, at p. 417.
31 See N. A. Owen and C. H. Schofield, 'Disputed South China Sea hydrocarbons in perspective', *Marine Policy*, 36(3), 2012, pp. 809–822.
32 Ibid.
33 D. T. Nguyen, *China's Fishing Ban in the South China Sea: implications for Territorial Disputes*', *RSIS Commentaries*, No. 89, Singapore: S. Rajaratnam School of International Studies, 9 June 2011.
34 Lyons and Davenport, 'South China Sea: limits to commercial fishing by claimants'.
35 L. Baguioro, 'Three nations sign pact for joint Spratlys survey', *Straits Times*, 15 March 2005.
36 J. Dosch, 'Managing security in ASEAN–China relations: liberal peace of hegemonic stability', *Asian Perspective*, 31(1), 2007, pp. 209–236, at p. 222.
37 T. Davenport et al., *Conference Report*, p. 37.
38 Ibid., p. 20.
39 B. Wain, 'Navigating tensions in the South China Sea', *Straits Times*, 18 November 2011.
40 A. San Pablo-Baviera, 'The South China Sea disputes: is the Aquino Way the "ASEAN Way"?', *RSIS Commentaries*, No. 4, Singapore: S. Rajaratnam School of International Studies, 5 January 2012.
41 J. Guintoand and D. T. Kate, 'Oil majors avoid Philippine bids for China-claimed sea blocks', *Bloomberg*, 31 July 2012.
42 San Pablo-Baviera, 'The South China Sea disputes'.
43 R. Beckman, 'The South China Sea disputes: how states can clarify their maritime

claims', *RSIS Commentaries*, No. 140, Singapore: S. Rajaratnam School of International Studies, 31 July 2012.

44 'Shoal mates: America's navy riles China in its backyard', *The Economist*, 28 April 2012.

45 M. Santos, 'Poaching triggers Scarborough stand-off', *Philippine Daily Inquirer*, 11 April 2012; M. Valencia, 'Current spat may be a sign of future tensions', *Straits Times*, 14 May 2012.

46 S. Tønnesson, 'China's changing role in the South China Sea: Reflections of a scholar's workshop', *Harvard Asia Quarterly*, 12(3–4), Winter 2010, pp. 18–30, at p. 26.

11 Joint development prospects in the South China Sea

Divergent and convergent forces

Vannarith Chheang

The disputes over the South China Sea between the claimant states Brunei, China, Malaysia, the Philippines and Vietnam have been the main flashpoints in the region and remain top of the regional security agenda, especially following the resurgence of tensions in the 2000s. There are varying approaches toward managing the disputes including joint development, which was initially proposed by the then Chinese leader Deng Xiaoping in the late 1980s when he suggested that the states put aside sovereignty disputes and focus on joint cooperation and development. However, there has been limited progress in implementing joint development due to a lack of strategic trust and confidence, and the absence of appropriate regional arrangements. This chapter reviews current developments and explores the divergent and convergent forces influencing the implementation of joint development in the South China Sea.

The South China Sea: regional strategic significance

The South China Sea has both regional and global strategic, security and economic significance because it is one of the busiest international sea routes and repository of energy and fishery resources in East Asia. The increasing national interests attached to the South China Sea, especially with regard to resources security and sea routes, have created a new level of economic and strategic competition between the claimant states. The South China Sea has been the subject of serious security concerns in the region and the situation has fluctuated depending on the level of mutual strategic trust and cooperation and sovereignty assertiveness between the claimant states.

Recent tensions in the South China Sea are a serious concern as the region has a high potential for security risks and wider regional security implications. The claimant states, particularly the Philippines and Vietnam, have expressed their concern over the increasing Chinese threat and China's assertiveness in the South China Sea and have called for the internationalization of the issue with the support and engagement of other major powers especially the United States.

However, from the Chinese point of view, disputes concerning the South China Sea should be dealt with between the parties directly involved, based on mutual trust, respect and benefits. During a press conference at the 2nd ASEAN Defence Ministers' Meeting-Plus in Brunei in August 2013, the Chinese Defense Minister stated:

> It is true that there are disputes between China and some ASEAN countries over territory, sovereignty, and the maritime rights and interests. However, these disputes are by no means the mainstream of regional security situation. These are not the problems between China and ASEAN. ASEAN is not a concerned party. Therefore, these disputes should not and will not undermine the overall relationship between China and ASEAN. As for the disputes, the Chinese side as always advocates that these disputes should be properly handled by the directly concerned countries. We oppose any actions and statements trying to confuse right and wrong in this regard of historical facts. And we oppose any attempt to internationalize, escalate, or complicate the disputes. We are ready to work together with the ASEAN countries to make active efforts to jointly maintain regional peace and stability.[1]

The South China Sea has become a strategic game between the major powers in the region and this is threatening the role of the relevant regional institution – ASEAN. ASEAN's centrality in shaping regional architecture has been questioned with regard to the South China Sea due to lack of unity and consensus among its member states. The failure of the 45th ASEAN Foreign Ministers' Meeting in July 2012 illustrated ASEAN disunity on such sensitive and divided issues. Different countries have different calculations of and emphasis on national interests. Almost all ASEAN member states are interested in and determined to build closer relations with China and they are cautious about taking any position that could harm their bilateral relations with China. Other areas of cooperation need to be implemented and the unresolved disputes in the South China Sea should not spill over into these other fields of cooperation.

Some countries have raised concerns about the freedom of navigation and sea lines of communication (SLOC) in the South China Sea since they could threaten their long-term economic and strategic interests. The concern comes from China's nine-dashed line claims over the South China Sea and the rebalancing strategy of the United States in the region. In addition, different understandings and interpretations of the freedom of navigation are further complicating the issue, in particular over exclusive economic zones (EEZs).

The reality is that freedom of navigation in the South China Sea has been normal and stable without interruption. However, a common understanding and application of the concept of freedom of navigation in the South China Sea is required and such a concept should not be politicized and monopolized. With regard to the safety issue, piracy, maritime terrorism and extreme natural events remain the key challenge in the South China Sea. Regional cooperation in coping with the safety issue is increasing. Information sharing and capacity-building mechanisms are the two main areas of regional cooperation.

Convergent forces

Rules based

Various approaches and mechanisms have been developed to contain and possibly manage the tensions in the area. In 2002, China and ASEAN adopted a Declaration on the Conduct of Parties in the South China Sea (DOC) and in 2011 they adopted the guidelines to implement the DOC. In 2012, ASEAN issued a six-point joint statement on the South China Sea and China, and in September 2013 ASEAN started official negotiations on the code of conduct for the South China Sea.

The DOC is so far the leading regional cooperation tool dealing with the South China Sea. It provides a legal and cooperation framework for the concerned parties. For the legal framework, the emphasis is on the Charter of the United Nations, the 1982 UN Convention on the Law of the Sea (UNCLOS), the Treaty of Amity and Cooperation in Southeast Asia, the Five Principles of Peaceful Coexistence and other universally recognized principles of international law which shall serve as the basic norms governing state-to-state relations.

The Guidelines for Implementation of the DOC add several new elements to the DOC, for example that the progress of the implementation of the agreed activities and projects under the DOC shall be reported annually to the ASEAN–China Ministerial Meeting, that the decision to implement concrete measures or activities of the DOC should be based on consensus among the parties concerned, and should lead to the eventual realization of a code of conduct, and that the services of the experts and eminent persons are welcomed if necessary.

As we move toward the realization of the code of conduct (COC), consideration needs to be given to reinforcing the principles of international laws, especially UNCLOS, and to reemphasizing security identity and cooperation to manage and solve disputes based on peaceful means and mutual trust and interests. Elements of preventative diplomacy and crisis management are also required, and the recent establishment of hotline communication between China and Vietnam could be expanded to include all the claimant states.

Trust based

At the strategic level, there are different confidence-building measures in both bilateral and multilateral dimensions. The Treaty of Amity of Cooperation (TAC), the DOC in November 2002 and the Guidelines for the Implementation of the DOC in July 2011 are regarded as the key regional tools to maintain peace and stability in the South China Sea.

As far as the interstate behavior and confidence-building measures are concerned, the DOC focuses on freedom of navigation in and flights over the South China Sea, peaceful means, without resorting to threat or the use of force, self-restraint and the preservation in their current condition of the presently uninhabited islands, reefs, shoals, cays and other features.

For cooperation mechanisms, the DOC encourages dialogue and exchange of views as appropriate between the defense and military officials of the states, ensuring just and humane treatment of all persons who are either in danger or in distress, notifying, on a voluntary basis, other parties concerned of any impending joint/combined military exercises and exchanging, on a voluntary basis, relevant information.

Non-traditional security cooperation is the key factor for confidence-building measures in the region. The cooperation area includes marine environmental protection, marine scientific research, safety of navigation and communication at sea, search and rescue operations, combating transnational crime, including but not limited to trafficking in illicit drugs, piracy and armed robbery at sea, and illegal traffic in arms.

Bilateral and multilateral cooperation on fishery, environmental and biodiversity conservation, and other non-traditional security issues seem to be the areas that need to be improved and strengthened. Such cooperation on less sensitive issues can lead to trust and confidence-building. ASEAN and China have worked hard to cope with the South China Sea issue in the spirit of friendship, good neighborliness and mutual understanding and interests. Both multilateral and bilateral mechanisms have been exercised and applied. Economic cooperation and integration, confidence-building measures and diplomacy are believed to be the key to managing and solving the conflict over the South China Sea.

Economic cooperation

By integrating both trust- and rules-based approaches, the dispute can be effectively managed. Solving the sovereignty disputes in the South China Sea is impossible in the foreseeable future; it is therefore necessary, given the complexity of the issue, to target the low hanging fruits first. Joint cooperation and development between the claimant states are the most achievable outcomes.

At the economic level, it is believed that through economic interdependency the potential for conflict among nation states can be reduced. In the mid-1980s, Deng Xiaoping proposed an economic approach to the South China Sea by 'shelving disputes and seeking joint development'. This philosophy is still relevant and could be the correct path toward regional cooperation. Joint exploration, research and development should be the core for cooperation in the South China Sea. For instance, on 14 March 2005, China, the Philippines and Vietnam signed a tripartite Joint Marine Seismic Undertaking.

In 2010, ASEAN and China signed the China–ASEAN Free Trade Agreement (CAFTA) to promote trade and investment. Now China has become the top trade partner of ASEAN while ASEAN is ranked third in terms of trade with China. Trade volume between China and ASEAN in 2010 was 36 times what it was in 1991. The value of ASEAN–China trade reached US$318.6 billion in 2012, up 13.6 percent from the 2011 figure of US$280.4 billion. If the trade value continues to increase at this rate, it is estimated to hit an all-time high of US$500 billion in 2015.

In addition to CAFTA, there are other de facto and functional economic cooperation schemes in the region, in particular the Pan-Beibu Gulf Economic Cooperation (PBG), which aims to integrate and link economic centers in the region especially in those countries bordering the South China Sea. The PGB comprises China, Vietnam, Malaysia, Singapore, Indonesia, Brunei and the Philippines. It has significantly contributed to building strategic trust and confidence among the claimant states of the South China Sea.

The feasibility study on economic cooperation between China and ASEAN, which was approved by the 14th ASEAN–China Summit in 2012, provides an additional momentum to strengthen economic ties between China and its Southeast Asian neighbors. It focuses cooperation on infrastructure development, ports and logistics, trade and investment facilitation, agriculture, tourism, environmental protection, biodiversity and industrial cooperation. Infrastructure connectivity has gained more attention from the regional countries especially the Nanning–Singapore Economic Corridor (NSEC). NSEC aims to link China with an ASEAN connectivity master plan. It also tries to promote capital flow into the less developed countries in the region, especially Cambodia, Lao PDR, Myanmar and Vietnam, in order to reduce the development gap in the region. The NSEC focuses more on hardware than on software development. The corridor, stretching about 5,000 km, covers expressways, waterways and air routes. A rail connection between Kunming and Singapore has been one of the projects actively implemented by the funding support from China to complete the missing links between China and Lao PDR and Myanmar, Thailand–Cambodia and Cambodia–Vietnam.

Maritime connectivity, which currently includes economic cooperation projects and people-to-people contacts between China and other claimant states in Southeast Asia, positively contributes to building mutual understanding and political trust. China takes a proactive approach to promoting regional maritime connectivity. At the Bali meeting in November 2011, China created a maritime cooperation fund of US$472 million to develop a 'maritime connection network' with Southeast Asian nations. Such a cooperation fund can be enlarged and expanded to cover broader areas of cooperation between China and ASEAN especially in ports connectivity and people exchanges.

Regional mechanisms

The rapid development of regional arrangements centering on ASEAN both in scope and scale have contributed to maintaining peace and stability in the wider East Asian region. The Asian Regional Forum (ARF) established in 1994, the East Asia Summit established in 2005 and the ASEAN Defence Ministers' Meeting-Plus (ADMM-Plus) established in 2010 are the key regional security forums discussing emerging regional security issues and cooperation. These mechanisms, although they are not designed to solve regional conflicts, play a significant role in building strategic trust through routine dialogues and joint efforts in addressing non-traditional security issues. The recent ADMM-Plus joint military exercises hosted by Brunei in 2013 reflect the political will of the member states to promote strategic confidence and mitigate regional security challenges through trust-building and cooperation.

The 20th statement of the ARF in July 2013 stated that:

> The Ministers underscored the importance of maintaining peace and stability in the South China Sea and noted the ASEAN Statement on the Six-Point Principles on the South China Sea. The Ministers stressed the importance of peaceful settlement of disputes through friendly consultations and negotiations by sovereign states directly concerned in accordance with universally recognized principles of international law, including the 1982 United Nations Convention on the Law of the Sea (UNCLOS). The Ministers welcomed the collective commitments of ASEAN Member States and China to fully and effectively implement the Declaration on the Conduct of Parties in the South China Sea (DOC), including the Guidelines for the Implementation of the DOC and to work towards the adoption of a code of conduct in the South China Sea (COC) on the basis of consensus.[2]

Divergent forces

The nature of sovereignty disputes in the South China Sea cannot be solved without mutual strategic trust and common interests. It is a long-term issue; therefore it requires a long-term solution and vision. However, the current development dynamics in the South China Sea reflect the high level of uncertainty and complexity in reaching concrete steps to solve the disputes within a win-win scenario.

Unresolved sovereignty disputes and nationalism are key stumbling blocks in promoting joint development cooperation in the South China Sea. Increasing strategic assertiveness and defense modernization are creating strategic mistrust between the claimant states. The perceived power and strategic competition between China and the United States in the region further complicate the existing regional tensions and distrust.

Tensions in the South China Sea have been on the rise since the late 2000s when various confrontational incidents took place between China and Vietnam, and China and the Philippines, and following the US's rebalancing strategy toward Asia. The increasing assertiveness of China, the active engagement of the US and the gradual strategic indirect intervention from other middle power countries have fueled political distrust between the claimant states, which prevents them from realizing the possibility of joint development projects in the South China Sea.

Conclusions

The South China Sea disputes need to be peacefully managed through different means and approaches. It is a gradual process and things need to be changed from a zero sum game to a win-win position for all the parties; from a blame game to frank dialogue and negotiation; from sticking to one's position to the understanding of motivations; from strategic competition to strategic and economic cooperation and integration; and from nationalism to regional citizenship and interests.

Although there is certain level of strategic mistrust and differences, peace and development are the mainstream and guiding principles of regional cooperation. A peaceful and stable environment, freedom of navigation, international cooperation in addressing non-traditional security issues and joint development are the common interests of the claimant states and other countries, and it is through these means that international trade and the supply of energy and raw materials can be safely conducted.

Thus the approach to the South China Sea issue needs to be holistic. It should combine both economic and strategic dimensions and try to find asymmetric value for cooperation and solutions based on regional interests and the principle of good neighborliness. Joint development cooperation is one approach that can be used to build trust and confidence, based on which win-win cooperation can be realized. Joint development needs to override sovereignty disputes. In other words, the claimants are required to put aside sovereignty issues and focus on joint development cooperation.

Notes

1 Available at http://iipdigital.usembassy.gov/st/english/texttrans/2013/08/20130829281946.html#axzz2e0MMTG5a.

2 Ministry of Foreign Affairs of Japan, at http://www.mofa.go.jp/mofaj/area/asean/arf/pdfs/cs_1307_en.pdf.

Part IV

Towards the future

12 Political will and joint development in the South China Sea

Irene Chan and Li Mingjiang

China and some of its Southeast Asian neighbors – Vietnam, the Philippines, Malaysia and Brunei – have reached an impasse over their competing South China Sea claims. Regional tensions were pushed to new heights by the increasingly confrontational positions taken by the claimants, in particular China, the Philippines and Vietnam. Claimants are also divergent in their pursuit of resolution mechanisms – Manila and Hanoi have actively courted support from the United States and lobbied the Association of Southeast Asian Nations for a multilateral conflict resolution mechanism, while Beijing prefers to resolve the disputes bilaterally although it is agreeable to the multilateral approach. On the other hand, political hardliners, empowered by the growth of domestic nationalism, are pushing governments for a tougher stance on such claims and in the process are further diminishing prospects of conflict resolution.

Given that there are already in existence successful bilateral joint developments on the exploitation of offshore oil and gas deposits straddling overlapping maritime boundaries within the Asia-Pacific region, such a development has been strongly recommended as the best way forward in the South China Sea impasse. However, Townsend-Gault also observed that '(t)he states of the region are not prepared to reduce their differences to legal questions, much less seeking adjudication on issues such as sovereignty'.[1] Legal avenues for resolution, in terms of both principles and machinery, do exist, but they are underutilized due to the strategic and political reluctance of claimants. This underscores Ong's observation that

> it must always be borne in mind that the possibilities for joint development or any other arrangements of co-operative nature will depend very much upon … a clearly defined political will towards the negotiation of such an agreement by the governments concerned. A prerequisite for the adoption of such a stance in favour of co-operation would most certainly be friendly bilateral relations between these countries.[2]

Chief among the many challenges hindering the pursuit of joint development are the claimants' ill-defined political will and increasingly strained relations between China and the other Southeast Asian claimants. The impact of these factors on reaching a joint agreement was evident in the drafting of the Declaration on the

Conduct of Parties in the South China Sea and the current negotiation of a binding code of conduct for the South China Sea.

Bearing in mind the historical backgrounds of each South China Sea claimant and the complicated regional geopolitics, it is little wonder that politics and national pride get in the way of reaching a joint development agreement, let alone establishing an effective mechanism. This chapter will examine the claimants' early interest in South China Sea energy resources and how the importance of such resources has affected the political will and domestic receptivity of the five claimants of the South China Sea toward the negotiation for joint development. The complexity of geopolitics within the Asia-Pacific region will also be examined. The chapter concludes that joint development between the five rival claimants, while not impossible, is unlikely in the foreseeable future.

Early interest in South China Sea energy resources

What sparked off early interest in energy resources in the South China Sea? Who were the early players in the pursuit of energy resources in the South China Sea? How did their interest play a part in generating the South China Sea disputes? This section identifies the early players and briefly outlines the motivations behind their interest in exploiting energy resources in the South China Sea.

It has been argued that the trend of increasing national claims to exclusive exploitation of natural resources from the seabed and subsoil was triggered in 1945 following a proclamation asserting jurisdiction and control over such resources by US President Harry Truman. 'Other states, and particularly developing states, almost immediately took advantage of the Truman Doctrine's implicit invitation to promulgate comparable claims.'[3] Granted that there was a heightened awareness of the rights of statehood, developing states in East Asia undoubtedly saw the oceans as 'an opportunity to claim large areas of previously unowned space as a means of access to a wealth of resources'.[4] Therefore, by ensuring that developing coastal states would not lose their sovereign rights over maritime spaces to former colonizing states who had exploited those areas first, the 1958 doctrine of continental shelf provided them with a windfall addition to national estate.

In 1965, the United Nations Economic and Social Commission for Asia and the Pacific established an intergovernmental body, the Committee for Coordination of Joint Prospecting for Mineral Resources in Asian Offshore Areas (CCOP), which began a decade of extensive seismic survey of East Asia's continental shelves. The immense offshore hydrocarbon potential of the East Asian region, particularly the South and East China seas, was thus revealed.[5] It provided the impetus for hydrocarbon exploration and exploitation in the South China Sea which bordered the member states of Malaysia, the Philippines, Vietnam and China.[6] For example, the offshore oil hunt in Malaysia began in earnest in 1967 and several major oil and gas strikes gave Malaysia prominence as a potential crude oil exporter as early as 1969.[7] Likewise for the Philippines, serious offshore oil exploration began in the mid-1970s. Exploration in the Palawan-Sulu seabed in 1976 resulted in the discovery of the Nido oil field, which began commercial production in 1979. Shortly after, the Cadlao and Matinloc oil fields off Palawan were discovered in the early 1980s. In the case of Vietnam, offshore oil exploration began in 1968 with assistance from the CCOP, which sent a team of specialists from Imperial College London to Saigon to help with the Vietnam Offshore Exploration Project.[8]

In addition, oil emerged as an important political and economic weapon during the 1973 oil crisis. It has been argued that the use of oil as a political weapon is one of the reasons why the Philippines is encouraging local exploration to reduce dependency on oil imports from OPEC.[9] As much of the world's oil lies in Islamic hands, the outbreak of Muslim separatist rebellion in the Philippines in 1972 prompted a fear of subjugation to international pressure from OPEC on behalf of its Muslim minorities. The second oil crisis, which followed in 1979, exacerbated perceptions of scarcity and insecurity in importing countries with rising economies, particularly the Southeast Asian littoral states. The trauma of the oil crises played a significant role in spurring the initial development of oil resources in the region for local use.

Apart from fulfilling local needs and providing local revenues, the primary objective of oil operators, foreign and regional, in the South China Sea has always been to obtain oil to be sold in foreign markets for profit. According to a prominent Chinese analyst, China took advantage of the first international oil crisis in 1973 by exporting crude oil to Thailand, the Philippines and other Asian countries to help cultivate a favorable regional environment for modernization.[10] Japan's establishment as the world's second largest economy in 1968 was another factor in the drive for oil exploration and exploitation in the South China Sea. As one of the world's largest oil and liquefied natural gas importers, Japan was the principal market for producers in the South China Sea area during the 1970s and 1980s. Its economic and political impact on regional producers is tremendous, even though Japan only imports about 20 per cent of its oil from this region. For instance, Japan was been the largest customer for Brunei's oil exports since 1972.[11] On the other hand, the normalization of Sino-Japanese relations during the early 1970s resulted in a long-term trade agreement between the two countries in 1978, which might have sparked early Chinese interest in exploring in the South China Sea after China's crude oil peaked in 1985.[12]

Oil and gas exploitation is an important source of export earnings, foreign direct investment and, to a lesser extent, employment in many developing countries. The primary benefit from development of the oil and gas sector is its fiscal role in generating tax and other revenue for the government. Government revenue from the oil and gas sector is derived from a variety of tax and non-tax instruments. The government's share of economic rent is primarily collected through production-based or profit-based arrangements. In some countries, the government may participate more directly in oil and gas projects by taking an equity interest. The most traditional method of government revenue extraction is in the form of a royalty/tax regime where the government grants concessions to foreign oil companies and draws bonuses from the moment of signature. One such 'signature bonus' amounting to US$5 million was paid by the Royal Dutch Shell Company to the Republic of Vietnam in the early 1970s.[13]

The fiscal role of the oil and gas sector was significant in supporting the civil war efforts and the war economy of South Vietnam between 1970 and 1975.[14] Two years before the fall of Saigon to the North Vietnamese, the South Vietnamese government invited 27 international oil companies to bid for some 30 offshore blocks available for lease. By 1975, in addition to the Royal Dutch Shell Company, a total of 12 US oil firms had won the bids for 13 offshore blocks in the South China Sea of approximately 21 million acres.[15] Capitalizing on the civil strife in Vietnam and buoyed by the prospects of oil in the South China Sea, the PRC seized the Paracels in 1974. South Vietnam's blossoming oil and gas industry and the international oil companies' offshore discoveries were of implicit value to Hanoi and its Soviet ally, thus setting the stage for the eventual military clash between Vietnam and the PRC in 1988.

Currently, regional interest in intensifying exploitation in the South China Sea is rising – with China, the Philippines and Vietnam as forerunners in the race to tap the possibly huge oil reserves. In 2012 alone, China National Offshore Oil Corp tendered 22 blocks in undisputed waters of the South China Sea, in addition to the nine disputed blocks within Vietnam's exclusive economic zone.[16] Two out of the three blocks, known as Area 3 and Area 4, straddling the Reed Bank Basin and Northwest Palawan Basin offered by the Philippines in the last phase of the country's biggest petroleum exploration tender in 2012, fell within China's nine-dashed line claim.[17] Although claimants such as Malaysia and Brunei have remained on the sidelines of the recent tensions over the South China Sea, both countries have numerous blocks within the infamous nine-dashed line claim that face potential conflict with China. According to an equity analysis of Malaysia's oil and gas sector in 2006, there were as many as 17 open exploration blocks offshore of Sarawak and nine offshore of Sabah available for review pending release dates from Petronas.[18]

Domestic politics as an impediment to compromise

Joint development of energy resources in a disputed area is not a new concept in East Asia.[19] The South China Sea claimants have repeatedly voiced their willingness to work toward joint development/cooperation and even formed a special Technical Working Group on Resources Assessment and Ways of Development (TWG-RA) in 1993 to study the assortment of joint development models around the world and to learn from them what could be applied to the South China Sea area. However, the TWG-RA has not been able to solve the inherent problems of joint development: (1) the zone for joint development; (2) the subject of the joint development – marine conservation, environmental protection, fisheries, energy resources, marine scientific research and so forth; (3) the mechanism for such joint development; and (4) the participants in such activities.[20] Former Indonesian diplomat Hasjim Djalal pointed out, 'While it might be relatively easier to formulate a bilateral agreement on Joint Development, it would be more difficult to work on a trilateral or multilateral Joint Development agreement. Many people are talking about the concept but many details still did not make much sense. In fact, the JD concept meant different things to different people.'[21]

As East Asia assumes the driver's seat for global economic development, control over resources becomes an increasingly nationalist issue as it signifies a state's wealth and strength. As proven in the 1973 oil crisis, resources such as hydrocarbons and minerals can also be used as economic and political weapons.[22] With news reports touting far higher hydrocarbon reserves than previous estimates, the importance of the South China Sea has grown exponentially in a region where countries regard energy security as a top priority.[23] The current South China Sea impasse can be seen as the result of national pride restricting regional governments' ability to cooperate on tension-defusing initiatives and cooperative activities. At the same time, domestic nationalist pressure also blocks efforts to cooperate and to de-escalate incidents. The South China Sea claimants have yet to clarify their claims and willingness to cooperate on joint development. It can be observed that some claimants tend to clarify their claims through their respective national legislations. Djalal argued that such clarifications are ineffective in settling disputes as national legislation tends to consolidate and harden the national position while weakening future political will to seek a solution or a compromise.[24] This behavior can be attributed to the fact that the leaders of such countries have to satisfy their domestic audiences and political agenda.

In this section, we discuss how domestic politics influences the political will of the South China Sea claimants toward negotiations for joint development of energy resources in disputed areas, with particular interest in the cases of China, the Philippines and Vietnam. Malaysia and Brunei will be mentioned only briefly as their claims are significantly smaller than those of the former claimants and these two countries face the least opposition from China with regard to their energy exploitation activities, both joint and individual, in the disputed areas of the South China Sea.

China

Currently, China has arrived at neither a unified domestic understanding of its claim in the South China Sea nor a commonly accepted approach to the South China Sea dispute. This in turn affects its political will to negotiate for joint development. China's ambiguous South China Sea claim and its indefinite support for cooperative activities are further complicated by domestic politics in China. The domestic political environment is as conflicted over the South China Sea as the general Chinese public. Compromise in the form of joint development faces opposition and different views from maritime law enforcement agencies and the Chinese military, especially the navy. While the Chinese navy flexes its muscles with military drills near disputed waters, Chinese maritime law enforcement agencies are given a much freer rein in implementing a heavy-handed approach. With their inclination to regard the South China Sea as China's proposed or actual jurisdictional waters, agencies such as the Fisheries Law Enforcement

Command and the China Marine Surveillance have stepped up their efforts to protect Chinese maritime interests, particularly in energy resources, and are more willing to use forceful means to block or interfere in the energy exploration and exploitation activities of other claimant countries in areas that fall within the nine-dashed line claim.

The Chinese Ministry of Foreign Affairs is also embroiled in the conflicted domestic political environment. It appears to be less active within the Chinese policy-making system and is seen to be merely a diplomatic mouthpiece for China. It has little effective control over the decision-making process, particularly in times of crisis and friction. The Ministry of Foreign Affairs seems to be making up for its lost interests in bureaucratic politics by appearing to be more hard-line than before on the South China Sea issue. The Chinese Ministry of Foreign Affairs itself caused the latest uproar over the South China Sea dispute with the release of a controversial map printed on its new electronic passport. The map, printed on the inside pages of the passport, shows an outline of China which includes the South China Sea, hemmed in by dashes.[25] The new Chinese passport is one of the latest contradictory diplomatic moves to have negatively impacted friendly relations with the Philippines and Vietnam – thus placing yet another roadblock, albeit minor, in the path of joint development.

The role of Chinese national oil companies is also vital in affecting China's political willingness to negotiate for joint development. Drawing from the experiences of Petronas, PetroVietnam and the Thai PTT Exploration and Production Public Company in the Malaysia–Thailand and Malaysia–Vietnam joint development models, Chinese national oil companies could act as agents of diplomacy and assist in forging joint development in disputed areas in the South China Sea. However, following the lapse of the 2005–2008 Joint Marine Seismic Undertaking (JMSU) with the Philippine National Oil Company and PetroVietnam, the China National Offshore Oil Company (CNOOC) has taken unilateral action to claim the energy resources and stepped up its efforts in exploiting parts of the South China Sea. In particular, the CNOOC has helped to demonstrate China's political willingness to 'go it alone' with its deployment of CNOOC981, China's first deep-water drilling rig, near the disputed Paracel Islands archipelago in May 2012. China's national mouthpiece, Xinhua, cited CNOOC Chairman Wang Yilin as saying that such drilling rigs are symbolic as 'China's mobile national territory and strategic weapon for promoting the development of the country's offshore oil industry'.[26]

The popular domestic views in China on the South China Sea issue also have a significant negative impact on China's political willingness to engage in joint development with the other claimants. The Chinese media plays a part in leading Chinese popular opinion with confusing and expansive interpretations of China's claim in the South China Sea being raised. The Chinese media uses extremely loose terms to describe China's claims in East Asian seas such as water/ocean/maritime territory and territorial seas, and has raised claims that China is entitled to 3 million km^2 of sea area, which includes the 2 million km^2 within the nine-dashed line in the South China Sea.[27] The Chinese media also practises the habit of sending intimidating messages to the other claimants, in particular the Philippines and Vietnam. Therefore, the general Chinese public, including certain Chinese international relations experts who are unfamiliar with maritime affairs, seem to believe that China has sovereignty over the entire South China Sea.[28]

Chinese nationalism and hard-line popular opinion over the South China Sea dispute serves as a serious constraint for Chinese decision-makers. However, the foundation for rising nationalism and hard-line beliefs on territorial disputes is laid by the Chinese educational system. Chinese history and geography textbooks continue to depict the southern-most point of Chinese territory at the James Shoal (*zeng mu an sha*) and schools encourage nationalism and reinforce hard-line positions on territorial disputes by encouraging students to express their patriotism in class and even by holding photography exhibitions in schools to showcase Chinese opposition.[29] Public opinion that the single-party government is too weak in safeguarding national sovereignty and pride does constrain its will to commit to concrete plans for joint ventures as the party struggles with increasing socio-economic discontent and the maintenance of its political legitimacy. During the recent Scarborough Shoal standoff, a survey conducted by the *Global Times* on the attitude of the Chinese public in seven cities showed that nearly 80 percent of respondents were supportive of using military means to counter 'foreign provocations and encroachments' of Chinese sovereignty.[30]

Vietnam

Currently, the ruling Vietnamese Communist Party (VCP) faces a high rate of nationalist sentiments over its disputes with China and it also faces allegations that Hanoi is selling out Vietnamese sovereignty and economic interests to Beijing.[31] The Sino-Vietnamese feud over disputed islands has already led to two armed conflicts in 1974 and 1988, which resulted in China's occupation of the Paracel Islands. Considering that the countries fought a brief border war in 1979 and that border skirmishes were common along the formerly disputed Sino-Vietnamese land border throughout the 1980s, it is difficult for both Hanoi and Beijing to convince the Vietnamese public that China will refrain from military force and settle sovereignty disputes amicably.[32] Vietnamese insecurity is further compounded by threats of invasion run by Chinese state-affiliated media and cyber threats launched by Chinese netizens.[33]

The legacy of past conflicts raised the stakes and increased the political and emotional sensitivity of the sovereignty issues in Vietnam. The impact of nationalism on Vietnam's political will to consider joint development can be seen in the fact that the VCP tolerated anti-China demonstrations in Hanoi and Ho Chi Minh City for 11 consecutive weeks, following a maritime altercation in May 2011. This is in stark comparison to similar Vietnamese protests in 2007, which were dispersed after two weekends. It has been argued that the VCP's decision to turn a blind eye was largely to assuage mounting nationalist pressure and to demonstrate the extent of public outrage in Vietnam to Beijing.[34]

Due to the fact that there is a strong pro-China faction within the VCP keeping alive Sino-Vietnamese ideological solidarity, China and Vietnam have maintained a direct channel of communication in the form of a Joint Steering Committee of their ruling parties.[35] Direct access to Chinese party officials has allowed the VCP to compartmentalize the South China Sea dispute and quickly repair frayed relations with China. However, the opaqueness of this direct access and the VCP's traditional diplomatic deference to its Chinese counterpart (driven by its ideological fundamentalism) has also led to suspicions among the Vietnamese public that the VCP is taking orders from the Chinese officials. Led by anti-imperialist party chiefs, the VCP made three attempts to draw an ideological alliance with China during the 1990s and early 2000s, but was rebuffed by China.[36]

It is interesting to note that at the height of the 2011 anti-China protests, 20 prominent old guards of the VCP, including the former ambassador to China, Major General Nguyen Trong Vin, the chairman of the Vietnam Union of Scientific and Technical Associations, Ho UyLiem, and retired government officials from the Prime Minister's Research Board, submitted a petition to Vietnam's Politburo and National Assembly calling for greater transparency of the Sino-Vietnamese relationship and for the leaders to 'commit to national interests above all others'.[37] For instance, they demanded that the government clarify the background, content and legal validity of the 1958 letter regarding alleged Vietnamese support for China's extension of its territorial waters. This correspondence between Premier Pham Van Dong and Chinese Premier Zhu Enlai was said to be the source of intentional Chinese misinterpretation.[38]

It is worth noting that in 1999 and again in 2000, the VCP Party General Secretary, Le KhaPhieu, paved the way for the conclusion of two Sino-Vietnamese pacts on land borders and on maritime borders in the Tonkin Gulf after making several concessions to the Chinese.[39] Since then, a wave of popular resentment has erupted as independent bloggers and dissidents criticized the move as the latest sell-out of national sovereignty to China.[40] The mounting suspicion was eroding the VCP government's political legitimacy and casting doubt on possible cooperation with China in joint development of the disputed areas in the South China Sea.[41] In addition, Vietnam's 2012 maritime legislation, which states its jurisdiction over the disputed Paracel and Spratly Islands and stipulates that all foreign naval ships entering these areas must notify Vietnamese authorities, has since been challenged by Chinese non-compliance. The Vietnamese government is obliged to respond resolutely to any violations of its law or risk losing credibility further in the eyes of the Vietnamese public.

One of the reasons why the nationalist domestic audience regards China as Vietnam's primary competitor is because Vietnam has the largest overlapping claims in the South China Sea with China. Vietnam's consideration for joint development is also hindered by China's overwhelming economic influence in the country. Apart from a rapidly increasing trade deficit with China in recent years it has been argued that as much as '90 percent of important works like power, metallurgical, chemical, bauxite and titanium mining plants, etc. in the form of EPC (Engineering, Procurement and Construction) are in the hands of Chinese contractors'.[42] Given the archaic issue of corruption in Vietnam, allegations of impending Chinese economic encroachment reaffirmed widespread belief that the VCP is selling out national interests to China. Thus far, the VCP's simplistic explanations of traditional friendship and geographic proximity seem to be losing their effect in reassuring its domestic political audience.

The marine economy is not solely about mineral exploitation and the Vietnamese government is also under domestic pressure to protect its fishery industry, as it is a leading contributor to the country's GDP. According to official statistics, Vietnamese fishermen caught a total of 2,622.2 thousand tons of fish, shrimp and other marine creatures in the South China Sea in 2012.[43] China's fishing bans, which have been enforced unilaterally since the late 1990s, have also sparked fears of negative economic effects that could be caused by Chinese encroachment of the South China Sea. Vietnam and the Philippines have routinely protested the arrival of large Chinese fishing fleets, under the protection of the infamous Fisheries Law Enforcement Command, which carry out unregulated fishing that threatens to deplete fish stocks in the South China Sea.[44] For the VCP leadership, like its Chinese counterpart, nationalism is a double-edged sword, providing it added advantage in resisting Chinese pressure while limiting its options in negotiating for a joint development resolution to the South China Sea dispute.

The Philippines

In comparison with China and Vietnam, the Philippine government faces considerably lesser constraints from nationalism as national focus centres on the Muslim insurgency in the southern Philippines rather than on territorial sovereignty in the South China Sea. It seems that only high-profile incidents at sea such as the 2012 Scarborough Shoal standoff catch the eye of the media and public. The Aquino government faces nationalist opposition toward its decision to seek US support in the face of Chinese challenges from political elites and the business community, but national sentiments regarding China remain positive in general, even though China's Foreign Ministry spokesperson, Hong Lei, and the Chinese media have accused the Aquino government of stirring up anti-China sentiments in the Philippine public.[45]

In a recent survey conducted by an independent Philippine research firm on public opinion of the handling of the South China Sea dispute, a majority of the 1,500 respondents from 77 provinces stated that they were satisfied with the way Aquino has handled the dispute.[46] Querying further the public opinion of possible solutions for the dispute with China, the survey showed that 33 per cent of the respondents opted for diplomacy over a show of force from both parties; 20 per cent supported the suggestion for negotiations between the Philippines and China for a joint venture on environmental protection or resource development; another 11 per cent chose international arbitration on the dispute; and only a minority of 8 per cent preferred to seek US assistance.[47]

While renewed Chinese assertiveness over the South China Sea dispute during the last two years has contributed to a climate of distrust and apprehension, the apprehension toward joint development with China is largely attributed to the personal leadership styles and political agenda of current Philippine President Benigno Aquino III. Aquino departed from the 'golden age of partnership' with China, hailed by his predecessor, Gloria Macapagal Arroyo, to the current state of brinkmanship.[48] He has been more outspoken than Arroyo on defending the Philippine's territorial claims, and has publicly appealed for US assistance with China's challenge in the South China Sea dispute. His anti-corruption crusade against the former regime and its links to corruption-tainted Chinese investment deals and loans may have influenced his distrustful attitude toward China. Joint development has become harder to pursue for the current Aquino government following accusations that the Arroyo government sold out Philippine sovereignty in the 2005–2008 JMSU in return for corruption-tainted Chinese loans and investments. Corruption scandals arising from the Zhong Xing Telecommunication Equipment Company and NorthRail project deals signed by the Arroyo administration also reawakened long-held views among Filipinos that link ethnic Chinese to corrupt practices.

The JMSU's constitutionality was questioned in the Philippines after Arroyo was found to have acted on the political interference of well-connected advisors and authorized decisions outside of the usual administrative and diplomatic channels involving the foreign affairs, defence and energy departments. The JMSU agreement lapsed in 2008 and was not extended by the Philippines, in spite of Chinese interest in pursuing it. Aquino reportedly told the Philippine press that the JMSU with China and Vietnam should not have happened as it compromised Philippine territorial sovereignty.[49] He also publicly blamed the JMSU for the worsening of the dispute in the West Philippine Sea.[50]

Currently, the Aquino government seems to be sending out signals that it is hesitant to approve joint ventures with China. For instance, approval from Malacañang (Presidential Office) is still pending for CNOOC's farm-in agreement with the Philippine National Oil Company Exploration Corporation signed in 2006 for Service Contract 57, which covers an area of 7,200 km^2, located in undisputed waters offshore Northwest Palawan, west of the Calamian Islands. Although the Philippine Department of Energy announced in August 2011 that approval would be given shortly after the agreement had been reviewed for administrative issues, executive approval remains elusive over a year later.

It is interesting to note that joint development of all other natural resources (agricultural lands excepted) with another country is potentially unconstitutional. According to Article VII of the 1987 Philippine Constitution, 'exploration, development, and utilization of natural resources shall be under the full control and supervision of the State'. Therefore, the Philippine government is technically only allowed to 'directly undertake such activities' or 'enter into co-production, joint venture, or production-sharing agreements with Filipino citizens'.[51]

Although the Philippine economic growth of 7.1 per cent in the third quarter of 2012 exceeded earlier forecasts of 5.4 per cent, the country is still facing structural economic difficulties and does not have sufficient resources to fund such an expensive project.[52] Hence, critics and political analysts have warned against joint development for the fear of being outmaneuvered by China.[53] However, given the renewed bilateral tensions between Beijing and Manila, it seems that the Aquino government may have far less political inclination to amend the Constitution to allow for joint development with the other claimants, particularly China.

Political will prevails – the cases of Malaysia and Brunei

In contrast with Vietnam and the Philippines, nationalist pressure on the Malaysian and Bruneian governments to act against China over their South China Sea disputes is minimal. It is our contention that this boosts their political will to accept or propose joint development undertakings with China in the disputed waters of the South China Sea. Using the case of Malaysia and Brunei, we will try to justify the importance of reducing nationalistic impulses and cultivating political will for cooperation.

Malaysia has made three successful attempts at joint development of hydrocarbon resources in the Gulf of Thailand and in the South China Sea, namely the 1990 Malaysia–Thailand Joint Development Area, the 1992 Malaysia–Vietnam Commercial Agreement Area and the 2009 Malaysia–Brunei Commercial Arrangement Area. Suffice it to say that each attempt took a tremendous amount of political will on the part of Kuala Lumpur to bring to fruition. For instance, Malaysia and Thailand took 15 years to overcome both legal obstacles and oscillating political will to realize the implementation of their joint development agreement.[54] Analysts have noted that the Thai and Malaysian prime ministers who supported and signed the Memorandum of Understanding for joint development lost office shortly thereafter and negotiations were stymied by differences in their successors' leadership styles and priorities.[55]

It should be pointed out that nationalist sentiments in Malaysia are not dormant. Malaysia has its fair share of domestic issues but little of its tumultuous communal politics seem to affect its leadership's political will to seek joint development and cooperation. Hence, Malaysian leaders were again afforded the luxury of political will to compromise in the case of the Vietnamese–Malaysian model. At this point, we would like to highlight that sensitivity over its maritime jurisdiction does exist in Malaysia, as with any rational claimant to disputed waters. Nationalism does come into play in limiting the Malaysian government's political will in seeking cooperation and hardening its stance, particularly in the case of its maritime dispute with Singapore.[56]

From the mid-1980s, Malaysia began hydrocarbon exploration activities in the Gulf and subsequently signed three petroleum contracts with foreign operators in areas overlapping those claimed by Vietnam. One of the Malaysia's operators, Hamilton, made a discovery of an estimated 1.1 trillion cubic feet of gas reserves in the Malaysian–Vietnamese overlapping area and reported that the Bunga-Orkid-1 well located within the overlapping claims area showed a test rate of 4,400 barrels of oil per day.[57] The announcements led to Vietnamese protests in May 1991. However, Vietnam expressed its willingness to negotiate with Malaysia in conformity with international law in a note sent to the Malaysian Foreign Ministry on 30 May 1991.[58]

In the absence of raging domestic nationalist sentiments, Malaysia suspended all petroleum exploration and exploitation projects carried out by its national petroleum company, Petronas, during negotiations with Vietnam. The first round of Malaysian–Vietnamese negotiations in Kuala Lumpur on 3–5 June 1992 succeeded in determining the area in which the two sides agreed to apply a joint development model in a spirit of understanding and cooperation, without prejudice to the final delimitation. Vietnam made a compromise on technical and economic grounds to allow Malaysian-appointed operators to continue exploration activities in the agreement area. The two parties quickly found an acceptable solution for extracting petroleum resources. Four years after the conclusion of the Malaysian–Vietnamese commercial arrangement, the first petroleum was extracted from the Bunga Kekwa field on 29 July 1997.

Nationalism as a factor hindering political will for joint development is not strongly evident in the case of Brunei. As Brunei's claim in the South China Sea overlaps the most with Malaysia's, it 'views its territorial claim as a bilateral issue with Malaysia and by implication does not recognize China's claims'.[59] In March 2009, Malaysia's joint petroleum development agreement with Brunei was reached when the two countries settled their land and maritime boundary issues after six years of negotiations. As relations between Brunei and Malaysia are harmonious, there had been little impetus for them to settle such boundary issues until 2003 when they came to a near armed conflict over mutually claimed waters. Apart from the fact that there is immense oil wealth in the Borneo seabed, it has been observed that Malaysia chose a confrontational stance towards Brunei for various reasons such as the autocratic leadership style of then Prime Minister Mahathir Mohammed and a heightened sensitivity to its maritime jurisdiction.[60]

China's relations with Brunei and Malaysia – hope for joint development?

Brunei and Malaysia are the two countries that face the least instances of diplomatic protests from China. On the other hand, Brunei has benefitted from China's policy to enhance its energy security. Though China displays a traditional tendency to pick on a militarily and economically weak rival, Brunei does not share the same unfortunate fate as the Philippines because China, driven by its insatiable thirst for energy resources, has actively sought to improve bilateral relations over the last decade. It is interesting to note that, in spite of tumultuous relations with Vietnam and the Philippines in the last two years, Chinese leaders and diplomats such as Hu Jintao, Jia Qinling, Sun Jiazheng and Yang Jiechi have kept up efforts to improve relations with Brunei by Chinese commitment to deepen bilateral ties and further strengthen economic cooperation, particularly in the energy sector.[61] In 2011, the two countries reaffirmed mutually beneficial cooperative ties with the signing of a Memorandum of Understanding on cooperation in the energy sector.[62]

Malaysia was the first claimant to develop the disputed islands for eco-tourism in 1991 and Chinese reaction was moderate, with half-hearted complaints about the construction of an airstrip on the atoll. However, China reserved its comments on the whole project and maintained its silence even when the resort construction began in earnest in 1992. Although Beijing strongly condemned Vietnamese inspection tours of the Vietnamese-held Spratlys in 1989, it was conspicuously silent over the visit to the Malaysian-occupied atoll of Terumbu Layang-Layang by Malaysian King Sultan Azlan Shah in May 1992. When Malaysia again erected structures on Terumbu Peninjau (Investigator Shoal) and Terumbu Siput (Erica Reef) in 1999, China's response was equally low-key.

Although Sino-Malaysian relations are relatively good, China did raise a formal objection against Malaysia's joint submission on the issue of extended continental shelf in the South China Sea with Vietnam to the Commission on the Limits of the Continental Shelf in 2009. It is interesting to note that, once again, there seemed to be no Chinese diplomatic or media reactions to the signing of a joint resource development agreement between Malaysia and Brunei over Blocks CA1 and CA2 within the Baram Delta, some 100 km northwest of the Bruneian coast in December 2010.[63] In comparison to its vociferation reactions over surveys and tenders by the Philippines and Vietnam, China also seems to have remained silent on four of Malaysia's 2012 promotion blocks, namely the SK-303B, SK-304A (partial), DWF and DW2D blocks, which fall within its nine-dashed line claim.[64]

Regardless, Malaysia shares an enduring benign and reciprocally productive bilateral relationship with China which began with the Mahathir administration. Mahathir's successors, Abdullah Badawi and Najib Razak, have continuously given deference to China over issues such as Taiwan and Xinjiang, and stressed the use of diplomacy as a preferred means to manage the South China Sea disputes. Malaysia's goodwill towards China is reflective of the political and economic priorities of the Barisan Nasional government. In reciprocation, China offered a US$25 billion contract to Malaysia's state-owned oil company Petronas in July 2006 to supply up to 3.03 million metric tons of liquefied natural gas (LNG) annually to China for 25 years.[65] Given that it was Petronas' first LNG deal with China, the deal was touted as a major breakthrough for the Malaysian oil company into China's energy sector. The signing of such agreements between China, Brunei and Malaysia underscored the three claimants' shared regard for actual cooperation rather than confrontation and has interesting implications for the future development of Sino-Malaysian and Sino-Bruneian South China Sea relations.

Conclusions

This paper has analyzed nationalism as one of the crucial impediments for the initiation of any joint development project in the South China Sea. What makes joint development unlikely in the foreseeable future is the fact that there is almost no political will for cooperative action in the South China Sea. The disputes and tensions in recent years have entailed a political atmosphere that makes it very difficult for the parties concerned to even discuss issues pertaining to joint development. It is no surprise that even suggestions for maritime cooperation in some of the less sensitive areas, such as cooperation in marine scientific studies and conservation, have received little positive response. Rising nationalism has become a powerful political weapon against any possibility of joint development in the South China Sea.

All claimant states are increasingly interested in exploring and exploiting the energy resources in the South China Sea primarily for the consideration of economic benefits. It is no exaggeration that almost all claimant states have made plans, short or long term, to further utilize the energy resources, and some claimants, more than others, are strongly interested in acting unilaterally. There is scant evidence to show that any claimant party is genuinely ready to pursue joint development with other parties in hunting for energy in the disputed area. In addition, technical issues, such as identifying an area for joint development and finding an appropriate mode of cooperation as in the Malaysia joint development experiences with Thailand and Vietnam, may impose additional barriers for bilateral or multilateral cooperation on energy exploitation.

Given the enormous difficulties that exist for joint development, it would seem logical to address the sources of those barriers before joint development becomes part of the policy agenda. For the time being, perhaps in the coming years as well, efforts to push for joint development as a means to calm or mitigate the security situation in the South China Sea are unlikely to produce any positive result. Before a serious policy deliberation on joint development can emerge, claimant states must tackle the daunting task of cooling down tensions in the South China Sea, cultivating the political will for cooperation and reducing nationalistic impulses in each of their domestic societies.

Notes

1 Ian Townsend-Gault, 'Legal and political perspectives on sovereignty over the Spratly Islands', 1999, available at http://community.middlebury.edu/~scs/docs/Townsend-Gault.pdf (accessed 20 December 2013).
2 David M. Ong, 'The 1979 and 1990 Malaysia–Thailand joint development agreements: a model for international legal co-operation in common offshore petroleum deposits?', *International Journal of Marine and Coastal Law*, 14(2), 1999, pp. 207–246, at p. 213.
3 Lea Brilmayer and Natalie Klein, 'Land and sea: two sovereignty regimes in search of a common denominator', *Faculty Scholarship Series*, Paper 2523, 2001, available at http://digitalcommons.law.yale.edu/fss_papers/2523 (accessed 15 November 2012), p. 720.
4 Ibid, pp. 712–713.
5 UNDP Project Manager, 'The offshore hydrocarbon potential of east asia: a decade of investigations (1965–1975)', in United Nations ESCAP, *CCOP Technical Bulletin* (Bangkok), no. 11 (October 1977), pp. 1–66. Although international oil companies had been quietly exploring for oil in the South China Sea prior to the CCOP's establishment in 1965, the CCOP as a regional multilateral organization is significant for creating greater governmental awareness of oil and gas exploration in the South China Sea.
6 See B. A. Hamzah, *The Oil Sultanate: Political History of Oil in Brunei Darussalam*, Kuala

Lumpur: Mawaddah Enterprise Sdn. Bhd., 1991. Negara Brunei Darussalam (hereafter, Brunei) did not feature in many of the CCOP surveys. As Brunei was a British Protected State, Britain had effective control over Brunei external affairs before its independence in 1984. Its first major offshore field, Southeast Ampa, was discovered by British-owned Brunei Shell in 1963, earlier than the CCOP surveys. The driver for Brunei's exploration and exploitation for energy resources in the South China Sea will be discussed later in this section.

7 Phiphat Tangsubkul. *ASEAN and the Law of the SEA*, Singapore: Institute of Southeast Asian Studies, 1982, p. 85.

8 Khương HữuĐiều, '1968: the very beginning of Vietnam's off-shore oil & gas development', a translated excerpt from Tran Van Khoi, *DầuHỏaViệt Nam 1970–1975*, available at http://huongduongtxd.com/offshoreoilexploration.pdf (accessed 12 November 2012).

9 Roderick O'Brien, *South China Sea Oil: Two Problems of Ownership and Development*, Singapore: Institute of Southeast Asian Studies, 1977, p. 2.

10 Zha Daojiong, 'China's energy security: domestic and international issues', *Survival*, 48(1), Spring 2006, pp. 179–190.

11 Saiful Islam and Sumimaru Odano, 'LNG exports from Brunei to Japan', *CRR Working Paper* No. A-20, March 2010, Center for Risk Research, Faculty of Economics, Shiga University, Japan. As a result, the development of Brunei's liquefied natural gas (LNG) operations was geared for the Japanese market. Brunei's first LNG cargo was exported to Japan in 1972. Japan has a long-term contract with Brunei to purchase a significant percentage of its LNG exports until 2015.

12 See Laura Newby, *Sino-Japanese Relations: China's Perspective*, London: Routledge, 1988. As early as 1972, Japan sought to establish a trade agreement with China, based on the concept of a direct linkage between the level of Japanese export of steel to China and the level of Japanese oil imports from China. The eight-year Long-Term Trade Agreement of 1978 called for China to export 8–9 million tons of coal and 47.1 million tons of crude oil in exchange for US$7–8 billion of plant and technology and US$2–3 billion of construction materials and machinery from Japan.

13 O'Brien, *South China Sea Oil*, p. 5.

14 See Louis Wesseling, *Fuelling the War: Revealing an Oil Company's Role in Vietnam*, London and New York: I. B. Tauris, 2000; R. Thomas Collins, Jr., *Blue Dragon: Reckoning in the South China Sea*, Oakton, VA: Ravens Yard, 2002.

15 Collins, Jr., *Blue Dragon*, p. 22.

16 'China's CNOOC tenders another 26 offshore blocks, many in South China Sea', *Reuters*, 28 August 2012, available at http://www.reuters.com/article/2012/08/28/china-cnooc-blocks-idUSL4E8JS03R20120828 (accessed 9 October 2012); PetroVietnam, 'Announcement of PetroVietnam to the international petroleum contractors', available at http://www.pvdtraining.com.vn/news/announcement-of-petrovietnam-to... html (accessed 9 October 2012).

17 IHS Jane's, South China Sea Strategic Map (updated 2012).

18 Hwang DBS Vickers, 'Malaysia equity research', *Sector Focus*, 28 June 2006, available at http://www.einvest.com.my/Archive-CompanyFocus/2.%20Sector%20Focus/2006%20Sector%20Focus/Oil%20&%20Gas%2020060628.pdf (accessed 6 November 2012), p. 9.

19 The 1974 Japan–South Korea Agreement, the 1979 and 1990 Malaysia–Thailand Joint Development Agreements, the 1989 Timor Gap Treaty between Australia and the Republic of Indonesia and the 1992 Memorandum of Understanding (MoU) between Malaysia and the Socialist Republic of Vietnam, who are fellow Spratlys claimants. This MoU resulted in a successful joint development between Malaysia and Vietnam, known as the PM-3 Commercial Arrangement Area, which has been extracting hydrocarbons from six offshore fields within the 1350 km^2 overlapping zone of the

South China Sea claimed by Malaysia and Vietnam since July 1997. See Offshore Technology.com at http://www.offshore-technology.com/projects/pm3/ (accessed 5 October 2012).

20 Hasjim Djalal, *Preventive Diplomacy in Southeast Asia: Lessons Learnt*, Jakarta: Habibie Center, 2002, p. 78.

21 Ibid., p. 79.

22 See Karen R. Merrill, *The Oil Crisis of 1973–1974: A Brief History with Documents*, Bedford: St. Martin's Press, 2007; Fiona Venn, *Turning Points: The Oil Crisis*, Boston: Addison-Wesley Longman, 2002.

23 'US report touts South China Sea riches', *Taipei Times*, 9 February 2013.

24 Hasjim Djalal, *Preventive Diplomacy*, p. 95.

25 Aljazeera.com, 'New China passport stokes diplomatic ire', *Asia-Pacific News*, 26 November 2012, available at http://www.aljazeera.com/news/asia-pacific/2012/11/2012112615540332910.html (accessed 26 November 2012).

26 'Cnooc deploys oil rig as weapon to assert China sea claims', *Bloomberg*, 10 May 2012, available at http://www.bloomberg.com/news/2012-05-09/cnooc-deploys-oil-rig-as-weapon-to-assert-south-china-sea-claims.html (accessed 26 November 2012).

27 Wang Qian, 'China to dive into mapping seabed', *China Daily*, 14 September 2011; Wang Xinjun, 'China one step closer to developing aircraft carrier', *China Daily*, 1 August 2011; 'Refitting aircraft carrier not to change naval strategy', *China Daily*, 27 July 2011; Zhang Zixuan, 'Cultural relics discovered under sea', *China Daily*, 17 May 2011.

28 Second author's interviews with over 50 Chinese scholars since 2009.

29 First author's interviews with 30 Chinese high-school and college students who participated in the Anti-Japanese protests within China in September–October 2012.

30 http://news.enorth.com.cn/system/2012/05/05/009169236.shtml (accessed 12 October 2012).

31 Carlyle A. Thayer, 'South China Sea: China's rejuvenation and Vietnamese nationalism', *Thayer Consultancy Background Brief*, 21 March 2013. (*Thayer Consultancy Background Briefs* are archived at Scribd.com.)

32 See Ramses Amer, *The Sino-Vietnamese Approach to Managing Boundary Disputes*, Maritime Briefing, vol. 3, no. 5, Durham: International Boundaries Research Unit, University of Durham, 2002; Min Gyu Koo, *Island Disputes and Maritime Regime Building in East Asia: Between a Rock and a Hard Place*, New York: Springer, 2010.

33 Vietnam was sufficiently disturbed by a Chinese invasion hoax that went viral online to lodge a formal protest to Beijing. 'China's netizens menace Vietnam', *The Australian*, 11 September 2008.

34 John D. Ciorciari and Jessica Chen Weiss, 'The Sino-Vietnamese standoff in the South China Sea', *Conflict and Security*, Winter/Spring 2012, pp. 61–69.

35 This direct contact between the two ruling party centers has been established since 1947. See Sophie Quinn-Judge, 'Rethinking the history of the Vietnamese Communist Party', in Duncan McCargo (ed.), *Rethinking Vietnam*, London: RoutledgeCurzon, 2004; Ian Jeffries, *Contemporary Vietnam: A Guide to Economic and Political Developments*, Abingdon: Routledge, 2011.

36 Alexander L. Vuving, 'Strategy and evolution of Vietnam's China policy: a changing mixture of pathways', *Asian Survey*, 46(6), 2006, pp. 805–824.

37 VietnamNet Bridge, 'Patriotic personalities make proposals on defense and development', 16 July 2011, available at http://english.vietnamnet.vn/fms/special-reports/10501/patriotic-personalities-make-proposals-on-defense-and-development.html (accessed 20 November 2012).

38 Ibid.

39 Zachary Abuza, 'The lessons of Le Kha Phieu: changing rules in Vietnamese politics', *Contemporary Southeast Asia*, 24(1), April 2002, pp. 121–145.

40 Lyall Breckon, 'Beijing pushes "Asia for the Asians"', *Center for Strategic and International Studies*, 4(3), October 2002; 'Vietnam jails three bloggers for "anti-state propaganda"', *Jakarta Globe*, 24 September 2012; 'Vietnam bloggers face trial for "anti-state propaganda"', *Democracy Digest*, 21 September 2012, available at http://www.demdigest.net/blog/2012/09/vietnam-bloggers-face-trial-for-anti-state-propaganda/ (accessed 22 November 2012).

41 'A liberal faction in the Vietnamese Communist Party?', at http://freedomforvietnam.wordpress.com/2010/08/23/a-liberal-faction-in-the-vietnamese-communist-party/ (accessed 25 November 2012).

42 VietnamNet Bridge, 'Patriotic personalities'.

43 General Statistics Office of Vietnam, 'Social-economic situation in 2012: fishing production', available at http://www.gso.gov.vn/default_en.aspx?tabid=501&thangtk=12/2012 (accessed 20 July 2013).

44 'China's power play will up East Sea ante: analysts', *ThanhNien Daily*, 31 May 2013, available at http://www.thanhniennews.com/index/pages/20130530-china-power-play-will-up-east-sea-ante-analysts.aspx (accessed 7 July 2013).

45 'China paper accuses Manila over S. China Sea "plot"', *Reuters News*, 3 July 2012; Yang Jingjie, 'Manila provocation blasted', *Global Times*, 10 May 2012.

46 The Laylo Report, 'Pinoys worried about PH-China sea dispute', Pedro Laylo, Jr., 22 September 2012, available at http://thelayloreport.wordpress.com/ (accessed 20 November 2012).

47 Ibid.

48 Renato Cruz De Castro, 'China, the Philippines, and U.S. influence in Asia', *AEI Online*, 6 July 2007, available at http://www.aei.org/article/foreign-and-defense-policy/regional/asia/china-the-philippines-and-us-influence-in-asia/ (accessed 5 October 2012); Genalyn Kabiling, 'Arroyo vows to boost RP-China partnership', *Manila Bulletin*, 5 June 2010, available at http://www.mb.com.ph/node/260606/arroyo-vow (accessed 5 October 2012); Paterno Esmaquel II, 'Why China prefers Arroyo over Aquino', *Rappler*, 24 July 2012, available at http://www.rappler.com/nation/9128-how-china-views-aquino,-arroyo (accessed 5 October 2012); Subhash Kapila, 'South China Sea: China escalates brinkmanship to dangerous levels', at http://www.eurasiareview.com/09082012-south-china-sea-china-escalates-brinkmanship-to-dangerous-levels-analysis/ (accessed 5 October 2012); Andy Hoffman, 'High-stakes brinkmanship on South China Sea', *Globe and Mail*, 11 April 2012, available at http://www.theglobeandmail.com/news/world/high-stakes-brinkmanship-on-south-china-sea/article4106335/ (accessed 5 October 2012).

49 'JMSU with China, Vietnam "shouldn't have happened"', *ABS-CBN News*, 4 January 2011, available at http://rp3.abs-cbnnews.com/nation/01/04/11/pnoy-jmsu-china-vietnam-shouldnt-have-happened (accessed 10 October 2012).

50 Aurea Calica, 'Aquino says JMSU with China worsened Spratly dispute', *Philippine Star*, 6 July 2011.

51 The 1987 Philippine Constitution, Article VII – National Economy and Patrimony, Section 2.

52 'Philippines economic growth better than forecast', *BBC News*, 28 November 2012, available at http://www.bbc.co.uk/news/business-20521862 (accessed 29 November 2012).

53 'Sovereignty first', *Philippine Daily Inquirer*, Editorial, 21 May 2012, available at http://opinion.inquirer.net/29219/sovereignty-first (accessed 29 October 2012); Jojo Malig, 'MVP warned on China energy deal in Spratlys', ABS-CBN News.com, 5 July 2012, available at http://www.abs-cbnnews.com/-depth/07/05/12/mvp-warned-china-deal-spratlys (accessed 29 October 2012); Riza T. Olchondra, 'Pangilinan may drop China from exploration venture', *Philippine Daily Inquirer*, 28 June 2012.

54 Nguyen Hong Thao, 'Joint development in the Gulf of Thailand', *IBRU Boundary and Security Bulletin*, Autumn 1999.

55 Ong, 'The 1979 and 1990 Malaysia-Thailand joint development agreements'.

56 Singapore and Malaysia had a 29-year maritime dispute over Pedre Branca, a rocky outcrop on which Singapore has maintained a lighthouse since colonial times. The case was heard by the International Court of Justice. In May 2008, the ICJ ruled in favour of Singapore. This case was largely responsible for the country's heightened sensitivity over maritime jurisdiction with Brunei in the following months.

57 J. R. V. Prescott, *The Gulf of Thailand: Maritime Limits to Conflict and Cooperation*, Kuala Lumpur: Maritime Institute of Malaysia, 1998, p. 14.

58 Nguyen Hong Thao, 'Joint Development in the Gulf of Thailand'.

59 Ian Storey, 'China's thirst for energy fuels improved relations with Brunei', *Jamestown Foundation China Brief*, 5(24), available at http://www.jamestown.org/single/?no_cache=1&tx_ttnews%5Btt_news%5D=3913 (accessed 20 October 2012).

60 See Jeffrey J. Smith, 'Brunei and Malaysia resolve outstanding maritime boundary issues', *LOS Reports*, 1, 2010, pp. 1–4.

61 'China's top political advisor makes 4-point proposal to further China-Brunei ties', GOV.cn, 20 April 2012, available at http://english.gov.cn/2012-04/20/content_2118434.htm (accessed 15 November 2012); PRC Embassy in Republic of Indonesia, 'Yang Jiechi met Brunei Second Minister of Foreign Affairs and Trade Lim Jock Seng', Embassy Updates, 7 July 2012, available at http://id.china-embassy.org/eng/sgdt/t950305.htm (accessed 15 November 2012); 'Brunei, China affirm strong bilateral ties', *Borneo Post Online*, 13 August 2012, available at http://www.theborneopost.com/2012/08/13/brunei-china-affirm-strong-bilateral-ties/ (accessed 15 November 2012); 'HM pleased with close China ties', *Brunei Times*, 8 September 2012, available at http://www.bt.com.bn/news-national/2012/09/08/hm-pleased-close-china-ties (accessed 15 November 2012).

62 Rachel Thien, 'Brunei to increase oil exports to China', *Brunei Times*, 24 November 2011.

63 'M'sia, Brunei ink historic pact for joint oil exploration', *The Star*, 13 December 2010.

64 IHS Jane's, South China Sea Strategic Map (updated 2012).

65 'China signs LNG deal with Petronas', *People's Daily Online*, 31 October 2006, available at http://english.peopledaily.com.cn/200610/31/eng20061031_316642.html (accessed 15 November 2012).

13 China's national interests and the law of the sea

Are they reconcilable?[1]

Stein Tønnesson

There are three main disputes in the South China Sea: over navigational rights, the sovereignty to islands and national maritime boundaries. It shall be argued here that it is in China's national interest to separate the three disputes from each other, and give priority to negotiating maritime boundary agreements with its neighbours. The tortuous issue of sovereignty to islands may continue to be shelved. If China enters into serious boundary negotiations on the basis of the law of the sea, then the other regional countries are likely to support its current view that the freedom of navigation does not include military exercises or scientific surveys of the seabed. Joint development schemes for hydrocarbons should be reserved for those areas that are directly affected by the sovereignty disputes to islands, and priority should be given to reducing these areas to the smallest possible size. This argument is based on an assessment of China's need for territorial integrity, national security, energy security, environmental sustainability, regional stability and peaceful development. In order to achieve a stable regional environment, China will have to recognize the sovereign rights of other claimant states to resources within their exclusive economic zones (EEZs). If the other claimants are reassured on this point, they are likely to accept Chinese proposals for joint management regimes for fisheries in certain defined areas. China may also seek a role for its energy companies in exploring for oil and gas through joint ventures on the continental shelf of its neighbouring countries. If China does not enter into serious boundary negotiations but continues to insist on joint development schemes in areas that other countries, with good basis in the law of the sea, consider as part of their EEZ, then China will risk political isolation in its own home region.

What is a national interest?

National interests are not objectively given but need to be defined by policy-makers. Yet there are limits to what can be construed as a national interest. The concept denotes interests that are truly national. The interests of individuals, parties, provinces, companies or sub-national religious or ethnic groups are not national, although it may be in a country's national interest to satisfy them. The national interest is also not international or global. International diplomacy may lead to the definition of shared interests among several or many nations. Such interests may thus be both national and regional or global at the same time but this does not make the national interest as such regional or global. National governments are set to defend the national interest. The word 'interest' denotes something that is materially or otherwise essential for the preservation of the nation as a unit, or in other ways advantageous for the nation as a whole. The term could lose some of its meaning if it were to include normative values or obligations, although they often influence political choices. National interests are not necessarily non-negotiable. A government may choose to downplay or give up one interest in favour of another. Thus it may be in a country's self-interest to make territorial concessions in order to obtain a peaceful environment, or make room for economic development.

The following Chinese national interests are at play in the South China Sea:

- territorial integrity (for islands and maritime zones)
- national security
- energy security
- environmental security
- regional stability
- global respect
- peaceful development.

These interests shall be discussed below in so far as they have a bearing on China's South China Sea policy.

Three disputes

China is engaged in three main legal disputes in the South China Sea. Their importance has steadily increased as more countries have become involved, sea lanes have become busier, fish stocks have dwindled and prospects of finding oil and gas have come to the fore. Meanwhile, patriotic emotions in several countries have focused on small islets as a sacred national heritage, and its rising economic and maritime power has made the People's Republic of China the central player in all these disputes.[2]

One dispute concerns navigational rights. It pits China against the USA. The two countries disagreed on this point at the United Nations Conference on the Law of the Sea 1973–82 (UNCLOS III). China argued that military vessels need permission from the coastal state if they wish to conduct exercises, reconnaissance or intelligence operations inside another country's EEZ. The USA insisted that EEZs are 'international waters' as far as navigation is concerned and that there can be no restrictions on the freedom of navigation for either civilian or military vessels. The laying of communication cables, for instance, is explicitly allowed under the law of the sea. The coastal state has sovereign rights only to *the resources* in the EEZ and on its continental shelf. Other countries can thus only be prohibited from commercial activities. Some of the countries around the South China Sea, such as Malaysia, Thailand and Vietnam, share the Chinese view, although the support given by seafaring nations to the conclusion of the UN Convention on the Law of the Sea (UNCLOS) in 1982 was premised on a recognition that EEZs should be treated as international waters as far as navigation both on the sea and in the air was concerned. In defiance of this principle, the maritime law adopted by Vietnam's National Assembly in June 2012 includes a clause allowing it to prohibit threatening military activities by foreign countries in its EEZ.[3] However, as long as China's neighbours see a need for the US Navy to counter-balance China's rising power, they are unlikely to try to prevent US military activities or provide active support to the Chinese view.

The second dispute is over sovereignty to islands: the Paracels, Spratlys and Scarborough Shoal. Pratas Island is not internationally disputed but occupied by Taiwan on behalf of China. The PRC often lists Macclesfield Bank (Zhongsha Qundao) as a part of its sovereignty claim, but since it is not above water at high tide it is legally speaking a part of the seabed, and can thus not be the object of a sovereignty claim. The Paracels are claimed by China and Vietnam. China has controlled the north-eastern part since 1946 – first by the Republic of China (ROC), and later by the PRC – and the south-western part since 1974, when China conquered it by force from the Republic of Vietnam (South Vietnam). North Vietnam resented the Chinese invasion of what it saw as Vietnamese territory but could not issue any open protest since it needed Chinese support in its war of national unification. China, Taiwan and the Philippines all claim the Scarborough Shoal (Huangyan), a group of six tiny rocks that China sometimes sees as constituting a part of Macclesfield Bank (although they are far away from it and with deep sea in-between).

The most complex dispute concerns the Spratlys, which consist of some 35–40 island features and many reefs and shoals, grouped together in a number of atolls with huge distances between them. China and Taiwan claim all of the Spratlys. So does Vietnam. The Philippines claims most of the islets – except the westernmost ones – as part of a 'Freedomland' (Kalayaan). Malaysia claims three island features located inside its claimed EEZ. Brunei also claims an EEZ in the area, including one island feature.

The third legal dispute concerns the delimitation of the maritime zones that are authorized by UNCLOS 1982, which all the countries with claims in the South China Sea have signed and ratified: a 12 nm territorial sea, 12 nm contiguous zone, 200 nm EEZ and 200 nm continental shelf. The shelf may extend even further through natural prolongation. Whereas the coastal state holds sovereignty in its territorial sea (but must allow innocent passage by foreign ships), it does not hold full sovereignty in the EEZ but has sovereign rights to its resources.

The same three disputes are also present in the East China Sea, but the conditions there are less complex.[4] The dominant dispute is between China and Japan although South Korea claims an area in the north and Taiwan has a strong interest in the south. The East China Sea has just one disputed group of features, the Diaoyu/Senkakus. To delimit the continental shelf in the East China Sea is thus much simpler than in the South China Sea. It is a matter of disregarding or reducing the impact of the disputed Diaoyu/Senkaku rocks so they have just a 12 nm territorial sea or just a minor EEZ, and then striking a compromise between the Japanese median line principle and the Chinese claim based on the natural prolongation of its continental shelf out to the Okinawa trough.[5] The big obstacle to conflict resolution in the East China Sea is not so much complexity as the historically based hostility between China and Japan, which Deng Xiaoping and some of Japan's former leaders tried to overcome, but which has since returned with a vengeance. The East China Sea dispute is a greater danger for international security than the dispute in the South China Sea since it involves two major powers, one of which is a US ally.

Before discussing *how* the boundary disputes may be resolved, we shall look at *why* China needs to resolve them. What are China's main national interests in the South China and East China Sea?

Territorial integrity

Every nation is strongly concerned about its territorial integrity. Yet history is full of changes in the geographical composition of states, often as a result of war. Sometimes whole territories have seceded to form an independent state or they have been annexed or colonized by another state. Such changes are always extremely conflictual. When territories are taken by force the psychological effects of such actions may reverberate through generations if not centuries. As M. Taylor Fravel has shown, the PRC has understood how dangerous it is to have unresolved border disputes and has been prepared in the past to make territorial concessions in peaceful negotiations when pursuing its greater goal of securing a stable environment. This has mainly been the case when Beijing has negotiated from a position of strength. The Chinese government has also seen clear border agreements as a way of ensuring internal stability in ethnic minority areas. Agreed borders make it less likely that other countries will provide support to would-be rebels.[6] Beijing has thus signed land border agreements with Burma (1960), Nepal (1961), North Korea (1962), Mongolia (1962), Afghanistan (1963), Pakistan (1963), Russia (1991, 2004, 2008), Tajikistan (1991, 2002), Kazakhstan (1994, 1997, 1998), Kyrgyzstan (1996, 1999), Laos (1991) and Vietnam (1999).[7] In 2000, China displayed the same wisdom in the maritime domain when agreeing with Vietnam on a maritime boundary in the Gulf of Tonkin, where later an agreement was also reached on the management and exploitation of resources in the area.[8]

Nations are particularly concerned to demonstrate their sovereignty in areas that are seen as part of their national heritage but not under their physical control. Thus Argentina is deeply concerned with its quest for the British-controlled Malvinas (Falkland Islands), the Republic of Cyprus with its sovereignty over territory occupied by Turkey since 1974, and China with the status of Taiwan. China has defined the question of Taiwan's reunification with the mainland as a 'core interest' for which it expects all other nations to provide support. China also defines the integrity of Xinjiang and Tibet as 'core interests'. These huge territories, which enjoy special autonomous status, are seen as threatened by separatist movements who might receive aid from hostile foreign powers. Other countries are warned in the strongest possible terms against any interference in China's internal affairs. This is standard state behaviour. China has also applied normal strategic behaviour when prioritizing the creation and development of the Shanghai Cooperation Organization, with the goal of ensuring stability in Central Asia.

The Taiwan issue is relevant in our context for three main reasons: Taiwan is situated between the South China Sea and the East China Sea and has strong interests of its own in both areas. Taipei has basically the same sovereignty and sovereign rights claims as the PRC on behalf of China. And Taiwan is in physical control of both Pratas Island and Itu Aba (Taiping Dao), the largest of the features in the Spratlys (Nansha Qundao). Taiwan is also actively promoting the Chinese sovereignty claim to the Diaoyu/Senkakus.

During President Obama's visit to China in November 2009, it was agreed that the USA and China would respect each others' 'core interests', and in 2010 it was reported that Chinese diplomats had hinted in talks with US counterparts that (parts of) the South China Sea should be considered a Chinese core interest. This caused a stir when it was leaked to the press. It was later denied by Chinese spokespersons, and it remains uncertain what was meant by the suggestion, if ever there were one.[9] What could conceivably be considered a core national interest is not the tiny Spratly Islands or the Scarborough Shoal but perhaps the area immediately south of Hainan, where the PLA navy has a submarine base. As mentioned above, in the Chinese view – and also in the view of several other coastal states – a coastal country has the right to prohibit military reconnaissance or exercises in its EEZ, although this is not the standard interpretation of the law of the sea among experts in international law.[10]

To define a certain interest as 'core' may be risky since this makes it almost non-negotiable. The intention is to affect the behaviour of foreign governments but the effect may instead be to tie one's own hands. If a disputed sovereignty claim is defined as 'core' then this may prevent a government – even future governments – from seeking compromises with other states even when it might be in the national interest to do so. This observation should be kept in mind when we now consider China's main national interests at sea.

National security

We shall begin with national security and apply a narrow understanding of the term as 'military security'. It is a basic assumption in realist international relations theory that every state must safeguard its national security not just against the known intentions of others but also against their capabilities, both their current and likely future ones. No nation in a basically anarchic world can trust that another nation will remain benevolent. National security may be secured through friendly relations, alliances or military capabilities. China has not entered into any military alliance since the breakdown of its alliance with the Soviet Union in the 1960s – just partnerships. Yet there can be no doubt that Chinese policy-makers are thinking in realist terms. They do their best to build both defensive and offensive military capabilities. At the time when Deng Xiaoping was China's paramount leader, he assessed the world situation on the basis of the prevailing rivalry between US imperialism and Soviet social imperialism and found that China could enjoy a period of peace without having to spend huge resources on its military.[11] This allowed the Chinese government to channel most of its resources into market-driven economic growth, and thus lay a basis for the prosperity that many Chinese now enjoy. Since the end of the Cold War, however, and notably in the most recent decade, China has invested huge resources in modernizing its armed forces, with acquisitions and production of a range of precision-guided missiles, advanced aircraft, fast-going ships and silent-going submarines. Only a limited part of the resources has been invested in intercontinental missiles and nuclear weapons. Substantial resources have gone to land-based short to medium range missiles deployed along the Taiwan Strait. China has also invested in fighter jets, a range of naval vessels and also modern vessels for its several civilian maritime agencies.[12] When Xi Jinping took over as China's new leader in 2012–13 one of his reform initiatives was to put several maritime agencies under the authority of the State Oceanic Administration.[13]

The number and quality of China's destroyers, frigates and submarines have grown rapidly, and this may have made it impossible for the US navy to repeat what it did in 1995 when it entered the Taiwan Strait undetected with aircraft carriers. In 2012 China launched its first aircraft carrier, and is engaged in building several more. The growth in China's military capabilities has dramatically changed the balance of force in the Taiwan Strait. It is no longer conceivable for Taiwan to defend itself alone against a Chinese attack, which would not take the form of an invasion but of a rain of missiles destroying the Taiwanese economy.[14] The only way that a Chinese decision to use force against Taiwan could fail to secure victory would be if the USA launched a preventive attack against China's land-based missiles or decided to retaliate immediately after an attack had begun. The growth in the number of advanced Chinese submarines (some of which are nuclear) in the East China Sea and the South China Sea has also changed the balance of force, and has led other countries to invest in their own submarines. Vietnam is buying Russian-made Kilo class submarines, and Taiwan has plans to build its own.[15]

The proliferation of submarines is the single most destabilizing factor in the region. This is also what makes the Sino-American dispute over maritime rights so important. The USA consistently refers to the principle of 'freedom of navigation' as an argument for conducting naval and aerial reconnaissance right up to the outer limit of the Chinese 12 nm territorial sea so it can follow every movement of Chinese submarines. This was behind the US insistence that the military reconnaissance vessel *USNS Impeccable* had the right to operate south of Hainan when China tried to chase it from the area in March 2009. China's overall aim is most likely to build a capacity for denying the US and other foreign navies access to the semi-enclosed South China Sea, East China Sea and Yellow Sea – within its 'first island chain' – so the Chinese navy can dominate its proximate waters. This is both for defensive reasons and for the purpose of projecting power beyond this chain of islands, which runs from the Japanese main islands to Okinawa, the Philippines, the Spratlys and the Malacca Strait. While building a capacity to deny access for foreign navies to these 'brown waters', China has also started to build a 'blue water' navy with a capacity to project power on the high seas.[16] Although one or a few aircraft carriers cannot threaten the US navy's 11 modern carrier groups, Chinese aircraft carriers could impress or intimidate its neighbouring countries, and serve as the beginning of a long-term build-up with the aim to dominate the Western Pacific. While the construction of aircraft carriers does not enhance but rather reduces China's national security in the short term,[17] this may still be a judicious long-term strategic investment *provided that* China uses other means to avoid any clash with the USA. To build a carrier force with a capacity to challenge the superiority of the US navy, whose aircraft carriers are being continuously replaced with newly built ships and replenished with first rate technology and highly trained crews, would require several decades of construction and training. The most demanding task may well be to train a sufficient number of pilots to take off from and land on the decks of the carriers. This requires constant practice, and there will be many accidents along the way. In order to make sense, China's investment in aircraft carriers thus presupposes that China is able to keep its peace with the USA for at least two more decades. This must be a peace that Washington feels sufficiently confident about to refrain from actions aiming to obstruct the further expansion of the Chinese economy and military forces. This will require astute reassuring diplomacy on the part of Beijing, with substantial elements of confidence-building, as part of a grand strategy.

How does this relate to China's sovereignty disputes in the South China Sea and East China Sea? Do the sovereignty disputes over the tiny rocks or islets in the Scarborough Shoal, the Diaoyu/Senkakus or the Spratlys offer valuable opportunities for China to gain experience with tactical operations when handling incidents between fishermen and coastguards or maritime surveillance vessels from neighbouring states? Are these islets important strategic assets? The answer to both questions is no.

While small clashes or stand-offs at sea may serve the particular interests of coastguards and maritime surveillance services, who improve their budgets and gain new modern ships as well as domestic popularity, cold-headed Chinese naval strategists are bound to see these sovereignty disputes and their related incidents as a nuisance, drawing resources away from the navy's main strategic tasks. The incidents instil fear among China's neighbours and lead them to invest more in their own military capabilities, thus adding new complications to China's projection of power. The Japanese and South Korean navies are already modern and well trained, more so than the Chinese. Singapore and Malaysia have quite impressive naval forces, and Vietnam is catching up. All of them could be future adversaries. The sovereignty disputes also draw unsolicited attention from the USA and other external governments and navies, such as those of India and Russia. China risks becoming a 'lonely power'.[18]

Patriotic emotions may prevent people from realizing that the rocks and islets in the Spratlys are of little strategic value. Modern satellite technology makes listening posts in such places redundant. Any occupied islet is a sitting duck, easy to subdue, destroy or invade and impossible to defend in war. From a purely military point of view it is an advantage for China that Vietnam and the Philippines are wasting resources on keeping a number of Spratly islets occupied and that the bill for keeping up the Chinese sovereignty claim to Itu Aba (Taiping Dao) is footed by Taiwan. If Vietnam were to place cruise missiles in the Spratlys then they would represent a threat against the Chinese navy but then it would be preferable for Vietnam – just as for China – to place any cruise missiles either on well-protected land installations or on fast-going ships rather than on an exposed reef. The possession of small islets does not provide a key to controlling the sea. Strong navies and air forces do. The only perceivable strategic value of the Spratly islets is in an offensive scenario. If a country controlling the Spratlys were planning to invade the nearby Philippines, Brunei or East Malaysia, then a surprise attack could benefit from pre-established bases in the archipelago. Hence if China were at some point to occupy and fortify the Spratlys, this would thoroughly scare up the governments and public opinion in those three countries and compel them to invest heavily in their national defence and external alliances.

Why has China so far not taken any Spratly island by force but just established a symbolic presence on a limited number of reefs? My guess is that this is not because of modesty or lack of resources. The likely reason is that China's naval commanders think in strategic terms and not as narrow-minded patriots. Any sensible grand strategy would dictate China to play down its conflict with its neighbouring countries. Unless China intends to move so close to the USA that a wedge can be drawn through the US–Japan alliance, China needs to reassure its neighbours, including Japan.

If China makes the sensible choice to concentrate on a strategy of access denial, that is, to project sufficient power from its coast to make it impossible for hostile foreign forces to penetrate the semi-enclosed seas inside the first chain of islands, then it needs stable relations with Japan, the two Koreas, Taiwan, the Philippines, Malaysia, Singapore and Vietnam. The less these countries feel threatened by China the more room there will be for China to quietly build up its power projection capabilities without being exposed to counter-balancing behaviour. If China instead spends substantial resources on building a blue water navy, then it will be even more important to maintain good relations with its neighbouring states. The reasons for this are threefold. First, China will then be more vulnerable in its home waters since resources are diverted to expensive aircraft carrier construction. Second, the USA will then most likely adopt counter-measures. Third, as mentioned above, in order to be successful a blue water naval construction programme requires several decades of peace with the USA. It will be much easier to uphold such peace if China also has peace with its neighbours, including those who are US allies. Under stable and peaceful conditions China could expect support from some of its neighbouring states for its opposition to uncurtailed US freedom of military navigation within its EEZ – but this would of course mean that Vietnam and the Philippines could also curtail Chinese military operations inside their EEZs.

What would be the best scenario in the South China Sea from the point of view of Chinese naval strategy? The best would be to not just shelve or downplay the boundary disputes but resolve them. If China could add secure maritime boundaries to its secure land borders (the border with Bhutan and India are exceptions), then there would be less risk that a rise of Chinese military power would lead to a confrontation with Japan and/or the USA. Even if Chinese strategic planners consider such a confrontation to be inevitable it would be to China's advantage to postpone it until China could be confident of winning. And then the implication for the East China Sea and the South China Sea is the same: China needs secure maritime boundaries. Thus, if Chinese naval commanders think in grand strategic terms, and not as short-sighted patriots or lobbyists for greater budgets, they must be eager proponents of conflict resolution.

Energy security

Mainland China is in the enviable position, compared with Japan, South Korea and Taiwan, of not being completely dependent on imported oil and gas. Its energy situation is quite similar to the USA's. China has abundant coal deposits, and still produces about 40 per cent of the enormous amount of oil it consumes. It also has huge amounts of shale gas that could greatly enhance its national energy security. The countries that depend the most on oil from the volatile Middle East are Japan, South Korea, Taiwan and some of the European countries, not the USA or China. The fact that China began in 1993 to import more oil than it exported, and today imports 60 per cent of its oil, does not mean it *depends* on imported oil. In a time of crisis it could drastically reduce its private consumption and thus maintain its national security.

To be overly concerned with national energy security is not – at least in peacetime – in any country's national interest since this leads to costly over-investments. It is doubtful that China's investments in African oil production or in pipelines through Central Asia and Myanmar make sense from the point of view of national energy security. Pipelines can be security risks since they are easy to sabotage. The decision to construct oil and gas pipelines through Myanmar may reflect the particular interests of Yunnan province and the China National Petroleum Corporation (CNPC) more than the national interest of China as a whole.[19] Yet all of these costly investments have been backed up by the seemingly compelling argument that China needs to diversify its oil imports in order to reduce its imports on sea lanes dominated by the US and Indian navies and running through the vulnerable chokepoint of the Malacca Strait before crossing the South China Sea.

It remains unclear if there are any substantial deposits of oil under the unexplored parts of the South China Sea.[20] The richest oil province in the area is just north of Borneo. It has already been tapped for decades by companies operating under concessions from Brunei and Malaysia. Oil produced on the continental shelf of Vietnam has been exported to Japan and China and has contributed much needed revenue to a country that has only modest foreign currency reserves. However, Vietnam's limited offshore oil reserves would not have made much difference to China's energy security if China had owned them. To gain control over oilfields off the Vietnamese coast is hardly a goal worth fighting for, no matter how much there might be. The wise thing to do is to recognize Vietnam's EEZ and import oil from Vietnam.

China's energy security would benefit from any oil discoveries in the South China Sea regardless of who had the sovereign rights to them, simply because the oil would not need to travel the long distance from the Gulf or East Africa. From a detached point of view it is far from vital that the hydrocarbons are located on China's continental shelf. The extra gain to be derived from having sovereign rights to the resources would be in the form of revenue but China's main need is not to further increase its money earnings or currency reserves. The main thing for China is the oil and gas itself. It would not be much of a problem if it were imported from Vietnam, the Philippines or Malaysia as long as it could be securely shipped or piped to China. If maritime boundaries could be agreed upon, the neighbouring states would probably be ready to invite the China National Offshore Oil Company (CNOOC) to partner in joint ventures with their national oil companies. The establishment of joint ventures could even be part of a negotiated package. This would be a much safer solution than so-called joint development areas (JDAs) where the sovereignty dispute is left unresolved. One of the problems with JDAs is that it is sometimes just as difficult to agree on whether or not an area is disputed as to settle on a boundary.[21] Another problem is that JDAs cannot be under the jurisdiction of any single country, so a whole separate body of law must be built up, with a special tribunal, in order for investors and lenders to feel secure.

The oil sector is characterized by huge high-risk investments. Oil companies are used to taking risks but need to know that they will benefit if oil is discovered. This requires a clear legal regime. They are therefore reluctant to explore for oil in disputed areas. In disputed areas they may sign up to concessions, and may also 'shoot some seismic', but when push comes to shove they prefer to stall instead of drilling. This tendency is heightened by the fact that many holes drilled in the undisputed parts of the South China Sea have been dry. Oil companies need a clear, unambiguous legal regime to protect their interests. This is best achieved within delimited national zones no matter whether the oil company in question is private or state owned. The executives of the CNOOC, Sinopec and CNPC will understand this just as well as their private partners abroad. Both from the perspective of their corporate interests and from the point of view of China's energy security, a maritime boundary system is to be preferred.

Environmental security

Care for the environment now counts more than before in calculations of the national interest, not least in China, where environmental problems could derail the country's development. The Chinese government well understands that this also pertains to the sea. China and the other littoral nations of the South China Sea and the East China Sea have a shared interest in living up to their moral obligation, as mentioned in UNCLOS, Article 123, to cooperate in protecting the marine environments, and in managing the living and non-living resources. To protect dwindling fish stocks and effectively prevent the use of illegal fishing methods is a matter of urgency. The coastal states must also be prepared to handle possible oil spills from a tanker in distress.[22] All of this requires clarity as to who carries responsibility for the various parts of a semi-enclosed sea. Such clarity is normally obtained through maritime delimitation. Sufficient clarity could also be achieved through the establishment of joint environmental management areas (JEMAs), to which each participating country must allocate a certain amount of resources. A JEMA might conceivably be established in the Spratlys' immediate surroundings but the most efficient way to take care of the environment is most probably to delimit the sea into national zones.

Regional stability

A stable regional environment has long been the aim of China's policy towards its neighbouring states. Regional stability is important for a number of reasons related to economy, culture and security.[23] If China and the USA were to draw closely together, and maintain good relations with India and Russia, then China could perhaps afford to lean heavily on Japan, the Philippines or Vietnam and get away with it. However, as long as China faces a US–Japan security alliance, the Philippines can draw on US treaty obligations and Vietnam can move closer to the USA while maintaining its traditional friendships with Russia and India. China's official policy of 'peaceful development', as propagated in Hu Jintao's time as China's leader, reiterated the traditional Chinese 'good neighbour policy'. China effectively pursued this policy in the 1990s and the first half of the 2000s. It encouraged the expansion of ASEAN to include Vietnam, Laos, Myanmar and Cambodia, took part in developing the ASEAN+3 and ASEAN Regional Forum consultative frameworks, as well as the East Asian Summits. It overcame its reluctance to discuss the South China Sea multilaterally when agreeing with ASEAN on a Declaration on the Conduct of Parties in the South China Sea (DOC) in 2002, and it entered into a free trade agreement with ASEAN. All of this improved the standing of China throughout Southeast Asia, reducing past apprehensions.[24]

However, most of this was lost once the South China Sea disputes flared up again from 2008 onwards. A low point was reached in 2012, when China relied on Cambodia to prevent the other ASEAN member states from making a joint statement including mention of a recent Sino-Philippines stand-off at the Scarborough Shoal.[25] That event itself, coming on top of a series of incidents between China, the Philippines and Vietnam over fishing and oil exploration during 2011, was a tactical victory for China since it managed – without using force – to obtain the withdrawal of a Philippines military vessel and then to seal off the lagoon with a rope and maintain a quasi-permanent Chinese presence. Strategically, however, the tactical victory was most probably a setback. The Philippines abandoned its former rather pro-Chinese attitude, based on appreciation of business opportunities, and undertook a determined effort to seek US support, bring back the US navy to its former bases, and, build up its own military capabilities. The Philippines also gained the courage needed to utilize a legal opening in Article 287 of UNCLOS to refer certain aspects of China's South China Sea policy to an Arbitration Tribunal, a move that led to strong Chinese protests and for some time derailed the process of consultations between China and ASEAN. China refused at one point to enter into further talks with ASEAN over developing a code of conduct (COC) agreement, unless the Philippines was shut out. No international organization would of course shut out one of its members for such reasons. All of this damaged Sino-ASEAN relations and strengthened the need felt not just in the Philippines, but in Vietnam, Indonesia and Singapore as well, for an increase in the US military presence. For China, the greatest danger is not perhaps US interference but what Zbigniew Brzezinski has called 'the disturbing possibility that a revitalized Asia may slide into the kind of nationalistic fervour that precipitated conflicts in 20th-century Europe over resources, territory or power'. President Jimmy Carter's national security advisor at the time when the USA and China established diplomatic relations in 1978–1979 now sees the proliferation of nationalist sentiments as a greater threat to stable US–China relations than any hostile intentions on the part of either China or the USA.[26] There are plenty of potential flash points where nationalist sentiments are at play: North Korea vs. South Korea, China vs. Japan, China vs. India, Vietnam vs. China. If governments incite or allow nationalistic fervour to proliferate further it could perceivably spin out of control and make it difficult to abstain from reckless behaviour vis-à-vis other states.

Any Chinese diplomat with experience of dealing with ASEAN countries must realize the urgent need to return to China's good neighbour policy. There should be agreement on that score both from those who might see it as a temporary tactical device to ensure China's continued rise and from those who see it as a way to permanently enhance China's respected status both in its own region and in the wider world. It is in China's national interest to further strengthen ASEAN as an organization that has never been directed against China but instead has sought to enhance cooperation between its members and China. To sow dissension within ASEAN is likely to weaken China's general standing in the region.

Respected status

Three overlapping and sometimes conflicting worldviews may be discerned in contemporary Chinese thinking about its position in the world. The first is based on China's historical status as a highly developed and ancient civilization. China is not a normal nation, but a great civilizational power for whom everyone should show due respect. If other nations fulfil this obligation, then China will reciprocate generously, and refrain from unwanted interference.[27] This worldview is more hierarchical than egalitarian but there is no strict hierarchy, no imperialism, just a sense of who is situated at the centre. If everyone knows their place in the inherited order of things, then peace will be preserved. The second worldview is based on the twentieth-century principle of national sovereignty and non-interference in other countries' internal affairs. This core idea, essentially European by origin, is crucial not just for China but for many developing countries. They resent the post-Cold War tendency in the West to allow interventions in other country's internal affairs under principles such as 'responsibility to protect'. The continued importance of the non-interference principle was a key message in a speech given by China's new president Xi Jinping to the State Institute of International Affairs in Moscow during his first tour abroad as President in March 2013.[28] The third worldview is more emancipatory. It emphasizes how China has grown from a humiliating position in the second half of the nineteenth and the first half of the twentieth century to the world's second greatest power. As such it does not just represent its own interests but is in the forefront of the struggle of all developing nations to obtain their share of global prosperity and influence. The global system of trade, finance and governance must be reformed to better reflect the interests of developing countries. A common denominator of all three worldviews is an expectation to be shown due respect as a central, sovereign and influential major power.

Tensions between the three worldviews tend to make it difficult for Chinese policy-makers to define their identity clearly in world affairs and form a coherent grand strategy.[29] There is also a traditional reluctance to think in terms of grand strategy. China sometimes just follows the unpredictable flow of events, seeking to manoeuvre in ways that maximize Chinese interests. China seeks at one and the same time to revive its central historical role, protect its national sovereignty and build a global agenda for change through active participation in multilateral institutions. China seeks to influence its global economic and security environment through bilateral and multilateral diplomacy in frameworks such as the United Nations, the Group of 20 (G20), the World Trade Organization (WTO), the International Monetary Fund and cooperation among the BRIC countries (Brazil, Russia, India and China). China's on-going rise is sometimes compared to the former rise – and fall – of the Soviet Union. While it was more awesome militarily than China is today, the Soviet Union had little influence outside its own system of alliances since it did not immerse itself in the institutional order that regulated international and transnational interactions. These global institutional frameworks gained in importance after the demise of the Soviet Union. China took an active part in that process and is today one of the three main players in global economic decision-making, together with the EU and the USA. This makes China a more respected global power than the Soviet Union ever was.

To preserve and develop the status and influence it has gained globally China must demonstrate its respect for international law. It is in China's national interest to do so, and the law of the sea is a case in point. This is not to stretch the concept of national interest too far. If China is not seen as a nation that lives up to its legal obligations it will find it difficult to realize its foreign policy goals with diplomatic means. Diplomatic leverage is of course a key national interest in itself. China has both signed and ratified UNCLOS. When it was negotiated during 1973–82, the PRC made its second breakthrough in global international diplomacy (the first was at the Geneva conference on Indochina in 1954) as a proponent of the interests of coastal developing states against the 'hegemonic' maritime powers (USA, USSR, UK). China shared in the joy of the world's coastal states when obtaining recognition for the principle of a 200 nm continental shelf and EEZ.[30] China formally ratified UNCLOS in 1996. It will mean a great deal for the status enjoyed by China both in its own region and globally for it to live up to its treaty obligations and recognize sovereign rights not only in its own maritime zones but also in those of its neighbours.

Peaceful development

The last national interest to be discussed is perhaps the most important one from the perspective of the Chinese nation. This is China's own social, economic and cultural development. The main factor behind China's high standing in Asia and the world is the phenomenal economic growth it has achieved since it introduced market economic reforms in 1978. Growth has happened through integration in the global division of labour, with flows of foreign direct investments to China's growth zones, market access for China in Europe and North America, and access to advanced technology from Japan, Europe and the USA. China's 2001 membership of the WTO was a major diplomatic achievement. The Middle Kingdom's integration in the global economy has also allowed it to build a capacity for innovation, which may help it avoid the middle income trap and jump to a new level of development and become a world leader in several sectors, such as 'green technology'. Yet the challenges are enormous. There are still large pockets of poverty in the country. Inequality has been growing between regions and social groups. There is a huge 'floating population' working and living in areas far away from its registered place of residence. Pollution is rampant and there are calls for drastic measures to protect the environment. China must urgently preserve and economize its water resources. Low levels of fertility and the one-child policy are leading to such ageing of the population that today's children will face a colossal task in feeding and caring for the old. The state must mobilize resources to finance expensive social security and health systems. The task of managing a highly complex modern economy requires radical administrative reforms. Abuse of power and corruption reduce public respect for the government and the Communist Party. These are just some of China's development challenges, which will not be automatically resolved by letting loose market forces. The market must be governed by a competent, efficient government, and this requires a conscious political strategy both for China's internal development and for its external economic interactions.

Asia's main economic powerhouse is not Southeast but Northeast Asia. A key national interest for China in the economic field is therefore to maintain and institutionalize a system of mutually beneficial trade and investments between Japan, South Korea and itself – including Hong Kong, Macao and Taiwan. China needs a proactive policy in free trade negotiations and cannot leave the initiative to the USA with its Trans Pacific Partnership idea, which excludes China. Although the Southeast Asian countries are less important than the major Northeast Asian economies in the context of trade and investments, they also have sizable markets and are important sources of raw materials. Chinese companies have invested heavily in the Philippines, Vietnam and other Southeast Asian countries, some of whom have cheaper labour than China itself. They have now taken over some labour intensive industries. At the other end of the prosperity ladder, Singapore plays an essential role as a hub of trade and finance.

The South China Sea disputes have led to growing fear in the Southeast Asian countries of their economic dependence on China. They have noticed the Chinese prohibition against imports of Philippines' bananas during the Scarborough Shoal stand-off and China's harsh reactions when the Philippines brought China in for the Arbitration Tribunal in January 2013. Several Southeast Asian countries are now afraid to become targets of Chinese economic sanctions. This has led them to look for alternative investors and trading partners. Although this may be of marginal importance in Beijing, it does affect south-east China, and is clearly not in China's national interest. It would be dangerous for China to seek comfort in the fact that the above fears are not felt in all the countries of ASEAN: Cambodia and Thailand have not lost any of their confidence in China. But cherry-picking supportive Southeast Asian countries is a less rewarding strategy for China than the generally pro-ASEAN policy it pursued from the mid-1990s to the mid-2000s.[31]

We must assume that Chinese investors and companies operating in Southeast Asia, if able to make their voice heard in Beijing, are speaking up for conflict resolution. China's maritime disputes with the ASEAN claimants have grown out of proportion to become a major irritant in China's regional policy, bringing setbacks in many domains. Anti-Chinese sentiments have been voiced publicly, notably in Vietnam. They have become a key problem for the Vietnamese Communist Party. It cannot bow to pressure from China without provoking popular protest and losing its national legitimacy.

Why China needs to be proactive

It seems that every single one of China's main national interests – except territorial integrity within a maximalist interpretation of China's 'maritime territory' – points towards a need for a sustained effort to resolve the disputes at sea. So far China has pursued a policy of calculated ambiguity concerning its claims in the South China Sea, thus keeping all options open while expanding its capabilities. With regard to the East China Sea, however, China took a huge step forward in December 2012 when submitting its calculation to the United Nations Commission on the Limits of the Continental Shelf of the extension of its continental shelf out to the Okinawa trough.[32] This may form a basis for tough future negotiations with Japan, who builds its heavily overlapping claim on the median line principle. In the South China Sea, however, China has not yet made known its precise claims but has maintained its calculated ambiguity in protest notes to the UN Secretary General against other countries' claims.[33]

While it may seem astute to leave the initiative to others while keeping one's own options open, this is only the case if China's primary aim is to maximize its maritime territory. As argued above, a dogged pursuance of this aim is bound to undermine China's quest for national security, energy security, a stable neighbourhood, global respect and continued peaceful development. If China were able to enter into serious boundary negotiations with the other claimant states, then this would enhance China's national security, reduce the neighbours' temptation to invite US interference, remove hesitation in other countries to integrate economically with China, enhance China's energy security if exploitable oil and gas is found in the South China Sea, and deepen respect for China in the global domain by demonstrating its commitment to international law and removing fears of 'maritime assertiveness'.

Since this argument is so logically overwhelming it cannot but be surprising that China has not pursued the same wise policy at sea as on land – except in the Gulf of Tonkin. Even that successful negotiation with Vietnam in 2000 did not lead to a sustained effort to build a case for resolving disputes in other parts of the South China Sea. China was lukewarm to attempts by ASEAN to negotiate a legally binding COC. China has also stuck to – or returned to – a principle of negotiating only bilaterally, although a comprehensive solution of the disputes in the South China Sea must require both bilateral and multilateral talks.

Why has China been vague and reactive instead of clear and proactive? Why did it not use the confidence obtained in its relationship with ASEAN to move forward? Why, from 2008, did it allow tension to grow again to unprecedented levels? One frequently heard explanation is that the Chinese government is influenced by nationalist public opinion. The following statement is often heard: 'No Chinese leader can afford to compromise China's sovereign rights in the South China Sea!' This is unconvincing. Concessions made by the PRC in past border negotiations have not led to uproar or revolt. A strong and confident government is able to explain to its population a need to make territorial concessions. It seems likely that China's ability to make concessions will increase as its power and self-assuredness grows.

Another possible explanation for China's recent reactive policy could be a mistaken assumption that adversaries will be more forthcoming as China becomes more powerful. The idea may be that an armada of modern maritime surveillance ships and naval vessels will soften adversaries and make them more prepared to accept Chinese terms. This is an illusion. The other claimants are instead likely to arm themselves and seek support from the USA, India, Australia and, in Vietnam's case, Russia. China's neighbours know the law of the sea and feel strong in their entitlement to a 200 nm EEZ and continental shelf measured from their main coasts. National psychology must also be taken into account. Just like China itself its neighbours are unlikely to make concessions from a position of weakness. The more China's power grows the more insecure and apprehensive its neighbours will feel – unless they are reassured – and the less likely they are to give up what they see as their right. Their maritime territories will tend to be perceived as matters of national survival.

Three additional factors may contribute to explaining why China has not adopted a more strategically proactive constructive diplomacy in the maritime domain. One is lack of co-ordination and the relative political weakness of the Ministry of Foreign Affairs in Chinese decision-making.[34] The other two factors need some further discussion. They are the Taiwan issue and the U-shaped line.

The role of Taiwan

In order to launch a sustained diplomatic effort to resolve the disputes in the South China Sea, the PRC needs to coordinate its policy with the ROC (Taiwan). The provincial government in Hainan, which has administrative responsibility for the South China Sea, could play a facilitating role in laying the groundwork for such coordination. It is necessary for several reasons. First, Taiwan occupies Pratas Island (south-west of Hong Kong) and Itu Aba (Taiping Dao), the largest of the Spratlys (1,000 m long; 400 m wide). Second, the ROC formalized China's sovereignty claims in the aftermath of the Second World War, and also published the first version of a map with a controversial U-shaped line. The ROC has considerable knowledge of the oceanography, geology and legal history of the South China Sea and could make major contributions if allowed to take part in talks. Third, Taiwan is located between the Chinese mainland and the Philippines, so the establishment of maritime boundaries between China and the Philippines must involve Taiwan. Fourth, if China were to enter into serious South China Sea talks without any Taiwanese involvement, then the ROC might challenge the results and play on patriotic Chinese resentment. Fifth, it might be attractive for the PRC to allow the ROC a recognized status as a separate entity within a 'one-China negotiating team', since this might be a step on the way to reunification. To realize this potential is admittedly a tall challenge, and the weak popular support for the Kuomintang party among the Taiwanese electorate makes it impossible at present for the ROC to enter into a 'one-China game'. This could, however, change.

The U-shaped line

A priority task for China and Taiwan with regard to the South China Sea is to clarify the meaning of the U-shaped line, which first appeared on an official ROC map in 1947 or 1948, and has since become standard on virtually every map produced in Taiwan and mainland China. There are many competing interpretations of the map, both in the PRC and in the ROC.[35]

The most extreme view is that the whole area inside the line is Chinese sovereign maritime territory. Legally speaking this is an absurd proposition since in that case there would be no need for the baselines that Taiwan and mainland China have drawn along their coasts.[36] A controversial archipelagic baseline drawn by the PRC around the Paracels would also be redundant if the whole area inside the U-shaped line were Chinese internal waters. The U-shaped line would then constitute the baseline.

The next view is that the U-shaped line encloses China's territorial sea. This is also irreconcilable with international law, since the territorial sea is clearly defined in UNCLOS as a 12 nm zone measured from the coastal baselines. The PRC has adopted national laws with provisions for a 12 nm territorial sea measured from its baselines. The ROC has done likewise.

The third interpretation is that the U-shaped line institutes a special 'historical waters' regime, based on the fact that these waters have been used historically by Chinese fishermen. The problem is that the same waters have been used by fishermen from other countries as well. The principle of 'historical waters' may have a basis in international law only as regards bays where fishermen from one country have had privileged access. This could be the case in a bay enclosed by the territory of just one nation but is impossible to imagine in a semi-enclosed sea surrounded by several sovereign states.

A fourth interpretation is that the U-shaped line represents the Chinese EEZ boundary, which is further away from the main Chinese coasts than 200 nm because the Paracel and Spratly archipelagos are Chinese and are entitled to a 200 nm EEZ. This argument has been underpinned by the PRC's drawing of archipelagic baselines around the Paracels, but China has fortunately not done the same around the Spratlys. It is difficult to argue that the original meaning of the U-shaped line was to denote an EEZ boundary since the EEZ did not yet exist as a concept when the map was first published. The fourth interpretation can also hardly be reconciled with contemporary international law since the Paracels and Spratlys are not considered in the eyes of the law to be groups or archipelagos but a collection of individual features. Only archipelagic states, such as the Philippines and Indonesia, have the right to use archipelagic baselines. In addition the Paracels and Spratlys do not satisfy the criterion set in UNCLOS with regard to the required ratio of land to water that is a condition for a status as an archipelagic state.

A fifth interpretation, which seems to be actively explored in China at present, is that the U-shaped line represents a claim to certain 'historic rights' that defy or overlap with other nations' sovereign rights. These historic rights are not necessarily exclusive or sovereign, but they do give Chinese fishermen a right to fish and its energy companies a right to exploit oil and gas – or at least take part in such exploitation. The historic rights argument is innovative and would require a revision of the law of the sea. Such revision is unlikely to receive much support from other parties to the UNCLOS. If China decides to pursue the historic rights argument, then it will probably prolong the stalemate in the South China Sea and make conflict resolution even harder.

The last and only reasonable interpretation of the U-shaped line is the one stated in China's official letter of protest to the UN Secretary General on 7 May 2009, to which a map with the U-shaped line was attached.[37] The letter said that the U-shaped line meant a claim to all islands inside it and their 'adjacent waters'. If 'adjacent waters' can be understood as the maritime zones that can be derived from the islands on the basis of provisions in UNCLOS, then this does provide an opening for resolving the disputes. However, the same letter to the UN also mentioned the term 'relevant waters', a concept that could leave the field open for trying to define more expansive 'historic rights'.

A precondition for a constructive diplomatic effort towards conflict resolution in the South China Sea is that China and Taiwan clarify that the U-shaped line means a claim to all islands inside it (Paracels, Spratlys, Scarborough Shoal) and to their maritime zones. In a letter to the UN Secretary General on 14 April 2011, China made it clear that it considers the Spratlys as capable of generating the full suite of maritime zones. The letter does not, however, clarify whether the Spratlys have this capacity as a group or if the zones must be derived from each individual island.[38]

Priorities in conflict resolution

If we imagine – optimistically – that mainland China and Taiwan are able to establish a 'one-China' team to talk with the other claimants and that they clarify the meaning of the U-shaped line, then the question remains of where to begin a process of conflict resolution.

It is common to assume that the dispute over sovereignty to the Spratly Islands must be resolved before it is possible to define EEZ or continental shelf boundaries in the South China Sea, and that the dispute over the Diaoyu/Senkakus must be resolved before the same thing can happen in the East China Sea. This is not necessarily so. A central proposition in this chapter is that the three main disputes – over navigational rights, sovereignty to islands and delimitation of maritime zones – may and should be handled separately, although they are interlinked.

It is clearly in the national interest of China to delink its quarrel with the USA over military reconnaissance from its disputes with neighbouring states over sovereignty to islands, and over fishing and oil exploration. The more the three kinds of disputes are mixed up, and the more China's neighbours see a need for a heavy US naval presence, the more external interference there will be in the South China Sea and the harder it will be for China to build international support for its attempts to curtail military reconnaissance activities in the EEZ.

To delink the sovereignty disputes over islands from the disputes over maritime boundaries is an uncommon proposition. Indeed, it is normal to assume that the resolution of sovereignty disputes to islands must precede the delimitation of maritime zones since the law of the sea is based on the principle that 'land commands water'. Maritime zones are always determined on the basis of distance from land, including islands. Yet this chapter argues that the key to conflict resolution is precisely to disassociate as much as possible the island disputes from maritime delimitation. This is for three reasons. The first is that the island disputes are so complex and emotional that it is hard to imagine any solution in the foreseeable future, except through impartial adjudication or arbitration, a method China has expressly said it will not accept. The second reason is that all of the disputed islands are so small that their effect on maritime delimitation will in any case be modest. They are islets rather than islands. The third reason is that it must be possible to confine the disputed maritime zones to the areas around the disputed islets, while proceeding to draw national boundaries in the rest of the sea, on the basis of distance from the mainland coasts and coasts of major islands such as the

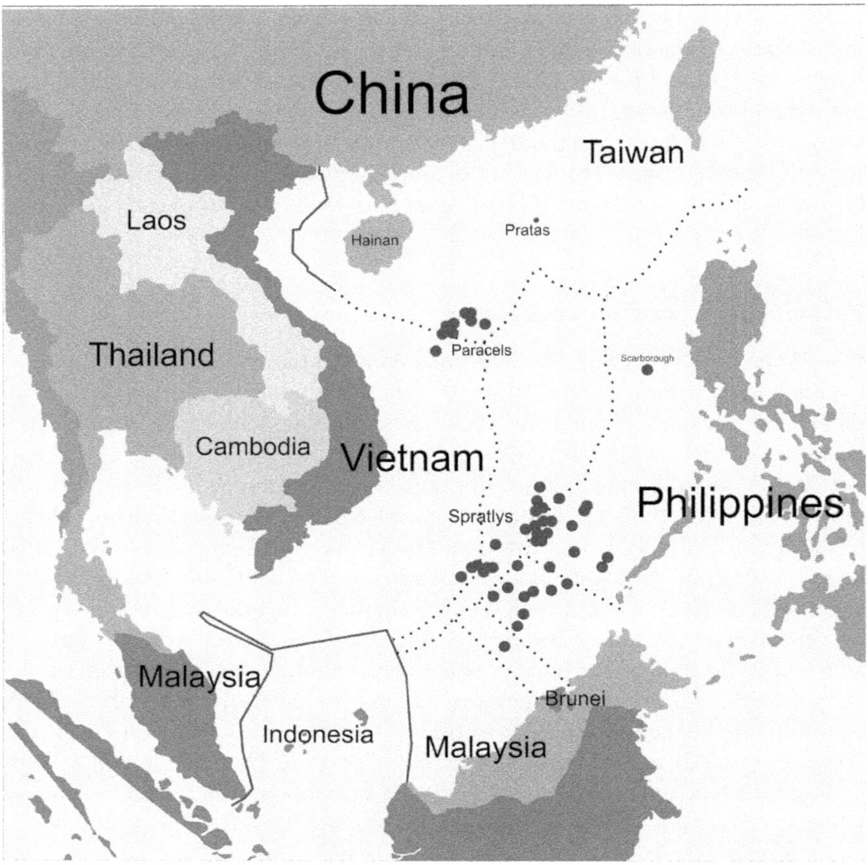

Figure 13.1 Rough delimitation of the South China Sea (full lines are agreed borders; dotted lines are estimated preliminary EEZ boundaries, before islands are taken into account; dark circles are 12 nm territorial waters around each islet)

Ryukuyus, Taiwan, Hainan, Luzon, Palawan, Borneo, Natuna and Con Dao. The disputed waters around the disputed islets could then be placed under a regional joint environmental protection regime.

The usual way to delimit maritime zones in waters where boundaries may be affected by the presence of small islets is to first disregard the islets and draw preliminary boundaries on the basis of distance from base points on the main coasts. In those cases where the EEZs overlap, one will draw a preliminary equidistant median line. For the approximate preliminary delimitation of 200 nm EEZs in the South China Sea, following this method, see Figure 13.1.

After the first rough delimitation, small islets may be given a certain modifying effect depending on their size and location. The most immediate modifying effect is that all features surrounded by water and being above water at high tide are awarded a 12 nm territorial sea. If they are located inside another country's EEZ then they may form an enclave, although this is not considered desirable since it may dilute responsibility for resource management. If sovereignty to an islet with a 12 nm territorial sea is disputed, then the whole enclave is of course disputed. The next issue to consider is whether the islet in question satisfies the criterions defined in Article 121.3 of UNCLOS for having a right to extended maritime zones. Article121.3 says that rocks that cannot sustain human habitation or an economic life of their own shall have only a 12 nm territorial sea.

From a non-partisan pragmatic perspective the optimal way to resolve the disputes over maritime delimitation is to decide that all the Diaoyu/Senkakus, Spratlys and Paracels, as well as the Scarborough Shoal, are unable to sustain human habitation or an economic life of their own. This would immediately reduce the disputed waters to include just these rocks, shoals and reefs, and their 12 nm territorial seas. Maritime delimitation would be greatly facilitated. Another effect in the South China Sea would be to leave a 'doughnut' of high seas in the middle, outside 200 nm from all mainland coasts. The presence of Hainan and Taiwan will help China gain sovereignty to resources in most of the northern half of the South China Sea. If Beijing could gain acceptance for according Pratas and some of the Paracels a status as being able to sustain human habitation or an economic life of their own, then the Chinese EEZ and continental shelf could be extended to a sizable part of the doughnut, including the whole of Macclesfield Bank (Zhongsha Qundao). However, to try the same in the Spratlys would complicate matters enormously since they are far away from China, near the coasts of the Philippines, Brunei and Malaysia, do not constitute real islands and are not controlled by the PRC. It has occupied just underwater reefs, three of which include small rocks that stick above the water at high tide. All the islets that might satisfy conditions for generating zones beyond 12 nm are occupied by Vietnam, the Philippines, Malaysia or Taiwan. If China were to accept that all the Spratlys can have no more than a 12 nm territorial sea, then it would also have to accept that it cannot get sovereign rights to resources in the southern part of the South China Sea. While this may be a bitter pill to swallow, it is probably the one big concession China needs to make in order to resolve its maritime boundary conundrum. In the East China Sea it is Japan that must swallow this pill by agreeing that the Diaoyu/Senkakus cannot be used as a basis for extending the Japanese EEZ and continental shelf.

The above may seem utopian but we should keep in mind that maritime boundary disputes cannot be resolved through the use of force. China may of course decide to conquer the Spratlys by force. The loss of lives will be modest since these islets are populated mainly by soldiers and occasional fishermen. But the use of force would provoke intense adverse reactions and make conflict resolution impossible for a long, long time ahead. Under such circumstances it would probably not be possible to exploit any oil or gas in the area. This would be too risky. China would be forced to divert valuable resources to fortifying strategically irrelevant islets at a substantial distance from its nearest naval bases and airports.[39]

China – regardless of what has just been said – seems likely to stick to its guns and remain unwilling to concede as much as it ought to if pursuing a grand strategy based on a cool assessment of its national interests. China may object to the usual procedures for maritime delimitation. It may suggest instead to start by defining maritime zones around the disputed islets, building on the assumption that either one or several can generate an EEZ and continental shelf. This would be a controversial proposition but could still make sense. One could begin by drawing equidistant lines between the mainland coasts and the nearest islets, and include full 200 nm EEZs measured from the Paracels and the Spratlys in those areas where they would not overlap with EEZs measured from mainland coasts, and do the same for the Diaoyu/Senkakus (thus fulfilling the aspirations of Japan). In the South China Sea this would absorb much of the doughnut, which would fall inside the EEZs of the Paracels, the Scarborough Shoal and the northern Spratlys. These equidistant lines would then mark the maximum extent of what could conceivably be part of the Spratly, Paracel and Scarborough Shoal EEZs vis-à-vis the coasts of the Philippines, Malaysia, Brunei and Vietnam. These countries would argue, with solid basis in international law, that an equitable boundary between their coasts and the nearest islet in the Paracels, Spratlys or Scarborough Shoal could not be equidistant, given the discrepancy in the length of their relevant mainland coasts and the short coasts around the islets. Thus the boundary between the disputed zones around the islets and these major countries' undisputed coastal zones would have to be drawn quite near the islets. Many precedents for this kind of equity can be found in earlier maritime delimitations. The Sino-Vietnamese Gulf of Tonkin agreement from 2000 might also be referred to as a precedent. It accorded the Vietnamese Cat Long Vi Island a 15 nm EEZ (12 nm territorial sea + 3 additional nm EEZ). Cat Long Vi is much larger than any of the Paracel or Spratly islets and has a population of several hundred Vietnamese.[40]

Through multilateral negotiations it might in this way be possible for the claimant states to confine the disputed maritime zones to a limited area around the Spratlys and Paracels and Diaoyu/Senkakus. The remainder of the seas would belong to the EEZs of the country with the nearest coast – provided that the distance does not exceed 200 nm.

In dealing with maritime delimitation China will be inclined to maximize the zone around the Paracels in order to include as much as possible of the northern half of the sea in an EEZ under its own de facto control. A complicating factor in this endeavour is the existence of the Vietnamese claim to the Paracels, which China does not recognize.[41] This has hindered any discussion of the Paracels between Chinese and Vietnamese representatives. This complicated the process leading to the DOC in 2002 when Vietnam tried to insist that the Paracels must be explicitly included under the agreement. Vietnam is unlikely to give up its claim to the Paracels, even in a situation where China has something important to yield in return. Any decision by a Vietnamese leader to give up the Paracels could easily be seen as treasonous by the Vietnamese public. The Vietnamese government is perfectly aware, however, that Vietnam will never de facto get back the Paracels from mighty China. This is unrealistic. The way for China and Vietnam to get around the Paracels problem would be for each side to uphold its claim to undisputed sovereignty while agreeing on a maritime zone around the Paracels. On the western side this zone would include only limited territory beyond 12 nm (since any further extension would overlap with the Vietnamese EEZ) and also on the northern side where it would overlap with the Chinese EEZ as measured from Hainan. On the east and south-eastern side, however, there would be no overlap. Hence the zone could even include Macclesfield Bank. China would not get Vietnam's de jure recognition of its sovereign rights in the zone around the Paracels but Vietnam would understand that China's de facto control of the islands included the exploitation of resources in their EEZ and continental shelf. This would put an end to the many incidents that occur when Chinese patrol ships intervene to stop Vietnamese fishing.

China's interest is more difficult to define in the southern half of the South China Sea, simply because it does not control any of the Spratly Islands. China might seek to maximize the zone around the Spratlys in the same way as around the Paracels, in the hope of gaining control of these islands in the future. A more realistic prospect would be to persuade the other claimants to establish a regional joint management zone. However, since these are rather remote possibilities, and since the Philippines, Malaysia and Vietnam are unlikely to ever accept that the Spratlys are entitled to a full 200 nm EEZ and continental shelf, it would be more expedient for China to agree with the other claimants to establish just a patchwork of 12 nm territorial waters around each Spratly atoll. These zones would then remain disputed, while the rest of the southern half of the sea could be divided among the Philippines, Malaysia, Brunei and Vietnam. This kind of solution might allow the creation of a special regional authority to manage the resources in the Spratlys and their territorial waters, where China and Taiwan could have a role.

In the East China Sea an agreement to define a disputed zone around the Diaoyu/Senkakus would reduce the bilateral Sino-Japanese problem to a question of finding a compromise between the Japanese median line and the Chinese natural prolongation of the continental shelf line. To reach a result would be tough but in no way complicated. It would just be a matter of give and take.

All of this may seem utopian but then it is not necessary to know the end result at the start of the process. One may do as Deng Xiaoping counselled: 'Cross the river by feeling the stones with the feet.'

Two possible steps

There are two ways by which China may seek to start a process of conflict resolution in the South China Sea. Both may set useful precedents for how to handle the larger boundary disputes in the South China Sea.

The first is to negotiate with Vietnam a southward prolongation of the agreed boundary at the mouth of the Tonkin Gulf. This would be useful in two ways. From China's point of view it would be advantageous to prolong it in a direction that separates the Paracels from the Vietnamese coast. Although this would not force Vietnam to give up its sovereignty claim, it would allow Vietnam to tacitly demonstrate its understanding that it will never resume de facto control of these islands. This would be useful because it would open up the prospect for a subsequent agreement on an EEZ around the Paracels. The other great advantage of the prolonged line would be its deviation from the first of the nine dashes in the Chinese U-shaped line. By agreeing to a boundary that does not coincide with the first dash in the U-shaped line China would demonstrate that the line does not represent a claim to maritime territory, territorial waters or historical waters but just to the islands inside and their maritime zones. China could agree with Vietnam on the prolongation of the Tonkin Gulf boundary without even consulting Taiwan, since the Paracels are far away from Taiwan. Fortunately, there are on-going negotiations between China and Vietnam concerning the prolongation of the boundary from the mouth of the Tonkin Gulf.

The second step that could initiate conflict resolution and provide a useful precedent for resolving other issues would be to make an agreement with the Philippines on the status of the Scarborough Shoal. Not the question of who has sovereignty. The sovereignty claims here seem rather weak in law, and it is difficult to say which of the two rivals has the least weak case. So the sovereignty dispute could safely be set aside. What China and the Philippines could instead agree upon is the extension of the Scarborough Shoal's maritime zones. Since there is little doubt that the small rocks that stick up from the shoal fail to satisfy the criteria in UNCLOS Article 121.3 for having more than a 12 nm territorial sea, it should be relatively easy for the parties to delimit a 12 nm water zone around the disputed shoal, and thus significantly reduce the salience of the dispute. This would pave the way for the Philippines and China to negotiate their maritime boundary in the whole north-eastern part of the South China Sea, without having to bother with the question of who owns the Scarborough Shoal. China and the Philippines would in this way set a precedent for how to handle the smallest – if not all – of the Spratlys, as well as the Diaoyu/Senkakus. Any such agreement on Diaoyu/Senkaku or the Scarborough Shoal should ideally be joined by the ROC (Taiwan), since both the Sino-Philippines boundary in the north-eastern part of the South China Sea and the Sino-Japanese boundary in the southernmost part of the East China Sea must be affected by distances to base points on the Taiwanese coast.

Arbitration under UNCLOS

China's option to shelve the dispute over the Scarborough Shoal may have been lost in the stand-off between a Philippine warship and a number of Chinese maritime surveillance vessels and fishing boats in March–May 2012, and later by the legal action taken by the Philippines on 22 January 2013 under Article 287(5) of UNCLOS to bring China in for arbitration under Annex VII of the Convention. The Philippines requested that an Arbitral Tribunal handle its request and that it issue an award declaring 'that China's maritime claims in the SCS based on its so-called nine-dash line are contrary to UNCLOS and invalid'. The Philippines also required that 'China desist from activities that violate the rights of the Philippines in its maritime domain in the West Philippine Sea (South China Sea)'.[42] China refused to take part and will thus not have its own judge on the Tribunal. The Tribunal is in any case obliged to handle the Philippines request as a compulsory arbitration. In order to make this possible, the Philippines avoided taking up any question relating to such topic areas for which China declared in 2006 that it will not accept arbitration. The Arbitration Tribunal might still find legal grounds for dismissing the case. While some commentators have speculated that a legal victory for the Philippines could lead China to withdraw completely from UNCLOS – a move that would represent an enormous setback for global multilateral cooperation – it is actually also possible that the Arbitration Tribunal's conclusions might serve China's overall interests. By refusing to participate in the arbitration China maintains its policy of keeping all its options open. However, with regard to the U-shaped line, it could be useful for China if the Arbitration Tribunal helps it to clarify the meaning. It seems likely that the U-shaped line itself is not, as claimed by the Philippines, contrary to UNCLOS or invalid. This depends on how the line is interpreted. If it means what China said in its note to the UN Secretary General on 7 May 2009, namely a claim to all islands inside it and their 'adjacent waters' (which must be understood as their legitimate maritime zones), then there is no conflict between the U-shaped line and the Convention. There is no prohibition in the law of the sea against claiming insular features and marking those claims on a map. While the Philippines is probably right when stating that China's constructions on submerged reefs and low-tide elevations (which are legally parts of the seabed) are illegal, it is not equally obvious that the Philippines is right to say that China has claimed excessive maritime zones around six small features at the Scarborough Shoal and similar features sticking up from three underwater reefs in the Spratlys. Since these features are above water at high tide, they satisfy the legal definition in Article 121.1 of UNCLOS for constituting an island. They can thus be appropriated by states and made the subject of a sovereignty claim. The question of whether or not such small islands can generate extended maritime zones has not yet been finally settled in international law. For these reasons it seems unlikely that the Philippines will win a full victory in the Arbitration Tribunal. If the case is not dismissed then the Tribunal could come up with an award that China may find useful in the future. In this context perhaps the most important request made by the Philippines is for the Arbitration Tribunal to determine 'whether, under Article 121 of UNCLOS, certain of the maritime features claimed by both China and the Philippines are islands, low tide elevations or submerged banks, and whether they are capable of generating entitlement to maritime zones greater than 12 (nautical miles)'. If the Arbitration Tribunal takes up this challenge then this may have ramifications in many parts of the world. The ICJ failed to fully clarify the interpretation of Article 121.3 in its recent rulings in the 2009 *Black Sea* case pitting Ukraine against Romania and the 2012 *Nicaragua-Colombia* case in the Caribbean.[43] If the Arbitration Tribunal applies a strict interpretation of Article 121.3, then this could greatly facilitate maritime delimitation in the Spratly area and also reduce the importance of the dispute over the Diaoyu/Senkaku rocks in the East China Sea. In that case it would be

China/Taiwan that would benefit most from a decision to classify them as rocks with just a 12 nm territorial sea.

Conclusions

It is in China's national interest to launch a proactive policy with the aim to resolve its maritime boundary disputes in the East China Sea and the South China Sea. With regard to the East China Sea, China has already been proactive by submitting to the United Nations, in December 2012, a detailed calculation of the extension of its continental shelf out to the Okinawa trough. A similarly proactive policy in the South China Sea may be applied while continuing to shelve the sovereignty disputes over the Paracel and Spratly Islands and the Scarborough Shoal. Priority would instead be given to the delimitation of maritime boundaries, mostly through bilateral negotiations. This effort will require diplomatic stamina over many years. The Chinese leaders must acquire the courage to make substantial compromises, notably by recognizing the sovereign rights of other claimant states in their EEZs and on their continental shelf. The two main obstacles to overcome at the initial stage are as follows:

1. To establish a co-ordinated all-Chinese maritime negotiation team including representatives of the ROC (Taiwan), perhaps with Hainan province in a role as facilitator
2. To clarify the meaning of the U-shaped line.

Unfortunately there are few signs that either Beijing or Taipei is ready to consider any such initiative at the present stage but at least they consult each other informally. What is required is strong and secure leadership both in Beijing and Taipei. While a common approach is worked out between the PRC and ROC, the PRC could set a useful precedent by agreeing with Vietnam on the southward prolongation of their maritime boundary in the Tonkin Gulf. And China and the Philippines could agree to shelve their dispute over the Scarborough Shoal while agreeing that its six rocks can have just a 12 nm territorial sea. Such an agreement would set a precedent for making similar agreements later both for the Diaoyu/Senkakus and for all or most of the Spratly islets. This could make the work of the UN Arbitration Tribunal redundant or help it reach a sensible conclusion. If all or most of the Spratly Islands could also be defined as incapable of sustaining human habitation or an economic life of their own, then this would significantly reduce the amount of disputed waters in the South China Sea as a whole, and thus pave the way for bilateral boundary negotiations between its surrounding countries, and this would in turn contribute greatly to giving China a peaceful, secure environment so it can pursue a grand strategy based on a realistic assessment of its national interests.

Notes

1 This chapter is based on a paper presented to the conference 'Recent Development of the South China Sea Dispute and Prospects of Joint Development Regime', China National Institute for South China Sea Studies, Haikou, Hainan, 6–7 December 2012. The basic argument was also spelled out in Stein Tønnesson, 'Steps forward for China to resolve its disputes in the South China Sea', *Global Asia*, 8(2), Summer 2013, pp. 93–100.

2 The best classical English-language account of the history of conflict in the South China Sea is M. S. Samuels, *Contest for the South China Sea*, New York: Methuen, 1982. Another useful introduction is G. Austin, *China's Ocean Frontier: International Law, Military Force and National Development*, Canberra: Allen & Unwin, 1998. China's contributions to the United Nations Conference on the Law of the Sea 1973–82 (UNCLOS III) are examined in J. Greenfield, *China's Practice in the Law of the Sea*, Oxford: Clarendon, 1992.

3 'Vietnam introduces Maritime Law', *VietnamNet*, 17 July 2012, available at http://english.vietnamnet.vn/fms/government/24535/vietnam-introduces-maritime-law.html (accessed 31 March 2013).

4 Two good English-language books distinguish themselves by examining the South China Sea and East China Sea disputes, and comparing them: Austin, *China's Ocean Frontier* and R. Emmers, *Geopolitics and Maritime Territorial Disputes in East Asia*, Abingdon: Routledge, 2010.

5 Commission on the Limits of the Continental Shelf (CLCS): Outer limits of the continental shelf beyond 200 nautical miles from the baselines: Submissions to the Commission: Submission by the People's Republic of China, 14 December 2012, available at http://www.un.org/depts/los/clcs_new/submissions_files/submission_chn_63_2012.htm (accessed 7 September 2013).

6 M. T. Fravel, *Strong Borders, Secure Nation: Cooperation and Conflict in China's Territorial Disputes*, Princeton: Princeton University Press, 2008.

7 Bruce A. Elleman, Stephen Kotkin and Clive Schofield (eds), *Beijing's Power and China's Borders: Twenty Neighbors in Asia*, Armonk, NY: M. E. Sharpe, 2013.

8 Zou Keyuan, 'The Sino-Vietnamese Agreement on Maritime Boundary Delimitation in the Gulf of Tonkin', *Ocean Development and International Law*, 36(1), 2005, pp. 13–24, at p. 15. Nguyen Hong Thao, 'Maritime delimitation and fishery cooperation in the Tonkin Gulf', *Ocean Development and International Law*, 36(1), 2005, pp. 25–44 (map on p. 26).

9 J. A. Bader, *Obama and China's Rise: An Insider's Account of America's Asia Strategy*, Washington DC: Brookings Institution Press, 2012, p. 76. M. D. Swaine and M. T. Fravel, 'China's assertive behavior, part two: the maritime periphery', *China Leadership Monitor*, 35, 2011, p. 7, available at http://www.hoover.org/publications/china-leadership-monitor/by-date (accessed 7 March 2012).

10 P. Dutton (ed.), *Military Activities in the EEZ: A US–China Dialogue on Security and International Law in the Maritime Commons*, Newport, RI: Naval War College China Maritime Studies Institute, 2010. N. Klein, *Maritime Security and the Law of the Sea*, Oxford: Oxford University Press, 2011, pp. 46–55.

11 E. Vogel, *Deng Xiaoping and the Transformation of China*, Cambridge, MA: Harvard University Press, 2011, p. 523.

12 International Crisis Group, 'Stirring up the South China Sea (I)', *Asia Report*, 223, 23 April 2012; G. Till, *Asia's Naval Expansion: An Arms Race in the Making?*, London: International Institute for Strategic Studies, 2012.

13 D. Cohen, 'Politics as damage control for China?', *The Diplomat*, 20 March 2013, available at http://thediplomat.com/china-power/ (accessed 31 March 2013).

14 A. Friedberg, *A Contest for Supremacy: China, America, and the Struggle for Mastery in Asia*, New

York: W. W. Norton, 2011, pp. 7, 177. Interviews by the author in Taiwan, October 2011.

15 C. Thayer, 'Vietnam's security outlook', Presentation to International Workshop on AsiaPacific Security, National Institute of Defense Studies, Tokyo, 17–18 January 2012; 'Taiwan eyes indigenous submarine build', upi.com, 21 March 2013, available at http://www.upi.com/Business_News/Security-Industry/2013/03/21/Taiwan-eyes-indigenous-submarine-build/UPI-54951363881678/ (accessed 31 March 2013).

16 E. A. McVadon, 'China's navy today: looking toward blue water', in A. S. Erickson, L. J. Goldstein and C. Lord (eds), *China Goes to Sea: Maritime Transformation in Comparative Historical Perspective*, Annapolis, MD: Naval Institute Press, 2009, pp. 373–400.

17 R. S. Ross, 'China's naval nationalism sources, prospects, and the U.S. response', *International Security*, 34(2), Fall 2009, pp. 46–81.

18 John Lee, 'Lonely power, staying power: the rise of China and the resilience of US pre-eminence', *Lowy Institute Strategic Snapshot*, 10 September 2011, available at http://apo.org.au/sites/default/files/Lonely%20power%2C%20staying%20power.pdf (accessed 9 September 2013).

19 D. Steinberg and Fan Hongwei, *Modern China–Myanmar Relations: Dilemmas of Mutual Dependence*, Copenhagen: NIAS Press, 2012.

20 N. A. Owen and C. H. Schofield, 'Disputed South China Sea hydrocarbons in perspective', *Marine Policy*, 36, 2012, pp. 809–822.

21 Gao Jianjun, 'Joint development in the East China Sea: not an easier challenge than delimitation', *International Journal of Marine and Coastal Law*, 23, 2008, pp. 39–75.

22 For an overview of environmental and other threats, see S. Bateman, 'Regional maritime security: threats and risk assessments', in S. Bateman and J. Ho (eds), *Southeast Asia and the Rise of Chinese and Indian Naval Power*, Abingdon: Routledge, 2010, pp. 99–113, and Part IV of Wu Shicun and Zou Keyuan (eds), *Maritime Security in the South China Sea: Regional Implications and International Cooperation*, Farnham: Ashgate, 2009, pp. 205–261.

23 Cai Penghong, 'Regional maritime security environment: A Chinese perspective', in Bateman and Ho, *Southeast Asia and the Rise of Chinese and Indian Naval Power*, pp. 72–79.

24 R. Emmers, *Geopolitics and Maritime Territorial Disputes in East Asia*, pp. 102, 112. Zou Keyuan, *China–ASEAN Relations and International Law*, Oxford: Chandos, 2009, pp. 146–149.

25 C. A. Thayer, 'The China–Philippines face off at Scarborough Shoal: back to square one?', *e-International Relations*, 26 April 2012, available at http://www.e-ir.info/2012/04/26/the-china-philippines-face-off-at-scarborough-shoal-back-to-square-one/ (accessed 31 March 2013); F.-X. Bonnet, 'Geopolitics of Scarborough Shoal', *Les Notes de l'Irasec*, 14 November 2012.

26 Z. Brzezinski, 'Giants, but not hegemons', *New York Times*, 13 February 2013. For a Chinese perspective on US policies and activities in the South China Sea, see Wu Shicun, 'Opportunities and challenges for China–U.S. cooperation in the South China Sea', in A. S. Erickson, L. J. Goldstein and Nan Li (eds), *China, the United States and 21st-Century Sea Power: Defining a Maritime Security Partnership*, Annapolis, MD: Naval Institute Press, 2010, pp. 365–376.

27 D. Kang, *East Asia Before the West: Five Centuries of Trade and Tribute*, New York: Columbia University Press, 2010; D. Kang, *China Rising: Peace, Power, and Order in East Asia*, New York: Columbia University Press, 2007.

28 V. Soldatkin, 'In Moscow, new Chinese leader Xi warns against meddling', *Reuters*, 23 March 2013, available at http://news.yahoo.com/moscow-speech-chinese-leader-xi-warns-against-meddling-092547200.html (accessed 31 March 2013).

29 Wang Zheng, 'Does China have a foreign policy?', *New York Times*, 18 March 2013, available at http://www.nytimes.com/2013/03/19/opinion/does-china-have-a-foreign-policy.html?pagewanted=all&_r=0 (accessed 31 March 2013).

30 J. Greenfield, *China's Practice in the Law of the Sea*. See also Song Yann-huei and Stein

Tønnesson, 'The impact of the Law of the Sea Convention on conflict and conflict management in the South China Sea', *Ocean Development and International Law*, 44(3), 2013, pp. 235–269.

31 I. Storey, *Southeast Asia and the Rise of China: The Search for Security*, Abingdon: Routledge, 2011, pp. 96–98.

32 Submission by the PRC to the Commission on the Limits of the Continental Shelf (CLCS), 14 December 2012, available at http://www.un.org/Depts/los/clcs_new/submissions_files/submission_chn_63_2012.htm (accessed 31 March 2013).

33 The Permanent Mission of the People's Republic of China to the UN Secretary General, No. CML/17/2009, 7 May 2009, available at http://www.un.org/depts/los/clcs_new/submissions_files/mysvnm33_09/chn_2009re_mys_vnm_e.pdf (accessed 24 February 2012), and CML/8/2011, 14 April 2011, available at http://www.un.org/Depts/los/clcs_new/submissions_files/vnm37_09/chn_2011_re_phl_e.pdf (accessed 31 March 2013).

34 Wang Zheng, 'Does China have a foreign policy?'; International Crisis Group, 'Stirring up the South China Sea (I)'.

35 E. Franckx and M. Benatar, 'Dots and lines in the South China Sea: insights from the law of map evidence', *Asian Journal of International Law*, 2, 2012, pp. 89–118.

36 D. Dzurek, 'The People's Republic of China straight baseline claims', *IBRU Boundary and Security Bulletin*, 4(2), Summer 1996, pp. 77–87, at p. 85; M. T. Fravel, 'China's strategy in the South China Sea', *Contemporary Southeast Asia*, 33(3), December 2011, pp. 292–319, at p. 295.

37 The Permanent Mission … 7 May 2009.

38 The Permanent Mission … 14 April 2011.

39 Stein Tønnesson, 'Law trumps realpolitik in the South China Sea', *Asian Survey*, forthcoming.

40 Zou Keyuan, 'Sino-Vietnamese Agreement on Maritime Boundary Delimitation in the Gulf of Tonkin', p. 15. Nguyen Hong Thao, 'Maritime delimitation and fishery cooperation in the Tonkin Gulf'.

41 Song Yann-huei and S. Tønnesson, 'The Impact of the Law of the Sea Convention on conflict and conflict management in the South China Sea', *Ocean Development & International Law*, 44, 2013, pp. 235–269. S. Tønnesson, 'The Paracels: the "other" South China Sea dispute', *Asian Perspective*, 26(4), 2002, pp. 145–169.

42 'Statement by Secretary of Foreign Affairs Albert del Rosario on the UNCLOS Arbitral Proceedings against China to Achieve a Peaceful and Durable Solution to the Dispute in the WPS (West Philippines Sea)', 22 January 2013, available at http://www.dfa.gov.ph/index.php/newsroom/dfa-releases/7300-statement-by-secretary-of-foreign-affairs-albert-del-rosario-on-the-unclos-arbitral-proceedings-against-china-to-achieve-a-peaceful-and-durable-solution-to-the-dispute-in-the-wps (accessed 31 March 2013); 'Notification and statement of claim', presented to the UN and the Chinese ambassador, Manila 22 January 2013, available at http://www.dfa.gov.ph/index.php/2013-06-27-21-50-36/unclos (accessed 31 March 2013).

43 'Maritime Delimitation in the Black Sea (Romania v. Ukraine), judgment of 3 Feb. 2009', available at http://www.icj-cij.org/docket/files/132/14987.pdf (accessed 31 March 2013). 'Territorial and Maritime Dispute (Nicaragua v. Colombia), 19 Nov. 2012 judgment', available at http://www.icj-cij.org/docket/files/124/17164.pdf (accessed 31 March 2013).

14 Functional cooperation and joint development

A way ahead in the South China Sea

Rommel C. Banlaoi

Establishing a 'joint development regime' in the South China Sea remains contested because of the claimants' existing differences on definitional issues of joint development and on procedural concerns on how to implement it. Prospects for joint development became more uncertain at the conclusion of the 21st Summit of the Association of Southeast Asian Nations (ASEAN) in Phnom Penh on 19 November 2012 when Cambodia, a well-known ally of China, hijacked the agenda of the summit. Cambodia declared that ASEAN 'would not internationalize the South China Sea from now on' – a statement that the Philippines vehemently opposed.[1] The holding in Brunei of the 46th ASEAN Foreign Ministerial Meeting on 1 July 2013 and the 20th ASEAN Regional Forum Meeting on 2 July 2013 also failed to see real progress on the discussion on joint development other than a general statement saying that ASEAN and China will exert best efforts 'to reach an early conclusion of a Code of Conduct in the South China Sea (East Sea), which will serve to enhance peace, stability and prosperity in the region.'[2]

There is no doubt that differences among claimants continue to obstruct the pursuance of a joint development regime in the South China Sea. Despite these differences, all claimants agree in principle that there must be joint development in the disputed waters and land features in the South China Sea if a peaceful management of the conflict is desired.

This chapter contends that the ethnocentric, irredentist and primordialist outlooks of claimants pose tremendous obstacles for the pursuance of joint development. But claimants can surmount all these obstacles if there is a strong willingness among them to promote functional cooperation in the South China Sea. This chapter describes the principle of functionalism and discusses how functional cooperation can help facilitate the creation of a joint development regime as a way ahead for the peaceful management of the complex nature of territorial conflicts in the South China Sea.

Obstacles to joint development

Although all claimants endorse the general idea of joint development, they have varying understandings and contending definitions of the concept. Since the Deng

Xiaoping era, China has long adopted the idea of joint development to deal with territorial disputes by shelving sovereignty claims in the South China Sea.

However, other claimants reject China's idea of joint development as it offers areas close to other claimants. For example, Vietnam has objected to the decision of China to open up nine areas of the South China Sea to foreign partners for joint development because those areas are near Vietnam's Wan'an Bank.[3] Vietnam is interpreting China's concept of joint development in the following words: 'What is mine is mine, what is yours is mine and we are willing to share.'[4] For Vietnam, China's idea of joint development is not only problematic but utterly objectionable.

The Philippines also has its own concept of joint development articulated in its concept of Zone of Peace, Freedom, Friendship and Cooperation (ZoPFFC) in the West Philippine Sea (WPS)/South China Sea (SCS).[5] In its official paper, currently languishing, the Philippine government promotes '10 ways to ZoPFFC', to wit:[6]

1 Not the whole of the WPS (SCS) is disputed;
2 The area of dispute in the WPS (SCS) is specific, determinable and measurable;
3 The area of dispute can be determined and measured by clarifying the nature of, and distinction between 'territorial disputes' and 'maritime claims' in the WPS (SCS);
4 The nature of and distinction between 'territorial disputes' and 'maritime claims' in the WPS (SCS) can be clarified by: fiby:, recognizing the distinction between geological features (i.e. islands, rocks, low-tide elevations) and waters (including continental shelf); and, second, by applying the rules governing each of these elements in accordance with the United Nations Convention on the Law of the Sea (UNCLOS);
5 The dispute in the WPS (SCS) is principally on the relevant features (i.e., islands, rocks, and low-tide elevations). If ever there is a dispute on the water, this is principally caused by the dispute on the features. Under the principle of 'la terre domine la mer,' or 'the land dominates the sea,' he who owns the land also owns the sea around it. Therefore, if the owner of the land is disputed, then the sea around it could also be assumed as disputed;
6 However, the extent of adjacent waters projected from the island is limited, finite, determinable, definite and measurable under UNCLOS (i.e., Article 121, Regime of Islands);
7 Once the extent of adjacent waters is determined and measured in accordance with international law, specifically UNCLOS, then the extent of dispute both on the relevant features ['territorial dispute'] and maritime zones ['maritime claims dispute'] generated from the said features, can already be determined;
8 Once the extent or limit of the disputed area (relevant features + adjacent waters) is determined; the same can now be segregated from the rest of the non-disputed waters of the WPS (SCS);

9 The disputed area (relevant features + adjacent waters) can be segregated from non-disputed waters (and continental shelf) of WPS (SCS) by enclaving the said disputed area. Enclaving will literally operationalize the 'shelving of territorial disputes' and pave the way for effective and meaningful cooperation among the claimant countries in the WPS (SCS);

10 Therefore, joint cooperation in the Enclave (as Joint Cooperation Area) could be conducted among the claimant countries. Outside of the Enclave, the littoral states in the semi-enclosed sea can also engage in appropriate cooperative activities under Part IX of UNCLOS, while exercising their sovereign rights over these bodies of waters under Articles 3, 4, 55, 57, and 76 of UNCLOS.

Since not the whole of the WPS/SCS is disputed, the Philippine government recommends the separation of disputed and non-disputed areas to manage the conflict in the SCS. Non-disputed areas are waters and continental shelves 'beyond the disputed relevant features.'[7] In non-disputed areas, claimants can develop them unilaterally based on the principle of sovereign rights in accordance with the application of exclusive economic zone, continental shelf and other maritime zones provided for by UNCLOS.

Disputed areas are the Spratlys and the Paracels. The Philippine government explains that 'disputed relevant features (and their adjacent waters) could be segregated from the rest of the waters of the SCS by enclaving the said features. The adjacent waters of the relevant features could be determined by applying Article 121 of UNCLOS.'[8] To promote cooperation and avoid conflict in the disputed areas, the Philippine government recommends the pursuance of joint development by converting all disputed territorial features as 'enclaves' and declares these 'enclaves' as 'joint cooperation areas' (JCAs) that could be demilitarized (see Figure 14.1).

In the JCA, the Philippine government says that the following joint cooperative activities can be pursued: 1) joint development; 2) marine scientific research; 3) protection of the marine environment; 4) safety of navigation and communication at sea; 5) search and rescue operations; 6) humane treatment of all persons in danger or distress at sea; 7) fight against transnational crimes.[9]

President Benigno Simeon Aquino III summarizes the wisdom of ZoPFFC in the following words: 'What is ours is ours, and with what is disputed, we can work towards joint cooperation.' Department of Foreign Affairs Secretary Albert F. Del Rosario expounds the idea of ZoPFFC by saying, 'There is a need to segregate the disputed area from non-disputed area. What is ours is ours, and what is disputed can be shared.'[10]

China, however, has expressed strong opposition to ZoPFFC's concept of joint development as it vehemently challenges China's nine-dashed line claim. The Philippine paper on ZoPFFC even underscores that the nine-dashed line claim of China 'is bereft of any legal basis under international law.'[11] Del Rosario has even described China's nine-dashed line claim as 'the core of the problem'

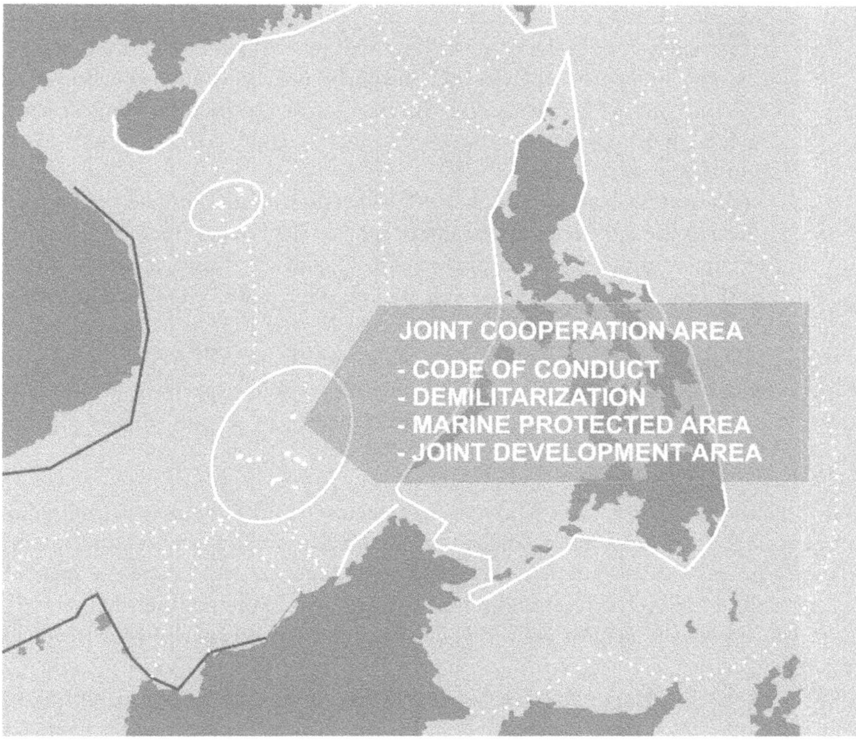

Figure 14.1 The Philippines concept for a joint development area in the South China Sea/West Philippine Sea

that must be 'subjected to [the] rules-based regime of UNCLOS.'[12] Though the Philippine government argues that the ZoPFFC proposal is consistent with the rules-based framework of managing international disputes, China vehemently opposes Manila's proposal because Beijing is not ready to bring the South China Sea disputes before international adjudication.[13]

Malaysia has also expressed its 'fundamental concerns' about the Philippine concept of joint development as described in ZoPFFC. Dato' Sri Anifah Aman, Malaysia's Minister of Foreign Affairs, issued an official statement arguing that the Philippine concept of disputed and non-disputed areas in the South China Sea could be a source of disputes, particularly in the context of the Sabah Problem.[14] Minister Aman raised the following points against ZoPFFC:

1. Malaysia has fundamental concerns with the Philippine's proposal on the Zone of Peace, Freedom, Friendship and Cooperation (ZOPFF/C);
2. The Philippines' proposal is premised on the need to segregate the disputed area from the non-disputed area. The issue is, what may be considered as being disputed by one party, is considered as an established

fact by another. Therein lies the source of the dispute to begin with. This is especially true in the case of the Philippines's claim over Sabah, whose integrity and sovereignty is recognized by the international community as being part of Malaysia. For this reason, this proposal cannot be used as a basis to address the South China Sea issue. To Malaysia, this is non-negotiable;

3. Malaysia emphasized that ASEAN's attention should instead be directed towards the effective implementation of the Declaration on the Conduct of Parties in the South China Sea (DOC) and the eventual realization of the Code of Conduct in the South China Sea (COC). We should not be distracted from this effort; and,
4. Malaysia strongly feels that it is not opportune for ASEAN to embark on such an ambitious endeavor, which is a non-starter and will be counter-productive to our genuine effort to maintain peace and stability in the South China Sea.[15]

Cambodia joined China and Malaysia in rejecting ZoPFFC and the Philippine concept of joint development. When the media asked the Cambodian Foreign Minister for his take on the issue, he reportedly laughed and raised the issue of duplication. Though the Cambodia Foreign Minister explained that his government was not totally against ZoPFFC, he stressed the need to avoid the problem of duplication.[16]

In other words, claimants have not reached a commonly agreed definition of joint development. Claimants in the South China Sea have problems agreeing on the concept of joint development because they remain intransigent concerning their ethnocentric, irredentist and primordialist outlooks. These points of view put the South China Sea in a remorseful state of seemingly perpetual trouble.[17]

Ethnocentrism is a worldview that promotes an outlook from a hard-line ethnonationalist standpoint. It is a self-centered worldview that distinguishes the 'self' from 'others.' This sense of 'self' and 'others' has permeated sharply into a bitter clash of sovereignties in the South China Sea.

Ethnocentrism propels claimants to pursue unilateral actions in their selfish efforts to advance their respective national interests. These unilateral actions, which trigger more misunderstanding among claimants, are seen in their continuing fortification of their existing facilities in the occupied land features, intensified maritime patrols and independent exploration of natural gas and oil resources in the disputed body of waters.[18] Ethnocentrism also encourages claimants to use UNCLOS as a sovereignty enhancing rather than conflict management measure in the South China Sea.[19]

Irredentism reinforces the ethnocentrism of claimants. Irredentism endorses a position expressing a tough claim on territories on the basis of strong historical rights and long ethnic associations. It justifies occupation of territories claimed by other states by using historical and ethno-nationalist narratives that are believed to be 'indisputable' and 'uncontestable.' Most claimants have irredentist claims on disputed territories in the South China Sea.[20]

Due to ethnocentrism and irredentism, claimants also develop a primordialist position on the South China Sea disputes. Primordialism is a paradigm in studying ethnic conflicts. But it can also be used to analyze territorial conflicts. Primordialism promotes the idea that a certain territory has belonged to a certain ethnic group 'since time immemorial' by virtue of an effective presence and continuing activities in the said area. This idea is based on the concept of a 'homeland territory' or 'ancestral domain' that belongs to a certain ethnic group that regards the said territory as its ancient abode. Some claimants in the South China Sea regard the waters and the land features therein as an important component of their homeland territory and an integral part of their ancestral domain. Primordialism strengthens the ethnocentric and irredentist position of claimants in the South China Sea.

As a result of ethnocentrism, irredentism and primordialism, there seems to be 'irreconcilable differences' between claimants in the South China Sea. These differences are not easy to resolve as ethnocentric, irredentist and primordialist outlooks create a hard-line, more often than not counter-productive, position on territorial conflicts. The modern concept of territorial sovereignty sanctified by the realist theory of international relations solidifies this hard-line perspective. Shelving sovereignty claims to promote joint development in the South China Sea is next to impossible because of hard-line convictions on the part of claimants, propelled by ethnocentrism, irredentism and primordialism.

If claimants remain hard line in their positions and outlooks, it will be difficult to pursue joint development and promote the peaceful resolution of the South China Sea disputes in the foreseeable future. Hard-line positions increase the risk of armed conflicts among claimants, a dreadful scenario that all claimants do not want to occur, particularly amid their rising stakes in the South China Sea.[21]

Functional cooperation: prospects for joint development

Claimants can escape the abyss of possible armed conflicts if they are willing to traverse an alternative path offered by the functional theory of international relations. Functionalism is the reverse of ethnocentrism, irredentism and primordialism; it pays more attention to common or shared interests than to the selfish interests of players in international politics. Rather than focus on competition and conflict as exemplified by realist theory, functionalism privileges cooperation and collaboration among states as promoted by liberal theory. While the functional approach may appear naive in the context of the harsh reality of international politics, this alternative perspective can really make sense if a peaceful and cooperative management of the South China dispute is desired by all parties concerned.[22]

The functionalist approach grapples with the process of regional cooperation and integration. It also provides measures for the peaceful resolution of territorial conflicts. The approach is based on the benign assumption that cooperation in functional areas limits the possibility of war and armed conflicts among sovereign nations. As the habit of cooperation in functional areas deepens and widens, prospects for conflict resolution and regional integration becomes more and more promising, which may in turn lead to a more stable and peaceful regional and international security environment.

Cooperation in low politics

David Mitrany introduces and popularizes the functionalist approach in his book *A Working Peace System.*[23] Otherwise known as functionalism, the functionalist approach offers an alternative approach to the management of inter-state conflicts through cooperation in *low politics* and non-controversial areas.[24]

Mitrany believes that the attainment of world peace and regional security can be made possible through cooperative undertakings in various functional areas such as education, health, economics, environment, science and technology, culture and sports. He argues that international conflicts can be avoided and managed through international cooperation not among political elites but among technical people with no political agenda or political motives such as engineers, scientists, economists, academics and medical specialists. These are members of the world's epistemic communities whose interests are driven by the acquisition of knowledge for the benefit of all humankind.

Mitrany adheres to the idea that cooperation among technicians brings more cooperation as they carry a non-controversial agenda acceptable to all parties concerned. Experts and technical people also have the capability to develop common standards, by virtue of their respective disciplines, to guide their cooperative undertakings.

Cooperation among experts and specialists

According to Mitrany, the complexity of governmental systems in the twentieth century has increased the technical/functionalist tasks facing governments.[25] Highly trained specialists or experts other than politicians can best address these tasks. In the context of the South China Sea disputes, experts and specialists are in the best position to promote joint development.

Mitrany believes that 'the emergence of technical issues would lead first to the felt or perceived need for collaborative action, devoid of a political, or conflictual, content' and therefore can be assigned to technical experts 'whose approaches were essentially based on apolitical considerations.'[26] Cooperation among political elites, on the other hand, is hard to prosper, according to Mitrany, as they carry controversial agendas such as security and politics. Political elites seldom agree with each other not only because of their varying political motives and agendas but also because they view security and politics from different philosophical and ideological perspectives. Thus, to promote joint development in the South China Sea, politicians are urged to refrain from articulating a hard-line nationalist rhetoric in order to create a political environment conducive to cooperation among experts and specialists.

The doctrine of ramification

Crucial to the understanding of Mitrany's functionalist approach is the *doctrine of ramification*. The doctrine states that 'Successful cooperation in one functional setting would enhance incentive for collaboration in other fields.' The doctrine also posits that the 'perceived need in one functional task would itself contribute to a change in attitudes in favor of even greater cooperation over a widening spectrum of issues.'[27]

Guided by the doctrine of ramification, Mitrany emphasizes that the broadening and widening of cooperation diminishes the prospect for and will eventually eliminate war through an incremental transformation from adversarial and hostile to cooperative and amicable patterns of behavior. The transformation of behavioral patterns is incremental or gradual because the *ramification effect* takes time. Apparently, the doctrine of ramification works in tandem with the *doctrine of incrementalism*, which also states that the broadening and widening of cooperation is a gradual process. In this context, the idea of a joint development regime is not something that can be created overnight. It needs quality time for claimants to appreciate the idea and internalize its value in the peaceful management of conflicts in the South China Sea.

The neo-functionalist approach

Another variant of the functional approach is the neo-functional approach, first introduced by Ernst Haas and later adopted and improved by Philippe Schmitter, Leon Linberg, Joseph Nye, Robert Keohane and Lawrence Scheineman.[28] In his *The Uniting of Europe*, Haas identifies the political, social and economic forces that led to the creation of the European Coal and Steel Community, the forerunner of the European Union.[29] Haas argues that the decision to integrate Western Europe is not based on altruistic considerations but on the expectations of gain or loss held by dominant groups and forces within the unit to be integrated. Thus, neo-functionalism overcomes the naivety of functionalism by adopting some tenets of realism.

Cooperation among relevant elites

Unlike Mitrany, who places prime importance on the role of technical people and experts, Haas posits that European integration has proceeded as a result of the work of relevant elites in the government and private sectors who supported integration for pragmatic but compassionate considerations.[30] In the case of the European Coal and Steel Community, for example, the removal of barriers to coal and steel trade would increase markets and profits beneficial to stakeholders. Haas underscores that elites 'anticipating that they will gain from activity within a supranational organizational framework are likely to seek out similarly minded elites across national frontiers.'[31] This leads to more cooperation that meets the pragmatic needs of elites who matter in decision-making.

In the case of the South China Sea, joint development will not only satisfy the scientific and academic needs of experts; it will also meet the interests of political and economic elites who should be convinced that cooperation is beneficial for them and for all humankind.

As a result of the learning process of cooperation, Haas assumes that power-oriented governmental activities may eventually lead to a welfare-oriented action – a functionalist-oriented action. As players realize the importance of cooperation through increased commitment to a larger organizational unit, the learning process of cooperation may lead to greater integration.[32] Haas points out that the 'Integrative lessons learned in one functional context would be applied in others, thus eventually supplanting international politics.'[33]

The spill-over effect

Important to the understanding of Haas' neo-functionalist approach is the concept of *spill-over*. The spill-over effect, or what Mitrany calls the ramification effect, states that cooperation in one functional area may lead to further cooperation in other areas that may include the political area. This 'gradual politicization' of relevant players may lead to the deepening and widening of the integration process.

In the 'gradual politicization process', functional issues previously considered 'technical' and 'non-controversial' become 'political' because in reaction to initial 'technical' purposes, relevant players eventually agree to apply the spectrum of political means deemed appropriate to attain them.[34] Thus, the 'gradual politicization process' resulting from joint development activities can transform the South China Sea from a sea of conflict to a sea of peace and prosperity. This idea is consistent with the 2002 DOC and the proposed regional code of conduct in the South China Sea.

Managing conflicts in the South China Sea the functionalist way

There are functional areas where experts and elites in China and in ASEAN claimant states can cooperate to manage conflicts in the South China Sea. Marine scientists in China and ASEAN claimants states involved in various types of research in the South China Sea can contribute to the management of conflicts. Cooperation between the Philippines and Vietnam on maritime and ocean concerns provides exemplary practices on how a potential conflict area can be an area of cooperation 'with vast potential benefits to the different stakeholders.'[35] China–Vietnam fishery cooperation in the Gulf of Tonkin also offers some good lessons.[36]

Marine scientists in these countries can also learn useful lessons from groups of marine scientists engaged in research in the Baltic Sea, the North Sea, the Mediterranean Sea, the Arctic Sea and the Antarctic Ocean. These groups of marine scientists advance the idea of marine regionalism, which provides a framework for coordinated marine scientific research in various parts of the world's oceans.

Managing the South China Sea conflicts: lessons from other seas

In the Baltic Sea, marine scientists have been involved in various forms of cooperation in marine policy.[37] These marine scientists have played a vital role in enacting national legislation in various regional agreements aimed to manage disputes over continental shelf boundaries in the Baltic Sea.[38] Disputes have also been mitigated by a web of both bilateral and multilateral agreements initiated by experts and specialists who have gained the support and respect of political leaders.

In the Mediterranean Sea, marine scientists have taken an active part in numerous cooperative actions by the coastal states to protect the environment. They participated in the establishment of the Barcelona Convention for the Protection of the Mediterranean Sea and its five protocols.[39] Cooperation in the Mediterranean Sea has also promoted regional integration despite the growing maritime nationalism of concerned states.[40] In the North Sea, marine regionalism may also be seen through the efforts of marine scientists and experts to develop a comprehensive sea-use planning that aims to promote cooperation for the international administration and management of the area.[41]

The Antarctic Treaty is an excellent model from which marine scientists in the South China Sea may learn many lessons[42] and can serve as a practical model for resolving disputes in the South China Sea. The Antarctic Treaty, which was signed in 1959, calls for the eventual demilitarization of the area. The 12 claimant states are strongly urged to prohibit 'any measures of military rule, such as the establishment of military bases and fortifications, the carrying out military maneuvers, and the testing of any types of weapon' in the demilitarized Antarctic Ocean.[43]

The Antarctic Treaty also upholds the collective utilization of the resources in Antarctica. For any disputes that may arise, it mandates the use of 'negotiation, inquiry, mediation, conciliation, arbitration, judicial settlement, or other peaceful means of their own choice' to manage conflicts in the area.[44]

What is notable in the Antarctic Treaty model is the vital role played by experts and scientists in convincing political leaders to eschew political issues in the area and to start cooperating in functional areas. Through their reliable scientific findings, experts and scientists push for the collective protection of the Antarctic Ocean for the benefit of all claimant states. Instead of competing for the resources of the Antarctic, experts and scientists propose a model that upholds the collective utilization of Antarctica and its resources through 'joint management.' Experts and scientists also uphold the idea of making the Antarctic a pristine world park and 'a center for peaceful scientific inquiry.' Thus, the Antarctic Treaty guarantees the collective governance of the Antarctic Ocean.

Marine scientists and functionalism in the South China Sea

Having learnt lessons from the other seas, particularly the Antarctic Ocean, marine scientists engaged in scientific research in the South China Sea have now put forward a proposal to declare the disputed area a neutral area and convert the South China Sea into a marine park.[45] This proposal is based on the scientific findings that the South China Sea is a known breeding ground for tuna fish and other fish resources that migrate into nearby fishing areas of claimant states.

Marine scientists also describe the South China Sea as 'the center of marine generic richness and diversity in the world' and a macro-ecosystem characterized by 'high bio-diversity and fisheries productivity' due to the 'intrinsic connectivity of coral reefs, sea-grass, and mangrove forests.'[46] Because the South China Sea is the locus of complex ecological connectivities, the area has been considered a 'savings bank' of all claimant states.

By turning the South China Sea into a neutral international marine park, marine scientists and experts firmly believe that 'all claimants could continue to benefit from the living resources emanating from the area.'[47] By so doing, they argue that 'a host of potential conflicts could be avoided,' including the tens of millions of dollars being spent annually on maintaining garrisons of troops to guard against other claimant states.[48]

Conclusions

Territorial conflicts in the South China Sea could be peacefully resolved if claimants were to pursue the concept of joint development. However, claimants have definitional problems on joint development because their outlooks are shaped by ethnocentrism, irredentism and primordialism. These outlooks make it hard for claimants to shelve sovereignty claims in order to create a joint development regime in the South China Sea. It is essential for claimants to overcome their ethnocentrism, irredentism and primordialism if they truly want to implement joint development.

Functionalism offers an alternative approach to facilitate the creation of a joint development regime in the South China Sea. It upholds an incremental process that can facilitate the peaceful management of territorial conflicts by promoting cooperation among experts, scientists and specialists. Functionalism has proven its merits in resolving conflicts elsewhere. If claimants are willing to abandon their ethnocentrism, irredentism, and primordialism, functional cooperation can provide a way forward in the South China Sea.

Notes

1 Ben Bland, 'Regional tensions flare at ASEAN summit,' *Financial Times*, 19 November 2012.

2 *Joint Communiqué 46th ASEAN Foreign Ministers' Meeting*, Bandar Seri Begawan, Brunei Darussalam, 29–30 June 2013.

3 For this issue, see 'Beijing offers South China Sea oilfields for joint development,' *Want China Times*, 27 June 2012, at http://www.wantchinatimes.com/news-subclass-cnt.aspx?id=20120627000141&cid=1102&MainCatID=11 (accessed 21 November 2012).

4 Tran Truong Thuy, 'Recent developments in the South China Sea and evolution of Vietnam's claims and positions,' paper presented at the Forum on South China Sea, organized by the Carlos P. Romulo Foundation in Makati City on 17 October 2011.

5 This section is based on Rommel C. Banlaoi, 'Philippine solution to the South China Sea problem: more problems, less solutions?,' paper presented at the International Conference on 'Security Environment of the Seas in East Asia: From the East and South China Seas – Power Shift and Response,' organized by the Ocean Policy Research Foundation, The Nippon Foundation and the S. Rajaratnam School of International Studies at Marina Mandarin Hotel, Singapore, 28–29 February 2012.

6 *Philippine Paper on ASEAN–CHINA Zone of Peace, Freedom, Friendship and Cooperation (ZoPFF/C) in the West Philippine Sea (WPS)/South China Sea (SCS)*, at http://webcache.googleusercontent.com/search?um=1&hl=en&client=safari&rls=en&tab=iw&q=cache:XwxT_QtzQwsJ:http://nghiencuubiendong.vn/trung-tam-du-lieu-bien-dong/doc_download/364-philippine-paper-on-asean-china-zone-of-peace-freedom-friendship-and-cooperation-in-the-south-china-sea+zone+of+peace+freedom+friendship+and+cooperation+(zopff/c)&ct=clnk (accessed 5 December 2012).

7 Ibid.

8 Ibid.

9 Ibid.

10 Ibid.

11 Ibid.

12 Albert F. del Rosario, 'On West Philippine Sea', delivered at the ASEAN Foreign Ministers' Meeting in Bali, Indonesia on 15 November, 2011, available at http://www.gov.ph/2011/11/15/the-secretary-of-foreign-affairs-on-the-west-philippine-sea-november-15-2011/ (accessed 5 December 2012).

13 Aileen S. P. Baviera, 'The South China Sea disputes: is the Aquino way the "ASEAN way"?,' *RSIS Commentaries*, No. 4, Singapore: S. Rajaratnam School of International Studies, 5 January 2012.

14 Dato' Sri Anifah Aman, 'Zone of Peace, Freedom, Friendship and Cooperation (ZOPFF/C),' press statement during the ASEAN Ministerial Meeting held in Bali, Indonesia, 15 November 2011.

15 Ibid.

16 Rey O. Arcilla, 'Two-track approach,' *Malaya*, 22 November 2011, at http://www.malaya.com.ph/nov22/edrey.html (accessed 21 November 2012).

17 For an insight on how 'troublesome' the situation in the South China Sea is, see Alice D. Ba, 'Staking claims and making waves in the South China Sea: how troubled are the waters?,' *Contemporary Southeast Asia*, 33(3), December 2011, pp. 269–291.

18 For an analysis of unilateral facilities development in the South China Sea, see Rommel C. Banlaoi, 'Renewed tensions and continuing maritime security dilemma in the South China Sea: a Philippine perspective,' in Tran Truong Thuy (ed.), *The South China Sea: Cooperation for Regional Security and Development*, Hanoi: Diplomatic Academy of Vietnam, 2010, pp. 143–159.

19 See Xavier Furtado, 'International law and the dispute over the Spratly Islands: whither UNCLOS?,' *Contemporary Southeast Asia*, 21(3), December 1999, pp. 384–404.

20 The irredentist positions of claimants in the South China Sea are best described in Mark J. Valencia, Jon M. Van Dyke and Noel A. Ludwig, *Sharing the Resources of the South China Sea*, Leiden: Martinus Nijhoff, 1997.

21 See Clive Schofield and Ian Storey, *The South China Sea Disputes: Increasing Stakes, Rising Tensions*, Washington DC: The Jamestown Foundation, 2009.

22 Sam Bateman and Ralf Emmers (eds.), *Security and International Politics in the South China Sea: Towards a Cooperative Management Regime*, New York and Abingdon: Routledge, 2008.

23 David Mitrany, *A Working Peace System*, London: Royal Institute of International Affairs, 1943.

24 David Mitrany, 'The functionalist approach to world organization,' *International Affairs*, XXIV, July 1948.

25 See James E. Dougherty and Robert L. Pfaltzgraft Jr., *Contending Theories of International Relations: A Comprehensive Survey*, 4th ed., New York: Addison-Wesley Educational, 1997, Chapter 10.
26 Ibid., p. 422.
27 Ibid.
28 For a more elaborate discussion, see Dougherty and Pfaltzgraft, *Contending Theories of International Relations.*
29 Ernst Haas, *The Uniting of Europe: Political, Social and Economic Forces, 1950–1957*, Stanford: Stanford University Press, 1958.
30 Ibid., p. 13.
31 See Dougherty and Pfaltzgraft, *Contending Theories of International Relations*, p. 423.
32 Ibid.
33 Robert Pfatlzgraft, Jr., *Britain Faces Europe, 1957–1967*, Philadelphia: University of Pennsylvania Press, 1969, p. 48.
34 Dougherty and Pflatzgraft, *Contending Theories of International Relations*, p. 423.
35 Henry S. Bensurto, Jr., 'Cooperation in the South China Sea: views on the Philippines–Vietnam cooperation on maritime and ocean concerns,' in Tran Truong Thuy (ed.), *The South China Sea*, pp. 293–302.
36 Li Jianwei and Chen Pingping, 'China Vietnam fishery cooperation in the Gulf of Tonkin revisited,' in Tran Truong Thuy (ed.), *The South China Sea*, pp. 303–318.
37 For an excellent reference on joint cooperation in the Baltic Sea, see Detlef Jahn, Marko Joas and Kristine Kern (eds.), *Governing a Common Sea: Environmental Policies in the Baltic Sea Region*, London: Earthscan, 2008.
38 See Ton Ijlstra, 'Development of resource jurisdiction in the EC's regional seas: national EEZ policies of EC member states in the Northeast Atlantic, the Mediterranean Sea, and the Baltic Sea,' *Ocean Development and International Law*, 23(2–3), 1992, pp. 165–192.
39 Ibid. See also Mark Valencia, Jon M. Van Dyke and Noel A. Ludwig, *Sharing the Resources of the South China Sea*, Hawaii: University of Hawaii Press, 1997, p. 150.
40 See J. L. Suárez de Vivero and J. C. Rodríguez Mateos, 'The Mediterranean and Black Sea: regional integration and maritime nationalism,' *Marine Policy*, 26(5), September 2002, pp. 383–401.
41 See North Sea Region Programme at http://www.northsearegion.eu/ivb/content/show/&tid=130 (accessed 17 December 2013).
42 For an excellent reference, see Davor Vidas, 'Emerging law of the sea issues in the Antarctic Maritime Area: a heritage for the new century?,' *Ocean Development & International Law*, 31(1–2), 2000, pp. 197–222.
43 See Article XI, Section 1 of the 1959 Antarctic Treaty.
44 Ibid.
45 John W. McManus, 'The Spratly Islands: a marine park alternative,' *ICLARM Quarterly*, 15(3), July 1992, pp. 4–8. See also his 'The Spratly Islands: a marine park,' *Ambio*, 23(3), 1994, pp. 181–186.
46 Miguel D. Fortes, 'The role of marine environmental science in the Western Philippine Seas,' University of the Philippines Marine Science Institute, unpublished, 1999.
47 McManus, 'The Spratly Islands: a marine park alternative,' p. 6.
48 Ibid.

15 Beyond oil and gas

Alternative fields and models of joint management[1]

Nong Hong

Given the complex nature of the territorial and maritime disputes in the South China Sea (SCS), a temporary arrangement is considered the most practical solution pending the final dispute settlement. Joint development is a concept that is mostly discussed and referred to as 'inter-state cooperation' over the offshore oil and gas in a designated sea area under dispute among related parties. Until now successful practices have only been developed bilaterally. However, it is unpredictable how joint development could be managed multilaterally even though there have been trilateral attempts in areas with overlapping claims, such as the 2005 China–Philippines–Vietnam trilateral agreement on seismic survey in the sea area around the Spratlys.

This chapter will address several questions: Is joint development the last straw for temporary arrangements? How realistic and feasible is the implementation of joint development in the South China Sea? If the prospect of joint development of non-living resources is unpredictable, what are the alternative areas for a broader concept of joint development or joint management?

The joint development regime and its applicability in the SCS

To break the stalemate of the SCS dispute and to access new oil and gas is in the interests of both China and the other claimant states. The late Chinese leader Deng Xiaoping started the Chinese movement in this direction in the early 1990s, when he initiated his famous proposal to 'shelve disputes and go for joint development' in the SCS. This proposal ran largely along the lines of code of conduct agreements such as the 1992 Manila Declaration and United Nations Convention on the Law of the Sea (UNCLOS) Article 123, which also called for cooperation in SCS development. The term 'shelving the disputes' (*gezhi zhengyi*) is understood to apply to the disputes over maritime jurisdiction rather than those concerning territorial sovereignty.[2] Adoption of a joint development arrangement would be a pragmatic, provisional measure to solve the disputes peacefully and in conformity with the common interests of China and its neighboring countries.[3]

Response from other SCS states

There have been a number of official indications of support for a bilateral joint development solution. In May 1994, the then Chinese Premier Li Peng, in discussions with the then Prime Minister Mahathir of Malaysia, endorsed this approach.[4] In June 1994, the Speaker of the Philippines Congress proposed joint development with China in the Rhhed Bank area.[5] Indonesian Ambassador-at-Large H. H. Djalal, in June 1994, toured the countries involved in the dispute to suggest 'freezing' the question of sovereignty and establishing relations.[6] In July 1992, Qian Qichen, the then Foreign Minister of the PRC, elaborated China's position of 'shelving dispute and going for joint development' at the 25th ASEAN Foreign Minister Meeting in Manila. These statements may be related to affirmations, such as the decision of the Vietnamese National Assembly in June that all parties should refrain from the use of force to settle the dispute which reinforces the 1992 Manila Declaration.[7] On 26 November 1996, China's former President Jiang Zemin, in talks with his Philippine counterpart Fidel Ramos, agreed that China and the Philippines should 'shelve differences' over the Spratly Islands and work together to build confidence and develop the disputed area jointly.[8]

Scholars and governmental officials in the ASEAN countries have also expressed their views on joint development in the SCS. Hasjim Djalal, a senior Indonesian diplomat, has written a paper on the relevance of joint development to the SCS.[9] Another Southeast Asian perspective was reflected in a paper published by two Philippine scholars as they argued that 'interest in the concept of joint development stems not only from its relevance to the large number of bilateral maritime boundary disputes in the region, but from its possible usefulness in the seemingly intractable multiple claim area of the Spratlys.'[10]

The problem of implementation

Some argue that the Chinese appeal for joint development was at the outset and remains today an ambiguous concept without any specific information on how to interpret the suggestion.[11] Lee states that

> China has never specified exactly what it means by 'joint development', nor has China clarified where such joint development might take place. Furthermore, at the multilateral workshops, the Chinese delegation has had a limited mandate, and been allowed only to discuss joint development schemes which do not infringe on China's territorial claims.[12]

However, those who are skeptical about China's lack of a clear plan on joint development should also look at the potential external obstacles to its implementation. First, the involvement of major powers outside of this region has added complexity and internationalization to the Spratly dispute, thus setting potential obstacles for the implementation of joint development. The US is the most powerful player due to its great strategic interest in Southeast Asia. After the September

2001 terrorist attack on Washington and New York, the US government strengthened its military presence and control in the SCS. Another key extra-regional actor is Japan. The Japanese military force has been stretched to the SCS by establishing cooperation with some ASEAN countries in non-traditional security fields. Beginning in Southeast Asia to promote its 'orientation' policy, India has, to a large extent, improved its comprehensive relationship with ASEAN. India has held military exercises in the SCS in the past and has recently expressed interest in doing so again in the future. Working in this way to restrict China's role in the area, India has become one of the latest players to become involved in the SCS dispute.[13]

Second, it is also difficult to define the area for joint development in the SCS because of overlapping sovereignty and jurisdictional claims. Hence, these problems have largely restricted the implementation of joint development in the SCS. The engagement of oil companies from outside of the SCS region also brings difficulties to joint development efforts in the area. So far, there are more than 200 oil companies involved in oil and gas exploitation in the SCS, most of which are from the US, the Netherlands, the UK, Japan, France, Canada, Australia, Russia, India, Norway and South Korea. These oil companies have made significant financial and technical investments in the region. The engagement of these oil companies will undoubtedly enhance the complexity and internationalization of the SCS dispute and become a potential drawback for joint development in this area.

Some argue that the Timor Gap model could be applied in the SCS. However, direct adoption of a Timor Gap model for the Spratlys would raise major difficulties. Taiwan could not be a party to such an agreement due to its non-recognition by the PRC and the other states involved. Military action has already been taken in the Spratlys. The occupation of a substantial number of the islands by military forces raises the additional obstacle that the states involved would be most reluctant to withdraw them. As Yu[14] and Dzurek[15] point out, the Spratlys present much greater legal complexities than the relatively straightforward bilateral situation between Australia and Indonesia. Resource development has already begun in the Spratlys and may be far advanced by the time practical negotiations begin. It is much more difficult to negotiate a joint development zone when oil and gas has already been found in substantial quantities.

The oil companies of the Philippines, China and Vietnam signed a landmark tripartite agreement (the Joint Marine Seismic Undertaking, JMSU) in March 2005 to conduct a joint seismic survey of oil potential in disputed areas of the SCS.[16] In a joint statement, the three parties affirmed that the signing of the agreement was in accordance with the basic positions held by their respective governments to turn the SCS into an area of peace, stability, cooperation and development in accordance with UNCLOS and the Declaration on the Conduct of Parties in the South China Sea (DOC).[17]

The signing of the agreement was commonly regarded as the Chinese initially putting into practice Deng Xiaoping's proposal. It shows the three nations taking active measures to fulfill the DOC. Some experts hailed the fact that China,

Vietnam and the Philippines, in a spirit of mutual benefit, flexibility and pragmatism, have cut a new path to peacefully settle the disputes in the SCS, and set an example for other countries to handle such kinds of issues.

Does the JMSU represent a profound breakthrough in the long-running territorial dispute? At this stage it is too early to tell. On the one hand, the JMSU represents a willingness to put aside competing sovereignty claims and engage in joint exploration for much needed energy resources. As such, it is an important confidence-building measure envisaged by the 2002 DOC. An encouraging sign is that none of the other disputants – Malaysia, Brunei or Taiwan – has objected to the JMSU (according to the Philippine Department of Foreign Affairs, all ASEAN members have been briefed on the agreement's contents).[18] On the other hand, the three disputants have emphasized that the JMSU is a commercial agreement that does not change their basic territorial claims. No further progress is scheduled after the three-year survey, proving that how to solve the obstacles facing the implementation of joint development still remains a tough question for the claimant states of the SCS.

Are the non-living resources of joint development areas the only model of temporary arrangement? Is resource a curse or an opportunity for cooperation? How realistic and feasible is the implementation of joint development in the South China Sea? If the prospect of joint development of non-living resources is unpredictable and not easy to achieve, what are the alternative areas for a broader concept of joint development or joint management? The following section will explore these questions.

Environmental security as a driving force of cooperation in the SCS

In general, environmental interdependence is both a source of conflict and an opportunity for international cooperation. If the political actors address serious environmental problems as security matters, they are more likely to put them at the top of the agenda and deal with them in a satisfactory manner, that is, to cooperate and find solutions that are acceptable to all parties involved. The direction of the development, whether it leads to conflict or cooperation, is to a large degree a question of how the decision-makers perceive the situation.

Securitizing the environment in the SCS

The environmental security aspect is pertinent in the SCS. Since 1990 a series of workshops on 'Managing Potential Conflicts in the SCS' have been held in Indonesia under the auspices of the Research and Development Agency within the Department of Foreign Affairs. The initiative is the brainchild of Ambassador Hasjim Djalal of Indonesia, a leading authority on ocean affairs and one of the most influential participants at the Third United Nations Conference on the Law of the Sea. A detailed strategy for its implementation was worked out by Dr Djalal and Ian Townsend-Gault, co-directors of the project. The regional scientific community of maritime experts succeeded in initiating, suggesting and formulating policy choices in the UN Environment Programme projects as well as in the SCS workshops. Unfortunately, governments of the region have prevented these attempts from leading to real political action.[19] Environmental knowledge has reached most countries of the region. Environmental ministries are in place, environmental laws and regulations formulated, environmental NGOs and IGOs undertake numerous projects, and environmental experts are allowed to meet on a free basis across borders, particularly within ASEAN. However, even though governments talk and act in an environment-friendly manner, marine environmental problems are still not dealt with efficiently. Fishermen catch less fish along the coasts, coral reefs and mangroves are destroyed throughout the region, and pollution from traffic at sea, from land-based industries and from the growing cities of the region keeps flowing untreated into coastal waters, and so on.[20] The environmental experts try to inform their governments about risks and challenges, but so far the governments of the region have not been prepared to prioritize management and protection of the marine environment. There are a number of possible explanations for why the governments of the region do not follow expert advice. First, during the last two decades a situation has emerged where China is facing its Southeast Asian counterparts in a contest for natural resources and sovereignty to islands. Latent conflicts have been brought to the surface, and threaten to destabilize the region. Thus, high politics, vital state interests, are at stake. Approaches emphasizing narrow state interests and power politics score rather high in describing state interaction in this region, whereas explanations emphasizing cooperation and the influence of non-governmental actors score rather low in comparison.[21] But this is not to say that environmental experts have no influence at all; it is rather that their influence is limited to agenda-setting and the framing of issues raised for discussion. Marine scientists have been influential in attracting the interest and attention of governments and decision-makers, and also in promoting knowledge about the environmental situation, but still this knowledge is not reflected in state policies for various reasons.[22] Second, domestic conditions also prevent governments from taking part in regional environmental initiatives. These domestic factors are closely related to the level of economic development. As experienced in relation to the 'Indonesian haze,'[23] economic and administrative inadequacies prevent government policies from being effective. Indonesia's neighbors also remain reluctant to express 'enough is enough.' The 'Asian way' of interacting within the ASEAN community implies that all members have to refrain from commenting on internal affairs in a neighboring country. The 'Asian way' allows the ASEAN countries, as well as other Asian nations clinging to the 'Asian way', to give priority to short-sighted national interests even though it may harm the interests of neighboring countries.

The Copenhagen School claims that any specific matter can be non-politicized, politicized and securitized. An issue is non-politicized when the state does not address it and when it is not included in the public debate. An issue becomes politicized when it 'is part of public policy, requiring government decision and resource allocations or, more rarely, some other forms of communal governance.'[24] Finally, a political concern can be securitized through an act of securitization. This refers to a process in which 'an issue is framed as a security problem.'[25] Securitization 'is the move that takes politics beyond the established rules of the game and frames the issue either as a special kind of politics or as above politics' and it 'can thus be seen as a more extreme version of politicization.'[26] De-securitization, on the other hand, refers to the reverse process. It involves the 'shifting of issues out of emergency mode and into the normal bargaining processes of the political sphere.'[27]

In general, marine environmental problems do not feature prominently on the agendas of most SCS countries. Based on the securitization theory of the Copenhagen School, environmental problems should now be securitized if we wish to put them at the top of the agenda among the SCS countries and address them in an effective manner. If serious environmental problems were defined by the political actors as security matters, then they would most certainly be given higher importance. Then environmental security issues could be used as a driving force of cooperation in the SCS. This driving force could be strengthened as the link between the oceans and climate change is receiving greater international attention. At the opening of the World Ocean Conference in May 2009, the Intergovernmental Panel on Climate Change and other scientific sources highlighted ocean changes associated with climate confronting small islands and coastal communities, such as ocean warming, sea level rise and changes to ocean circulations.[28] The gradual awareness of the critical link between marine environment and climate change thus highlights the importance of securitizing the marine environment in the SCS.

Environmental security as a driving force to stimulate cooperation in the SCS

How can security considerations function as driving forces for regional cooperation? One very important aspect related to this is that driving forces cannot function as such without being perceived by the political actors as high politics. Hence the concept must be related to the general perceptions of the politicians. The actors must recognize and perceive the link between high politics and marine environmental security in the SCS. It is the issue of politico-military security that is most likely to generate calls for closer international cooperation in the SCS. To a large degree, one may say that security questions have been a driving force for continued regional integration in Southeast Asia.[29] Increasingly, problems of environmental security will play a similar role. The littoral states of the SCS are to a large degree interdependent when it comes to questions of the marine environment. If they fail to find common solutions to environmental problems they may end up in violent conflict with each other. Regional environmental problems may be considered in terms of shared hazards and shared resources: both categories are now poised to acquire significant integrative potential. The problems are growing, and so are the potential gains of cooperation.[30] It is therefore necessary to ask whether there are signs of epistemic communities playing such a role in relation to marine environmental cooperation in the SCS region. Studies on the role of experts in relation to environment, security and international cooperation in the SCS region are as yet limited. Around the Mediterranean and the Baltic, authoritative regional communities of scientists have emerged and these communities were influential in establishing ocean governance systems for those seas.[31] Generally, authoritative expertise and data are a vital basis for any community or group of policy-makers dealing with the environment. Scientists who have the ability to think ecologically and in broad terms can play an important role in the development of ocean governance systems.[32] The impact of scientific advice is more likely to be greater where decision-makers are uncertain about environmental problems.[33] This is the case with the SCS. There is a general lack of qualified information on the sea and its resources. There are, however, several factors impeding a possible scientific impact on environmental policies in the SCS. At the outset, heavy emphasis on vital state interests and national sovereignty does not leave much room for independent scientific advice on how to formulate environmental policies in the region. For the time being, the climate is dominated by high politics. This obviously hampers the influence of expert advice.

The dependency on the sea for its resources, as a means of transportation and for foreign exchange earnings, from fishing and tourism, and so on, and the fact that the littoral states of the SCS are heavily interdependent in relation to the use of the resources, should imply that international cooperation is the only sensible policy alternative for the future. However, knowing that today there is a perceived contradiction between environmental considerations and international cooperation on the one hand and the emphasis on vital state interests and national sovereignty on the other, what will it take to make the political actors feel compelled to cooperate? The concept of 'environmental security' may be part of the answer.

According to this concept there is no contradiction between international environmental regimes and vital national interests. Rather, international cooperation on environmental resources is the only way to secure vital national resources for the future. Dealing with environmental problems usually requires some pooling of state sovereignty on behalf of common ecological security. The linkage between political/military security and environmental security arises from the fact that we are living in an interdependent world. The destinies of nations are becoming intertwined in ever more complex ways. Sensitivity and vulnerability are two key concepts related to the phenomenon of interdependence. In general, the sensitivity and vulnerability of states in an interdependent world create a need for policy coordination to reduce the effects of vulnerability and regain control. So far, this has been of importance primarily in relation to political/military security. However, the conceptualization is equally valuable where environmental security is concerned. A trans-border ecosystem out of control creates the need to cooperate between states so as to reduce further vulnerability and regain control.[34]

On environmental security matters, states never have been, nor will they ever become fully sovereign. This is particularly evident when it comes to international policy on pollution. Trans-boundary pollution of waterways raises the question of whether polluting activities within the boundaries of one state should remain the exclusive jurisdiction of its government. Alternatively, is the sovereignty of a state compromised when its environment is degraded by pollutants emanating from neighboring countries?[35] These are among the points that need to be emphasized by scientific experts when asked for advice by the policy-makers in the SCS region. It all points in the direction of the need for further international cooperation.[36]

The main question is whether common marine environmental problems could be a driving force for further cooperation in the SCS, within ASEAN and between ASEAN, China and Taiwan. The recognition of strong environmental interdependence is one of the strongest driving forces for regional cooperation and integration outside Europe today. We know that in organizations like ASEAN, and between ASEAN and China, pragmatic interests are not sufficient to move the cooperation process forward. A driving force is needed. It is possible that, if defined as security matters, grave regional marine environmental problems could provide the necessary driving force for future cooperation in the SCS. For the political leaders of the SCS states to perceive environmental problems as security matters, they must learn that they are. Teaching the political actors about the relationship between environment and security in the SCS region may therefore be an important task for the communities of concerned scientists in the region.

Fisheries cooperation as a first step toward SCS dispute resolution

Stability can be achieved through joint cooperation undertaken at the lowest levels of contact in the SCS, even as major political disagreements remain unresolved. A prime example of joint cooperation can be found in the field of fisheries management, an area in which cooperation among the littoral states is encouraged. Fisheries cooperation might be one practical option to avert outright conflict in a region that seems perpetually on the edge of hostilities.

The SCS meets the criteria set out in Article 122 of UNCLOS defining the term 'semi-enclosed sea':

> 'enclosed or semi-enclosed sea' means a gulf, basin or sea surrounded by two or more States and connected to another sea or the ocean by a narrow outlet or consisting entirely or primarily of the territorial seas and exclusive economic zones of two or more coastal States.

Because the SCS is semi-enclosed, any change in the ecosystem of the sea will have significant impact on the whole area. It is generally recognized that the living resources in the SCS area migrate from one exclusive economic zone (EEZ) to another, particularly those highly migratory species such as tuna and other shared stocks. It is interesting to note that most of the fishery resources in the SCS region are either shared stocks such as scads and mackerels that migrate across the EEZs of more than one coastal state or highly migratory species, especially tuna, whose migratory patterns sometimes cover a vast area of the ocean. Common stocks of scads and mackerels are believed to occur along the coasts of the Gulf of Thailand and the eastern region of the SCS.[37]

Each country may already have its own assessment of its living resources in its EEZ, assuming that the definition and delineation of each EEZ is clear. The problem is that many of those EEZ boundaries are not well defined or mutually agreed upon by the relevant parties. Likewise, there are various conflicting claims to islands that complicate and defer the determination of the EEZ boundaries. For this reason, many experts and scholars are convinced of the need to cooperate on the assessment of the living resources in the SCS area without regard to jurisdictional boundaries.

Article 123 of UNCLOS regarding enclosed and semi-enclosed seas provides that

> States bordering an enclosed or semi-enclosed sea should co-operate with each other in the exercise of their rights and in the performance of their duties under this Convention. To this end they shall endeavour, directly or through an appropriate regional organisation:
>
> (a) to coordinate the management, conservation, exploration and exploitation of the living resources of the sea;
> (b) to coordinate the implementation of their rights and duties with respect to the protection and preservation of the marine environment;
> (c) to coordinate their scientific research policies and undertake where appropriate joint programmes of scientific research in the area;
> (d) to invite, as appropriate, other interested States or international organizations to cooperate with them in furtherance of the provisions of this article.

Therefore, all parties concerned should be aware that fish are migratory and fishery resources are exhaustible, and thus that rational use of the SCS and the preservation of its marine environment are important to all parties. Therefore, cooperation among littoral states in the region is essential. In order to avoid overfishing or depletion of resources, conservation measures have to be taken. Such measures are not possible without regional cooperation and require close coordination among the parties concerned especially in a semi-enclosed sea.

As Kuen-chen Fu puts it, conservation and management of the SCS fishery resources is a complicated issue, which it is not possible for a single state among the SCS countries to resolve alone.[38] A joint effort is thus essential, particularly in consideration of the fact that the state of the SCS fisheries has worsened while the demand for fisheries has escalated. Kuen-chen Fu suggests that there is an urgent need for a more effective regional cooperation scheme for fishery resources conservation and management. Wang argues that fishery cooperation could be the most feasible course of action for the littoral states since, through cooperation, fishery resources could be properly conserved and managed so that economic waste and over-exploitation may be avoided.[39] Without affecting jurisdictional boundaries as laid down in UNCLOS, it is certainly possible to have regional joint fishery management of the SCS as the starting point for further cooperation. If all states in this region treat cooperation as a key step toward achieving mutual benefit, then the future for such a regional cooperation mechanism is assured.

It is obvious that while some fishery resources of the SCS are still under-exploited, most are heavily exploited. Therefore, fisheries development should be accompanied by a rational resource management mechanism. To date, however, not a single resource management method has emerged that would work efficiently over the whole area. Even within the zones of each littoral state's jurisdiction, rational resource management mechanisms are not apparent. One of the reasons for this is the problem of overlapping claims among the littoral states. The other reason is that none of the littoral states has sufficient stock assessment data available to support a rational resource management mechanism.[40]

Wang suggests that, in view of the situation with respect to living resources in the SCS, cooperation toward management and conservation of fishery resources should start with defining and minimizing disputed areas;[41] then a joint committee could be established to manage the fishing-related issues.[42] In the meantime, definition and determination of fish stocks and allowable catches of living resources in the region should proceed.

In this respect, cooperating on managing and conserving fisheries resources is especially significant because fish are migratory, and often highly migratory. Moreover, overfishing is a serious and pressing problem in the region. In this regard, a maritime boundary cannot entirely protect a state's fishery resources from encroachment, because fishery resources can migrate beyond the state's territorial or fishing zones, and overfishing beyond its borders can also affect the fish stocks within its territorial boundaries. Therefore, a proper management mechanism, subject to natural conditions, is necessary for the coastal states to keep stocks at sustainable levels. This is especially important for the littoral states of the SCS. Because this region is a semi-enclosed sea, any change in fishery policy-making could have far-reaching effects on fishery resources in the area.

In the SCS region, it is not difficult to locate opportunities for cooperation. Military cooperation, joint development on hydrocarbon resources, marine scientific research, marine environmental protection and fisheries cooperation are all options. To date, however, disputes surrounding possible hydrocarbon resources in the area and actions in favor of conservation and management of fishery resources have been delayed. Nevertheless, conservation and management of fishery resources could be the starting point for cooperation in this area and could have a 'spill-over effect' to other areas of cooperation. Accordingly, the next step depends on the littoral states' political will and determination to pursue cooperation in this matter.

UNCLOS as a framework for ocean governance in the SCS

UNCLOS provides an integrated legal framework on which to build sound and effective regulations on the different uses of the ocean. Whether or not we choose to call UNCLOS a constitution for the ocean, it does articulate a system of ocean governance.[43] It does not specify in detail when and how fishers can harvest living resources in the EEZs of coastal states or what the terms of leases for deep seabed mining will be. What it does do, however, is to create procedures, though sometimes contentious, for arriving at collective decisions about such matters. This is precisely what we expect a constitution or constitutive agreement about governance to do. Rainer Lagoni argues that UNCLOS is no constitution in the sense of the usual terminology of the law of states. Notwithstanding this, it is the principal legal instrument that provides the framework for the public order of the oceans and seas.[44] This function has to be taken into account during its interpretation and application by the state parties. Moreover it determines its systematic role for the integration of all international treaties relating to the oceans and seas into such an international public order.

A constitutional perspective suggests that UNCLOS was not intended to be comprehensive to the extent that there would be no need to create further law.[45] This means that, although UNCLOS made use of 'vagueness, ambiguity, and silence' at certain points and in respect of certain controversial matters,[46] it could be regarded as legally effective to the extent that it provides clearly for a system within which to address substantive issues as they arise. The goal of a constitution is to provide for a system of governance rather than to deal with all substantive matters. UNCLOS refers in almost 70 provisions to the possibility that the subject in question may be governed by another international instrument, bilateral or multilateral, anterior or posterior.[47]

In *Ocean Governance: Sustainable Development of the Seas*, UNCLOS was highly praised by Christopher W. Pinto as follows:

> In considering the extent to which existing international institutions are adequate to the task of making a reality of the concept of sustainable development in the field of marine resources, the obvious starting point is the 1982 UN Convention on the Law of the Sea. Designed to reflect elements of the 'New International Economic Order' and to establish the legal content of the concept of the 'common heritage of mankind,' the Convention gives expression precisely to those elements of universal participation, equity and balanced reciprocal obligation, transference of funds, science and technology to the developing countries, and regulation of access to shared natural resources, that are also inherent in the concept of sustainable development.[48]

Although UNCLOS may be perceived to have certain shortcomings, it is comparatively effective in the SCS in terms of its internal coherence. Rather than a compulsory channel to settle disputes, UNCLOS is seen more as a framework within which regional ocean governance can be used as an approach to address the disputes.

A regional system of ocean governance – which presupposes some concepts of shared, rather than self-centered, sovereign authority – would mean not only more intensive and transparent consultations among ASEAN members and China on a full range of ocean issues, but also a more ready willingness on their part to accept and institutionalize a strategic notion of regional security based on a comprehensive system of ocean security. 'Regional ocean governance' simply means the comprehensive process of sustainable development of and for the oceans at the regional level. Its underlying premise reiterates the core principle of UNCLOS that 'the problems of ocean space in a region are closely interrelated and need to be considered as a whole.'[49] Like ocean governance at the global level, regional ocean governance has two prerequisites: sustainable development norms and sustainable development institutions. While in the SCS there is no overall policy on ocean governance per se, it could be said that the building blocks for this policy are already in place. A consideration of the normative framework for ocean sustainable development in the region would show that the regime of comprehensive security envisioned by the UNCLOS process finds support in the ocean management regimes of ASEAN and China – enhancing, directly or indirectly, the substantive framework of sustainable development and/or comprehensive security embodies in UNCLOS. The elements of a regional regime of ocean governance consist of several distinct strands of ocean management norms and standards which have become integral to the international law of ASEAN and China. Mention may be made, first, of the DOC, which may be considered as setting forth the broad framework of regional cooperation which could very well be extended to the oceans, or applied in the context of the expanded and integrated ASEAN+1 program on marine affairs.[50] The norms and standards elaborated under these agreements specify the concrete aims and the various forms of regional cooperation, as well as the norms of conflict-avoidance and peaceful settlement of disputes.

As Desilva points out, the first step to ocean governance is to draw up a framework agreement which will contain elements of the general principles and policies, of the special program and sub-regional and bilateral agreements.[51] It should be functional and effective in resolving environmental problems and fostering strong regional cooperation and coordination of appropriate cost-effective actions. The framework instrument must include, among other elements:

- the use of sound science incorporated into policy-making processes to foster ecological and economic soundness;
- laws, policies and actions that are effective in terms of ecological improvements. Ecological ineffectiveness also results in waste of scarce financial resources. Ecologically effective actions must be based on sound science and not on perceptions or political considerations;
- cost-effective actions;
- economic valuation of environmental goods and services as a tool for sound development planning;
- decision-making after gathering all relevant knowledge/information for the purpose. This improves the effectiveness of decisions and it also improves cooperation;
- promoting and building a base on consensual knowledge. This is particularly true where progress on regional cooperation is stalled or slowed due to complexities or uncertainty surrounding the issue;

- good communication both vertical and horizontal for effective cooperation;
- periodic assessment and review and revision of actions as required, ensuring that they are effective. Where assessments indicate problems, they need to be revised; and
- a flexible approach that allows for the inclusion of new information.[52]

The DOC may be cited as such a framework agreement on ocean management in the SCS region. The consistency with which it has been invoked in ASEAN and China does make it an authoritative basis for conflict avoidance and cooperation in the region: in addition to its call for restraint and a peaceful resolution of the overlapping territorial claims, the declaration invites all parties involved 'to explore the possibility of cooperation in the SCS relating to the safety of maritime navigation and communication, protection against pollution of the marine environment, coordination of search and rescue operations, efforts toward combating piracy and armed robbery, as well as collaboration in the campaign against illicit trafficking in drugs.'[53] The ASEAN members pledged to 'seek an early, peaceful resolution' of the dispute and to 'explore ways and means to prevent conflict and enhance cooperation in the South China Sea consistent with the Treaty of Amity and Cooperation, the ASEAN Declaration on the South China Sea of 1992, as well as international law, including the UN Convention on the Law of the Sea.'[54]

Conclusions

Joint development, as a temporary arrangement pending the final settlement of maritime delimitation, has been proposed in the contested South China Sea. However, given the recent development of the disputes and the lack of mutual trust among the claimant states, the implementation is hard to achieve. I question whether oil and gas is the only option for the concept of the joint development regime and propose a three-part model of joint management for the purpose of enhancing confidence-building and regional cooperation: 1) environmental security as a driving force of cooperation in the SCS; 2) fisheries cooperation as a first step toward SCS dispute resolution; and 3) UNCLOS as a framework for ocean governance in the SCS.

Notes

1 Part of this chapter is drawn from Chapter 6 of my book entitled *UNCLOS and Ocean Dispute Settlement: Law and Politics in the South China Sea*, Abingdon: Routledge, 2012.
2 See Wu Shicun, 'Certain reflections on joint development in the Nansha (Spratly) Islands,' in Zhong Tianxiang, Han Jia and Ren Huaifeng (eds.), *Proceedings of the SCS Workshop (2002)*, Hainan: Hainan Institute for the SCS, 2002 (in Chinese), pp. 69–78, at p. 72.
3 Ibid., p. 73.
4 'Premier Li Peng met with Prime Minister Mahathir of Malaysia', *People's Daily*, 13 May 1994, p. 1.
5 'Timeline of major events of China-Philippines diplomacy (1975-present),' China.org.

cn, 28 February 2012, at http://cn-ph.china.org.cn/2012-02/28/content_4841408.htm.

6 Personal communication.

7 Nayan Chandra, 'The new nationalism,' *Far Eastern Economic Review*, 9 November 1995, p. 22.

8 *Straits Times*, 27 November 1996, p. 3.

9 Hasjim Djalal, 'The relevance of the concept of joint development to maritime disputes in the South China Sea,' *Indonesian Quarterly*, 27(3), 1999, pp. 178–186; see also Zou Keyuan, *China's Marine Legal System and the Law of the Sea*, Leiden/Boston: Martinus Nijhoff, 2005, p. 99.

10 Aileen S. P. Baviera and Jay L. Batongbacal, 'When will conditions be ripe? Prospects for joint development in the South China Sea,' *Chronicle*, 4(1–2), 1999, available at http://www.up.edu.ph/cids/chronicle/articles/chronv4n1and2/infocus08baviera_pg3.html (accessed 1 November 2004).

11 Knut Snildal, 'Petroleum in the South China Sea – a Chinese national interest?,' thesis submitted in partial fulfillment of the requirements for the award of the Cand Polit degree at the Department of Political Science, University of Oslo, 30 June 2000.

12 Lee Lai To, 'The South China Sea, China and multilateral dialogues,' *Security Dialogue*, 30(2), 1999, pp. 165–178, at p. 167.

13 Clive Schofield and Ian Storey, 'Energy security and Southeast Asia: the impact on maritime boundary and territorial disputes,' *Harvard Asia Quarterly*, 9(4), 2005, pp. 36–46.

14 Peter K-H. Yu, 'A critique of the three proposals for "solving" the Spratlys dispute: a Chinese view from Taiwan,' *Issues and Studies*, 31(1), January 1995, pp. 63–76.

15 D. J. Dzurek, *The Spratly Islands Dispute: Who's On First*, Maritime Briefing, vol. 2, no. 1, Durham: International Boundaries Research Unit, University of Durham, 1996.

16 Schofield and Storey, 'Energy security and Southeast Asia.'

17 Ibid.

18 Schofield and Storey, 'Energy security and Southeast Asia.'

19 Tom Næss, 'Environment and security in the SCS region,' master's thesis, University of Oslo, 1999, available at http://www.duo.uio.no/sok/work.html?WORKID=5092.

20 Næss, 'Environment and security in the SCS region.'

21 Ibid.

22 Ibid.

23 The haze, caused by forest fires burning in Indonesia's Kalimantan and Sumatra islands, has caused health problems across the region, dented tourism, hurt precious wildlife and damaged food sources in affected areas. Indonesia is viewed as the main culprit in this environmental crisis, but the trans-boundary problem holds lessons as well for neighboring countries preoccupied with fast-paced growth.

24 Næss, 'Environment and security in the SCS region,' p. 23.

25 Ibid., p. 75.

26 Ibid., p. 23.

27 Ibid., p. 4.

28 Sam Bateman and Mary Ann Palma, 'Coming to the rescue of the oceans: the climate change imperative,' *RSIS Commentaries*, No. 80, Singapore: S. Rajaratnam School of International Studies, August 2009.

29 Karin Dokken, 'Environment, security and regionalism in the Asia-Pacific: is environmental security a useful concept?,' *Pacific Review*, 14(4), 2001, pp. 509–530, at p. 509.

30 Ibid., p. 523.

31 Peter Haas, *Saving the Mediterranean: The Politics of International Environmental Cooperation*, New York: Colombia University Press, 1990; Ronnie Hjorth, 'Baltic Sea environmental cooperation: the role of epistemic communities and the politics of regime change,' *Cooperation and Conflict* 29(1), 1994, pp. 11–31; Tom Næss, 'Environment and security in

the South China Sea region: the role of experts, non-governmental actors and governments in regime building processes,' final thesis in political science, University of Oslo, 1999, available at http://www.sum.uio.no/southchinasea/.
32 Dokken, 'Environment, security and regionalism in the Asia-Pacific,' p. 523.
33 Peter Haas, 'Introduction: epistemic community and international policy coordination,' *International Organization*, 46(1), 1992, pp. 1–37.
34 Dokken, 'Environment, security and regionalism in the Asia-Pacific,' p. 524.
35 Dokken, *Environment, Security and Regional Integration in West Africa*, Oslo: Unipub, 1997, p. 89; Marvin S. Soroos, *Beyond Sovereignty: The Challenge of Global Policy*, Columbia: University of South Carolina Press, 1986. See also Dokken, 'Environment, security and regionalism in the Asia-Pacific,' p. 524.
36 Dokken, 'Environment, security and regionalism in the Asia-Pacific,' p. 524.
37 Kuan-Hsiung Wang, 'Bridge over troubled waters: fisheries cooperation as a resolution to the SCS conflicts,' *Pacific Review*, 14(4), 2001, pp. 531–551, at p. 536.
38 Fu Kuen-chen, 'Regional cooperation for conservation and management of fishery resources in the South China Sea,' in John Wong, Zou Keyuan and Zeng Huaqun (eds.), *China-Asean Relations Economic and Legal Dimensions*, Singapore: World Scientific, 2006, pp. 219–243.
39 Wang, 'Bridge over troubled waters,' pp. 536 and 542.
40 A. Dwiponggo, 'Project proposal on regional fisheries stock assessment in the South China Sea,' paper presented at the Second Working Group Meeting on Resource Assessment and Ways of Development in the South China Sea, Jakarta, Indonesia, 5–6 July 1993, pp. 1–2.
41 Mark J. Valencia, Jon M. Van Dyke and Noel A. Ludwig, *Sharing the Resources of the SCS*, Leiden: Martinus Nijhoff, 1997, pp. 205–206.
42 Wang, 'Bridge over troubled waters,' p. 544.
43 Oran Young, 'Commentary on Shirley V. Scott "The LOS Convention as a constitutional regime for the ocean",' in Alex G. Oude Elferink (ed.), *Stability and Change in the Law of the Sea: The Role of the LOS Convention*, Leiden: Martinus Nijhoff, 2004, pp. 39–46, at p. 42.
44 Rainer Lagoni, 'Commentary,' in Elferink, *Stability and Change in the Law of the Sea*, pp. 49–52, at p. 51.
45 J. R. Stevenson and B. H. Oxman, 'The future of the United Nations Convention on the Law of the Sea,' *American Journal of International Law*, 88, 1994, pp. 488–499, at p. 492.
46 A. Pardo, 'The new law of the sea and some of its implications,' *Journal of Law and the Environment*, 4, 1987, pp. 3–15, at p. 13.
47 R. Wolfrum, 'The legal order for the seas and oceans,' in M. H. Nordquist and J. Norton Moore (eds.), *Entry into Force of the Law of the Sea Convention*, The Hague: Martinus Nijhoff, 1997, pp. 161–185, at p. 161.
48 Christopher W. Pinto, 'The United Nations convention on the law of the sea: sustainable development and institutional implications,' in Peter Bautista Payoyo (ed.), *Ocean Governance: Sustainable Development of the Seas*, Tokyo: United Nations University, 1994, accessed at http://archive.unu.edu/unupress/unupbooks/uu15oe/uu15oe06.htm#ii.%20the%201982%20un%20convention%20on%20the%20law%20of%20the%20sea.
49 UNCLOS, Premise.
50 The 1995 Bangkok Summit Declaration asserts that 'cooperative peace and shared prosperity are the fundamental goals of the ASEAN.'
51 Vice Admiral John C. Desilva, Pvsm, Avsm. (Retd), 'Conflict management and environmental cooperation in the South China Sea,' at the 8th Science Council of Asia Conference Joint Project: 'Security of Ocean in Asia' , 29 May 2008, Qingdao, China, p. 7.

52 Ibid.
53 Dong Manh Nguyen, 'Settlement of disputes under the 1982 United Nations Convention on the Law of the Sea: the case of the South China Sea dispute,' Fellowship on the Law of the Sea New York, December 2005.
54 1995 ASEAN Summit Declaration (Bangkok), 15 December 1995.

Index

For Product Safety Concerns and Information please contact our EU representative GPSR@taylorandfrancis.com
Taylor & Francis Verlag GmbH, Kaufingerstraße 24, 80331 München, Germany

www.ingramcontent.com/pod-product-compliance
Ingram Content Group UK Ltd.
Pitfield, Milton Keynes, MK11 3LW, UK
UKHW020014200926
475702UK00014B/1877
* 9 7 8 1 1 3 8 6 8 5 1 2 3 *